Selfless persons

Selfless persons

Imagery and thought in *Theravāda* Buddhism

STEVEN COLLINS

Lecturer in the Study of Religions, Department of Theology and Religious Studies, Bristol University

CAMBRIDGE UNIVERSITY PRESS

Cambridge
London New York New Rochelle
Melbourne Sydney

Published by the Press Syndicate of the University of Cambridge
The Pitt Building, Trumpington Street, Cambridge CB2 1RP
32 East 57th Street, New York, NY 10022, USA
296 Beaconsfield Parade, Middle Park, Melbourne 3206, Australia

First published 1982

Printed in Great Britain at the Pitman Press, Bath

Library of Congress catalogue card number: 81–16998

British Library Cataloguing in Publication Data

Collins, Steven
Selfless persons: Imagery and thought in
Theravāda Buddhism.
1. Hinayana Buddhism – Doctrines
2. Self (Philosophy)
I. Title
294.3'422 BQ7235
ISBN 0 521 24081 6

Contents

	Preface	*page* ix
	Introduction	1
Part I	**The cultural and social setting of Buddhist thought**	27
1	The origins of rebirth	29
1.1	Buddhism and early Indian religion	29
1.2	Time: *saṃsāra*	41
1.3	Action and the person: *karma*	53
1.4	Timelessness: *mokṣa (nirvāṇa)*	58
2	Varieties of Buddhist discourse	65
2.1	Buddhist thought in context	65
2.2	Different ways of talking about 'self' and 'person'	71
2.3	Elements of personality and (not-)self	78
Part II	**The doctrine of not-self**	85
3	The denial of self as 'right view'	87
3.1	Different kinds of 'right view'	87
3.2	Arguments in support of *anattā*	95
3.3	The denial of self as a strategy in 'mental culture'	111
4	Views, attachment, and 'emptiness'	116
4.1	Views and attachment	117
4.2	The Unanswered Questions	131
4.3	Quietism and careful attention	138
Part III	**Personality and rebirth**	145
5	The individual of 'conventional truth'	147
5.1	'Conventional' and 'ultimate truth'	147
5.2	*Attabhāva* 'individuality', *puggala* 'person'	156
5.3	House imagery	165

6 'Neither the same nor different' 177
6.1 'A person is not found' 178
6.2 Images of identity and difference 185
6.3 Self and other: compassion 188

Part IV Continuity 197

7 Conditioning and consciousness 199
7.1 The construction(s) of temporal existence 200
7.2 The stations of evolving consciousness 213
7.3 Vegetation imagery 218

8 Momentariness and the *bhavaṅga*-mind 225
8.1 'Impermanent are conditioned things' 226
8.2 The 'ultimate' extent of a lifetime: momentariness 234
8.3 The *bhavaṅga*-mind 238
8.4 River imagery 247

Conclusion 262

Notes 267
Bibliography 310
Glossary and index of Pali and Sanskrit terms 318
General index 321

For Claude Grangier

Preface

This book is a revised version of my thesis, 'Personal Continuity in Theravāda Buddhism', approved for the D.Phil. degree at Oxford University in 1979.

I am glad to be able to thank all those who have helped me to produce the book. The original thesis was written at Wolfson College, Oxford, and the revision for publication at Exeter College, Oxford, during my all-too-brief tenure of a Junior Research Fellowship there. The University of Bristol have kindly given me a small award to help toward pre-publication costs. I am grateful to these three institutions for providing me with a home during the course of writing the book.

My debts to individuals are many. Margaret Cone helped me through my first steps in the Pali language; conversations with Paul Williams and Alexis Sanderson have many times given me valuable guidance, correction, and stimulation. The examiners of the thesis, Clifford Geertz and Friedhelm Hardy, made valuable criticisms and suggestions for revision, which I have tried to incorporate into this revised version. To two men, above all, I owe a personal and intellectual debt which cannot be adequately conveyed by the references to their work in this book. Richard Gombrich, my *upajjhāya*, taught me Sanskrit, and as my D.Phil. supervisor gave me a level of help, advice and encouragement beyond anything I could have expected or hoped for. Michael Carrithers, my *kalyāṇa-mitta*, has with unfailing kindness over the last six years given me the benefit of his sensitive understanding of anthropology and of Buddhism. To adapt a familiar Buddhist formula: if there is any intellectual merit in this book, I transfer it to the reputation of these two friends and teachers.

I could not have written this book in the way that I have done without the help of my wife. She has read through every draft of every section with immense care and critical understanding, and if I have achieved any measure of clarity and self-awareness in the ordering and presentation of my ideas, it is thanks to her. I dedicate the book to her in love, gratitude and respect.

Bristol 1981

Introduction

This book is offered to the reader as an essay in the history of ideas. The particular tradition dealt with here is that of *Theravāda* Buddhism, a tradition whose ideas were conceived and elaborated in India and in certain Indian-influenced cultural settings in South and South-east Asia. In presenting my account of this tradition, however, I wish immediately to make two points. Firstly, in speaking of a 'history' of ideas here I will try to follow the advice and example of Louis Dumont (as indeed on many other occasions in this study): 'The history of India must be read in an Indian way. It is better to seek first, by a synchronic study, to grasp the fundamental configurations or structure which constitute the framework in relation to which history – apart from the pure sequence of events – is defined.'[1] Secondly, although the particular subject-matter, and the treatment of it I have considered appropriate, are *prima facie* concerned only with India and with Buddhism, I hope very much that the book will be read with an awareness that this specialist Indological appearance is meant to be only skin-deep. Naturally, I have had to address myself to particular issues which the relevant scholarship, Indological and anthropological, has raised hitherto; indeed, I hope that on this level the book will be coherent simply as a contribution to the solution of certain classic problems in the study of Buddhist culture. However, my main interest is philosophical; the imaginative world of *Theravāda* Buddhism, and *a fortiori* of the Indian culture of which it is essentially a part, are of great depth and complexity, and their speculative thought derives from concerns and presuppositions radically different from those of western philosophy. Such an alien tradition, however, is important for us not *in spite of* but precisely *because of* these differences, and the difficulty we have in understanding them.

I think that a great deal of contemporary philosophy, particularly in the English-language tradition, suffers from a lack of historical and social self-awareness. I want to argue that philosophical reflection should not proceed in abstraction from intellectual history and anthropology, from the investigation and comparison of cultures. Just as anthropology hopes, by means of the ethnographic study of other societies, eventually to illuminate both the specific nature of our own society and the general nature of all societies, so I think our philosophy should hope eventually to illuminate both the specific nature of its own inherent concerns and presuppositions, and perhaps the general nature of human thought (if such exists), by studying the intellectual history of its own, *and of other* traditions. Let me quote the remarks of two anthropologists whose work has greatly influenced me. Louis Dumont, acknowledging the influence on himself of Marcel Mauss, writes:

> Let us consider here another of Mauss' conclusions, whose importance might escape one because of the form in which it is expressed: 'Aristotelian categories are not the only ones which exist. We have first to make the largest possible catalogue of categories.' There is little doubt for those who know Mauss that 'make a catalogue' means nothing less than to experience those categories, to enter into them, to elaborate them into social facts . . . If I am not mistaken, in anthropology, properly scientific categories are only born . . . from a contradiction between our categories and the categories of others, from a conflict between theory and the data. I think that it is for this reason that Mauss did not want a philosophy, that is to say a speculation with insufficient concepts, but an inventory of categories equivalent to the construction of scientific concepts.[2]

Clifford Geertz, writing of the difficulties of a truly empathetic understanding, which would see things 'from the native's point of view', has the following to say, which is relevant both to the general intellectual position I am trying to describe, and to the particular topic of this study:

> The concept of person is, in fact, an excellent vehicle by which to examine this whole question of how to go about poking into another people's turn of mind. In the first place, some sort of concept of this kind, one feels reasonably safe in saying, exists in recognizable form within all social groups. Various notions of what persons are may be, from our point of view, more than a little odd. People may be conceived to dart about nervously at night, shaped like fireflies. Essential elements of their psyche, like hatred, may be thought to be lodged in granular black bodies within their livers, discoverable upon autopsy. They may share their fates with *doppelganger* [sic] beasts, so that when the beast sickens or dies they sicken or die too. But at least some conception of what a human individual is, as opposed to a rock, an animal, a rainstorm, or a god, is, so far as I can see, universal. Yet, at the same time, as these offhand examples suggest, the actual conceptions involved vary, often quite sharply, from one group to the next. The Western conception of the person as a bounded, unique, more or less integrated motivational and cognitive universe; a dynamic centre of awareness, emotion, judgment, and action organized into a distinctive whole and set contrastively both against other such wholes and against a social and natural background is, however incorrigible it may seem to us, a rather peculiar idea within the context of the world's cultures. Rather than attempt to place the experience of others within the framework of such a conception, which is what the extolled 'empathy' in fact usually comes down to, we must, if we are to achieve understanding, set that conception aside and view their experiences within the framework of their own idea of what selfhood is.[3]

I hope that the project of investigating the specificity of Buddhist thinking about self, persons, and their continuity, the task of coming to terms with the particular nature of its intellectual and social content, will help to enable us to hold up a mirror to our own thinking on these subjects. In the study which follows I will describe the way in which I think *Theravāda* thinking has arisen from its historical and cultural context. I will suggest that it embodies as a basis for thought certain specific conceptual constructions and hypotheses; constructions and hypotheses which are addressed to quite specific (and socially derived) concerns, all of which became finally crystallised, as it were, into a schematic religious dogmatism. Doing this, I hope, will help us to appreciate how western thinking about persons, selves, their nature and their activities, itself also represents a specific historical and cultural product, addressing its own particular concerns and embodying its own particular conceptual constructions and hypotheses as the basis for its thought. (The two crucial areas here, I suppose, are Christian soteriology and the individualist presuppositions of economic and socio-political thought.)[4]

There seems to me to be a strong tendency in contemporary philosophy – at least in some parts of the English-language tradition primarily influenced by Wittgenstein – to accord to different cultures, under the names perhaps of 'forms of life' or 'language games', a kind of immunity from external historical or sociological criticism and comparison. This tendency, exaggeratedly and self-protectively tolerant, is encouraged by the tacit but frequent assumptions that *for us* what one might call (paraphrasing Chomsky) 'the intuitions of the native English thinker' should be the arbiter of philosophical correctness, and that it is the conceptual and linguistic habits of 'common-sense' to which we should look for enlightenment on philosophical issues. The approach I am suggesting, on the contrary, will see these 'intuitions', and the 'common-sense' constructed out of them, as merely problematic data; data, moreover, whose implicit presuppositions and particular concerns must be investigated and made explicit by appropriate historical and social-anthropological scholarship. In the pages which follow I will try to confront the native English thinker with certain aspects of the mental universe as it appears to the Buddhist mind. The result of thus placing oneself, for a moment, in a Buddhist world (in Mauss' terms of 'experiencing Buddhist categories'), will be, I hope, to widen a little the cultural horizons in which both our common-sense and our philosophy set their ideas of the person and of selfhood. It is this fundamental project to which my study of Buddhism is directed.

So much for the content of the book: its form results from my approach to two classic problems in the study of Buddhism. In the first place, there is the doctrine of 'not-self' (Pali *anattā*, Sanskrit *anātman*). I will let three distinguished contemporary *Theravāda* Buddhists introduce the doctrine. All of them are writing in English for a western audience, and they show admirably, I think, the importance which the denial of self has for Buddhists themselves, and some of the perhaps unexpected implications and consequences which Buddhism supposes the opposing belief in the existence of a self to have. Rāhula, a learned and authoritative Sinhalese monk, writes:

> What in general is suggested by Soul, Self, Ego, or to use the Sanskrit expression *Ātman*, is that in man there is a permanent, everlasting and absolute entity, which is the unchanging substance behind the changing phenomenal world. According to some religions, each individual has such a separate soul which is created by God, and which, finally after death, lives eternally either in hell or heaven, its destiny depending on the judgement of its creator. According to others, it goes through many lives till it is completely purified and becomes finally united with God or *Brahman*, Universal Soul or *Ātman*, from which it originally emanated. This soul or self in man is the thinker of thoughts, feeler of sensations, and receiver of rewards and punishments for all its actions good or bad. Such a conception is called the idea of self.
>
> Buddhism stands unique in the history of human thought in denying the existence of such a Soul, Self, or *Ātman*. According to the teaching of the Buddha, the idea of self is an imaginary, false belief which has no corresponding reality, and it produces harmful thoughts of 'me' and 'mine', selfish desire, craving, attachment, hatred, ill-will, conceit, pride, egotism, and other defilements, impurities and problems. It is the source of all the troubles in the world from personal conflicts to wars between nations. In short, to this false view can be traced all the evil in the world.[5]

Malalasekera, an active Sinhalese lay Buddhist and statesman, tells us that:

> this is the one doctrine which separates Buddhism from all other religions, creeds, and systems of philosophy and which makes it unique in the world's history. All its other teachings . . . are found, more or less in similar forms, in one or other of the schools of thought or religions which have attempted to guide men through life and explain to them the unsatisfactoriness of the world. But in its denial of any real permanent Soul or Self, Buddhism stands alone. This teaching presents the utmost difficulty to many people and often provokes even violent antagonism towards the whole religion. Yet this doctrine of No-soul or *Anattā* is the bedrock of Buddhism and all the other Teachings of the Buddha are intimately connected with it . . . Now, what is this 'Soul' the existence of which the Buddha denies? Briefly stated, the soul is the abiding, separate, constantly existing and indestructible entity which is generally believed to be found in man . . . it is[regarded as]the thinker of all his thoughts, the doer of his deeds and the director of the organism generally. It is the lord not only of the body but also of the mind; it gathers its knowledge through the gateways of the senses . . . Buddhism denies all this and asserts that this belief in a permanent and a divine soul is the most dangerous and pernicious of all errors, the most deceitful of illusions, that it will inevitably mislead its victim into the deepest pit of sorrow and suffering.[6]

Nyanatiloka, a German who went to Ceylon, became a monk and a leading figure in modern 'reformed' Buddhism there, and who was a prolific translator and interpreter of *Theravāda* tradition, adapts a canonical pattern of exposition in saying that:

> there are three teachers in the world. The first teacher teaches the existence of an eternal ego-entity outlasting death: that is the Eternalist, as for example the Christian. The second teacher teaches a temporary ego-entity which becomes annihilated at death: that is the annihilationist, or materialist. The third teacher teaches neither an eternal nor a temporary ego-entity: that is the Buddha. The Buddha teaches that what we call ego, self, soul, personality, etc., are merely conventional terms not referring to any real independent entity. And he teaches that there is only to be found this psychophysical process of existence changing from moment to moment . . . This doctrine of egolessness of existence forms the essence of the Buddha's doctrine of emancipation. Thus with this doctrine of egolessness, or *anattā*, stands or falls the entire Buddhist structure.[7]

I shall not be concerned to come to any final evaluation of the *anattā* doctrine, nor thus to decide whether 'the entire Buddhist structure' is to stand or fall. Rather, in examining the doctrine, I shall wish to elucidate how it appears in the texts, what it asserts, what it denies, and what it fails to assert or deny; and, perhaps most importantly, I shall wish to study what role or roles it plays in the varieties of Buddhist thought and practice, what function or functions it might have for those who profess allegiance to it and whose religious activity is patterned on it. The problems raised *for us* by the doctrine are naturally legion, and I shall try to show what, in the indigenous categories of Buddhist thought, corresponds roughly to an answer to them. Amongst other things, we will want to know how Buddhism can conceive or explain experience, action, and moral responsibility, without a real subject or agent; what rationale for action it can provide for the *Theravāda* practitioner himself; and – the main thread on which this book is woven – how there can be any coherent Buddhist account of personal identity and continuity, both in its general form, and in the particular case of rebirth (since of course Buddhism shares with all other major indigenous Indian religious traditions a belief in reincarnation).

The second classic problem which has determined the form of this study is that of 'Buddhism and Society'; more properly said, the problem of the relation between the content of Buddhist doctrine as it is found in the scriptural tradition of the Pali Canon and the other kinds of religious thought and practice found in what we call 'Buddhist societies'. This is, indeed, a problem which has had important repercussions in a wide intellectual sphere; along with the doctrine of not-self which we have just seen, Buddhism does not accept any idea of an omnipotent, eternal God, and although it accepts the existence of certain types of superhuman being, it does not accord any crucial religious value to human interaction with them. Thus, there is no place for worship, prayer, nor for many other things which are usually included *by definition* in the category of 'religion'. Durkheim's[8] realisation of this, and his insistence that therefore 'religion in society' must be defined in some other way (in his case, in terms of 'the sacred and the profane'), has been very widely influential in social anthropology and in all comparative and historical study of religion. I am not at all concerned with the matter of definition; the important factor here is the ubiquitous co-existence of Buddhism with other more 'popular' forms of religious thought and practice which centre on rituals aimed at gaining some benefit or avoiding some threatened harm from local gods, spirits, and so on. Spiro[9] has happily termed this 'culturally patterned interaction with culturally postulated superhuman beings'. These rituals differ from place to place, and generally have little or nothing to do with canonical Buddhism. However, by far the largest proportion of those whom we call by any other criterion 'Buddhists' (or, more importantly, who call themselves 'Buddhists') happily integrate into their religious activities as a whole both practices oriented towards canonical Buddhism, such as feeding monks, and these other more 'popular' practices. Whatever the nature of the particular practices, moreover, the aim of them all is the future well-being of the person who performs them, or perhaps of another (such as a dead relative) to whom the 'merit' gained by the ritual is donated.

If these 'popular' Buddhist activities are to have any sense for those who participate in them, we must necessarily assume that, in relation to the person performing the ritual, to any possible recipient of 'merit', and to any gods or spirits to whom the ritual might be directed, there exists some feeling – not necessarily or even usually articulated – for the continuing existence and importance in this life and thereafter of oneself, of others, and of gods. Given the precisely contradictory doctrines of intellectual Buddhism, our interpretative problem might then be described as that of grasping adequately and holistically the relation of the stricter, intellectual kind of Buddhist thought and practice to the actual thought and practice of most Buddhists.

We are lucky to have seen, within the last decade, a number of anthropological studies which together provide a satisfactory intellectual framework in which we can take account of all the varieties of Buddhism found in Buddhist societies. (I shall return to this presently.) I should stress that I am not myself writing as an anthropologist. I am interested primarily in the thought of canonical Buddhism, and only secondarily with problems in the anthropological study of Buddhist society as it affects our understanding of that thought. Accordingly, my concern will be to investigate how the fact of social differences in thought and practice are taken account of *by Buddhist doctrine itself*, and how they affect it. That is, I shall study the question of whether and how the psychological and philosophical analyses of Buddhist thought ignore or include the dimension of social and individual differentiation. I can indicate the answer to this in a preliminary way now: not only does the intellectual tradition take account of what it imagines to be the social and psychological reality of actual Buddhists, but also it is precisely this dimension which gives us the key structures by which we will understand the *Theravāda* account of personality and continuity as it was developed, given the initial postulate of the denial of self.

Readers of the scholarly literature on these questions will no doubt be familiar with most of the arguments raised and positions adopted. I will here review briefly some of the most influential opinions, in order to situate my own account within the history of western scholarship.

With regard to the first problem, the denial of self, we can classify most opinions into two groups: those who refuse to believe that the 'real' doctrine taught by the Buddha is what the canonical teaching of *anattā* appears to be; and those who do accept that the doctrine of *anattā* is what the Buddha taught, and that it means what it appears to say, but who then deduce from it a final evaluation that Buddhism is 'nihilistic', 'pessimistic', 'world-' and 'life-denying', and so on.

In the former group, a number of different approaches have led to the same conclusion. Perhaps the most flamboyant was Mrs Rhys Davids, who achieved a great deal of sound scholarly work for the Pali Text Society but came finally to believe that these canonical texts do not represent the 'original gospel' of the Buddha. She began to claim that the Buddha taught the way to a 'More' in man; that is, an unseen self or soul, 'the very man', who was more than the visible 'instruments' of body and mind. Relying on what she saw as 'evidence . . . overlooked by Buddhists, whose ignorance of their Canon (only now in the process of translation into South Asiatic vernaculars) must be met with to be realized' she thought that it was

> clear that the object of the utterance [i.e. one of the forms of the denial of self] was clearly to warn the new fellow-teachers never to identify the self, soul, very man with his parts or instruments, namely, body or ways of mind. They were to see that this (body, mind) 'is not of me, that I am not it, that for me it is not the self'. But the Buddhist inference from it has for centuries been the adding: this self being neither body nor mind, there is no self. Logically this is quite unwarranted.

She then asks 'How then is the self so oddly denied, denied even today, in orthodox Southern Buddhism?', and answers that it was the work of 'monasticism', which came to construe the doctrine as a 'pure nihilism', adding curiously that 'no cult of that kind could long persist in India without dishonour and discredit'.[10] Her husband had remarked more soberly, some forty years earlier, that

> the position [of not-self] is so absolute, so often insisted on, so fundamental to the right understanding of primitive Buddhism, that it is essential there should be no mistake about it. Yet the position is also so original, so fundamentally opposed to what is usually understood as religious belief, both in India and elsewhere, that there is a great temptation to attempt to find a loophole through which at least a covert or esoteric belief in the soul, and in future life (that is of course of a soul), can be recognised, in some sort of way, as part of so widely accepted a religious system. There is no loophole, and the efforts to find one have always met with unswerving opposition, both in the *Piṭakas* [i.e. canonical texts] themselves and in extra-canonical works.[11]

A similar approach to Mrs Rhys Davids' is followed by Christmas Humphries, founder of the Buddhist Society in England, and whose voluminous writings on Buddhism have been very widely distributed and influential. Blending a background in theosophy with a particular view of the *Mahāyāna* Buddhist tradition (that is, Buddhism in Northern Asia), he feels of the *anattā* doctrine that

> the difficulties in its understanding are inherent, for it is the Self which is striving to understand itself, and they are not made any easier by the persistent attempts of members of the *Theravāda* school, in the West as well as the East, to substitute a cold and dreary doctrine of their own which is unknown to the Pali Canon . . . Now, the Buddha nowhere denies the *Ātman* doctrine as originally taught [that is, as he has just explained, in the early Hindu texts, the *Upaniṣads*, where the *Ātman* is ultimately identical with the Cosmic Spirit, *Brahman*, which is 'the *absolute* principle which is common to and unites man and the Universe'] but only in the degraded form of an 'immortal soul' which separates man from man.

Humphries seems untroubled by any difficulties in understanding the doctrine, however, as the following entries in his *Popular Dictionary of Buddhism* make clear:

> *Ātman:* The Supreme SELF;* Universal Consciousness; Ultimate Reality. The divine element in Man, degraded into idea of an entity dwelling in the heart of each man, the thinker of his thoughts and doer of his deeds, and after death dwelling in bliss or misery according to deeds done in the body. For Buddhist attitude to *Ātman* conception see *Anattā* (q.v.).

> *Anattā:* The Doctrine of the non-separateness of all forms of life, and the opposite of that of an immortal and yet personal soul. As applied to man, it states

* As the quotations I give here show, in this context, capital letters seem often to be imbued with profound and mysterious significance. Neither Sanskrit nor Pali script uses them, nor any equivalent, and so they are useless as an instrument for our interpretative understanding.

> that there is no permanent ego or self in the five *skandhas** which make up the personality. The Buddha, however, nowhere denied the existence of an ego or soul, but taught that no permanent entity, not subject to *anicca* and *dukkha* [impermanence and suffering] can be found in any of the human faculties. That which pertains to any human being is not immortal; that which is immortal and unchanging is not the possession of any one human being. The reality behind the flux of *saṃsāra* [rebirth] is an indivisible unity . . .[12]

Professor Zaehner, a converted Roman Catholic who confessed privately to finding Buddhism 'an alien tradition',[13] was prevented by scholarly discipline from imputing quite so directly to Buddhists a belief their texts ubiquitously deny; but nevertheless, his view of Buddhism, conditioned by a Jungian-influenced sensibility to other religions, tended always to speak of the denial of self as merely 'the elimination of ego'. This formulation leads the way for him, as for so many others, to suggest that there is a Self, or Real Self behind the (small) self or ego. Thus he speaks of 'the Buddhist convention of using the word "Not-self" to mean something other than the Ego which has direct experience of both the subjective self and of objective phenomena'; and declares that 'the Buddha . . . recognizes that there is an eternal being transcending time, space and change; and this is the beginning of religion. Moreover the Hindus, overwhelmingly, and the Buddhists when they are off their guard, speak of this eternal being as the "self".' (As if an entire cultural tradition could somehow adopt a deceptive pose!)

Modern intellectual Hinduism, reacting against the Christian missionary effort, has often claimed that 'all religions are one' – and that Hinduism is inexpugnably valuable because it alone recognises this fact. Exponents of this view generally follow the particular Hindu school called *Vedānta*, for which the essence of the human individual self, called *Ātman*, and the Ultimate Reality of the Universe, called *Brahman*, are the same; the approach is then that since all religions are 'really' saying the same thing, Buddhism's denial of self must refer to a 'small', 'selfish' ego, and not to the magisterial cosmic *Ātman*. Thus, for Radhakrishnan, the Buddha 'repudiates the popular delusion of the individual ego and disputes the reality of the surface self . . . It is the false view that clamours for the perpetual continuance of the small self that Buddha refutes.'[14] Similarly Coomaraswamy finds that

> there is nothing . . . to show that the Buddhists ever really understand the pure doctrine of the *Ātman* . . . The attack which they led upon the idea of self or soul is directed against the conception of the eternity in time of an unchanging individuality; of the timeless spirit they do not speak, and yet they claim to have

*Body, feelings, sensations, 'mental formations', and consciousness. I shall discuss this analysis in Chapters 2 and 3.

disposed of the theory of the *Ātman*! . . . Buddhist dialectic . . . is directed to show that things are 'Empty'; when their component elements are recognized, there is no remainder, but only the 'Void'; he who realises this, attains *Nibbāna** and is freed. But we cannot distinguish this 'Void' or 'Abyss' from that *Brahman* which is 'No thing'.[15]

Recently the Indian scholar K. Bhattacharya, in a work which quotes frequently from Radhakrishnan, Plotinus, Schopenhauer, Jaspers, and others, as well as from Indian and Buddhist texts, attempts to show that the 'Real', 'Absolute' (etc.) of all these systems is the same, indescribable 'spiritual *Ātman*', whose nature is best grasped and expressed by silence.[16] It is, perhaps, as if entering a room full of people sitting in peaceful (or exasperated!) silence, one were to be able to conclude that they were all thinking 'the same thing'.

As I shall discuss in Chapter 3, perhaps the most frequent way in which the denial of self is presented in the texts is by placing the word *anattā*, 'not-self' in apposition to terms referring to any or all of the perceivable and conceivable aspects of human beings. Thus, for example, 'consciousness is not-self'.† The way is then open for interpreters to claim that if X Y Z (body, consciousness, or whatever) are 'not the self', then the self can, or must, be something else. This argument has been put forward by many scholars, a notable example in Germany being Georg Grimm, himself a Buddhist enthusiast.[17] The justifiably renowned Austrian scholar Frauwallner[18] followed a similarly common, though less positive, path in taking *anattā* as merely the strategic denial of any definite description of self, without affirming or denying the existence or non-existence of some transcendent, indefinable self. Like many others, he emphasised the occasional remarks in the texts to the effect that there is no point in discussing the problem of the existence or non-existence of the self, or the Buddha, after enlightenment, since such discussion is useless, or indeed a positive hindrance, to actual religious practice. Thus, finally, Buddhist metaphysics could be reduced to a kind of pragmatic agnosticism in which the self is not so much denied as declared inconceivable. *Anattā* then simply advises against uselessly trying to conceive it.

These examples will perhaps suffice to show something of the variety of positions adopted by those who see some other 'real' doctrine or attitude behind those apparently intended by the teaching of *anattā*. The other kind of approach, which accepts that in doctrine and attitude the denial of self is what it appears to be, but which then charges Buddhists

* The Pali form of Sanskrit *nirvāṇa*.

† See Chapter 3.2.1 for discussion of the linguistic form of *anattā*, and the possibilities for translation.

with 'pessimism', 'nihilism', or whatever, has naturally been widespread amongst those unsympathetic or opposed to Buddhism, in India as in the west. I will quote three examples, all, indeed, taken not from opponents of Buddhism but from illustrious Buddhist scholars.

The question of what is meant by the denial of self naturally leads, as we have already seen, to the question of what is involved in the idea of final *nirvāṇa*. For those who accept the literal meaning of *anattā*, this often means that *nirvāṇa* is conceived as a simple death; *nirvāṇa* at the end of a series of lives is comparable in this view, perhaps, to the modern western view of death at the end of a single life – a complete annihilation. Thus the French scholar Bareau, one of the greatest Buddhist historians, writes of *nirvāṇa* as the 'absolute' state beyond birth, death, and change:

> Is it pure nothingness [*pur néant*], as all its definitions lead one to believe and as all the opponents of Buddhism represent it? The latter's faithful deny this and describe it, on the contrary, as eternal and ineffable beatitude. They deny also that the saint who has entered it and who has broken off all relations with the world here below no longer exists. Nevertheless, one must really admit, if the person is nothing but a changing collection of phenomena, of transitory elements, that when all these have disappeared, nothing remains. Only the Personalist schools* could maintain that the person, because it is not truly identical with the elements which compose it, subsists in *nirvāṇa*. But again, the state in which it remained, after the complete cessation of all its psychic and biological functions, must have resembled a profound and dreamless sleep, a complete unconsciousness. To people who, like all Indians, believed themselves to pass without ceasing, without rest, immediately, from one existence to another, that is to say from one series of states of consciousness to another, that eternal and complete peace of psychic nothingness [*néant psychique*] must have seemed desirable, whereas it has always terrified people in the West.[19]

In a similar vein, Oldenburg, a German much of whose work at the turn of the century both on Buddhism and on Brahmanical religion has yet to be surpassed, holds overall the position that the logic of the Buddha's teaching leads to a view of *nirvāṇa* as 'nothing' (*das Nichts*) or 'a vacuum' (*ein Vakuum*), but that this was withheld in 'the official teaching of the Church' (*die offizielle Kirchenlehre*) so as not to deter the weak-minded. Thus 'the answer, to which the premises of the Buddhist teaching tended [is]: the self [*das Ich*] is not. Or, what is equivalent: the *Nirvāṇa* is annihilation [*die Vernichtung*] . . . [But] why present to the weak the keen edge of the truth: the prize of the delivered man's victory is nothingness?'[20] From this he arrives finally at the view that the 'official teaching' of Buddhism is a kind of pragmatic agnosticism, in the manner of Frauwallner which we have already seen. The Russian Stcherbatsky, a great scholar of Buddhist philosophy and logic, speaks straightforwardly

* For some remarks on whom see Chapters 5.2.3; 5.2.4; 6.1.1.

of 'lifeless *nirvāṇa*', a state which was 'life's annihilation', comparable to the extinction of a fire when its fuel is exhausted.[21] (This is, indeed, a common Buddhist metaphor.)

It seems to me that a great deal of the confusion on this issue arises from a need felt by many with strong religious convictions, and by some neutral scholars, to come to some final conclusion of their own – in terms, necessarily, of their own indigenous categories of thought – on the reality depicted by the conceptual products of other cultures. That is, in relation to my present concern, once certain translations of Buddhist terms are accepted, and one speaks of 'self', 'person', 'death', 'rebirth', 'release', 'enlightenment', and so on, it is as if the task is simply to make a judgement of our own on the relations, logical or otherwise, between these concepts, and on the 'ultimate reality' to which they are taken to refer. As might be expected from my earlier remarks on the investigation and comparison of cultures, I shall try to adopt a different approach. The scholar must, I think, *qua scholar* eschew all such questions and concerns (even though as an individual thinker or believer he may or may not want to arrive at a personal conclusion). The task of scholarship is endlessly to investigate, by any and every academic discipline which proves necessary, the words in which beliefs and doctrines are presented, the categories of thought which they express, and the function or functions which they might have in the life and thought of those who hold them.

Accordingly, in Parts I and II (Chapters 2–4), I shall develop an analysis of the Buddhist doctrine of not-self as a soteriological strategy. Using Weber's distinction between the religious specialist and the ordinary man, the 'virtuoso' and the 'religiously unmusical', I will argue that the denial of self in fact represents a linguistic taboo; but a taboo which is applied differently by different Buddhists, according to their position on the continuum from ordinary man to specialist. For ordinary men, the doctrine is not a matter of immediate, literal, and personal concern. As a socially institutionalised system of symbols, Buddhist theory functions as a reference point which orients, and provides a criterion for, the general religious outlook and practices of the ordinary Buddhist; in this sense, the *anattā* doctrine's crucial importance is to provide an intransigent symbolic opposition to the belief system of the Brahmin priesthood, and therefore to the social position of Brahmins themselves. For Buddhist specialists, considered as a general category, the doctrine *is* taken literally and personally, and thus *anattā* represents a determinate pattern of self-perception and psychological analysis, which is at once the true description of reality – in Buddhist terms it 'sees things as they really are' – and the instrument by which the aspirant to *nirvāṇa* progresses towards, and achieves, his goal. Within the category of 'specialists' there are of course differences in emphasis. As we shall see, there is a difference between the way the denial of self is appropriated by the monk earnestly engaged in meditative reflection (which characterises the most practical form of treading the Buddhist Path), and the way it was appropriated, and elaborated, by the Buddhist scholastic, concerned with preserving and clarifying the conceptual content of Buddhist theory, but not necessarily with *himself* using it to attain *nirvāṇa*.

I shall distinguish two main forms of the soteriological strategy of *anattā*, corresponding to the two emphases of the doctrine as the true description of reality, or as an instrument of salvation. There is the 'right view' of not-self, which opposes other 'wrong views', and which forms part of the practice of 'mental purification'; and there is the 'no-view' approach, which imposes a certain moral and epistemological attitude towards the activity of conceptualisation *per se*, and which brings with it a particular, and peculiarly Buddhist, aesthetic of 'emptiness'.

As a preliminary to this presentation of the denial of self, I will devote Chapter 1 to tracing the development in pre-Buddhist India of the fundamental conceptions of the person and of time which inform Buddhist thinking; and of the categories in which it, like all other major Indian traditions, elaborated its ontology and psychology: *saṃsāra*, 'the round of rebirth', reincarnation; *karma*, the doctrine of action and the rewards, punishments, good or bad fortune, which it entails; and *mokṣa* (in Buddhism *nirvāṇa*), release from the round of rebirth, 'enlightenment'.

The second problem, 'Buddhism and Society', has evoked less controversy than the doctrine of *anattā*, and in my account I draw on what is slowly becoming a consensus of opinion among students of the subject about the way it should be approached. In the past, of course, many scholars concerned with the intellectual systems found in the textual traditions of Indian religion were content to approach the anthropological problem of the social and historical position of such thinking in the spirit of Monier-Williams, who distinguished between 'what may be called *true Buddhism* as taught by its founder' and 'its corruptions in some of the countries bordering on India and North-eastern Asia'. For him 'the corruptions and schisms of Buddhism are the natural and inevitable outcome of its own root-ideas and fundamental doctrines', since the 'primitive Buddhism' taught by the Buddha was at the same time too unnatural in contradicting 'the simple working of the eternal instincts of humanity' – examples he gives are marriage and worshipping a god – and had too 'tolerant, liberal and eclectic [a] spirit' to survive intact in the syncretic atmosphere of Indian religion.[22] Similarly, Sir Charles Eliot found that the criticism – that Buddhists are prone to corrupt their faith – is just, for their courteous acquiescence in other creeds enfeebles and denaturalises their own . . . Such statements as that the real religion of the Burmese is not Buddhism but animism are, I think, incorrect, but even the Burmese are dangerously tolerant . . . The weakness comes from an absence of any command against superstitious rites and beliefs.[23]

This kind of attitude to the realities of Buddhism in society is not confined to western scholars. It is found, for example, in the essays and the speeches of Anāgārika Dharmapāla, a crucially important figure in the modern history of Buddhism in Ceylon. Preaching a reformed, modernistic Buddhism in which a 'Return to Righteousness' would be based on Buddhist morality and psychology mixed with the findings of modern science, he declared:

The message of the Buddha I have to bring to you is free from theology, priestcraft, rituals, ceremonies, dogmas, heavens, hells and other theological shibboleths. The Buddha taught to the civilized Aryans of India 25 centuries ago a scientific religion containing the highest individualistic altruistic ethics, a philosophy of life based on psychological mysticism and a cosmogony which is in harmony with geology, astronomy, radioactivity and relativity.

Deploring the contemporary state of religious practice, he advises lay Buddhists to ignore the 'vulgar sciences' of 'astrology, occultism, ghostology and palmistry', holding that 'the occultists dabbling in mystery and esotericism bring down the human understanding into animalism . . . And this is especially so in India, the land of insane mysticism and animalising sciences.' Thinking (in 1920) of 'the past greatness of the Sinhalese race', he says that

the people have degenerated to an alarming extent. Religion they have forgotten. The *bhikkhus* [monks] have become pleasure loving, neglecting the study of the Higher Doctrine [that is, Buddhist psychology written in Pali] . . . devoting their time to poetical literature of an erotic kind in the Sanskrit language . . . Intelligent, educated, unselfish, patient, self-sacrificing *Upāsakas* and *Bhikkhus* [laymen and monks] are needed today to lead the ignorant, helpless Sinhalese Buddhists. In another ten years *pure Buddhism* will cease to exist in the historic island [my italics].[24]

Although he is without these exaggerated condemnations of popular religion, in both western and eastern thinkers, and does not make the assumption that the ideal form of Buddhism or Hinduism, as portrayed in their textual traditions, represents any actual historical reality, or any 'original' and 'pure' form from which popular practice has 'degenerated', Zaehner still takes the same fundamental sociological (or rather, non-sociological) attitude: 'one of the paradoxes of Hinduism has always been the yawning gap that separates its higher manifestations from the frankly superstitious and magical practices that go to make up the religious fare of the rural masses'.[25] I shall try to approach the problem, in relation to Buddhism, in the spirit advocated by Pocock: 'There is no "yawning gap" between beliefs which Professor Zaehner might think "superstitious" and the rarefied thought of the sectarian philosophies. These are interconnected not only in the minds of individual men but are interlinked through social relations to constitute that whole which is inevitably hidden from the student of texts.'[26] Although I am a student of texts, and not an empirical social scientist, my particular concern is precisely how far the theoretical texts of the Buddhist tradition reflect and incorporate what they see to be the social whole in which they operate. I will argue that the picture of social and psychological reality in which Buddhist theory sees itself as inserted is, albeit in simplified, schematised and idealised form, congruent with that developed by modern anthropologists working on the subject. Let me present this picture briefly by means of a number of interpretative categories, presented as dichotomies, or three-fold distinctions along a continuum. Clearly, any such tools of cultural research should not be used too simplistically, and they obviously do not represent directly and simply any separable 'levels' or 'entities' in cultural reality.

With this caveat, let me turn to the first distinction, which was made, as early as 1917, by de la Vallée Poussin, between what he called 'religions' and 'disciplines of salvation' in India. Of what he terms 'religions', he says that

> whatever be their diversity, all were 'made' to meet, and do meet in some manner, the needs of Man living in society, needs supernatural, moral and secular, needs individual and social. They teach a superhuman power, whatever be the nature and dignity of this power; they explain the duties of Man towards it, or, more uncompromisingly, the right *modus vivendi* of Man with it; they have prayers or formulas, sacrifices, sacraments. They are concerned with the welfare of the dead, and also with personal welfare in this life; they have devices and ceremonies for the work and the anxieties of everyday life, for illnesses and for sins, which are often another kind of illness. They teach a general rule of conduct, and penetrate the Law of family or of tribe.

But also

> side by side with the religions properly so called, there arose in India from about the seventh century B.C. – to last for many centuries, attracting thousands of adherents and exercising a strong influence on the Indian religions – a number of 'disciplines', with a special character of their own. They cannot be exactly described either as philosophies or as religions. We have to see what is the right name for them . . .
>
> In contrast with religions, the disciplines are made for ascetics, for ascetics only. Further they are purely personal or individualistic, that is they do not care for one's neighbour or for the dead. They are unsocial and often antisocial: they

deprecate and often prohibit marriage . . . they are not concerned with mundane ends at all . . .

In many respects they are widely different one from another . . . But they are sisters born from the same parents, namely disgust with life and love of mystery. If they do not agree concerning deliverance and the path to deliverance, they all pursue deliverance. The right name for them seems to be 'disciplines of salvation' or 'paths to deliverance'.[27]

The most important effect, for my present concern, of the mutual interaction and influence of these two systems, was the development of an intermediate range of thought and practice, such that certain symbols, ideas, and practices derived from the 'disciplines' came to be used for goals usually associated with the 'religions'. Thus, as the disciplines came to have a more settled social place and function, they came to incorporate as lesser aims in their total system such mundane goals as success in life, freedom from illness, and so on – and, most importantly, for the lay and non-ascetic supporter, the intermediate eschatological goal of better rebirth in the round of *saṃsāra*, rather than the complete escape from it into 'deliverance'. *This* is the crucial distinction within Buddhist practice which one must grasp if one is to understand its nature as a religion in society, and the way in which its theoretical analyses accommodate the facts of internal differentiation.

Building on the work of previous scholars, Spiro has distinguished what he calls 'the three systems of *Theravāda* Buddhism'. First, there is nibbanic Buddhism. This term, derived from the Pali *nibbāna* (Sanskrit *nirvāṇa*), refers to the ideal system of thought and practice leading to complete escape from rebirth, as it is depicted in the texts of the Pali Canon. The second system is that of kammatic Buddhism, derived from the Pali *kamma* (Sanskrit *karma*), which is concerned with acquiring, by good action and its soteriological rewards (*kamma*), a desirable future rebirth. Examples of such a rebirth would be as a god in one of the many heavens of Buddhist cosmology, or as a man in more fortunate circumstances. That these two soteriological systems are not ideologically distinct is shown by what is perhaps the most widely acknowledged goal of Buddhists nowadays, whether monks or laymen. It is generally considered impossible in our time to attain *nibbāna*, because of the prevalent corruption of the age; accordingly, one hopes for rebirth as a man (since release from rebirth cannot be attained except as a man) in the time of the coming Buddha Metteyya, as *nibbāna* will then be again a real possibility.

Apart from these two soteriological systems, Spiro distinguishes

still a third type of Buddhism, one which is concerned with man's worldly welfare: the curing of illness, protection from demons, the prevention of droughts, and so on . . . Since the latter is primarily concerned with protection from danger, I shall call it *apotropaic* Buddhism . . .

Having delineated three distinctive Buddhist systems, I do not wish to suggest that living Buddhism presents itself as packaged into three neat bundles of belief and practice. On the contrary, when first encountered, living Buddhism appears as a bewildering hodgepodge of beliefs and practices, some canonical and some non-canonical, which it is difficult to distinguish from those comprising the non-Buddhist religious systems found in all Buddhist societies, let alone from each other.[28]

This approach to the problem has been accompanied by the development of a more general interpretative dichotomy in anthropology, that of Redfield and Marriott between the 'Great' and 'Little' Traditions. The former refers to the common inheritance of a wide cultural area, transmitted in a definite form (in writing or mnemonically by specialists) – in our case, the literary tradition of the Pali Canon. The little tradition refers to local beliefs and practices, restricted to particular areas and transmitted orally – in our case, centring on interaction with local gods and spirits, apotropaic rituals, and the like. Many justified criticisms have been made of the more extreme formulations of this idea, and within anthropology itself it is certainly somewhat out-dated. In a study of Buddhism invaluable for this whole problem, *Buddhism and the Spirit Cults of North-east Thailand*, Tambiah remarks that such formulations

have been mistaken in two important respects: first, insufficient regard was paid to the fact that the great literary tradition is itself varied and has been both cumulative and changing; secondly, it has for some curious reason not been seen that contemporary live religion, even that observed in the village, incorporates a great deal of the literary tradition. *Brahman* priests, Buddhist monks, ritual experts and scribes in some measure deal with literary and oral knowledge transmitted from the past and which they themselves systematically transmit to their successors. And for the common people at large such texts and knowledge have a referential and legitimating function, even if they themselves have no direct access to them.[29]

Indeed, the great literary tradition of the Pali Canon not only contains whole texts – such as the *Jātakas*, 'Birth-Stories', which are legends of the Buddha's former lives, sometimes as an animal in stories which resemble Aesop's fables – which have little to do with the ideal Buddhist quest for *nirvāṇa*, but also there are many traces in the normative texts which deal with 'high' matters of psychology and morality, of the 'popular religion' of their time 'The North-east of India, roughly from 500 to 300 B.C.).[30] Clearly the internal differentiation of Buddhist culture is ancient, ubiquitous, and important.

It seems to me that the complexities, and potential misuse, of the great/little tradition distinction concern more immediately the ethnographer and social anthropologist than the intellectual historian. In social fact, the religion of Buddhist societies, as of Indian society generally, is and always has been a coherent and unified field, from which the 'pure' normative systems of ideas are abstracted – by intellectuals within the tradition as much as by western interpreters. However, for the systematic study of these ideas one has to accept, I think, a certain measure of artificial abstraction from social reality if one is to keep intelligibly to a single line of argument. Thus I will use the terms 'great' and 'little' tradition, not supposing them to represent real structures of Buddhist culture from the sociological point of view, but rather as a shorthand means of keeping an awareness of the social whole of Buddhism in the background, while I am discussing some of the complexities of Buddhist thought.

There is one final interpretative dichotomy which I will use explicitly, and presuppose implicitly, throughout the study which follows. This is Gombrich's,

> between what people say they believe and say they do, and what people really believe and really do . . . What people really do I shall call simply religious behaviour. What they say about their beliefs and practices I shall call 'cognitive' . . . What people really believe I am aware to be ultimately unknowable; but this does not mean that it is nonsense to talk about it. Only a pure behaviourist refrains from making inferences from what people really do to what they are thinking and feeling. If a lapsed Roman Catholic states that he has lost all belief in God, and yet is seen to cross himself at a moment of crisis, we infer from his actions that he is operating on an ideological system which differs from his explicit or conscious beliefs: he behaves *as if* he still believed in God. In old-fashioned terms, it is the religion of the heart, not the head. So I propose to call it 'affective' religion.

This distinction is particularly useful in connexion with Buddhism, precisely because so many of the central ideas of its ideal, normative system are counter-intuitive, and seem *prima facie* unlikely vehicles for the religious aspirations of the ordinary man in society. For example, Gombrich himself has used the distinction to account for different ideas and attitudes to the figure of the Buddha. Cognitively, the Buddha was a man who attained final enlightenment some 2500 years ago, and who, being both dead and during his life a preacher of the most extreme self-reliance in religious practice, is no longer available to assist the this- or other-worldly aspirations of present-day Buddhists. However, from observed behaviour towards relics and images of the Buddha (to which offerings, prayers, and the like, are addressed) one can conclude that he is – for the majority of ordinary Buddhists – affectively divine.[31]

I have said that the picture of social and psychological reality in which the Buddhist textual tradition sees itself as operating is congruent with what I have called the consensus of opinion among modern scholars. I said also that it is this dimension which allows us to understand the key structures of the *Theravāda* account of personality and continuity, given the doctrine of *anattā*. Let me now indicate, in brief outline, what my reasons are for arguing this. Firstly, the supposed psychological reality of the progression, along the Buddhist Path, from the self-interested and self-positing ordinary man to the self-denying and selfless ascetic virtuoso, makes use of categories similar to Gombrich's 'cognitive' and 'affective'. It is thus, according to Buddhism itself, only a first step cognitively to pay allegiance to the denial of self. To 'realise' the truth of it personally – both to understand it and to make it real – involves an affective change in personality and psychology only brought about by long and arduous practice. (I will discuss this in detail in Chapter 3.1.4.)

Secondly, in picturing both the relationship between its theoretical system and other modes of thinking in society, and the variety of linguistic forms in which 'self' and 'persons' are discussed, Buddhism uses a distinction between the categories of 'ultimate' and 'conventional' truth. Ultimate truth refers to those psychological and philosophical analyses contained in the canonical tradition which are held to be universally true: that is, it denotes the form and content of what are considered to be the crucial doctrines of the great intellectual tradition, to be used by the specialist meditator and scholar. Conventional truth – of which, of course, there is a very great deal in the canonical texts also, since they are not only tracts of psychology and philosophy – refers both to the general structures and to the particular local content of the various little traditions of Buddhist societies, which are used by the ordinary man (and indeed by the specialist when not dealing with matters of ultimate concern).

Accordingly, in Parts III and IV (Chapters 5–8), which deal with the accounts of personality, rebirth, and continuity generally, I will organise the material in terms of the distinction between ultimate and conventional truth, since only thus can we understand the particular nature and dynamic of Buddhist thinking. In addition, however, to using concepts which are explicitly part of Buddhism itself, and to investigating the conscious and rational structure of its ideas, I will develop an analysis of these ideas in terms of certain unconscious and non-rational patterns of imagery. I will argue that these patterns of imaginative and 'collective' representation might be seen to be fundamental not only to Buddhist intellectuals' thinking about personality and continuity, but also to much wider ways in which Buddhists at all levels of conceptual sophistication represent to themselves society, psychology, and cosmology. I will suggest that it is through these regularities in the imagination of *Theravāda* culture that we can best see Buddhism as a single cultural system, which includes in a single imaginative universe all the varieties of thought and practice, from the specialist intellectual and meditating monks, to the ordinary peasant-layman.

As I have already stated, I am not writing as an empirical social scientist; that is, in presenting these patterns of imagery, I have not used material drawn directly from fieldwork among modern Buddhists, but only from the content of the Pali Canon. I hope that in future anthropological researchers in Buddhist countries will find my work helpful, and will attempt to investigate the incidence of these patterns of imagery in the spontaneous verbal products of native informants. (We have no means of checking such 'popular' culture in the past; it is dead and unrecorded.) But the absence from my account of material gathered in direct fieldwork does not invalidate my claims for these patterns of imagery as the unifying fundamentals of 'Buddhist culture'. Obviously, the Buddhist Canon is itself, intrinsically and empirically, perhaps the most crucial part of 'Buddhist culture', and it can be taken, I think, to reflect directly or indirectly the whole spread of that culture. The intellectual content of the Canon is itself, as Durkheim would have said, a 'social fact'. Equally undeniable as 'social facts' are the two major aspects of Buddhist society which I have tried to relate to the imagery of the Canon: the institution of the monkhood with its necessary relation to the 'household' laity, and the fact of South Asia's being a peasant agricultural society. There is a good book waiting to be written on the relation between the psychological universe of the Buddhist Canon and the indigenous psychology of 'popular' culture in 'Buddhist' countries (if such exists as a separately specifiable entity). But the most important focus of my work is in philosophy and intellectual history.

I will conclude these introductory remarks by describing briefly the kinds of text found in the *Theravāda* tradition which contain the ideas I shall be discussing; and by attempting to suggest, rather impressionistically, the particular nature of this *Theravāda* tradition and its relation to the history of Buddhism as a whole. I will not want to write any kind of chronologically detailed history,[32] but rather to sketch something of the style in which the *Theravāda* presents its form of Buddhism, and some simple differences in the flavour of this kind of Buddhism in contrast with that predominant in the Northern, *Mahāyāna** traditions of Tibet, China, and Japan.

* *Mahāyāna*, the 'Great Vehicle' was the self-designation of various 'schools' who contrasted themselves with those of the *Hīnayāna*, 'Lesser Vehicle', of which the

The texts which preserve *Theravāda* doctrine for us display a quite specific variety in literary character. Traditionally, these texts are grouped into three collections, or 'Baskets' (*Piṭaka*), those of the *Suttā*, 'Stories' or 'Dialogues'; *Vinaya*, '(Monastic) Discipline' or 'Rules of Conduct'; and *Abhidhamma*, 'Further Doctrine'. Of these, for our purposes, the first two may be taken together;[33] in them, the kind of doctrinal matter with which I shall be concerned is presented in the form of narrative, as episodes in the life of the Buddha and his most famous monks. In appreciating these texts, their narrative form must constantly be borne in mind. Not only, as orally transmitted tales, do they have a particular form, in which repetitions, standard passages, formulae, and the like abound, but also very frequently the narrative framework gives a quite specific function and meaning to the doctrinal ideas it contains – and so this function and meaning can be wholly distorted if the narrative context is not preserved in interpretation. Although I will give some detailed examples of this,* for brevity I will have for the most part to discuss particular textual passages in abstraction from their context. As a general rule, let me recommend this: in connexion with any idea which seems puzzling, bizarre, profound, or whatever, the very first step in further understanding must be to seek the original text (or its translation) in order to set the idea in its context.

The *Theravāda Suttā* and its *Vinaya*, like the whole of its scholarly tradition, are preserved in Pali, a form of Middle Indo-Aryan. As far as can be told, from comparing these narratives with the corresponding forms preserved in Sanskrit, Tibetan, Chinese, and some other minor languages, there seems to be little drastic doctrinal or literary difference in the content of these 'early' tales, throughout the Buddhist world. Where a difference is seen, both in style and content, is in the later kinds of intellectual literature produced by the various traditions. In the *Theravāda*, later scholarly works can be divided into two main forms. The first is the third of the three traditional 'Baskets', the *Abhidhamma*, 'Further Doctrine'. This has its beginnings, visible also in the *Suttā*, in lists of analytic categories called *mātikā*; indeed, sometimes the three collections of texts are called *Suttā*, *Vinaya*, and *Mātikā*.[34] We have already met perhaps the most pervasive of these, the *khandhā* (Sanskrit *skandha*), 'categories', 'aggregates', 'constituents of personality', in

Theravāda, 'Way of the Elders', was but one. Although in fact it is other traditions (such as the *Sarvāstivāda* and *Sautrāntika*) which figure much more prominently in *Mahāyāna* texts as examples of the 'Lesser Vehicle', I shall for simplicity compare *Theravāda* directly with *Mahāyāna*, as it is the only *Hīnayāna* tradition to have survived as a socially institutionalised form, with an extensive textual corpus.

* See Chapter 4.2.3.

which the apparently unitary person is divided into five impersonal groups of elements. These lists take on a quite specific conceptual and psychological function in *Theravāda* soteriology,* but in a more general perspective they would obviously have been valuable in a predominantly oral culture – for both mnemonic and ritual (chanting) purposes – and are, indeed, by no means confined to Buddhism in early Indian religion.[35] The *Abhidhamma* textual corpus is a huge elaboration of this list-making form of preserving and extending doctrine. By far the largest part of these texts consists simply in lists of categories for analysing psycho-physical phenomena, each term in a list frequently being given its own list of synonyms.

The second of the two later forms of scholarly text is that of the commentaries. These were made on all kinds of primary material, whether *Suttā*, *Vinaya* or *Abhidhamma*, and mix a discursive, sometimes even narrative, explanatory style with that of the list-making, synonymous-category form. A modern (western) *Theravāda* scholar-monk, Ñāṇamoli, speaks of the 'three main layers' of doctrinal literature as follows, using his own image of a voyage of exploration in conceptual and mental space: 'The *Suttas* offered descriptions of discovery; the *Abhidhamma*, map-making; but emphasis now [in the Commentaries] is not on discovery, or even on mapping, so much as on consolidating, filling in and explaining. The material is worked over for consistency.'[36] The epitome of this last kind of scholarship is the *Visuddhimagga*, 'The Path of Purification', written in the fifth century A.D. by Buddhaghosa on the basis of existing Sinhalese commentaries,† and which is

> an exhaustive summary in Pali of Buddhist doctrine, still the best work of its kind. He [Buddhaghosa] then wrote commentaries in Pali on most works in the Canon. The Sinhalese books on which these commentaries are based have perished, because he superseded them. Though he may at first have intended only to translate them he in fact edited and systematized them. He quotes nearly every earlier work of Pali literature known to have existed. His interpretations are mutually consistent. To this day Buddhaghosa's Buddhism is in effect the unitary standard of doctrinal orthodoxy for all *Theravāda* Buddhists, whether or not they are educated enough to be aware of the problem.[37]

I shall quote extensively from the *Visuddhimagga* throughout the study which follows, in Part II when dealing with the denial of self, as giving explicitly the *Theravāda* view of what is contained implicitly in the earlier Suttā, and in Parts III and IV, dealing with the accounts of personality, rebirth, and continuity found in the later scholarly literature,

* See Chapters 2.3.2 and 3.3.2.

† According to the tradition, these Sinhalese texts were themselves based on Pali originals brought from India.

as being the finest example of that genre. (It is perhaps worth emphasising, in passing, this range in the kinds of text which form, to a greater or lesser extent in the various sections, the basis of my study. That is, not only for its own sake is it important to remember the difference in cultural ambience, in the kinds of questions asked and the answers thought appropriate, found in the various texts of the developing tradition; but also it is part of my argument for the significance of patterns of imagery in giving us a unified picture of the *Theravāda* imagination that the same patterns are found throughout the entire range of its literary tradition.)

The whole of this literary tradition, as I remarked, is written in the form of Middle Indo-Aryan called Pali. Throughout its history, for almost all *Theravāda* Buddhists, this has been a learned language, a *lingua franca* for education and scholarship, similar to Latin in the western Middle Ages, and indeed to Sanskrit in Indian culture as a whole. What Coulson says of Sanskrit and its use by the poet Kālidāsa and the theologian-philosopher Śaṃkara applies equally to Pali and its use by *Theravāda* scholars:

> By now [i.e. after the very earliest period] Sanskrit was not a mother tongue but a language to be studied and consciously mastered . . . On this point it may be useful to make a twofold distinction – between a living and a dead language, and between a natural and a learned one. A language is natural when it is acquired and used instinctively; it is living when people choose to converse and formulate ideas in it in preference to any other. To the modern Western scholar Sanskrit is a dead as well as a learned language. To Kālidāsa or Śaṃkara it was a learned language but a living one.[38]

Mahāyāna Buddhism in India came to use Sanskrit as the medium of its scholarship. Although thus both Pali and Sanskrit were learned but living languages for the scholarly traditions of the *Theravāda* and *Mahāyāna* respectively, there are, I think, significant differences in the cultural and historical connotations of this linguistic fact. This comes to light clearly if we trace the two traditions beyond the borders of India, into South-east and Northern Asia respectively. At least, using the linguistic point as a focus will enable us to trace at once the historical development of the two traditions and the major differences in the 'flavour' of the Buddhism they present.

Theravāda Buddhism has relied continuously and exclusively, in its great tradition, on Pali as the language of its sacred texts and as the medium of education and scholarship. Conversely, Pali itself has been almost exclusively confined to the texts of the *Theravāda* tradition. Throughout the history of *Theravāda*, in India and in its expansion over the surrounding areas of South and South-east Asia we call Ceylon,

Burma, Thailand, and Cambodia, there has been a continuous literary tradition of canonical texts, commentaries and sub-commentaries, written in a single and little-developing learned language. This can symbolise for us, and doubtless in historical fact was both cause and effect of, the peculiarly conservative nature of the *Theravāda* tradition. Linguistic conservatism of this sort was accompanied by a doctrinal conservatism, a lack of conceptual innovation of any depth; and a tendency rigidly to separate an unchanging 'pure' and 'ultimate' form of Buddhism contained in the Pali texts from the multitudinous variety of 'popular' and merely 'conventional' forms of culture and religion performed in the vernacular. Two modern examples can perhaps catch the spirit: we have seen the zealous reformer in Ceylon, Anāgārika Dharmapāla, urging a return to 'pure Buddhism'. For him a crucial part of this project was the promulgation of Pali texts and education in the language, since 'to understand the *Buddha Vacana* [the Buddha's teaching] a knowledge of Pali is essential'.[39] Similarly, many of the western monks in contemporary Ceylon, who practise in forest hermitages an austere form of meditative life based on the ancient texts, refuse to learn *Sinhala*, despite assiduously studying Pali, since the former would bring them too much into contact with the 'popular' religion they see as having nothing to do with their form of Buddhist life.[40]

All this contrasts strongly with the literary and linguistic history of *Mahāyāna* Buddhism. As I mentioned earlier, the early tales recorded in the Suttā (Sanskrit *Sūtra*) of all traditions seem to be very similar, as do the codes of monastic discipline, to the *Vinaya*. It is in the later scholarly literature that differences are seen. *Mahāyāna* scholarship did produce, like the *Theravāda*, catalogues of analytic lists and synonyms, in works of 'Further Doctrine', *Abhidharma*; and commentaries in exegesis of earlier material. It also produced, however, kinds of text the *Theravāda* did not. Among those produced in India, perhaps the most important are the 'Perfection of Wisdom' texts, *Prajñāpāramitā*, and new philosophical works, usually in the form of (verse) text and commentary. The former are very important for the aesthetic feeling, the style of *Mahāyāna* spirituality. They are usually voluminous and repetitive, concentrating on that part of the denial of self which stresses the sense of 'Emptiness'. I shall discuss this in Chapter 4, where I will argue that though this kind of feeling is not absent from *Theravāda*, it is not there very strongly emphasised. The latter new kind of literature, the philosophical texts, reflect the adoption of Sanskrit as the language of *Mahāyāna* intellectualism. It shows the entry of *Mahāyāna* into the wider and more variegated world of Indian religious thought and philosophy generally. These texts, unlike those of *Theravāda*, came explicitly to place themselves in, and argue in the terms of, mainstream Indian logic and philosophy, opposing themselves in detail to varieties of Hindu thought as well as to other schools of Buddhism. Such a position could hardly have made for, and did not in fact make for, a doctrinal single-mindedness, not to say isolation, of the conservative *Theravāda* sort.

It was not only the detailed intellectual adaptation of *Mahāyāna* thinking to Indian thought as a whole which produced more variation and flexibility in its doctrinal products. In all the many new developments in ontology and epistemology, in the characters of religious mythology and in the conception of the Buddha, I think we should see not only an increase in range and subtlety of purely Buddhist ideas, but a result of the readiness of *Mahāyāna*, in contrast with the unwillingness of the *Theravāda*, to include popular ideas and practices in what it is willing to call, without the simple and exclusivist dichotomy between ultimate and conventional truth, properly 'Buddhist' culture. The philosophy of *Mahāyāna* has, indeed, explicit and very good reasons for so doing;[41] but the immediate consequence is that the surface level of its textual discourse is accordingly very much more culturally extensive and complex than is that of *Theravāda*. The linguistic fact of adopting Sanskrit, and this accommodation to 'popular' religion, are themselves perhaps not entirely unconnected: for the form of the *Mahāyāna* relationship to its wider cultural milieu – roughly, and with exceptions, inclusivist and accommodating, through hierarchising into a totality, rather than exclusivist and dichotomising into an opposition – resembles far more the general form of the Sanskritic Hindu attitude to its wider cultural setting than it does that of the *Theravāda*.[42]

This flexibility of *Mahāyāna* comes to light clearly in its expansion beyond India into Northern Asia: doubtless part of the reason for its enormous missionary success in Tibet, China, and Japan was its willingness to accommodate and colonise the indigenous practices it found there. Where *Theravāda*, through its maintenance of a Pali textual tradition (amongst other things), remained oriented towards its Indian origins, the sacred texts of the *Mahāyāna Sūtras* and commentaries, as well as later works, were translated at an early stage into Tibetan and Chinese; these translations then became the Buddhist Canon of those cultures. Thus, Tibetan, Chinese, and finally Japanese *Mahāyāna* Buddhism developed away from the simply Indian cultural world, producing quite new – and equally valuable – forms of cultural expression. Again, a modern example will serve to catch the spirit. Anyone familiar with the introduction of Tibetan Buddhism into the west, particularly in America, will know that while preserving a great respect and concern for the maintenance of their Tibetan linguistic and cultural heritage, many teachers in the west are concerned to present their message in western languages, and in the terms of western thought.[43]

Such, roughly, is the nature and position of *Theravāda* in the history of Buddhism as a whole. Although I shall speak on occasion directly of *Mahāyāna* in the study which follows, I shall be consistently concerned only with *Theravāda*. Thus when the word 'Buddhism' appears without qualification, it should be taken as referring directly only to the *Theravāda* – though of course on many occasions what is said will be equally true of the *Mahāyāna* traditions.

Finally, a brief word about the style of the book. I have attempted to achieve two, perhaps incompatible, ends. First, I hope to have provided specialists in Indian and Buddhist studies with a new account of a familiar doctrine, and an account which treats the material exhaustively. I do not know of any major relevant passage in the texts which I have not discussed explicitly, and I have given comprehensive exemplification of the patterns of imagery I discuss. Secondly, I have also aimed to provide a picture of an alien cultural world for philosophers and intellectual historians which will be comprehensible without any previous knowledge of Buddhism or of Indian religion. I have, accordingly, repeated and summarised my argument during the course of the book in a way I would not have needed to do if I were writing only for specialists. I hope that specialists will not find the repetitions too unnecessary, and that non-specialists will not find the detail too exhaustive.

Part I

The cultural and social setting of Buddhist thought

1 The origins of rebirth

> If in Buddhism the proud attempt be made to conceive a deliverance in which man himself delivers himself, to create a faith without a god, it is Brahmanical speculation which has prepared the way for this thought.
>
> Herman Oldenburg (1882) p. 53

1.1. Buddhism and early Indian religion

In this chapter I shall do two things: first, I shall indicate, in outline, what I conceive to be the place in the general history of early Indian religion of the Buddha and his teaching. In doing this, I shall emphasise, within the general spectrum which seems to have existed, the particular tradition of Brahmanical thought and practice, arguing that it was this tradition which had the decisive intellectual influence on Buddhism, as indeed on all subsequent Indian thought. Secondly, I shall trace in some detail the evolution, within the Brahmanical tradition, of those fundamental categories of thinking in which Buddhism, and all other major Indian religions, have elaborated their ontology, eschatology and psychology. These categories are:

1. *saṃsāra* – 'the round of rebirth'. The idea that each person (however that is conceived) lives through a series of lives, which can occur in various forms both in this world and elsewhere.

2. *karma* – 'action', 'moral retribution'. The belief that it is action which causes this process of rebirth, and experience within it; the moral quality of actions performed previously – usually but not necessarily in past lives – determines the happiness or suffering experienced thereafter. This gives both one type of explanation of suffering and evil, and a possible rubric for religious and moral behaviour which tries to improve one's lot in the future. One may hope for rebirth in better circumstances, or for an escape from rebirth entirely.

3. *mokṣa* – 'release', 'liberation' (in Buddhism usually called *nirvāṇa*). This refers to the escape from rebirth, to an ultimate state variously conceived, but usually involving some or all of the qualities of freedom, bliss, transcendental knowledge, and power.

In relation to the general early history of Indian religion, we must place the figure of Buddhism against a background composed of two other elements: one, in diachronic focus, being the development of great tradition – Hindu and Buddhist – culture over the Indian sub-continent; the other, in synchronic focus, being the milieu of wandering religieux contemporary with the Buddha, composed of ascetics, mendicants, and teachers, out of which Buddhism arose first as a monastic movement, then as a 'church', perhaps the first of its kind in the history of religion.

1.1.1. The Brahmanical tradition

The first of these background elements has to do with what has been called the 'Sanskritisation' of India;[1] that is, with the increasing influence over the indigenous tribes of the sub-continent of the language, ideas, and practices of the Aryan invaders, and within this dominant group, of the Brahmin priesthood. This process began in the later second millennium B.C. in the hills of North-west India, and gradually extended over the whole country, until today the life of almost all Indians is permeated – to a greater or lesser extent – by Sanskritic culture. It is this Sanskritic culture which is denoted by that most vague of terms, 'Hinduism'. The textual evidence for the early stages of this process is the corpus composed of the *Vedas*, *Brāhmaṇas*, and *Upaniṣads*. I shall deal later in this chapter with some themes from the content of these texts. Here I wish to delineate their particular character as historical evidence. They are normative texts, giving a picture of religious practice as its Brahmanical authors wished it to be and to be seen. That is, they do not contain descriptive accounts of what the majority of people actually did and thought, but contain prescriptive recommendations as to how Brahmins wished people to act and view their action.

The relationship between the picture of 'Indian religion' given by these texts, and the general spectrum of religious practice as we know and presume it to have been, is difficult to describe accurately. We know that the kind of religious practice I have roughly characterised by the term 'little tradition' – cults of local gods, spirits, sacred places, and so on – was ubiquitous in ancient India, as indeed it has remained throughout South Asia. Equally, there is evidence that the great movements of devotional worship of a personal god, centred around the figures of Viṣṇu and Śiva, which first grew into prominence in the last few centuries B.C., drew on deep historical and cultural roots, particularly in the Dravidian South, which the Brahmanical tradition had not extinguished despite the central tendency of its system. Early Brahmanical religion had revolved around sacrificial ritual, and of course the place of the Brahmins within it, and was inextricably linked to the development of caste society. The main thrust of this early religion, before Brahmanism came to incorporate within itself the devotional movements, was increasingly to deny the importance of gods in favour of the sacrifice. The Brahmins, calling themselves 'the human gods',[2] sought to put in the gods' place their own sacrificial ritual, both as an explanation of the origin and significance of the universe, and as the sole vehicle of worldly or other-worldly advancement. Finally, in the seventh to sixth centuries B.C., in the *Upaniṣads*, the attainment of ultimate religious goals is said to be the result of human understanding and action, independent of any divine aid. At this later stage, the tradition came to place the highest value and prestige on the figure of the world-renouncing ascetic, who represented within himself structures of thought and imagination which had previously been related to the external ritual.

The development of Brahmanical thought and practice which culminated in this focus on the ascetic can be seen to follow a gradual and coherent path. Nevertheless, as I shall presently discuss, the phenomenon of world-renunciation in India seems also to have drawn on extra-Brahmanical roots, and to have been a social phenomenon wider than the Brahmanical interpretation of it. The particular doctrine of *saṃsāra*, the round of rebirth, shows the ambiguous historical situation of mutual influence between Brahmanical and non-Brahmanical parts of what is called 'Indian religion'. I shall trace the development of the idea, in Chapter 1.2 below, using only the content of the Brahmanical texts; I think it can be shown to grow naturally and logically out of the nature and concerns of Brahmanical sacrificial thinking. At the same time, one might agree with von Fürer-Haimendorf that 'the very fact that the concept of repeated rebirth and repeated death is peculiar to India and that it is absent among other Indo-European peoples, suggests that the gradual transformation of the earlier Aryan beliefs and practices occurred under the influence of certain indigenous concepts'. As well as providing ethnographic data from certain recently, and only partially, 'Hinduised' tribes to support the contention that 'traditional Hinduism . . . impinges to an ever-growing extent on aboriginal thought', he argues that

> the idea of an interminable series of 'Lands of the Dead' and the inevitable death of a person after a span of life in any such 'Land of the Dead', as it is still to be found in the belief of the Assam tribes [roughly in the area in which the Buddha preached] may have contributed to the development of the Hindu concept of successive existences in a chain of rebirths.

If we can project contemporary belief back into the past, assuming that 'the Aryans, moving eastwards down the Ganges valley, there came in touch with populations holding eschatological beliefs conceptually similar to those still found among some of the more isolated hill-tribes', then we can perhaps conclude that 'we have every reason to believe that concepts stemming from pre-Aryan civilizations have found their way into Hindu thought and scriptures, just as concepts of orthodox Hinduism have been assimilated by many of the primitive forest and hill-tribes'.[3]

The problem with taking this line of investigation any further, of course, is the fact that we simply do not know what the beliefs of such pre-Aryan tribes might have been; and while extrapolation from contemporary data may provide suggestive hypotheses, it will hardly do as historical evidence. I will, accordingly, restrict myself to the available sources – the Brahmanical texts – in drawing a picture of pre-Buddhist thought, on the following assumptions. These Brahmanic texts are normative and prescriptive, urging their authors' ideas and values on the rest of the population of ancient India. In the course of time, these ideas and values developed in a manner which may very well have been influenced – in unknown and perhaps unknowable ways – by the existence and content of pre- and non-Brahminised religious culture. Leaving aside further speculation on this issue, I take it that the intellectual influence of developed Brahmanical thought on Buddhism is due to the undoubted fact of the former's playing in India (to borrow a term from Gramsci,[4] used in connexion with western politics) a 'culturally hegemonous' role. That is, although the texts of that tradition by no means portray the historical reality of early Indian religion in its entirety, still they came to be taken as culturally prestigious, and provided an inescapable conceptual paradigm for speculative thought, just as both the facts and the ideology of caste society came to be inescapable for all political, social, and religious movements. (This is so even for those groups which, like Buddhism, were theoretically opposed to caste society – more usually simply to the place of the Brahmins within it.)[5] All movements came to settle down in practice to a *modus vivendi* with the Brahmin-derived hierarchy of social groups; in the same way, the general pattern of the belief system of *saṃsāra-karma-mokṣa*, as it developed in Brahmanical thought, was accepted by all major schools of Indian religious thinking, while even those minor trends which did not accept the overall pattern had specifically to refute it.

I shall give more detailed examples of the way I think Brahmanical thought was 'culturally hegemonous', in relation to Buddhist philosophy and psychology, in the later chapters of the book. A simple example here is provided by the use to which the very word *brāhmaṇa*, 'brahmin', is put in Buddhist texts. Whereas for Brahmanical thought it is being born a Brahmin in social fact which gives the highest status in religion (and indeed in everything else), for Buddhism it is the man who practises Buddhist precepts to their utmost who has the highest status, and who is therefore the ('true' or 'real') 'Brahmin'. That is to say, while the particular religious content has been changed, even reversed (typically from a Brahmanic social to Buddhist ethical emphasis), still the overall formal structure – here 'being a Brahmin' as the highest value – remains the same. This, I think, is the general form of the relationship of Buddhism to Hindu or, more precisely, Brahmanical thought. In what follows, I will try to show how Buddhist thought, both in its general tenor and in certain specific details, developed in this relation to the Brahmanical tradition; it did this both positively and negatively, by accepting or consciously rejecting specific ideas and more general and fundamental structures of thought and imagination.

Of course, at the same time as tracing the conceptual influence of one Indian great tradition on another, we must also be aware of direct influence on each great tradition from the little traditions in which both had necessarily to situate themselves. We have seen the hypothesis that the doctrine of *saṃsāra* in Brahmanical thought was influenced by little tradition ideas. I remarked earlier that the Pali Canon contains many traces of the 'popular' religion of its day – the North-east being relatively less Sanskritised at that time than the North-west. Buddhism subsequently competed with Brahmanism in the spread of what we now call 'Indian religion' over the southern half of the sub-continent and surrounding areas of South-east Asia, and its intellectual tradition accommodated itself and its theorising in a quite specific way to its socially and culturally wider setting. I shall later mention some particular details of this theorising in Buddhist psychology and cosmology, which show 'popular' influence.

1.1.2. Other styles of thought: asceticism

The second of the two background elements against which one must set the figure of early Buddhism, arising in the sixth century B.C., is the contemporary religious milieu, composed apparently of a great number and variety of wandering ascetics, holy men, more or less loosely grouped into 'sects' or 'schools' around particular teachers. As in the case of the Brahmanical texts, we must be wary here of the nature of the historical evidence for these 'schools' and their beliefs. The difficulty lies in the fact that the main evidence is contained within the Buddhist, and to a lesser extent Jain, texts themselves. These texts, like those of the Brahmanical tradition, are normative, and the other teachers and their ideas are described in them with polemical intent. It is thus difficult to get through to an historical reality which might have existed underneath the picture we receive from the tradition.[6] The milieu is referred to in Buddhist texts by the compound *samaṇa-brāhmaṇa*: *brāhmaṇa* may be taken to refer to 'orthodox' Brahmins and Brahmanical ascetics, *samaṇa* (Sanskrit *śramaṇa*) to refer to non-Brahmanical ascetics and religious teachers.[7]

There has been much debate on the origins of asceticism in Indian religion. Some have seen it as a development of certain aspects of the religious culture brought into India by the Aryan invaders; some as a phenomenon already in existence among the pre-Aryan indigenous tribes; and some as a reaction of the kingly or warrior class within Aryan society, the *kṣatriyas*, to the domination of religion by the Brahmin priesthood (though one wonders why kings or warriors should have initiated a movement of mystical and ascetic world-renunciation). Whatever its origins, if we confine ourselves to the effect which this general milieu is taken, by Buddhism itself, to have had on Buddhist thought, there are two aspects to mention: the ethical and the conceptual. In both cases, Buddhism characterises itself as a Middle Way between two extremes.

Ethically, Buddhism sees itself as taking a middle path between the two extremes of the ordinary man's enjoyment of (sense-)pleasure, and the intense self-mortification practised by many ascetics at the time (and indeed thereafter). As Basham puts it:

> Some ascetics were solitary psychopaths, dwelling in the depths of the forests, and suffering self-inflicted tortures of hunger, thirst, heat, cold and rain. Others dwelt in 'penance-grounds' on the outskirts of towns, where, like some of the less reputable holy-men of later times, they would indulge in fantastic self-torture, sitting near blazing fires in the hot sun, lying on beds of thorns or spikes, hanging for hours head downwards from the branches of trees, or holding their arms above their heads until they atrophied.[8]

In the legendary account of the Buddha's life, he is described as having practised asceticism of this kind, before coming to condemn it as fruitless, and not conducive to the moral and religious salvation he was seeking. The path he then taught his renunciatory followers thus avoided both this kind of extreme self-mortification and the simple immersion in self-indulgent sense-gratification seen as characteristic of the lay man-in-the-world.

Conceptually, the effects of this milieu on Buddhism were various; two may be emphasised. First, the picture Buddhist texts draw, of a large variety of small sects, each with their own ideas, all arguing with each other and sticking to their own particular 'views', provides the perfect foil for the image of the Buddha and Buddhist saints as peaceful unargumentative sages, whose 'silent wisdom' transcends philosophical bickering. This is a crucial part of the *anattā* doctrine, and I shall devote the whole of Chapter 4 to it. The second, and here more important, conceptual effect consists in the attitude taken towards those kinds of thought, amongst the apparently multitudinous variety of 'views' in existence at the time, which correspond roughly to what we would call 'materialism' and 'determinism'. Thus in its Middle Way of theory, Buddhism (as we have already seen exemplified by the modern monk Nyanatiloka) characterises itself as standing between two styles of thought. On the one hand there are those systems which postulate, and orient all their thinking and behaviour towards, an eternal and divine self or soul – including, *inter alia*, the Brahmanical tradition – and which Buddhism calls 'Eternalism'; on the other hand there is 'Annihilationism' which includes both straightforward, 'materialistic', conceptions of a self, soul, or person which exists but is destroyed at death, and also by assimilation any kind of thought which rejects the other-worldly/moral account of action – that is, in terms of *karma* and its rewards – examples of which I shall shortly give under the general heading of *Ājīvikism*.[9] This was a movement which contained within itself a variety of ideas, but all of them were based on a very strict form of determinism. ('Annihilationism' also includes, by implication, any 'nihilist', 'sceptical' or 'agnostic' attitudes to these matters, such as would not provide an incentive and goal for religious action.)[10]

Traditionally Buddhism has schematised other styles of thought either in terms of ordered lists of doctrines, arranged by means of their conceptual content, as in the very first *Sutta* of the *Suttā* Collection, the *Brahmajāla*; or in terms of particular personalities, usually a group of six, referred to as the Six Heretics – as in the second *Sutta* of the Collection, the *Sāmaññaphala* – each of whom is presented as 'the head of an order, of a following, the teacher of a school, well-known and of repute as a sophist, revered by the people, a man of experience, who has long been a recluse, old and well-stricken in years'.* I will first present some of their ideas, in the traditional Buddhist words and in the traditional way, as particular doctrines held by particular individuals; and then hazard some speculations on the possible place of some of these ideas in the wider picture of North-east Indian society at the time of the Buddha.[11]

Three of the Six Heretics seem to have been connected with the beginnings of the movement known as that of *Ājīvikism*. The most important of them is Makkhali Gosāla, who taught that

> there is no cause, no condition for the [moral] defilement of beings, they become defiled without cause or condition. There is no cause, no condition for the

* D.I.47. Rhys Davids' translation nicely captures the spirit of the Buddhist attitude. The word translated as 'recluse', *pabbajjito*, is the standard term, meaning 'one who has gone forth (from home to homelessness)', used to refer to those I have called ascetics or world-renouncers.

purification of beings, they are purified without cause or condition. No action of one's own, of another, or of any person has any effect . . . All beings . . . powerless, without strength or vigour, are changed by fate, [the] class of being [to which they belong] and [their own] nature, as they experience happiness or sorrow in the six classes of being . . . Through eighty-four thousand great cosmic aeons fools and wise [alike], wander through the round of rebirth before making an end to suffering . . . In the round of rebirth, with its appointed end and happiness and sorrow measured out as in a measure of rice, there is neither decrease nor increase, neither rise nor fall. Just as when a ball of string is thrown it unwinds to its [full] length, so fools and wise [alike] wander through the round of rebirth before making an end to suffering.[12]

Thus, 'the cardinal point in the doctrines of its [*Ājīvikism*'s] founder, Makkhali Gosāla, was a belief in the all-embracing principle of order, *niyati,** which ultimately controlled every action and all phenomena, and left no room for human volition, which was completely ineffectual'.[13] Pūraṇa Kassapa, similarly, is portrayed as denying moral retribution, teaching that no evil would be done by a murderer reducing all living beings to one mass of flesh, and that there was no good, or merit, in generosity, self-control, or truthfulness. A man on the south bank of the Ganges, murdering, wounding, torturing, did no evil, while a man on the north bank giving alms and performing sacrifice acquired no merit.[14] Pakudha Kaccāyana, whose ideas seem to have resembled those found in the South Indian form of *Ājīvikism*,[15] is said to have arrived at a similar rejection of a moral account of action through a form of atomism.

There are seven [elementary] categories, which are neither made nor commanded to be made, neither created nor caused to be created, barren [i.e. nothing is produced from them] firm as mountains and stable as pillars. They do not move, change, or harm one another, and one has no effect on the happiness or sorrow, or both, of the other. What are they? Earth, water, fire, air, happiness, suffering, and the soul† as seventh . . . Thus no man kills or causes to kill, hears or causes to hear, knows or causes to know. When one cuts a head apart with a sharp sword, no-one deprives anyone of life, there is simply a sword-cut passing between the seven categories.[16]

The 'soul' here should not be taken as an immaterial or spiritual category, for 'the *Ājīvikas* . . . at all periods of their history seem to have maintained the material nature of the soul'.[17]

A straightforward form of materialism was taught by another of the Six Heretics, Ajita Kesakambalī, who denied the existence of moral retribution of action like the others we have met:

There is no result or ripening of good or bad deeds . . . A man is made of the four elements; when he dies, the earth (in him) reverts back to the earth-category,

* The word translated in the quotation as 'fate'.

† *Jīva* from the root *jīv*, 'to live'; thus perhaps simply 'life'.

water to water, fire to fire, air to air, and the senses pass into space . . . At the break-up of the body fools and wise men alike are cut off, perish – they do not exist after death.[18]

These, then, are some of the beliefs alleged to have been held by non-Brahmanical religious teachers in the varied and seemingly colourful milieu contemporary with the Buddha. These kinds of belief, presented as they are, seem to me to present the historian with an *a priori* problem of sociological reconstruction. If we assume that the doctrines thus presented were actually a concern of the laymen who supported such teachers,* since they must needs have relied on lay support, then for whom did such seemingly harsh and rigid forms of 'determinism' and 'materialism' represent an ideal religious answer to their 'ultimate concerns'? In the light of the paucity of evidence, this is perhaps better phrased, and certainly more easily answered, thus: what styles of thought in society might such beliefs be taken to represent and personify? What forms of action might they have been taken to legitimate?

The data on which we can base an answer is, as I have said, meagre, fragmentary, and unreliable. What follows is a speculative picture which seems reasonable, and which at least has the merit of offering a plausible social and historical basis for these otherwise disembodied and apparently bizarre doctrines. In the sixth century B.C. the Ganges valley – scene of all these various teachers and doctrines – was characterised by a great increase in urbanisation, and in the development of trade and commercial prosperity. It seems reasonable to suggest that such a period of social and economic innovation would have seen corresponding cultural changes, and in particular have been receptive to the growth of a variety of new religious ideas.[19] Regardless of the question of its origins, the milieu of ascetic world-renunciation in the sixth century B.C. can be regarded as an existing vessel into which could be poured the new ideas which then developed, so that different individual teachers came to personify – in historical fact, doubtless, rather less schematically than in Buddhist texts – the varied and conflicting innovations in intellectual and religious culture.

We can, perhaps, hazard an attempt at some more detailed connexions. As Basham says 'the three heterodox sects which arise in this climate, Buddhism, Jainism and Ājīvikism, had much in common'. All three offered an alternative, or complement, to the popular polytheistic and sacred-place cults of a kind which opposed the Brahmanic magico-mystical ritualism of the sacrifice, whether this was 'inside' society as

* I shall, however, argue that the content of the most specialist and intellectual levels of Buddhist thought were *not* a concern of its lay supporters, save as orienting symbols.

ritual priests or 'outside' it as ascetics who had 'internalised' the sacrifice as a permanent way of life and imagination.

> The three new religions represent a recognition of the rule of natural law in the universe . . . Of the three systems that of the *Ājīvikas*, based on the principle of *niyati* as the only determining factor in the universe, perhaps represents a more thorough recognition of the orderliness of nature than do the doctrines of either of its more successful rivals.

The three systems share not only the conceptual fact of basing their cosmology and eschatology on universal orderliness and cosmic principles, but also, according to Basham, 'the greatest support for *Ājīvikism* seems to have come from the industrial and mercantile classes'.[20] We know that Buddhism, in its earliest stages, was associated with urban merchant groups,* as has been Jainism throughout its history. The two kinds of similarity, conceptual and socio-economic, are perhaps themselves connected. It is not absurd to think that new systems based on universal order and a kind of natural law should have appealed to commercial rationalism among the new urban merchant classes of the era.†

It was not only mercantilism in the cities which could have favoured the 'heterodox' sects (in opposition to 'orthodox' Brahmanism). The city nobility would perhaps have had an incentive to support them through their mutual opposition to the strength of the social position and political influence of the Brahmin priesthood. It is, in any case, this social group with which I think one should connect the second type of thought in non-Brahmanical asceticism I mentioned, that of 'materialism'. In the sixth century, 'A high standard of luxury was enjoyed by kings, nobles, and merchants, and many of the latter had amassed very large fortunes.'[21] In later Hindu literature, materialistic thinking is symbolised by a 'school' called the *Cārvāka*, founded by a legendary sage Bṛhaspati; the 'school' was also called *Lokāyata*, from the word *loka*, 'world', since the existence of any but this world was denied, and accordingly worldly ends were considered the only ones possible. The fourteenth-century compilation of 'systems', the *Sarvadarśanasaṃgraha*, remarks ruefully that

> most men, in the tradition of the Treatises on Policy and Pleasure, considering

* I shall, however, argue that as Buddhism has developed in history as a more widely institutionalised form, it has become essentially a phenomenon of agricultural, peasant culture. See Chapter 7.3 and Conclusion.

† Nor is it particularly original. We already have a classic of the sociology of religion connecting a belief, like that of the *Ājīvikas*, in ineluctable destiny and the 'work ethic' of early western capitalist commercialism – Weber's *The Protestant Ethic and the Spirit of Capitalism*. In the Indian case I am not suggesting any Weberian psychological structures connecting *Ājīvika* fatalism and mercantile attitudes.

wealth (or 'power') and pleasure the only human goals and denying (the existence of) anything belonging to another world, are seen to be followers of the *Carvāka* . . . In this view, the four elements, earth (fire, water, air) are the (only) categories. When these are changed into the form of a body, consciousness arises, like the power of intoxication when [certain ingredients] are mixed; when these elements are destroyed, consciousness ceases immediately. Thus this self [*ātman*] is only the body with the special characteristic of consciousness . . .[22]

Well-known examples of treatises on pleasure and policy (*kāma-*, *nītiśāstra*) are the *Kāmasūtra* ('written . . . for the sophisticated townsman'),[23] and recommending pleasure as the highest goal and describing elaborately how to achieve it; and the 'Treatise on Power' (or 'Wealth', *artha*) (*Arthaśāstra*) of Kauṭilya, which contains hard-headed and matter-of-fact, not to say ruthless advice to kings and politicians on how to acquire power and wealth, and how to keep it. Neither of these texts shows any real enthusiasm for other-worldly religiosity. Brahmanical thought – that which is usually presented as 'Indian' – has traditionally hierarchised these values, such that in ascending order there are *kāma*, 'pleasure', *artha*, 'power' or 'wealth', and *dharma*, '(caste) duty', with a superimposed and transcending fourth, *mokṣa*, 'liberation'. It seems clear, however, that here the situation is similar to that in the four 'stages of life' (*āśrama*), in which the opposition between householder and renouncer is reconciled into a temporal sequence (in which religious studentship is followed by the life of householder, then later by hermit life in the forest, and finally by the condition of the wandering ascetic) and as in the ideology of caste society as a whole. That is, Brahmanical thought is attempting (successfully for the most part) to resolve into a coherent sequence or hierarchy what was originally, and always in fact to a large extent, remained, a mutually conflicting set of alternatives.

1.1.3. Conclusion

These last remarks on the possible social background to some styles of ascetic thought are, as I said, very speculative, and as they stand certainly inadequate. Let me emphasise those points I think important, in summarising the whole background spectrum of early Indian religion as it affects our appreciation of Buddhist thought. In the first place, in what is generally referred to as the 'Sanskritisation' or 'Brahmanisation' of India, not only did the belief and practice of Brahmins impose itself on and colonise the society and culture of the indigenous tribes, but also the content, and still more the form, of the ideas developed by its intellectual tradition came to provide the fundamental paradigm for the conceptual activity of all other competing groups. Buddhism, arising at an early stage of this process, competed as an alternative great tradition with

Brahmanism for the role of the ultimately legitimating and orienting religious ideology *vis-à-vis* the multitudinous little traditions of the sub-continent and of surrounding areas of South-east Asia. The intellectual stratum of Buddhism worked with the basic paradigm provided by Brahmanical thought, accepting the overall form, while rejecting certain features. It was the developing Brahmanical interpretation of the sacrifice, and of the phenomenon of the world-renouncing ascetic, which came to provide, as I will try to show, the crucial ideas in which eschatology and psychology were conceived.

Despite this 'hegemony' of Brahmanical thought, we must recognise the existence of diversity in society and in thought at the time of the Buddha. Specifically, although the Brahmanical interpretation of world-renunciation and life in (caste) society, when transcribed into the metaphysical terms of liberation from and bondage to rebirth, came to provide the determining intellectual structure for all subsequent Indian religious thinking, still the historical evidence seems to bear witness both to the fact that asceticism was a social phenomenon wider than the Brahmanical interpretation of it; and to the fact of the existence, apparently within the ascetic milieu, of styles of thought which might suggest to us certain social and economic phenomena existing at the time of Buddha. These considerations might help us appreciate – imaginatively, indeed, more than historically – something of the variety which then, as always, existed in Indian society and its values, and thus help us to see the Brahmanical account of Indian thought and its values, as the normative, and not simply descriptive, ideology which it is.

Although I will organise my account of the 'hegemonous' early Brahmanical ideology in terms of its three main eschatological components – *saṃsāra*, *karma*, and *mokṣa* – I hope that the reader will bear in mind two other kinds of emphasis which cut across this indigenous categorisation. First, as a perspective on the subject-matter as a whole, there is the difference between developments of thought which the Brahmanical tradition can be imagined to have produced by itself, from its own intrinsic concerns, and those in which it seems to be reacting to, and accommodating, outside influence (the most obvious example being the lessening of importance, even rejection, accorded to the sacrifice by world-renouncing thought). Second, as a perspective within the subject-matter, there is a division between two (connected) areas of thinking which I would emphasise, but which the tradition does not; that is, between the development of ideas concerning the nature of time (and, correspondingly, timelessness), and that concerning the nature and construction of the human person.

1.2. Time: *saṃsāra*

1.2.1. The sacrifice[1]

Early Brahmanical religion revolved entirely around the sacrifice and attitudes towards it.[2] The *Vedas* give sacrificial hymns and prayers; the *Brāhmaṇas* directions for, and interpretations of, the sacrifice; while the *Upaniṣads* offer psychological and 'mystical' re-interpretations of it. The multifarious gods of the *Vedas* became less and less important in relation to the sacrifice; indeed they came to be seen as depending on it themselves for sustenance. Sacrificial activity, accordingly, came to be conceived not as the propitiation of a transcendent god or gods, but as itself a constructive power whose place in the cosmic scheme of things was essential.

The two Sanskrit terms which might be translated as 'the scheme of things' are, in the *Vedas*, *ṛta*, and in later classical Sanskrit, *dharma*. *Ṛta* means 'that which is fitted together, ordered', *dharma* 'that which is (to be) upheld, preserved'. Though in Vedic mythology the work of arranging and maintaining cosmic order is often attributed to a god or gods, this divine force is always seen more as that of a demiurge than as that of a creator god proper; and, always, divine ordering activity is to be supplemented by human effort. The very recitation of the hymns of the *Ṛg Veda* was thought to contribute to the task of 'maintaining universal Order and keeping the powers of nature operative',[3] while in the later *Atharva Veda* and in the *Brāhmaṇas*, where we enter more and more a magical world of analogical reciprocities, the Brahmanical sacrifice becomes the mesocosm through which are joined the divine/macrocosmic and human/microcosmic levels – just as the Brahmin priests themselves are the mediating point at which the social hierarchy is interlaced with the hierarchy of the cosmos. *Ṛta* and *dharma* denote, ambiguously, both the way the universe *is* ordered, and the way it ideally is, or should be ordered. In the theory of Cosmic Ages (*yuga*), developed from the fourth to the third centuries B.C.,[4] this idea became more explicit: originally in the 'Golden Age' men performed proper sacrifice, acted morally, caste rules were strictly maintained, there was no suffering or early death – in short the ideal *dharma* actually existed. In the present age, however, the last and degenerate stage of the cosmic cycle, men do not act rightly, the caste system is confused and impure, there is suffering and death – the ideal *dharma* is 'only' an ideal. At the early period of which I am speaking, however, the ambiguity between the two aspects of *ṛta*/*dharma* reflected simply the need for man to act – through sacrifice – if the ideal order was to be actualised and preserved; this was assumed to be done, and so no systematic cosmological or ethical inferences as to the state of the present age were drawn.

1.2.2. Time in general

According to Silburn's magnificent study of Brahmanical and Buddhist thought,[5] 'one does not find in the *Veda* any time in itself which would not be the work of a god or the result of sacrificial activity'. I am not concerned here with mythological cosmogonies of time, but rather with the way that time, once begun, is thought to continue as a process. The same duality of macrocosmic and microcosmic activity is found here: both men and gods act together in a project of continual renovation. This renovation is pictured in a number of different images: for example, as the perpetual weaving and re-weaving of a cloth by the two sisters day and night, or as the incessant turning of the wheel of the year, with its twelve (monthly) spokes. The image which is most influential here is that of the perpetual death and rebirth of the sun; each night it dies over the horizon, and enters the waters underground, where it becomes an embryo, before being reborn with the dawn. On earth, the sacrificial fire must repeat the activity of the sun, the cosmic fire: hence the need for constant sacrifice, and for oblations by Brahmins at dawn and dusk, the two crucial junctions of the sequence of days and nights. In any performance of the fire-sacrifice, the process of time is thus propelled forward once again, both for the whole of society and for the individual sacrificer:

> The central theme of the . . . ritual is the periodical regeneration of the cosmos, the winning of life out of death. In the classical system of the ritual, as presented in the *brāhmaṇas* and the *sūtras*, the pivot of the ritual is the *yajamāna*, the patron at whose expense and for whose sole benefit the ritual is performed. He is supposed symbolically to incorporate the universe – he is identified with the cosmic man Prajāpati.* The ritual culminates in his ritual rebirth which signifies the regeneration of the cosmos.[6]

From these motifs of ritual thinking, then, came the idea that it was only by incessant attention to the correct maintenance of the cosmic cycle by sacrificial action that a man could produce and order a sequence of time in which to live. For Brahmanical thinking, time and continuity were not simply and deterministically given to man; rather, they are the result of a constant effort at prolongation, a constant pushing forward of life supported by the magical power of the sacrifice.

1.2.3. *Amṛtam*: non-dying

It is this dynamic, constructive sense of time which makes clear the developments in eschatological thinking. The central concept around which these developments unfold is that of *amṛtam*. This word is 'usually translated "immortality" but in fact [denotes] "freedom from death,

* On whom see Chapter 2.3.1 below.

continuance of life" '.[7] If we translate the word as 'immortality', it might suggest a dichotomy between a divine, timeless existence without birth and death in contrast to the temporal life of man, which necessarily has both. This is not, however, the distinction between *mṛtam* and *amṛtam* – literally, 'death' and 'non-death'. There *was* an important strand in the early Vedic and Brahmanic tradition which emphasised an essential timelessness (or a timeless essence) both preceding and in some sense underlying the ordered human world of time; this is the immobile hub of the moving wheel[8] of time, the still point (*pada*) beyond the ceaseless movement of *saṃsāra* – derived from the root *sar* – 'run, hasten, flow, stream'. The famous Hymn of Creation in the *Ṛg Veda* (10.90) speaks of this timelessness as a point 'before' time began: 'There was neither death nor *amṛtam* then; there was not the beacon of night, nor of day.' *But* as these verses show, the essential timelessness is contrasted with time as the sequence of days and nights, in which are included both death and its avoidance, *amṛtam*, 'non-dying'. The timeless essence, beyond death and 'non-dying', in this poem celebrated but not described, becomes later in the *Upaniṣads* the *Ātman-Brahman* which lies behind both the ordered universe and the human being. *Amṛtam*, then, is part of the ordered world of time, and denotes for men and gods alike the avoidance of death, the prolongation of life.

Amṛtam is a term applied frequently to the gods, particularly to the fire-god Agni – better said, the fire-element and fire-sacrifice personified. It denotes, in addition to the gods' avoidance of death, their greater vitality and strength, swifter movement, and so on – that is, their possession in general of the same characteristics as men, but to an enhanced degree, rather than a wholly different mode of existence. The gods were once born, like man, and were not guaranteed *amṛtam*, avoidance of death. They are said to have attained it in various ways, all of them connected with sacrifice. In the *Vedas*, two classes of demi-gods, (the *Ṛbhus* and *Angirases*) were indeed born as men, but attained divine status and *amṛtam* by their sacrificial skill. In the *Brāhmaṇas*, all of the gods achieved 'non-dying' and victory over the demons by acquiring the sacrifice and fire, by singing sacrificial hymns, and by building the fire-altar. They are not free from continued dependence on the sacrifice: it is their food, indeed their life-principle, their *ātman*.

The dependence of gods on the ritual which sustains them is by no means confined to Indian religion – it was, indeed, stressed by Durkheim as one of the 'elementary forms' of religion everywhere.[9] What gives the idea importance here is the specific way in which the continuance of time and of life, the avoidance of death and attainment of 'non-dying', is brought about for the gods of early Brahmanical thought: that is, by a continual renovation or rebirth as the result of sacrifice. The sacrifice itself 'only survives in its results; considered in itself it dies completely . . . To celebrate a sacrifice, then, is to give birth to it and to kill it . . . The life of sacrifice is thus an infinite series of births and deaths.'[10]

The life of man shows exactly the same need for prolongation through sacrifice as that of the gods. When the term *amṛtam* is applied to men, however, it has a more specific sense than the vague 'non-dying' which it has when applied to the gods. It means a long 'full life' (*sarvam āyus*) of one hundred years: 'to have a complete term of life, that is a man's non-dying' (*amṛtatvam*), 'a hundred years, so much is *amṛtam*'.[11] On the many occasions in the texts when the plea for 'non-dying' is made, when the gods are asked to 'set us in *amṛtam*', or 'set *amṛtam* in us', we may interpret the request simply as 'keep us alive'. Thus 'those who give *dakṣinā* [the fee of the officiating sacrificial priests] have a share in *amṛtam*; givers of *dakṣinā* lengthen their lifetime'.[12] This acceptation of the word *amṛtam* is consonant with the general spirit of the earlier Vedic religion, which is – in contrast to the supposed 'pessimism' of later Indian thought – concerned not with escaping from life or securing existence after death, but with obtaining enjoyment and continuation of ordinary human life, with all its pleasures – wealth, cattle, strong sons, and the like, and above all a 'full life'.[13]

1.2.4. Existence after death

Both men and the gods, then, continue their life in time by the same means. The gods do so without foreseeable end, but for men there will always be a meeting with death, called 'the ender', even if they achieve a 'full life' of a hundred years. For Vedic man, death was always an evil.[14] Although existence after death is spoken of in the *Vedas*, it is never with any clearly delineated system of cosmology and soteriology. There is some suggestion, particularly in the later *Atharva Veda*, of a kind of hell for miscreants and enemies.[15] More usually, the dead who are remembered are said to live as 'the Fathers', with Yama the god of the dead, or sometimes with all the gods. This realm represents not so much an eschatological hope as a representation of the collective past of the whole people; 'the ancestors' as a group rather than a prospective state to which an individual can look forward with expectation and empathy. Ritual communication with the Fathers is possible, but only scant attention is paid to their mode of living outside their attendance at the sacrifice. That is, the hymns referring to the Fathers have a symbolic function within the ritual – evoking a sense of continuity between the generations (the ancestors as past sacrificers and present 'fathers', the present adult generation as present sacrificers and future 'fathers', and their descendants as future sacrificers) – rather than allotting to them a place in a scheme of eschatology proper. By this I mean a place in an organised system of destinies, to the individual attainment or avoidance of which hopes and efforts are directed.

A history of the evolution of such a scheme of eschatology is difficult to write, for two reasons. Firstly, we cannot look to the history of cosmology to find specifiable 'realms' of the living and the dead – 'the world of soteriology does not fit well with the world of systematic cosmology'.[16] This is always true in India, but is particularly so in the early period. Secondly, the word *loka*, which is used in what seem to be eschatological contexts and which is translated as 'world' or 'realm', has what Gonda calls an 'inherent vagueness'.[17] It does not necessarily refer to a particular spatial location at all, but often simply to a state of happiness and stability. Its earliest meaning seems to have been 'free, open space', or 'safe, sacred space', ideas which had a particular relevance for the early Aryan invaders.[18] Hence, the desire to 'gain a *loka*', when transferred from the conditions of this life to those hereafter, does not mean to wish for a specifiable place in a range of possible destinies obtained by different types of behaviour or religious practice, but rather a desire to prolong life into a more or less vaguely defined 'happy secure state' in the same way as one desired to have a continued happy life on earth.[19]

The 'worlds' which are spoken of in this way are given various names. We may reduce them to three: the World of the Fathers (*pitṛ-loka*), the World of the Gods, also called the Heavenly World (*deva-*, *svarga-loka*),[20] and the World of (Those who acquire) Sacrificial Merit (*sukṛtām*, *sukṛtasya loka*).

The Worlds of the Fathers and of the Gods. In the *Vedas*, the relationship between these two worlds was inconstant; sometimes the two were distinguished, sometimes coalesced. In the *Brāhmaṇas*, however, there is an increasing separation between the two. Now the World of the Fathers becomes increasingly a shadowy realm, about the stability and safety of which there can be no certainty.[21] About the World of the Gods, the Heavenly World, Gonda says that in matters of detail there are many uncertainties: thus 'there is for instance no unanimity with regard to the nature of the "position" of that "world" or to its exact relation to other ideas such as "immortality" or the "fulfilment of all desires"'. At the same time, however, 'it is with all clearness desirable apparent that it often denoted "the other world" conceived of as a state of bliss and happiness'.[22] Whereas the fathers are mortal, not free from suffering, and connected with darkness, and so a man who sacrifices before sunrise does not obtain 'a full life' (*sarvam āyus*), the gods are immortal, free from suffering, and connected with light, and so sacrifice after sunrise does produce 'a full life'.[23] Just as in the *Brāhmaṇas* the status of the gods falls, and they become less and less transcendent of mankind (and especially of the Brahmins), but dependent, like them, on the sacrifice, so too the goal of man's ritual aspirations rises, to become that of equalling the gods in status: 'he who sacrifices does so in order to win a place in the *devaloka*'.[24] The division between these two realms and the 'ways' to them[25] remained a constant motif in later Indian religion, and was an important element in the first formulations of an explicit scheme of rebirth, as we shall see.

The World of Sacrificial Merit. 'The *sukṛtāṃ loka*, the sphere or condition of those who have earned the rewards of well-performed rites (and so are entitled to such a special *loka*)', or the *sukṛtasya loka*, 'the sphere of ritual and religious merit',[26] is of crucial importance for the entire development of ideas which I am here concerned to trace. The word *sukṛt* is literally translated as 'well-doer'; *sukṛta* (neuter) as '(what is) well-done'. This refers not to a concept of virtue, piety, or the like, but to a straightforward concept of ritual efficiency: if the sacrifice is performed correctly, the action leaves a residue of merit, which though unseen must nevertheless produce automatically, future benefits for the sacrificer. In the *Vedas*, the *loka* to which such ritual action and merit gave access was associated both with the *loka* of the Fathers and with that of the gods. In the *Brāhmaṇas* – consonant with the gradual separation of these two *lokas* – the World of Sacrificial Merit is more often associated with the World of the Gods as the sphere in which continuance of life after death is anticipated. The gods themselves, naturally, are said to have gained this *loka* as the reward for correct performance of the sacrifice.

We have seen that the gods rely on the continual regenerating effect of the sacrifice for their enjoyment of 'non-dying'; and that this same power produced the continuity of life in time, during a human lifespan on earth. Both the sacrifice and its cosmic analogue, the sun, undergo a series of deaths – at the end of each particular ritual or day, respectively. The natural conclusion from all this is that those humans who 'die and are reborn (into the World of Sacrificial Merit shared with the gods)'[27] nevertheless are subject to the continual births and deaths of the sun and sacrifice in the sequence of time – for, as we have seen, 'non-dying' is a state within the sequence of time. This subjection to 'continual death' in time is what is referred to by the much-discussed term *punarmṛtyu*, 'repeated death'.[28] This term becomes increasingly frequent in the

Brāhmaṇas, and finally comes to refer to what is the obvious final conclusion of the whole development of ideas about life after death: just as in life in this world, the sequence of repeated deaths of sun and sacrifice was to be followed for a man by a final death at the end of his lifespan, so it came to be thought that in life in the *loka* after death, being subject to the repeated death of the process of time would be followed by another final death at the end of that new life.

The literature of the Brahmins always promised to those who made correct use of their ritual the higher of two alternative fates: in the first place, honoured remembrance as one of the Fathers in opposition to forgotten disappearance, or perhaps to ignominy in a hell; then, in the *Brāhmaṇas*, existence alongside the gods in the Heavenly World as a higher goal than existence as one of the Fathers. Now that such an extension of life in time, the promise of 'non-dying', was thought to be followed finally by a second final death, clearly a new eschatological goal could not be further extension of life into a third lifetime (*āyus*), in another *loka*, but would have to be complete escape from subjection to 'repeated death' in any world. We have, of course, arrived at the very threshold of the classical Indian view in which complete subjection to an endless sequence of births and deaths – in a word, *saṃsāra* – was opposed to complete escape from it – *mokṣa*. The way in which this idea was finally concretised in Brahmanical thought owed much to the interpretation given to the social phenomenon of world-renouncing asceticism. Before coming to include this dimension of the matter, however, we must see how the lower of the two fates, subjection to repeated death, came to be seen as an inevitable return to life on earth. This was not an arbitrary assumption, produced by its logical complementarity with the idea of complete escape from death, but was itself a natural extension of ideas. In order to show that this is so I must now retrace my steps a little.

1.2.5. The concept of *loka*

In discussing the various *lokas* envisaged in the *Vedas* and *Brāhmaṇas*, I have until now left unemphasised a vital ambiguity. I remarked above that the word *loka* can refer generally to a condition of happiness and stability; in fact, all the *lokas* I have referred to were on occasion said to be attained in the present life, either by material or familial success, or more frequently in the *Brāhmaṇas* by the entrance during the sacrifice into a *loka*, seen as a sacred sphere of ritual reality.[29] The sacrificer must die to the 'profane' sphere of normal existence and be 'reborn' through initiation (*dīkṣa*)[30] into the sacrifice, before returning to 'this world' at the conclusion of the ritual. Again, this idea is not confined to India, being one of Durkheim's 'elementary forms' of religion everywhere;[31] and again, in India the idea has a particular importance in the development of eschatological thinking. The fact that the same structures of thought and imagination represent both the temporal sequence of the sacrificial ritual and that of cosmological and eschatological destiny is quite clearly apparent in Brahmanical thought (as we shall see that it is in Buddhism, where the sacred reality of ritual is replaced by states of consciousness attained temporarily in meditation).* In the early period of Brahmanical sacrificial thinking, the two sides of the concept of *loka* can be seen in the image of 'paths' between different 'worlds', and in the idea of man's three births.

We have seen that such thinking was permeated by the idea of analogies between macrocosmic and microcosmic levels,[32] the sacrifice being the mesocosm which joined the two. Hence, the idea of 'ways' or 'paths' to the other worlds – along which a ritual god such as Agni (as I have said, better seen as the fire-element personified) carried gifts to the gods, or along which travelled, after death, those who gained access to the Worlds of Fathers or Gods – is used equally easily in the immediate sacrificial context. Both gods and fathers travel down these paths to be present at the sacrifice and to take their 'food', and men can travel up them, when attaining to a ritually sacred '*loka*' is expressed in spatial terms. It is vital, however, that the sacrificer travel back down again to rejoin the profane, social world. This concern to keep the 'sacred' and 'profane' spheres apart is an ubiquitous requirement of religious ritual; in the Brahmanical texts it is expressed by the idea that a man must return soon to 'this world', for a prolonged stay will result in madness, death, or exclusion from human society.[33]

The overlap of the sacrificial and eschatological aspects of the *loka* concept is developed in the notion of the 'three births' of a man: he is born first from his parents; for a second time when he performs the sacrifice – this means both the first 'initiation' (*upanayana*) into one of the three privileged classes of Aryan society which were entitled to the use of Brahmanical ritual, and also the initiation (*dīkṣa*) into each sacrifice which confirmed and continued this membership;[34] and lastly for a third time when he is placed on the funeral pyre: 'when a man is born (again) from there [into the next life] that is his third birth'.[35] If we remember that the eschatological side of 'being born into another *loka*' has developed to the point at which we left it at the end of the last section, with a second final death inevitable at the end of any life in a *loka* after death, it is now perhaps not surprising that, just as after a sojourn in a ritually sacred *loka* the sacrificer returns to human society,

* See Chapter 7.2.1.

so after a second lifetime in a *loka* after death, it is imagined that there is a return to earth, to the world of human society.

1.2.6. The return to earth

The journey back down the path to human life, when it was first described in the *Upaniṣads*, incorporated two other motifs found in the *Vedas* and *Brāhmaṇas*: first, the idea of the dispersal at death of the various parts of a human body into the material universe, and their being grouped around particular elements in the construction of a living human being; and secondly, the idea of the sun and moon as barriers between human life and a sphere which transcends it.

In connexion with the first of these two motifs, the basic idea, to which we shall return often throughout this study, is that the human person is an assemblage of different parts. Various passages speak of the return of these parts to their larger place in the universe. At death, a man's breath returns to the wind, his eye(-sight) to the sun, his bones to the plants, and so on; thus a hymn to preserve a man's life calls back his breath from the wind and his sight from the sun. When a man is cremated, 'he passes into the fire by his speech, into the sun by his eye, into the moon by his mind, into the quarters by his ear, and into the wind by his breath'.[36] When the time came to consider the re-creation of a body for rebirth on earth, this process was available – reversed – as a means. Different ideas are found as to the central force around which this regrouping of elements took place. Frauwallner[37] has well systematised these into three 'doctrines' – those of water, breath, and fire.

The water-doctrine. In the Vedic hymns there is frequent mention of the original cosmic waters which existed before the creation; in the *Brāhmaṇas*, the theme is also common, and there we find the further thought that water continues to underlie the creation of new life in the form of rain. The transformation of water in the life-cycle is explained sequentially as rain vivifying plants; men's consuming their sap, and drinking water, producing 'sap' in them (a sap which is both the physical water of the body and the enlivening of the 'vital airs'); this sap as semen producing a new body. If we add to this the notion, also found in the *Brāhmaṇas*, of the cremation of the corpse and its humidity rising to the sky as smoke, the cycle is complete.[38] As we shall see presently, this cyclical movement of earthly waters was connected with the phases of the moon.

The breath-doctrine. Speculations on breath and its significance have always been ubiquitous in Indian thought, from its earliest beginnings and throughout its history. A few examples from this early period can suffice. In the *Vedas*, when an enemy is cursed, the wish is expressed 'let him not live, let his breath [*prāṇa*] leave him!' The word *asu*, meaning 'life-breath', is that which goes to the god of the dead and the Fathers at death; *asunīti*, 'leading (away) the breath' is a term for the world of the dead, or its lord.[39] The word *ātman*, later so important as the essential self, is etymologically connected with the idea of 'life-breath', and the connexion is found explicitly: 'everything which, having *ātman*, breathes'. In the *Brāhmaṇas*, breath is synonymous with life; and in the *Upaniṣads*, in a version of the world-wide tale of a contest between the bodily functions, it is breath which wins, and so is recognised as their chief; all the other bodily functions revert to it during sleep.[40]

The fire-doctrine. We have seen that the macrocosmic fire of the sun was joined with the human world through the mesocosmic fire sacrifice. Here it remains only to specify the way in which the microcosmic fire of the human being was imagined. In the *Brāhmaṇas* the warmth of life, the difference between life and death, felt when the body is touched, is the result of the sun's kindling of the breath within. In the *Upaniṣads* food is 'cooked by the inner fire' – the same verbal root *pac* is used for the ripening of food by the sun, its being cooked over a fire, and its being digested in the stomach. This inner fire can be heard burning when the ears are stopped up.[41]

The sun and moon as barriers. Although the sun, the macrocosmic fire, is the source of life both in this way, and also in the larger sense in which the continual rebirth of the dawn provides time in which to live, nevertheless because of this very dependence of man on the sun, it can be seen as (potential) death. 'That one who is burning is death; because he is death, therefore the creatures on this side of him die, those gods who are on the far side are non-dying.'[42] The sequence of days and nights, it is said, although creating a man's lifetime, still, by revolving, destroy it. In this way, the sun is as much a barrier for a human 'fire-soul' as a macrocosmic aid to continued existence.

In a similar manner, the moon is seen in two ways. First as a vessel which, as it waxes and wanes, empties and refills itself with the life-giving liquid *soma*; this brings 'immortality' when drunk, and, as the symbol of vivifying water in general, brings life to the whole animate universe.[43] The moon is 'seed' and is equated with the year – frequently used to symbolise time in general – and all living beings. Secondly, it is seen also as a gate to the heavenly world, and along with wind (breath), water, fire, lightning, and the sun, one of the 'six doors of *Brahman*'. At the same time, obviously, since in the water-doctrine human life is dependent on water, the moon is a closed door, a barrier.

1.2.7. Rebirth in the early *Upaniṣads*

With these last ideas, the background to the appearance of explicit ideas of rebirth in the *Upaniṣads* is complete. The two fullest accounts are in the *Bṛhadāraṇyaka* (6.2.9–16) and *Chāndogya* (5.4.1–5.10.8). Both these passages are presented as ideas of nobles, *kṣatriyas*, indeed the *Chāndogya* version is said to be a teaching which has 'never before come to Brahmins'. Many, including Frauwallner himself, have taken this as evidence that in history the idea of rebirth developed, at least in some of its crucial details, outside the Brahmanical fold. Whether or not this was so – and it seems to me *a priori* possible that there might well have been reasons for the Brahmanical tradition to have preserved such remarks in its texts, other than their historical veracity – the evident fact that these passages are redolent with the themes of Brahmanical thinking as I have described it shows that these ideas are natural extensions of Brahmanical tradition, which were integrated into its ideology with perfect coherence. As Heesterman has said, non-Brahmanical or even non-Aryan influences on Brahmanical thought in these matters 'do not seem to have made a decisive irruption causing a break in the development of ritual thought. They seem rather to have fitted themselves into the orthogenetic, internal development of Vedic thought.'[44]

Both passages open with an account of the 'doctrine of the five fires'. Some minor details differ in the two versions, but the essential idea is the same. In the *Chāndogya* version:

> The yonder world is a (sacrificial) fire . . . in this fire the gods offer faith. From this oblation rises king Soma (the moon). The rain-cloud is a fire . . . in this the gods offer king Soma. From this oblation arises rain. The earth is a fire . . . in this the gods offer rain. From this oblation arises food. Man [*puruṣa*] is a fire . . . in this the gods offer food. From this oblation arises semen. Woman is a fire . . . in this the gods offer semen. From this oblation arises the foetus [in the *Bṛhadāraṇyaka*, 'the person' – *puruṣa*] . . . When born, he lives out his lifetime [*āyus*]. When he is dead, they carry him to the appointed place for the (funeral) fire – from whence indeed he came, from whence he arose.

The *Chāndogya* continues: 'So those who know this, and those who in the forest take up religious practice[45] with the thought that faith is (the same as) asceticism [*tapas*], they pass into the flame (of the funeral pyre).' From here they pass through the parts of the process of time connected with light (the day, the time of the waxing moon), to the sun: 'from the sun to the moon; from the moon to the lightning; there a man who is non-human leads them on to *Brahma*; this is called "the path leading to the gods"'. An earlier passage of the same *Upaniṣad* where this journey is found alone, adds 'this is the way to *Brahma*; those who go along it do not return to the human condition'.

The *Bṛhadāraṇyaka* version of this journey is the same except that at the lightning 'a man consisting of mind . . . conducts them to the *Brahma*-worlds. In this *Brahma*-world they live for long extents. For them there is no return.'

The alternative fate is described in *Chāndogya* as follows: 'But those in the village whose religious practice consists in (gaining) sacrificial merit, and alms-giving, they pass into the smoke.' From here they pass into those parts of the process of time connected with darkness, the night, the time of the waning moon, and from there

> into the world of the fathers; from there into the moon. That is king Soma – the food of the gods. The gods eat that. Having lived there as long as there is a residue (of sacrificial merit), they return again by the same path to space, from space to the wind; having become wind, they become smoke . . . mist . . . cloud; having become cloud there is rain. They are born here as rice and barley [etc.]; from here the escape is difficult: only if someone eats (them) as food and emits semen, can there be further progress. And so, those whose conduct here has been pleasant can expect to reach a pleasant womb – of a Brahmin, a *Kṣatriya*, or a *Vaiśya*.* But those of stinking conduct can expect to reach a stinking womb – of a dog, a pig or an outcast.

The *Bṛhadāraṇyaka* version of this journey is the same as far as the moon, where

> they become food. There the gods, as they say to king Soma 'increase, decrease', so they feed on them there. When that (period) has elapsed, they pass into space . . . wind . . . rain . . . earth. Reaching the earth they become food; again they are offered in the fire of a man, and from there they are born in the fire of a woman. Rising up again into the worlds, thus they circle round.[46]

Although these passages are clearly early versions of the classical *saṃsāra* idea, they still lack certain elements of the final Indian *Weltanschauung*. These are two: first, the higher of the two destinies is as yet still ill-defined. According to the *Chāndogya*, the path of the successful leads to the gods and *Brahma*, from whence there is no return; the *Bṛhadāraṇyaka* adds that one dwells there for 'long extents'. We are still partially in the world of the *Brāhmaṇas*, where successful ritual activity leads simply to a more or less 'endless' extension of temporal existence. This style of thinking has remained alive, for example in a theoretical form in Jainism, where released souls float to the top of the universe to remain in a state of purity and bliss forever; and in a simpler version in 'popular Buddhism', where final release, *nirvāṇa*, becomes a heaven above all the others.[47]

* That is, in one of the three classes who were allowed access to Brahmanical ritual.

The standard concept of final release in developed philosophical Hinduism, and in Buddhism, is that it is not the attaining of an endless heaven, but a state which cannot be described in temporal terms at all: it is an escape from the ordered cosmos and temporal extension altogether. It was in the idea of final release as a timeless contrast to *saṃsāra* that Brahmanical thinking both reacted to and inspired the social phenomenon of world-renouncing asceticism, and thus finally concretised the rebirth/release opposition. We have indeed already seen this idea prefigured in the *Upaniṣad* passages, in the dichotomy between those who perform sacrifice in the village and those who practise asceticism in the forest. Already in the development of ideas I have been tracing (particularly in connexion with the ambiguous concept of *loka*, where both the 'rebirth' through sacrificial initiation and the return to the human world were coalesced with the idea of membership of the privileged classes of Aryan society) the connexion of structure between the view of society and that of metaphysics and eschatology has been broached. Before dealing directly with this part of the matter, however, I must mention the second point in the classical Indian *saṃsāra-mokṣa* picture which is still lacking – that of *karma*, action and its rewards. We have seen, in the *Chāndogya* version given above, that those who are subject to rebirth on earth can attain different births, according to their 'conduct' (*caraṇa*). Insofar as this might refer solely to the merit acquired through sacrificial action, the previous discussion will suffice as an explanation. Here, however, we seem to be moving towards the developed *karma* concept, in which all types of action are important, not just the sacrificial. Accordingly it is the idea of *karma*, and its generalisation, to which I now turn.

1.3. Action and the person: *karma*

1.3.1. The creative power of sacrifice: magical automatism

Throughout the preceding pages, the idea of the power of ritual action has been apparent: the nature of the universe (*ṛta*, *dharma*) was seen to depend on the sustaining efforts of gods and men, and every extension of eschatological hopes took place in terms of good results to be expected from sacrificial action. The various *lokas* had to be maintained, in a general sense, by ritual action,[1] and of course their attainment by the individual depended on his particular sacrificial record; this is most obviously the case with the *loka* whose very name enshrines the idea, the World of (Those who have acquired) Sacrificial Merit.

The fundamental point to be remembered in connexion with the workings of sacrifice and reward is its automatic, and quasi-material nature. The metaphor I have just used, of a sacrificial 'record', suggests perhaps the idea of an estimate made by a schoolmaster or judge, and so might be appropriate for monotheistic eschatologies, where final judgement is in the – free – hands of such a 'cosmic arbitrator' god. In the Brahmanical context, however, we are never far from the world of magic; by this I mean simply that the ritual hymns and gestures are not of the nature of a supplicatory prayer, but of a spell, which, if correctly carried out, must automatically have the desired effect, since the analogies and correspondences are simply and unambiguously in the nature of things. It is this quality of the *Weltanschauung* which allows a *Brāhmaṇa* to speak at one and the same time of a *loka* as the 'space' made by building bricks for the sacrifice, as the sacred reality brought about in the ritual, and as the 'world' which he hopes to gain after death: 'when he performs the initiation, he indeed pours out his own self, as seed, into the fire-pan, the womb; and when he becomes initiated, he makes for himself that *loka* beforehand, and he is born into the *loka* made by him; hence they say "man is born into the *loka* made (by himself)"'. If we describe this, as does the translator, as a play on the word *loka*, we make the subtle but crucial mistake of not realising that for the sacrificer (assuming that the rite is correctly performed) building a space with bricks, bringing into being a sacred reality, and creating merit for the next life are all accomplished, with equal facility, by one and the same action.[2]

1.3.2. The (reborn) person constructed by sacrifice

The ways in which it was imagined that performance of the sacrifice and the merit thus obtained actually created a new life, and the person reborn in another world, were various. The earliest notion seems to have been that of something called *iṣṭāpūrta*, a word of difficult etymology, referring to the offerings made to the gods and to the officiating priests, offerings which awaited the sacrificer in the next life.[3] A frequent image had it that the sacrifice created a 'store' or 'treasure-house' of good deeds, which could be drawn on in the life to come.[4] Often there is quite a physicalistic ring to the passages, connected with the idea of maintaining a body by food. Proper performance of the sacrifice brought food in this life and merit for the next; the sacrifice became the body in the next life, the *ātman*; 'making the sacrifice into his self, the sacrificer seats himself in the heavenly world'.[5] Merit, and the new body, could, however, decay; the sequence of days and nights could 'consume' (*dhayanti*) them, and food was put with a corpse so that the Fathers could consume that, rather than the dead man's good deeds. This kind of physicalistic attitude to the working of sacrificial merit will no doubt remind the student of Indian religion of the later Jain conception of *karma* – a wholly physical 'stuff', particles of which stick to the immaterial soul (*jīva*) and keep it weighed down in the world of rebirth.

The idea I would like to stress here, which will also remind the Indologist of later speculations, both Hindu and Buddhist, is that of the person created by sacrifice as a *composite*. We have already met the idea of the elements which compose a human being returning to their places in the macrocosm at death – eyes to the sun, breath to the wind, and so on. This idea is elaborated in two hymns of the *Atharva Veda*, where the various parts of the body are assembled into a composite (*sambhāra*).[6] As we shall see, in Buddhism it is 'formations' or 'constructions' (Pali *saṃkhāra*) which in the process of *karma* and rebirth, create that composite which is the human being and which is wrongly imagined to be a 'self'. In the early Brahmanical texts, we can see many precursors of that conception, which use terms like *saṃkhāra* (Sanskrit *saṃskāra*), derived from the verbal roots *kṛ* and *saṃs-kṛ*, 'to do', 'make' (thus *karma*), 'construct', and so on. We have already met the *sukṛtāṃ/sukṛtasya loka*, the World of Sacrificial Merit.

In the *Brāhmaṇas* the sacrificer comes into being in the next world with a body which is 'constructed' (*saṃskrīyate*) out of the Vedic hymns. The person who exists in the *loka* obtained by sacrifice – as we have seen, this means at one and the same time both 'sacred, ritual reality' and a 'world' after death – is a composite creation: it is made up (*saṃskṛta*) during the ceremony, and is a composite put together by the priest's verses from breath, mind, speech, and hearing (*ātmānaṃ samastaṃ saṃskurute*). This is a theme repeated in the *Upaniṣads*: the priest 'makes the person, consisting of the sacrifice, made of actions' (*aiṣṭikaṃ karmamāyam ātmānaṃ saṃskaroti*). The very word *sukṛta*, as we have seen used to refer both to the results of sacrifice and the world in which they are enjoyed, is applied to the human being: in the beginning 'Being' made for itself (*svayam akuruta*) an *ātman*, and that is why an *ātman* is called 'well-made' (*sukṛtam*). All the parts of the body and their cosmic equivalents (nostrils and the wind, eye and the sun, etc.) were put together into the human being when a person (*puruṣa*) was brought to them: 'they said "well done!" – indeed a person is a thing well-done ("well-made")'.[7]

1.3.3. *Karma* generalised: from ritual to ethics

So far, in connexion with the early idea of *karma*, we have seen that sacrificial ritual created, automatically, that composite which is the human being. We have not yet met with one of the central aspects of the developed *karma* conception: that the *quality* of the next life is determined by the quality of previous actions. There may be an early hint of this in the Vedic idea of differences in status of the Fathers;[8] there are passages also where good health in the next world and even good eyesight there are hoped for – but therefore not expected automatically. If differences in the quality of the next life were imagined, there would scarcely be any other cause for them in the world of the *Brāhmaṇas* than ritual success or failure; but it seems simply to be the case that this aspect of the matter was left unexplored. This may well have been because success or failure in ritual matters is not a thing which admits of degrees: either the sacrifice is performed perfectly, and so is automatically efficacious, or there is a mistake, in which case the whole performance is useless, or even positively harmful. To arrive at an idea of action which admits of differences in quality, it was necessary for the concept of *karma* to be generalised to include all actions, and thus for it to extend from the sphere of ritual manipulations to that of behaviour in general; that is, to ethics. (We might also say that all action thus became ritualised.)

It has been argued[9] that the ethicisation of a formerly magical, and morally neutral, eschatological scheme is a universal pattern in religious evolution. In India the thorough ethicisation of the *karma* idea owed much to the teachings of Buddhism; but even in pre-Buddhist times, the beginnings of the trend can be seen. These beginnings reflect that divergence between the intrinsic concerns of Brahmanical thinking and non-Brahmanical influence on it, of which I have spoken.

On the one hand, the period of the *Brāhmaṇa* texts saw an attempt by the Brahmins to appropriate conceptually, for themselves and their ritual, power over every facet of life. Thus every phenomenon, both cosmic and psychological, found an 'intermediary' analogue in the sacrifice, and sacrificial terminology came to be used to explain and describe these phenomena in themselves. We have seen the five-fire doctrine in which the course of birth and death was seen as an inter-connected series of sacrificial fires, and how fire-imagery was used to describe the warmth of life, digestion, and so on. These ideas were extended to depict the course of a lifetime as a large-scale course of the daily pattern of sacrifice. One of the five 'great sacrifices'[10] was the *Brahma*-sacrifice, which consisted in the recitation of Vedic passages: here the spoken recitation was the 'oblation' offered in the 'fire' of breath. In a similar way, the wind – macrocosmic counterpart of the breath – was said to be a sacrifice, which has the two 'paths' of mind and speech: the mind of the Brahman priest who oversaw the ritual, in silence, and the speech of the priests who performed the recitation.

On the other hand, the extension of a sacrificial quality to everything came to be mingled with the idea that, if everything was a form of sacrifice, there was then no need for particular, external rituals. Naturally, such an idea would draw strength from, and give strength to, those kinds of specialist religious practice which dispensed with, or opposed, the place of Brahmanical ritual in religious life. In this connexion we encounter what has been called the internalisation of the sacrifice in the life of the renouncer.[11] In non-Brahmanical religion, the life of the renouncer and his support by the laity simply replaces the support of Brahmanical sacrifice by its patrons. Thus for Buddhism, the highest form of sacrifice is said to be the life of a monk.[12] In Brahmanical thought, the life of the world-renouncer outside society has an ambiguous relationship to the socially oriented sacrificial ritual. In the ideology of the four 'stages of life', it is relegated to a small, and harmless, period at the end of life while the main stages of life still require the usual rituals. For life-long ascetics, however, whether or not there is an explicit rejection of external ritual, the overwhelmingly important modes of thought and practice are those in which the external ritual is refracted into the inner life of the individual. Thus the *Kauśītaki Upaniṣad* (2.5) takes up the theme of speech and breath as sacrifice, but reverses the conclusion drawn from it:

> as long as a man is speaking, he cannot breathe: then he is sacrificing breath in speech; as long as he is breathing, he cannot speak: then he is sacrificing speech in breath. One offers these two endless, deathless sacrifices continuously, whether waking or sleeping. Whatever other oblations there are, are limited [or, 'have an end', *antavatyas*], consisting in (ritual) action [*karmamaya*]. Knowing this, the ancients [pre-Aryans?] did not offer the *Agnihotra* sacrifice.

The *Agnihotra* is perhaps the most important of all ritual obligations for the orthodox householder, being the oblation into the fire performed at dawn and dusk. Elsewhere, the *Agnihotra* sacrifice is re-interpreted as breath (Ch.U.v. 19–24), and though it is said that the external sacrifice is still performed, the knowledge that all beings, like all the bodily functions, 'sit around the fire-sacrifice (breath) as do children around their mother' means that even if food is offered to an outcaste, it is still an oblation in the 'breath-self' common to all men. It should not be thought that this necessarily implies an outright opposition to the caste system of Brahmanical society; rather it implies the beginnings of the alternative, and, in the Brahmanical interpretation, ultimately complementary, type of religious practice; that is, of those who 'went to the forest', dispensing with external rituals and caste-related social behaviour, leaving the social world of the village in order to make their entire life into a sacred ritual act.

If one's entire life is a sacrificial performance, then every action will have the results which sacrificial performance has – that is, every act will have its effect on the next life. When the idea of general *karma* appears for the first time in the *Bṛhadāraṇyaka Upaniṣad* it does so in contexts which perhaps show that the concept was first integrated only with difficulty into the 'orthodox', socially oriented form of Brahmanical thought. In the middle of a normal sacrifice the Brahmin Yajñavalkya is asked, when all the constituents of the phenomenal human being have gone back to the material universe, what happens to the person (*puruṣa*)? Discreetly, he takes his questioner aside – since the new concept did not have a place in the public sacrificial arena: 'what they spoke of was *karma*, and what they praised was *karma*. Indeed, one becomes good by good action, bad by bad action.'[13] Later, Yajñavalkya teaches the same thing, but quotes an objection: 'some say that a person is made by desire' (*kāma*). 'Desire' here should not be taken in the general moral sense with which we are familiar from later Hinduism and, especially, Buddhism; rather it is that concentrated attention within the sacrificial ritual, focussed on the desired object of sacrifice, which was held to be a necessary condition of attaining it.[14] Yajñavalkya continues: 'as is one's desire, so is one's intention [*kratu*]; as is one's intention, so one performs actions . . . (in the other world) reaching the end of whatever acts he did here, (a man) comes again to this world for (further) action'. It makes more sense here to understand that the speaker is taking what was originally sacrificial terminology and phrasing it in such a way as to have general application. This general idea of *karma* finds its way, as we have seen, into one of the earliest passages dealing explicitly with a system of rebirth, and is then found frequently in the later *Upaniṣads*.[15]

1.4. Timelessness: *mokṣa (nirvāṇa)*

The reader will doubtless be prepared for most of the themes of this section. We have seen that the hope of an ultimate soteriological goal came to require that it be a complete escape from the extension of life in time; and that the function of the sacrifice in extending life in time was associated in Brahmanical thought with the membership of caste society; and that the renouncing ascetic who was to attempt to leave both life in time and life in that society came to represent within himself ideas which had been related to the external sacrifice. We must here investigate a little further this emphasis on the inner nature of the individual renouncer; and the idea within the Brahmanical tradition which provided the centre around which were grouped these various aspects of its interpretation of world-renunciation: that of knowledge as power.

1.4.1. Knowledge as power

Attention was first drawn to this by Edgerton.[1] The basic idea is that knowledge of a thing gives power over it: this 'magic' power proceeds through the universal idea that knowledge of a thing's or person's name gives power over them,[2] to the assumption that of two magically correspondent things, action on one will immediately affect the other. This can operate on a simple level, as when a doll represents a person in whose likeness it is made, or in the multitudinous obscure identifications of things in the *Atharva Veda* and *Brāhmaṇas* (such as a cow with a person's life-breath); on a more sophisticated level, the parallelism between macrocosmic and microcosmic functions, which we have seen repeatedly above, can give man an effective power in the scheme of the cosmos itself. An early hymn, for example, which praises the cosmic 'breath' – that is, the wind – as the enlivening principle of the universe is itself used as a magic performance for long life, to prolong the 'life-breath' of the individual. All the pieces of 'magic' knowledge in the *Vedas* and *Brāhmaṇas* are sought for a particular end; this may be a mundane goal like defeating enemies or gaining wealth, or a more significant goal like attaining long life or rebirth in a *loka* after death. This instrumental aspect of knowledge remains fully alive throughout the spiritual and eschatological speculations of the *Brāhmaṇas* and *Upaniṣads*.[3]

From the idea that the attainment of particular sacrificial and eschatological goals proceeded from particular types of ritual performance or knowledge, it was a natural step to the hope that by knowing everything one could have power over everything. In the multitudinous variety of Brahmanical lore, clearly, this hope could not be fulfilled by a quantitative accumulation of knowledge; but the fact that each piece of knowledge, because it worked through a correspondence, was thought to be somehow appropriate to the desired result, gave rise to the hope that by finding a similarly appropriate essential correspondence between something known, and therefore within one's power, and the underlying principle of the universe itself, one might thereby know and control everything in the universe – including, of course, how to escape from death and 'repeated death'.

This desire found its fulfilment in the correspondence between the human soul, man's essential self (or however one translates the Sanskrit reflexive pronoun *ātman*), and the power behind the universe, *Brahman*. An infinite amount could be – and has been – said about this correspondence; I will restrict myself to those aspects of the idea which are germane to the notion of knowledge as power.

The word *Brahman* is undoubtedly polyvalent,[4] and it is perhaps fruitless to seek for a single basic meaning; but at least one of its meanings can be traced back to the *Atharva Veda*, where the idea of 'knowledge as power' was first extensively developed.[5] There, the neuter noun *brahman* means a 'charm' or 'incantation', that is, a Vedic hymn itself as an embodiment of magic power; the hymns themselves had power to bring about the desired end.[6] I mentioned above the idea that recitation of the Vedic hymns in a general sense helped to maintain cosmic order. In the time of the *Brāhmaṇas*, when the priests were engaged in extending the influence of their hymns and rituals over the entire range of the universe, it was natural that they should claim that their hymns derived power from an ultimate and all-embracing force behind everything. Thus from particular instrumental uses, such as freedom from illness, and injury to one's enemies, the hymns began to be seen as instantiating in their user power over the universe. Taken by itself, however, the term *brahman* suggests perhaps less the dynamic power to achieve goals, than the static support of things, that power which permeates everything and gives it solidity and strength.[7] What made this 'ground of things' into a potent, usable force was its being taken up by the sacrificer in the ritual act.

We have seen examples above of a frequent idea of the *Brāhmaṇas*: the sacrificer, in performing the ritual, makes the sacrifice his own self – *ātman*; that is, he creates himself anew by birth into the ritual *loka*, and in doing so perpetuates his life, both here and hereafter. At the same time, the sacrifice is said to be the same as *brahman*; that is, the efficacy of sacrificial power rests on the power which supports the whole universe. 'When the coals are glowing intensely, then indeed the fire is *brahman*':[8] the sacrificial fire expresses cosmic vitality, and re-vitalises the man who uses it. Clearly, if the sacrifice is the same as the self of the sacrificer, and as the power of the universe, it will not be long before these two are equated with each other.

1.4.2. The renouncing individual

The Brahmanical renouncer, then, sought that inner self called *ātman* as the means of gaining access to *brahman*, to universal control and power, by a life of rigid asceticism and self-control (*yama*, *niyama*),[9] which would find the 'inner controller' (*antaryāmin*).[10] In that search, the emphasis was on the 'mental sacrifice', or the sacrifice of the self (*ātmayajña*) – already in the *Brāhmaṇas* extolled as superior to sacrifice to the gods. The focus of religious life – for the specialist – is placed not on external ritual performances but on inner experience interpreted in the light of concepts and values derived from previous sacrificial speculation.

Heesterman has argued persuasively that this development represents the logical outcome of previous ritual thinking: 'the institution of renunciation is already implied in classical ritual thinking. The difference between classical ritualism and renunciation seems to be a matter rather of degree than of principle. The principle is the individualization of the ritual which could not but lead to its interiorization.' What he means by individualisation here is a change from a pre-classical agonistic form of ritual, which consisted of competition and exchange between two persons or groups, to the classical form, in which the patron (*yajamāna*) and officiating priests form a 'single unit', which operates for the sole benefit of the individual patron. Thus

> the development of brahminical theory, set off by the individualization of the ritual, did not stop at the point where the host–guest, protagonist–antagonist complementarity was fused into the single unit of *yajamāna* and officiants. It had to advance to its logical conclusion, that is the interiorization of the ritual which makes the officiants' services superfluous.[11]

We can see from the idea of knowledge as power that there would be a tension within the unit of patron and officiants, for two reasons. First, from the patron's point of view, the idea of *knowledge* rather than ritual *action* as the important power obviously threatened the performance of the rites:

> 'the knowledge of a procedure, its psychic image, is magically connected with the procedure itself. The knower, precisely through the fact that he knows – not because through his knowledge he acts skilfully and correctly, but by reason of the power of the knowledge in itself – possesses power over the entity or event known.' It is therefore even said to be unnecessary actually to perform a rite. If you know it you have as good as performed it; that is, you can be sure of the benefits which are promised to the performer; . . . That this doctrine in its extreme form is dangerous to the perpetuation of the actual performances, is obvious. All the more impressive is the fact that despite their absorbing interest in the rites, the *Brāhmaṇa* texts frequently do not shrink from drawing this conclusion.[12]

Secondly, from the officiating priests' point of view, as specialists holding the necessary ritual skills of performance and interpretation, such an increase in the significance of the interpretations would cause a distancing from the paying client. Although the idea of knowledge as a special constituent of the rites is mentioned in connexion with the patron, 'he who knows this, or he for whom, knowing this, the sacrificial rite is performed',[13] it seems fairly obvious that the developments in specialist knowledge of the significance of the rites – to which the *Brāhmaṇas* are devoted – would be the preserve of the specialist priests themselves. As the complexity of the rites increased, so too did the importance of the priest; not only because he knew what rites to perform, what chants to recite and so on, but, in the case of the *Brahman* priest, because his knowledge and sacred presence ensured that the performance was a success. Remaining silent, and concentrating his thought, he thus organised and sustained the ceremony as an efficacious act.[14] Consequently, from this point of view there gradually came to be a gap between the ritual experts, the priests, who 'knew' what was happening, and the paying client, the *yajamāna*, who remained in comparative ignorance.

We might say, then, that the new role of renouncer, in its Brahmanical interpretation, combined in itself the roles of priest and *yajamāna*: the forest ascetic not only tries to attain an esoteric knowledge of the true significance and meaning of the old ritual practices, but also hopes to gain for himself the benefits of his 'self-sacrifice'; 'interiorization meant the real fusion into one person of patron and officiant'.[15]

The 'one person' of the renouncer is henceforth, in Dumont's words, 'the agent of development in Indian religion and speculation, the creator of values'.[16] In a series of publications, Dumont has argued that in India it is not the ordinary man in society but the renouncer who represents an *individual* in the western sense – that is, not the biological person, the concrete human being, but the value-laden 'Individual' as autonomous moral agent and subject of the socio-economic institutions of free enterprise, equality, and liberty, and in each of whom is embodied the idea of abstract humanity. In India the ordinary man in caste society is defined by his position in the hierarchy; his human nature is particular, essentially linked to his position in the greater caste system, from which 'encompassing whole' all parts receive their specific value.[17]

For the individual renouncer as religious specialist, the search for ultimate control and power through realisation of the *ātman* (the idea of abstract humanity) was to bring escape from the ordered cosmos of time and rebirth altogether. Those early Upaniṣadic passages which first adumbrated the idea of rebirth explicitly were imprecise as to the fate of the successful. The *Kauśītaki Upaniṣad* repeats the idea of souls going to the moon at death. There they are asked a question: those who know, go further, those who do not, return to earth via rain to be reborn. The question is 'who are you?', and the correct reply is 'I am you', that is, both moon and soul are *brahman*. The man who knows this equivalence not only 'creates whatever he desires', and gains whatever *loka* he desires, but he is released from the effects of good or bad actions and so is not reborn in *saṃsāra*, but 'becomes *brahman*, becomes this all'.[18]

Such an absorption in 'the all', and such an escape from time into timelessness, as part of the conscious inner experience of individuals, doubtless is the sort of aesthetic feeling (variants of which seem to occur to virtuosos in many different religious cultures) which has been described – in western terms – as 'pantheistic mysticism'. In a wider sociological perspective, it is clear that this sort of feeling is available only to a few individuals whose aspirations and skills tend in that direction.

What turned this statistically unusual type of feeling into the commonly accepted ultimate religious goal in India was the particular social position and prestige of the world-renouncer and his quest.

1.4.3. *Saṃsāra/mokṣa*; village/forest; life-in-the-world/world-renunciation

We have seen that the earliest accounts of rebirth in the *Upaniṣads* made a distinction between the 'ignorant' village-dwelling ordinary man, who could only perform rites and acts of charity, and the forest-dwelling seeker of knowledge, who was not concerned with external ritual but with its 'real' cosmic significance. The opposition between village and forest is ancient and ubiquitous in Brahmanical thought. Malamoud has described the parallel between village and sacrifice on the one hand, and forest and renunciation on the other. In particular, he mentions the analogy between the ideas of the village and that of repetition.[19] This repetition means a group of related things: first, the perpetual repetition of ritual and social forms, caste rules and obligations, in contrast with the renouncer's progress (in theory) towards complete freedom and isolation (*kaivalya*, a term frequently used as a synonym for *mokṣa*); then, the repetition of social life imaginatively transcribed as the series of births and deaths experienced in the 'worlds' of sacrifice and *saṃsāra*. There is extensive parallelism between the act of renouncing the world of society, entering the ascetic life, and the initiation into the sacrifice which the sacrificer previously had undergone. The renouncer 'dies' to society – he has no longer a social status, indeed his funeral rites are performed – and is reborn into his new status of lone salvation-seeker, just as the sacrificer had to be reborn through initiation into the sacrificial *loka*. Just as, for the duration of the sacrifice, the *yajamāna* was outside the human *loka*, being charged with a profound but dangerous cosmic power, and was – as far as his membership of caste society was concerned – in an intermediate stage between life and death, so the renouncer, being outside caste rules, is an object of awe as holy, but is also impure, so far as normal social contact is concerned. Whereas the sacrificer, because his stay in the sacrificial world was temporary, in fact used the repeated birth and death of the sacrifice as a means of re-stating his membership of caste society, the renouncer – whose whole life is a sacrifice – is permanently outside society, never returning to the human 'world' from the sacred sphere into which his renunciation has put him.

We have seen how the same structure of thought came to represent the temporal sequence of the sacrifice and that of eschatological destiny. Now we can see that this same structure represents at once the ideas of repeated birth and death in the sacrifice, of repeated birth, through sacrificial initiation, into village society with its constant round of social ties and caste obligations, and of repeated birth and death in the eschatological scheme of *saṃsāra*. The forest-dwelling renouncer escapes them all. The ordered cosmos of caste relations in society – a 'cosmos' which had been imposed on the 'chaos' of pre-Aryan tribal India – and the freedom from social relations enjoyed by the individual renouncer are thus the visible 'facts' of daily experience, which are transcribed onto the eschatological sphere as *saṃsāra* and *mokṣa*.

The religious texts, both Hindu and Buddhist, which from this time on emphasised the *saṃsāra-karma-mokṣa* belief system (we should remember, of course, that this was never the *only* belief system of Indian religion), represent the thought of the renouncer (in Buddhism, of the monk). In Dumont's words again: 'we could say that transmigration not only transcribes the caste system imaginatively, but also establishes the relation between the renouncer, as an individual man, and the phantom-like men who have remained in the world and support him. Transmigration is the idea that the renouncer, turned towards liberation, has of the world he has left behind.' Similarly, in this relationship of mutual signification: 'without transmigration the liberation or extinction (*nirvāṇa*) which he [the Buddha] recommends would lose all meaning'.[20]

The development of thought that I have described in this chapter, the appearance in the Brahmanical great tradition of the ideas of *saṃsāra*, *karma*, and *mokṣa*, was complete before the time of the Buddha. This was the cultural world into which he was born, and it was with these conceptual tools that he articulated his message of salvation.

2 Varieties of Buddhist discourse

> It is necessary always to distinguish who 'they' are, who says what in what situation, and what the 'task orientation' of the various actors in the situation is, for 'religion' – in the form of esoteric ritual lore and theology – is differentially distributed throughout a society, or elements of it will be differentially distributed, or be available differentially to different actors.
>
> Peter Worsley (1968) reprinted in Robertson (1969) p. 224

2.1. Buddhist thought in context

In this section I will give a brief outline of the variety of Buddhist practice in South Asian society, in order to suggest the particular social position and role of the intellectual doctrines with which I myself shall be concerned in the rest of this book. In tracing the development of the belief system of *saṃsāra-karma-mokṣa* in Brahmanical thought, I argued, following Dumont, that the final concretisation of this conceptual world could only be understood in the light of a sociological apperception of the dichotomy between the man-in-the-world and the world-renouncer. In the Buddhist version of this conceptual world, the same dichotomy appears as that between the layman and the ordained monk; and it is this same dichotomy which is the fundamental ideological structure on which are erected the psychological and eschatological speculations which constitute the doctrine of not-self, and the analyses of personality and continuity made in its light. Social reality, of course, whether in 'Hindu', 'Buddhist', or any other culture, is always more complex than are the fundamental structures of ideology. In looking at the Buddhist texts, we shall have to try to remain aware both of the ideology and the wider realities which it represents and encompasses.

2.1.1. The social range of Buddhism

In Chapter 1 we saw two types of Brahmanical specialist: the ritual priest whose abiding concern was the socially oriented sacrifice, and the ascetic renouncer, conceptually oriented towards the abandonment of society. For descriptive sociology this dichotomy is obviously too simple, for although there is a clear difference between the social and caste status of those who have renounced and those who have not, nevertheless, in terms of the intellectual and religious interests of individuals and groups, there is a fairly large range of degrees of proximity to the conceptual and religious life of the ordinary man-in-society. For example, as bearers of the Sanskritic intellectual tradition, many Brahmins have become scholars, specialists in a wide variety of subjects, from grammar and linguistic analysis to poetics and beyond. Paradoxically perhaps, such a scholar – though 'officially' a householder – may in fact have less connexion with the ideas and interests of ordinary religious life in society than does the ascetic – nominally outside society – begging from village to village, in daily contact with ordinary people.

I do not wish to go further into the details of Brahmanical life and thought; suffice it to show from the example just given that the simple structures of Brahmanical ideology, such as 'householder' and 'renouncer', are not simply and directly related to all observable social realities. In the case of Buddhism, similarly, the difference in status between monk and layman is clear enough; we must, however, interpret a body of heterogeneous texts which both uses such simple ideological distinctions, and at the same time reflects more complex social reality. The tradition has recognised explicitly the difference between village-dwelling and forest-dwelling monks; and between book-duty and meditation-duty as monkish careers.[1] Ideologically, and generally in fact, the two distinctions can be taken to refer to the same two sets of monks; but the scholarly tradition of book-duty has at its most sophisticated level been housed in large city temples, which became like universities,[2] and whose immediate relation to ordinary village Buddhism might perhaps have merited the western gibe of 'living in an ivory tower'.

A brief summary of the range of Buddhist practice might be as follows. At the village level, there are a large number of different types of what we might call religious practitioners: magicians (black and white), astrologers, medical practitioners of various sorts, officiants at shrines to local gods and spirits, and a few (usually two or three) Buddhist monks. In different settings, these different types of practice may have more or less connexion with each other in the life of individuals and of groups in a village. Certainly, the 'village-priest' monk will have to live in symbiosis with these other concerns. Gombrich tells the instructive story of an arrogant young Sinhalese monk, whose refusal to accept such a symbiosis (through his contempt for the 'popular Buddhism' of 'devotion' as opposed to the 'true Buddhism' of 'philosophy') eventually made life in the village impossible for him, whence he had to return to the larger city monasteries of Colombo, where he had been educated.[3]

In the more urban social settings, monks will be congregated in larger temples, with a variety of social and even political functions; their

'Buddhist' practice will accordingly have less of an immediate and necessary relation to those other kinds of 'religious' practice found at the village level. A large sub-section of this population will be scholars, housed in monastic universities, whose main task is to preserve, comment on, and even elaborate Buddhist doctrine. Contrasted with these kinds of monk, in both village and city, is the virtuoso life of meditation. Monks of this sort may live alone or in small groups as hermits in the forest, or they may be collected in larger monasteries which are – unlike most – specially devoted to the practice of intensive meditation. Laymen support monks at all these levels, in all the different social settings, and will identify their own level of Buddhist practice and aspiration more or less closely with the monks' in each particular case.

Even this short and simplistic account of the variety of Buddhist practice is enough to alert us to the fact that the corpus of Buddhist literature might be found to reflect these differences in religious concern and aspiration, and to contain discourse with a correspondingly wide theoretical content and conceptual sophistication.

2.1.2. Literacy and the doctrine of *karma*

I will choose two topics to demonstrate how important is an awareness of the social variety in Buddhist practice for the understanding of Buddhist theory: literacy and the use of the doctrine of *karma*. We lack detailed accounts of literacy in all *Theravāda* countries: I will draw on Tambiah's[4] account of North-east Thailand. Tambiah shows that traditionally novice monkhood – in Thailand most frequently only a temporary state, lasting for a number of years in adolescence and early adulthood – has been the main avenue to the acquisition of literacy skills. Within village Buddhism, these skills are for the most part restricted to the preservation, through copying, of a small range of Buddhist texts; and to the learning of a fairly limited amount of material for use in ritual chants and sermons. Insofar as this material draws from the texts of the great tradition of Buddhism, it consists almost exclusively in stories of the Buddha's many lives (the canonical *Jātaka* stories), which are used to illustrate the moral and psychological exhortations of Buddhist sermonising.[5] The sermons, and the texts containing the stories to be used in them, will use the vernacular language of the particular community; the only Pali learned by a village monk is a very small collection of ritual chants, whose precise syntactic and semantic content is not necessarily understood (though of course the general meaning is).

In order for a monk to have access to the Pali texts whose ideas form the content of my own study, it is necessary to leave the village temple and to study further in monastic centres of increasing sophistication, culminating in the great universities of Bangkok. Clearly an individual monk following this path will become more and more a specialist, more and more remote from the roles, such as ritual expert, which the village monk fulfils. In Tambiah's own summary

> a monk who becomes engaged in Pali doctrinal studies is in all probability also one who becomes increasingly committed to following that kind of doctrinal Buddhism, which, if taken seriously, results in progressive detachment from the world and involves practising meditation and self-control and entering into mystical realms which promise *Nirvāṇa*. In other words, he tends to become a world-renouncer, and only a few are capable of engaging in this higher pursuit.[6]

The words 'if taken seriously' are important here, for of course a scholarly acquaintance with, and allegiance to, the conceptual content of Buddhist doctrine are not necessarily accompanied by the actual practice of meditation and the personal quest for *nirvāṇa* (as Buddhist preaching, naturally, tends to point out).

This account of literacy in Thailand cannot be straightforwardly generalised to all *Theravāda* countries, since the conventions of monks' lives differ – most obviously in the matter of temporary monkhood, which in Ceylon, for example, is virtually unknown. What can be generalised, however, is the fact that a deep knowledge of Pali doctrinal Buddhism is already, for the individual monk, a large step away from village Buddhism, and from preaching simple Buddhist ethics in the vernacular, towards a more specialist and potentially more intense and introjected commitment to Buddhist theory. Thus the type and complexity of Buddhist doctrine available to individuals – monks or laymen – varies with their social position, literacy skills, and their own individual aspirations. The complex psychological analyses of the Pali texts which constitute the doctrine of *anattā*, and still more the analyses of personality and continuity made in its light, are clearly situated at the highest end of this range of doctrine. It is important for us to realise not only that a very large proportion of Buddhists and Buddhist practice (considered in the most general sense of these words) has nothing to do with the specialist understanding and application of not-self; but also, *that the textual tradition of Buddhism reflects this state of affairs*. The written tradition of Buddhism contains, quite naturally and consistently, a wide range of discourse about psychology and continuity, suited to all the differences in religious practice and the use to which doctrine is put. Our understanding of Buddhist thought will be realistic only if we remain aware of this range of discourse.

The other topic I will mention – *karma* – shows the importance of studying not only *what* is believed, but also *how* beliefs are held. Here again, the Buddhist written tradition reflects the variety of Buddhist practice. Indeed, much of the way in which explanations in terms of *karma* are used by ordinary people is common both to Buddhism and Hinduism. Studies of village Buddhism[7] and of village Hinduism[8] have shown that the explanation of good and bad fortune, and the hope for worldly or other-worldly increases in good fortune, are formulated in a number of different ways, of which *karma* is only one. The different ways of dealing with these matters correspond to the different religious practitioners of village life whom I mentioned earlier. For example, bad fortune may be explained as the result of witchcraft or the revenge of an unpropitiated local deity; good fortune can result from the transference of 'merit' (accruing from religious performances) from others, or may be the consequence of successful propitiation of deities. Astrology is ubiquitous as an explanatory scheme; and insofar as psycho-physical facts are amenable to 'medical' technology, various types of medicinal reasons may account for troubles and sufferings of that sort. In Ceylon, as Obeyesekere has reported, traditional Indian Ayur-Vedic medicine is linked with concepts from the other explanatory schemes through the concept of *doṣa*: literally 'troubles', this also refers to the three humours (*tridoṣa*) of Ayur-Vedic theory, the imbalance between which is the focus of therapeutic analysis and treatment. Obeyesekere gives a list of *doṣas*, as follows:

preta doṣa . . . Troubles, generally sickness, caused by a mean ancestral spirit
yakṣa doṣa . . . Illness caused by demons
äsvaha/kaṭavaha dosa . . . Effects of the evil eye and the evil mouth
deyiyanne doṣa . . . *Doṣa* caused by the gods – e.g. punishments of wrong-doers by illness
hūniyaṃ doṣa . . . Consequences of sorcery
graha doṣa . . . Misfortunes, including illness, as a result of inauspicious planetary influence
karma doṣa . . . Misfortunes due to a person's bad *karma*.

As Obeyesekere remarks: 'none of these concepts is mutually contradictory; rather, a more limited concept is often contained within a larger one. The limited concepts generally pertain to disease, and the larger ones to a wider class of misfortunes.'[9] For the ordinary South Asian villager – whether layman or monk – counteracting or coming to terms with misfortune will utilise explanations from any or all of these levels. Lesser use of the lower, or, more rarely, the abandonment of them by any individual, represents a conscious attempt at self-assimilation to the sphere of Buddhist virtuosity. This is accomplished by the monk's approximation, in behaviour and attitude, to the ideal renunciatory image of monkhood, or by the layman's adoption of the role of *upāsaka*, a role which combines a certain amount of orthodox asceticism with the retention of lay status.[10]

It is not only modern anthropological study which has revealed the co-existence of *karma* with other systems of explanation. Literary study of early Brahmanical texts and Buddhist *Jātaka* stories,[11] and of a vast range of Hindu mythology,[12] shows that there have been alternatives to, and modifications of, the idea of *karma* from earliest times. There are several mentions in the *Theravāda* Canon of a list of 'diseases', or more generally 'things experienced', which are said to arise from a variety of causal factors, such as the bodily humours, change of season, and so on, in which 'the ripening of *karma*' is only one.[13]

The idea of *karma* is a very basic plank of the Buddhist doctrinal edifice; the theories of not-self and of continuity, which I will examine later, represent far more sophisticated and complex intellectual products. If *karma* is not an ubiquitous and uniform element of religious practice in Buddhist societies, how much less so will be such abstruse matters as not-self and continuity?

My point, then in outlining the social range of Buddhism, and in giving the examples of literacy and *karma* in elucidation of it, is this: 'Buddhism' does not represent a unitary system of belief and practice, and 'Buddhist texts' do not display a unitary type of discourse. I do not mean to suggest that there is any simple correlation between socially distinguishable types of practice and conceptually distinguishable styles of discourse. We must, however, as part of our attempt to understand Buddhist ideas, try to appreciate the function which the texts serve in the lives of Buddhists.

To anticipate my argument a little: the doctrine of *anattā* and the problems of personality and continuity explained in its light form only a part of the active religious life of virtuoso meditators and scholastic intellectuals. These two groups do not exhaust the range of Buddhist practice in South Asian society; and the textual passages which disallow any talk of unitary and persisting selves or persons, according to the doctrine of *anattā*, do not exhaust the range of discourse in which Buddhist teaching is carried out. Nor, indeed, is it the case that the theoretical discourse in which the doctrine of *anattā* and the explanations of personality and continuity are contained exhausts the range of psychological and behavioural concern of the individual Buddhist, however much of a meditative or scholastic specialist he might be.

So far, I have argued these points with regard to Buddhist doctrine *a priori*, and by analogy with Buddhist practice as revealed by anthropology. Let me now turn to the doctrinal texts themselves.

2.2. Different ways of talking about 'self' and 'person'

The preceding considerations suggested *a priori* that the doctrine of *anattā* can be of immediate concern only to a small number of Buddhist intellectuals; a study of the canonical texts shows clearly that the denial of self, the refusal to allow any 'ultimate' validity to personal terms which are taken to refer to anything real and permanent, is insisted on only in a certain specific kind of conceptually sophisticated theoretical context. The linguistic items translated lexically as 'self' and 'person' (in Pali *attā, purisa/puggala,* Sanskrit *ātman, puruṣa/pudgala* respectively*) are used quite naturally and freely in a number of contexts, without any suggestion that their being so used might conflict with the doctrine of *anattā*. It is only where matters of systematic philosophical and psychological analysis are openly referred to or presupposed on the surface level of discourse that there is imposed the rigid taboo on speaking of 'self' or 'person'. We shall see (in Chapter 5.1) that the later *Theravāda* tradition constructed a meta-linguistic explanation for this difference in the use of personal terms – that is, in terms of a difference between 'conventional' and 'ultimate' truth. Here I will give some examples of the way personal terms are used, in order to show how the textual and linguistic evidence parallels and confirms the sociological facts we have just encountered. For convenience, I will divide these uses into three groups. The first two of these groups are clearly separate from the third, as acceptable non-theoretical uses from unacceptable theory; they are differentiated from each other only by a gradual increase in the contextual importance attached to the reference to 'oneself', or the kind of 'person' one is. In many cases, examples of which I shall give, one must beware the pitfalls of literal translation into English, where the translation contains presuppositions and implications *not* found in the original Pali.

2.2.1. As reflexive pronoun: narrative

Attā is the regular reflexive pronoun in Pali, used in the masculine singular for all numbers and genders. Thus the phrases 'we restrain ourselves' and 'she enjoys herself' use the same pronominal form (masculine singular accusative *attānaṃ*). This is a usage common to all types of Indo-Aryan language, and is found in the Pali texts with as little reference to systematic metaphysics and psychology as has any simple reflexive form in any language. Syntactically literal translation, however, can seem to suggest otherwise: the phrase *suddham attānaṃ pariharati*

* As we shall see in Chapter 2.3.1, *ātman* and *puruṣa* were two of the most important terms used in Brahmanical thought for the self or person whose liberation from embodiment and rebirth was the ultimate religious goal.

can be translated literally as 'he carries about a pure self'. If this can be given any sense in English, it might seem to imply some more or less definite view of self. The phrase in Pali, on the contrary, simply uses the standard Buddhist idea of purity to describe a man who behaves with ethical correctness. We might translate as 'he bears himself in purity' or simply 'he keeps himself pure'. Any Buddhist saint, like the Buddha, 'sees in himself complete purity of bodily action'.[1]

Similarly, the word *attā* is often used as part of a compound, where elegant translation can avoid the use of the English word 'self' altogether. Thus *attānuvāda*, 'self-reproach', 'remorse'; *attavetana*, supporting oneself', 'earning a living'; *attādhīna*, 'master of himself', 'independent, free' (used of a recently liberated slave); *khematta*, 'at peace with himself', 'tranquil'; *rakkhitatta*, 'self-guarded', 'prudent'; *pahitatta*, 'self-willed', 'resolute'. Many other examples could be cited.[2] Often compounds of this sort oppose self and others. Thus a proud man 'exalts himself' and despises others; acting for 'one's own benefit' is contrasted with acting for that of others (for various different reasons); in moral life, both bad *karma* and purification are 'self-born', 'self-caused'; equally, 'no-one purifies another'. *Attakāra*, 'action of oneself', is contrasted with action 'by another', both of which are said to denote 'initiative'. Any view which denies 'action of oneself', 'of others', and 'of persons' generally is vigorously repudiated as a nihilistic and spiritually enervating heresy.[3] The standard way of opposing self and others, in the whole range of ethical and behavioural concern, is by means of the terms 'internal' or 'concerning oneself' (*ajjhattam*), and 'outside' (*bahiddhā*).

In all these passages, one should translate by normal English reflexive pronouns, if they are necessary at all, and not by any semi-theoretical locutions with the definite article – 'the self (Self)'. A particularly acute example of this is provided by a passage in which the Buddha comments on the remark of a king and queen that 'no-one is dearer than oneself'. He remarks (in verse) 'surveying the whole world in one's mind, one finds no-one dearer than oneself [or "than a man's self"]; as everywhere others hold themselves dear [literally "self is dear to others"] the man who loves himself should not harm others'. It would be possible to translate *attā* here as 'the Self', as if the idea were that a single cosmic self was shared by all (as in some *Upaniṣads*); but then the whole Buddhist ethical point would be distorted. The idea here is simply that since each person is naturally concerned with his own welfare, a truly moral agent should realise that to cause suffering to others is to cause them the same distress which the agent knows well enough in his own experience. Certainly this point is expressed with a play on the word *attakāmo*, 'self-lover', a word-play which is impossible in English; but we should not mistake literary elegance for a disguised reference to a theory of self which so many other passages are concerned to deny.[4]

In just the same way, the words *purisa/puggala* are used frequently in simple narrative contexts where the intention is simply to denote a particular person or persons; it would be an absurd mistranslation if one attempted to see in this use a reference to the pure monadic spiritual individual of the *Sāṃkhya* system, which is denoted by the Sanskrit equivalent *puruṣa*. In one simple example an 'ignorant person' (*purisa-puggalo*) is said to be reborn in circumstances congruent with his acts, whereas 'a monk in whom ignorance is destroyed' does not come to rebirth.*[5]

2.2.2. As religious exhortation: character description

We have seen in some of the examples just given that often ethical and religious injunctions or descriptions are expressed linguistically by a focus on 'oneself'. In passing from the use of 'self' or 'person' as a simple reference to the facts of men's reflexivity and individuality without any theoretical connotations, to their use as items of metaphysical and psychological analysis, we see a second, and, one might say, more resonant use of personal terms in Buddhist texts. These are found in contexts of spiritual education, where for various reasons concentration on oneself, either as the instigator of religious progress or as a particular character type, is the focus of interest. In a much-quoted passage, the Buddha tells some young men searching for a runaway courtesan that they would be better occupied 'searching for yourselves'.[6] It is quite wrong to translate this as 'searching for the Self' as some have done;[7] the Buddha is simply reiterating the universal message of religious teachers that happiness is not to be found in external pleasures, courtesans and the like, but in some more profound 'inner' beatitude. This general injunction to seek inner values is expressed by the phrases 'taking refuge in oneself', 'making oneself an island'. (Elsewhere, and with much the same practical meaning, it is said that one should make Buddhist teaching one's 'island refuge'.) The recommendation to seek self-control, equally ubiquitous in religious thought, is found in Buddhism in the phrase *attā hi attano nātho*; literally translated 'self is lord of the self', a more accurate rendering of the sense would be simply 'be your own master!' One should 'watch oneself', and be 'self-guarded'; a man who has succeeded in this is called 'self-developed', or '(spiritually) advanced' (*bhāvitatta*).[8]

Almost every tradition knows such recommendations, expressed in the

* For the commentarial meta-linguistic exegesis of this passage see Chapter 5.1.3.

general maxims to 'know thyself', 'look within', and so on – and in Sanskrit and Pali the reflexive use of *ātman/attā* in the singular is virtually unavoidable in phrasing such maxims. Thus, through Buddhist training one comes to 'know oneself' (*attaññū*).[9] Clearly this phraseology presupposes no technical picture of what will be found at the end of the search for self-knowledge.

In fact, according to Buddhist theory, the end result will be the final discovery that no real self exists, and the bliss of *nirvāṇa* will consist, amongst other things, in living out this sublime truth. During the course of religious training which is held to lead to this liberating discovery, the practitioner will find out a lot about the kind of character he has in this particular lifetime – better said, 'which he is'. This kind of self-knowledge is extensively discussed in Buddhism: the 'individuality' of each lifetime (as it apears to the unenlightened man) is sometimes called *attā*, more usually *attabhāva*, literally 'self-state'. (This is a very important term, of which I shall have much to say later, in Chapter 5.2. 1–2.) The karmic effects of similar actions will vary according to whether the person who performs them (both *puriṣa* and *puggala* are used) is 'developed' or 'undeveloped in behaviour, thought, and wisdom', whether he is 'great-' or 'small-souled' (*attā* is the term used) – that is, whether his character (the commentary glosses as *attabhāva*) is in general good or bad.[10] When an individual reaches *nirvāṇa*, for the rest of his lifetime he lives 'without craving, quenched, become cool, experiencing bliss, having become himself like Brahmā'.[11] The Pali of this last phrase is *brahma-bhūtena attanā*, which could bear the literal translation 'with self become *brahman*', as if in Upaniṣadic style. In fact, in Pali the prefix *brahma-* often simply means 'excellent'. If we wish to look for an interpretation which includes a reference to some 'divine' state, it is best here to see an analogy with the 'Divine Abidings' (*brahma-vihāra*), those meditative states where the monk suffuses himself and the rest of the universe imaginatively with loving-kindness, compassion, sympathetic joy, and equanimity. By doing this, the monk can become equal to the gods of the *Brahma*-heaven in happiness, for as long as the meditation lasts. When a liberated saint 'becomes himself like Brahmā', he attains such happiness throughout the rest of his life, as a continuous state of personality rather than temporarily acquired 'experience'.

Each 'individuality', then, at whatever level of spiritual attainment, has a particular character, describable in terms of karmic status or progress along the Buddhist Path. The word *puggala* is used very frequently in this sense to describe an individual 'person' or 'personage' in this way. A whole book of Buddhist scholasticism is devoted to enumerating lists of these different character types – the *Puggala-paññatti*, literally 'Designation of Persons', and the same kind of character description is frequent in the Suttas, especially the collection known as the *Anguttara Nikaya.* (I shall return to this in Chapter 5.2.3.)

If the Buddhist monk, as renouncing individual, is thus urged to remember that all religious progress or default 'comes from himself'; that he must 'look within' to 'know himself', to find out what kind of 'person' he is, then clearly in the course of his training he will have to reflect on himself, to take stock of his progress, to ensure that he is still striving earnestly and not deceiving himself in a state of self-satisfied inactivity or even misdeed. These ideas are found in the texts, and if we follow a little further the complexities of syntax in the Pali phrases which express them, we will come to see the transition from uses of personal terms which are acceptable and those which are not.

The word *attā* in the nominative singular is used to express much the same idea as the English 'conscience' (though without any psychological hypostatisation of it as an entity). Thus *attā attānaṃ upavadati*, 'one reproaches oneself', literally 'self reproaches self'. The question 'do you reproach yourself with regard to morals?' is asked immediately before what I will describe in Chapter 3 as the second argument in support of the denial of self. In one striking passage, self-reliance in moral evaluation and the ease with which self-deceit in it is possible are forcefully expressed: 'you know yourself, man, what is true and false! When you are obviously good you (seek to) make little of it; when you are being bad, you (seek to) hide it from yourself!' Translation here with the definite article, 'the self' ('Self'), as if a quasi-technical term, wreaks havoc with the sense.[12] It is in this same sense that one reads often that a man can be a 'friend' or 'enemy' to himself. This means that by good or bad conduct men produce future happiness or suffering for themselves. Thus, in the case of bad conduct 'what a man would do to his mutual enemy, that these men do to themselves by themselves'. The word translated as 'by themselves' is *attanā*, the (as usual, singular) instrumental case of *attā*. The same case is found in a phrase used of evil-doers, who are said to act with 'themselves as [as we would say in English, their own worst] enemy'. The instrumental *attanā* is often used to contrast what a man does 'by', 'in', or 'in relation to himself', with what he does to others, or advises others to do. It can be used to express the idea that a man achieves certain religious advances 'by his own efforts', and the idea that all men are 'in themselves', or 'inherently' subject to old age and death.[13]

The use of *attā* in two cases in the same sentence, or its use in an oblique case referring to the subject of the sentence, is, again, simply a fact of Indo-Aryan syntax structure, which in no way conflicts with or compromises the Buddhist doctrine of *anattā*. It is only by looking at the context of specific sentences and syntactic forms that one can see where and why *attā* is denied or refused validity. Let us compare two uses of exactly the same syntax, in the phrases 'they contemplate themselves by themselves well', or in reasonable English 'they practise strict self-examination' (*sādhukaṃ attanā va attānaṃ paccavekkhanti*), and 'by the self I know the self' (*attanā va attānaṃ sañjānāmi*).[14] The former occurs in a context where matters of discipline within the monkhood are being discussed. If a dispute arises over one monk having committed an offence, both the offending monk and his accuser are each to reflect on their unwholesome psychological state (both are caused to feel anger and distress), as a way of defusing the dispute and 'living at peace'. The phrase quoted is perfectly acceptable here as a means of referring to a kind of reflective self-analysis necessary for spiritual education and welfare. In the latter case, however, the phrase is given specifically as a kind of mistaken and harmful *theory*, in Buddhist terms a 'view', which is liable to occur to someone who does not pay 'careful attention'. (That is to say, who does not practise meditative reflection in the approved Buddhist manner.)* Because the *Sutta* in which this is found deals explicitly with *systematic* self-analysis and with theoretical 'views' used in meditative reflection, it is not foreign to the spirit of the Pali to translate *attā* here as 'the self', as I have done.

2.2.3. As theoretical construct – refused

This last example, where a particular use of the term *attā* is refused, gives us the essential clue to that kind of thought and discourse in which the denial of self, the doctrine of *anattā*, takes effect. It is thought and discourse in which a more or less definite theoretical system is in question, a system which has no direct link with any particular behavioural circumstances, but purports to offer a general and atemporal account of psychological structure and functioning. It is static, unalterable dogma which posits a permanent and reincarnating self or person which is the object of Buddhist censure. Thus, 'the doctrine of self' (*attavāda*) is one of the four forms of 'grasping' (the others are sense-pleasures, (mere) rule-and-ritual, and 'views').[15] 'Speculation about the [or "a"] self' (*attānudiṭṭhi*) is a term used in the Suttas (many synonyms are used in the later texts) for any specific views of self, all of which are rejected *tout court*.[16] In Chapter 1 we saw that in Brahmanical thought the final truth and goal of religious thought was that self (*ātman*) and universe (*brahman*) were essentially the same. In Buddhism, doctrines of self and

* I shall discuss this *Sutta* more fully in Chapter 4.1.1.

universe (in Pali the term is *loka*) are frequently connected. 'Views concerned with the doctrine(s) of self and universe' are to be renounced by the monk's practice of 'careful attention'. The view that 'self and universe are the same' is one of the 'net' of views in which a man can become entangled; and is said to be a form of 'anxiety about unreality internally'. The Buddha goes on to say that there is no 'grasping of a doctrine of self' or 'dependence on view' which will avoid 'distress, grief, suffering, sorrow, and unrest'. In later Buddhist texts, the word *puggala* 'person' comes to denote the theoretical idea of a permanent subject or soul, and accordingly it is argued that 'a person is not to be found'.[17]

It will be the task of Chapters 3 and 4 to elucidate in detail how and why no theoretical self is to be allowed, and of Chapters 5 and 6 to discuss why 'the person is not found'. Here I wish only to recognise what is the particular role in Buddhist thought generally played by the doctrine of *anattā*. One might well describe it, I think, as a linguistic taboo in technical discourse. We have seen that Buddhism has a wide range of internal differentiation in society, and I have suggested that technical philosophical and psychological discourse plays an active part in the religious life only of virtuoso meditators and scholastic intellectuals. Within the religious concerns even of these latter, this kind of technical discourse does not exhaust the range of ways in which personal terms are used. Accordingly, both for the ordinary non-specialist Buddhist (that is, of course, the majority) and for the specialist when dealing with the kinds of simple narrative or ethical/behavioural material I have outlined, we might say that the self is not denied – meaning that the words 'self' (*attā*) and 'person' (*purisa/puggala*) can be used without technical qualms. When the doctrine of *anattā* is insisted upon, for the non-specialist, it has the function of providing an intransigent symbolic opposition to Brahmanical thought. (I shall return to this point at the end of this chapter.) For the specialist scholar and meditator, the use of personal terms, as technical constructs in systematic analytical discourse, is quite simply disallowed, tabooed. There is, of course, a form of systematic analysis which replaces the use of 'self' or 'person' as technical terms – that of impersonal elements (*dhammā*). It is these elements which, collected together, are said to give the impression to the unenlightened that there is a self. At the same time, this kind of alternative theorising, as we shall see, does not represent the whole of the doctrine of *anattā*: equally important is the avoidance – for both moral and epistemological reasons – of using any theoretical constructs in whatsoever kind of systematic 'view'.

I spoke in the Introduction of the various kinds of approach to the doctrine of *anattā* which scholars and Buddhist enthusiasts have hitherto adopted. I hope it is by now beginning to be clear why I adopted the approach I outlined there. The intellectual position of specialist Buddhism is quite specific; despite its being a system which emphasises to an almost exaggerated degree individual responsibility in ethics (through the strict application of *karma*) and which offers a way to complete salvation (in *nirvāṇa*), there is a radical refusal to speak of a self or permanent person in any theoretical contexts. It is, I think, fruitless for a scholar to try to explain, in his own more or less technical terms, what this 'means' and what such a salvation can be. Rather, he should see Buddhism's ideological stance as a social, intellectual, and soteriological strategy. Among those Buddhists who are concerned with, and pay explicit allegiance to, the doctrine of *anattā*, it provides orientation to social attitudes and behaviour (particularly *vis-à-vis* Brahmanical thought and the ritual priests who purveyed it), to conceptual activity in the intellectual life of Buddhist scholastics, and to soteriological activity in the life of virtuoso meditators. Thus, anyone who accepts the Buddhist virtuoso Path accepts submission to the strategy, and applies the modes of psychological analysis to himself which Buddhist doctrine recommends. Other religious traditions have different views and different strategies, and it is open to the syncretistic thinker to construct his own explanation of the 'reality' to which they all might refer. Scholarship must remain silent, content to show the logic and function of the particular forms of words which each tradition has chosen to embody its message.

What scholarship can do is two-fold: first, to try to see what it was in the values and presuppositions of contemporary Indian religious thinking which allowed the Buddha to adopt this strategy; and second, to examine how it was and can be applied to the life and experience of the Buddhist monk. The latter I shall do in Chapters 3 and 4; to do the former I must complete the account I began in Chapter 1 of the Brahmanical ideas of personality and continuity, to see how Buddhism adopted and adapted that tradition.

2.3. Elements of personality and (not-)self

As we have seen, virtuoso religious thought in the Brahmanical tradition turned on the refraction into the life of the individual renouncer of structures of thought and imagination which had previously been related to the external sacrificial ritual. This had both behavioural and conceptual effects: the actual practice of such ascetic renouncers concentrated on the manipulation and interpretation of consciousness (or, in the modern vogue term 'experience'); and the conceptual interpretation (and hence conditioning) of that experience proceeded clearly and wholly in terms of those ideas developed through the sacrifice. Among these ideas the most important here, for my present purpose, are two: the ordinary psycho-physical personality, made up of a composite of different constituents, destined, and in the renouncers' thought, 'doomed' eternally to group and re-group themselves in the round of rebirth; and the indescribable vivifying support of the process, the 'self' (*ātman*) or 'person' (*puruṣa*), union with which, or realisation of which, could be achieved in the – 'mystical' – experience of the virtuoso practitioner, and which was the eschatological goal to which religious practice was aimed.

2.3.1. Elements of personality and the self/person

We saw in Chapter 1 how the human being was thought to be a composite of different constituents, which separate at death to return to their original place in the universe, and how this idea was used – in reverse – for the re-creation of the person reborn on earth. At the time of the *Upaniṣads*, religious thinkers continued and developed this pattern of analysis; so one finds in the *Upaniṣads* a large variety of different categorisations of the constituent parts of the person. Already in the *Brāhmaṇas*, a man is said to be made of five immortal and five mortal parts – respectively, mind, speech, breath, sight, hearing; hair, skin, flesh, bone, and marrow. These five immortal parts recur frequently in the same context in the *Upaniṣads*, sometimes with the addition of other senses, bodily functions, or more abstract ideas such as heart, consciousness, and wisdom.[1] A more complicated classification is found in the *Chāndogya Upaniṣad* (6.2f), where the three elements of heat, water, and food are combined in three different grades of refinement, with results which can be tabulated as shown here. Processes of interaction between

	heat/red	water/white	food/black
coarse	bone	urine	faeces
medium	marrow	blood	flesh
fine	speech	breath	mind

these elements account not only for sleep, hunger, and thirst, but also for the growth of the human being from, and reabsorption at death into, Being (*sat*).

Frequently, these lists look like early versions of the lists of the later *Sāṃkhya* school: for example, in ascending order, we find 'senses', 'objects of sense', 'mind' (*manas*), 'intellect', 'self' (*ātman*), 'the unmanifest', and 'the person' (*puruṣa*).[2] It has been thought that these passages reflect a 'proto-*Sāṃkhya* school'; but if we remember that the word *sāṃkhya* means 'enumeration' or 'discrimination', perhaps we might rather say that the later school appropriated as a proper name what was originally a general analytical tendency among religious thinkers. This discrimination refers both to the distinguishing of the different elements within one person, and also to the project of separating, both in theory and in practice, the essential self or person from the composite psycho-physical personality as a whole.

This essential self or person was the central element around which the kaleidoscope of psycho-physical constituents were arranged and re-arranged in the series of lives-in-*saṃsāra*. We have seen how the idea of such a 'central something' developed from naturalistic ideas of breath, water, and fire, to a more abstract notion of a vitality or vivifying force. In the *Upaniṣads*, a new element is added: this one might call the internalising, or subjectivising of the central something, to make of it the *Ursprung* of consciousness or mentality. Already in early times, mind (*manas*) has been said on occasion to fulfill roles which were associated with the other central elements; for as long as one possessed mind, one lived; at death the *manas* went to Yama, lord of the dead. Another hymn praises mind as the charioteer who controls men,[3] as 'wisdom', 'awareness' (*cetas*) and 'the support'; it is the 'undying light within' which experiences both waking life and dreams. In the *Brāhmaṇas*, release from the sequence of days and nights is given to one who 'looks down on (them) as on the turning wheels of a chariot'.[4]

The two major terms used in the *Upaniṣads* for the central something, both partake strongly of this tendency to be seen as the terminus of the subjective pole of consciousness. *Ātman*, as we have seen, was an outgrowth of ideas of a life-breath, combined with the motif of a 'fire-soul'. Progressively, however, this vital force became deprived of content, becoming, like *brahman* in the sacrificial-cosmic sphere, a support or ground of the person: the 'life-breath' (*prāṇa*), the hub on which all things are fastened as spokes, is itself based on the *ātman*, as is consciousness, speech, and so on. The *ātman* is no longer the breath, but 'he who breathes in (and out) with in- (and out-)breathing,' the seer of seeing, thinker of thinking; in short, the agent behind all the senses, and so naturally beyond description.[5]

Once there has arisen such an analytical distinction between the describable constituents of phenomenal personality and their indescribable vivifying support, naturally judgements of value arise in accordance. The sage Yajñavalkya tells his wife that one's spouse, wealth, the caste structure, indeed everything are not valuable for their own sakes, but because of the *ātman*.[6] It is the search for a contentless self, and denigration of the constituents of the phenomenal person which, among the renouncers for whom the search for this self was a matter of immediate personal concern, gave the theoretical parallel of, and justification for, the self-mortificatory practices of asceticism (*tapas*).

Asceticism of this sort is most immediately associated in the common picture of Indian religion with the figure of the *yogin*; and it was the theoretical elaboration of *Yoga* practice, along with the categories of the *Sāṃkhya* school, which made most use of the second term for the central something found in the *Upaniṣads*, the 'person' – *puruṣa*. Characterisation of the ultimate source of things as personal is as ancient and ubiquitous in India as the relatively impersonalised *ātman-Brahman* motif. In the *Ṛg Veda*, the *Puruṣa* hymn (10.90) tells of the sacrificial dismemberment of the primeval person, and the arising of the physical and social worlds from different parts of the body. The *Atharva Veda* tells of how the parts of the ordinary person were put together, and of their enlivening by Prajāpati – also called *brahman* – and 'the spirit having *ātman*'. In the *Brāhmaṇas* the figure of Prajāpati 'lord of creatures' is ubiquitous; like *brahman*, with whom he is identified, he is at the same time identical with the sacrifice, and the enlivening support of man, as well as being the cosmic man, whose dismemberment created the universe. For the Upaniṣadic thinkers, the central something is described as Prajāpati; the 'person' (*puruṣa*) who animates the inanimate (*acetana*) body is Prajāpati, who – originally alone – created and vivified all bodily functions. 'In the beginning this (all) was *ātman*, having the form of a person'; a person who is 'the shining, immortal Person in (everything external), and (who) with regard to the inner world is the shining immortal Person who is oneself here [*ayam ātmā*] – this is immortal, this is *brahman*, this is all'.[7]

It is this use of the sacrificial person, Prajāpati, as a term for the subjective 'self within' which reflects most clearly the interiorisation of the sacrifice in renunciatory thought. The internalisation of the aspect of sacrifice as self-denial – stressed by Hubert and Mauss as its main function in the social sphere[8] – added to the devaluation of all which is not self, produces both the ascetic practice of self-mortification, and the theoretical structure (concretised in *Sāṃkhya* thought) in which all parts of the psycho-physical person are but forms of the 'material world' (*prakṛti*), a world which imprisons and enslaves the real 'person' (*puruṣa*). In this way, the description of personality given by the system enshrines the abstraction of value from phenomenal personality which constitutes the aim of religious life and the criterion for its practice.

2.3.2. Elements of personality and not-self; *nirvāṇa*

The teachings of the Buddha, and of the Buddhist tradition, are both strikingly similar to, and significantly different from, this pattern. The general ideas of *karma* and *saṃsāra* are accepted in more or less the same sense. The Buddhist scriptures bear witness to a very thorough ethicisation of the idea of *karma*; we saw in Chapter 1.3.3 that already in pre-Buddhist times, the concept had been generalised from the sacrificial sphere to action in general. For Buddhism, this movement is continued, with a new emphasis on the intention (*cetanā*) with which actions are carried out. It is still *karma* which provides the motive force for the prolongation of life in time, in *saṃsāra*; the general idea of *saṃsāra* also is taken over, with some minor differences in the details of cosmology. A significant change of attitude towards the prolongation of life in time is apparent both in Buddhism and some of the later *Upaniṣads* contemporary with it. Whereas in the earlier Brahmanical literature the extension of life was a good, and even in the earlier *Upaniṣads*, although a lesser goal, still a desired one, in later Indian and Buddhist thought, rebirth in *saṃsāra* is considered – or at least is represented in the thought of the rénouncers whose ideas became culturally prestigious – as a form of suffering (*duḥkha*, Pali *dukkha*) in itself.[9]

In the conception of personality, Buddhist doctrine continues the style of analysis into non-valued impersonal constituents: indeed it is precisely the point of not-self that this is *all* that there is to human individuals. Examples are the two-fold 'name-and-form' (*nāmarūpa*); the four-fold '(things) seen, heard, thought, cognised';[10] the very widespread and influential five 'categories' (*khandha*), that is 'body, feelings, perceptions, mental formations, consciousness'; the six-fold 'sense-bases' (*āyatana*), that is, the five senses plus 'mind'; and on into the huge variety of classifications found in Buddhist scholasticism (*Abhidhamma*) – we shall soon become very familiar with these lists.

It is at this point that the differences start to become marked. There is no central self which animates the impersonal elements.* The concept of *nirvāṇa* (Pali *nibbāna*), although similarly the criterion according to which ethical judgements are made and religious life assessed, is not the liberated state of a self. Like all other things or concepts (*dhammā*) it is *anattā*, 'not-self'. Whereas all 'conditioned things' (*saṃkhāra* – that is, all things produced by *karma*) are 'unsatisfactory and impermanent' (*sabbe saṃkhārā dukkhā . . . aniccā*) all *dhammā* whatsoever, whether conditioned things or the unconditioned *nibbāna*, are 'not-self' (*sabbe dhammā anattā*).[11] Indeed no description of *nibbāna*, even in terms of simple existence or non-existence, was ever held to be true – in the sense of being universally applicable regardless of the psychological context.[12]

* On what does energise the human composite, the 'life-faculty' (*jīvitindriya*) see Chapter 8.1.2.

To use my own metaphor, the denial of self in whatever can be experienced or conceptualised – that is, in the psycho-physical being who is exhaustively described by the lists of impersonal elements – serves to direct the attribution of value away from that sphere. Instead of supplying a verbalised notion of what *is* the sphere of ultimate value, Buddhism simply leaves a direction arrow, while resolutely refusing to predicate anything of the destination, to discuss its relationship with the phenomenal person, or indeed to say anything more about it.

The arrival at that destination has two stages. First, there is the attainment of *nibbāna* during the individual's lifetime. This is the 'blowing out' (the etymological sense of *nirvāṇa*) of the flame of desire.[13] As Gombrich[14] has said:

> *Nirvāṇa* in life is the cessation of craving, alias greed-hatred-and-delusion, and is indescribable because it is the opposite of the process of life as we know it; to discuss it in isolation is futile because you have to understand what, according to Buddhist ontology,* is being negated. It is futile also for a more important reason: *nirvāṇa* is an experience, and all private experiences (e.g. falling in love) are ultimately beyond language (though they can to some extent be discussed with others who have had the experience). Experiences do have an objective facet. Objectively hunger is want of food, etc.; subjectively it is a kind of pain, imperfectly describable. My description of *nirvāṇa* as the cessation of craving is objective. As one cannot even fully describe the experience of the cessation of a toothache, the indescribability of *nirvāṇa* is unsurprising. For the convenience of discourse Buddhist saints did apply various kinds of epithets to it, and thus objectify and even reify what was for them the experience of the cessation of a process. Had they foreseen the confusion this would cause they might have kept silence.

As I mentioned earlier, some of the epithets used to describe this state make use of personal terms.

The second stage of arrival at *nibbāna* occurs at the death of the enlightened saint, in which the flames of life-in-*saṃsāra* die out through lack of fuel.[15] The word for 'fuel' here is *upādāna*, which also means 'grasping', or 'attachment'. A cognate term, *upādi*, denotes the 'fuel' or 'substrate' of life-in-*saṃsāra*. The first stage of *nibbāna* is called 'with substrate' (*sa-upādi-sesa*), the second 'without substrate' (*an-upādi-sesa*), since then the 'remaining fuel' of the saint's psycho-physical individuality is completely burnt out. It is this second *nibbāna* which the Buddhist tradition has resolutely refused to speak about, and where the simple submission to Buddhism as a strategy is most necessary. This may be disappointing for those who want to 'know what *nirvāṇa* is', but it must be accepted as the unequivocal answer of Buddhist intellectual thought.

* And, I might add, psychology.

If a man wants to know, he must try to reach the state himself and find out.

So much energy has been expended on trying to give a coherent, rational elucidation of the concept of final *nibbāna*,[16] to so little point: as far as the individual practitioner of Buddhism is concerned, this *nibbāna* is completely beyond rational elucidation, and must simply be taken on trust. As far as Buddhism as an ideological system in a social milieu is concerned, we must recognise, as Gellner has advised,[17] that the irrationality of certain concepts may itself have a specific social function. The social function of the irrationality of final *nibbāna* is, I would suggest, the preservation of the Buddhist tradition as an Indian religious system separate from, and in certain crucial respects opposed to, the Brahmanical one. Just as socially the Buddhist tradition has provided an alternative to the Brahmanical religion of the sacrifice, with its supposed cosmic significance, so, too, psychologically Buddhism has refused to recognise the microcosmic correlate of the sacrifice in Brahmanical thought, the 'self' or 'person' within. The absolute indescribability of *nirvāṇa*, along with its classification as *anattā*, 'not-self', has helped to keep the separation intact, precisely because of the impossibility of mutual discourse. The opposition between Buddhist and Brahmanical ideas is expressed clearly and symbolically by the reversal of fire-imagery. For Brahmanical thought, the fire of the cosmos-sacrifice-self is the focus of all value; virtuoso practice to gain 'release' involves burning off the distracting bodily and mental accretions to this inner self by the heat of asceticism (*tapas*). For Buddhism it is the cooling of the fire of craving by the detached practice of the Middle Way between sensual indulgence and asceticism which is the task of the virtuoso search. Thus, both the fire of desire, and the fire of life-in-*saṃsāra*, go out. Throughout Buddhist thought, we must recognise this reaction of opposition to Brahmanical ideas and practices: the denial of self (*ātman*) is the most fundamental example, and symbol, of this attitude.

Part II

The doctrine of not-self

3 The denial of self as 'right view'

> This me is an empirical aggregate of things objectively known. The *I* which knows them cannot itself be an aggregate, neither for psychological purposes need it be considered to be an unchanging and metaphysical entity like the Soul, or a principle like the Pure Ego, viewed as 'out of time'. It is a *Thought*, at each moment different from that of the last moment, but *appropriative* of the latter together with all that the latter called its own. All the experiential facts find their place in this description, unencumbered with any hypothesis save that of the existence of passing thoughts or states of mind.
>
> William James (1950) pp. 400–1

3.1. Different kinds of 'right view'

In Chapter 2, I showed that although Buddhism finds certain ordinary uses of the words *attā*, *purisa*, and *puggala* unexceptionable, it objects strongly to their use in any theory which posits a real, permanent self or person as the agent behind action or the subject of experience. In Buddhist terminology such a theory is called a 'view' (*diṭṭhi*); and there are two main ways in which Buddhist teaching seeks to counter what it sees as mistaken views. One approach, which might be described as quietistic, recommends exclusive concentration on religious practice, avoiding any speculative thought which goes beyond immediate questions of morality or meditation. I will deal with this approach, and the 'silent wisdom' to which it is held to lead, in Chapter 4. For the present, I will be concerned with the other means of countering mistaken views; that is, by condemning them as 'wrong view' (*micchādiṭṭhi*), and contrasting with them an opposing theory – in this case, that of impersonal elements (*dhammā*) – which is correct: 'right view' (*sammādiṭṭhi*).

The opposition between right and wrong views is not confined to the topic of theories of a self, but is found widely throughout Buddhist teaching. Before discussing the specific arguments which are used to oppose self-theories, therefore, I shall discuss briefly the wider range of uses to which this opposition is put.

3.1.1. As 'pro-attitude'

The first and most simple sense in which right view is opposed to wrong view is that of having a correct attitude to one's social and religious duties, in the light of the belief system of *karma* and *saṃsāra*. By the time the Buddhist Suttas were collected, these ideas had changed from being the particular concern of Brahmanical sacrifice and ascetic renunciation, to being ideas which had influence over the whole range of Indian religious life. The Buddha's own insistence on *kamma** must have contributed to this process. A frequent example of wrong view in this sense is given by the following refrain:

> There is no (gain from making) gifts, offerings, sacrifice; there is no fruition, no ripening of good or bad deeds; this world and the other world do not exist; there is no (benefit from duties towards) mother and father; there are not beings of spontaneous birth;† there are not to be found in the world ascetics and brahmins who, living and practising rightly, proclaim (the existence of) both this world and the next, having personally experienced them by superior knowledge.[1]

The corresponding affirmation of these things is right view. In the *Apaṇṇaka Sutta*,[2] the Buddha gives a long list of wrong views, whose contradictories, being right, constitute a teaching which is 'sure'. They are: firstly, the refrain quoted immediately above, then the view that good and bad actions have no karmic result, then the view that human good and bad fortune has no cause, being simply matters of chance, then that there is not 'formlessness throughout' (explained by the commentary as referring to a kind of heaven), and lastly that there is no cessation of rebirth (that is, *nibbāna*). There are, he explains, two reasons for accepting the right view which contradicts these beliefs. In the first place, an 'intelligent man' will reason that whether or not they are right, still a man who holds such a right view will enjoy in this life the praise of other 'intelligent men'; if they are right, then he will enjoy both this praise, and in future lives the karmic benefits of the views and the actions recommended in them.[3] In the second place, by holding such wrong views, a man 'sets himself in opposition' to those *Arhats*,[4] or saints, who know that in fact the opposite is true. In each case, the Buddha says that the fact that there is another world, *kamma*, and so on, is the reason why belief in them is right view. In a similar way, in the *Pāyāsi Sutta*,[5] the monk Kassapa teaches Pāyāsi that he should believe there are 'another world, beings of spontaneous birth, and result of actions', because, amongst other things, recluses in the forest endowed with the magic power of the 'divine eye' *see* these things to be the case.

* The Pali form of Sanskrit *karma*.

† That is, beings reborn in a heaven without the intermediacy of parents. This is an important point in the cosmology of *kamma*.

In these passages, clearly, the belief system of *karma* and *saṃsāra* is being recommended as a simple religious faith. Holy men can know that it is true, but the ordinary man must take it on trust. The Buddhist term for the appropriate attitude here is *saddhā*, commonly translated as 'faith'. Provided it is remembered that the Christian attitude toward faith as a virtue for its own sake is out of place in the Buddhist context, such a translation is reasonable. A more precise rendering would be 'confidence (in the truth of doctrines not personally experienced)', since in Buddhism and all Indian religion it is always said to be in principle possible for any individual to experience personally the truth of such doctrines, by himself becoming an ascetic and undergoing the necessary practices.

To hold right view in this first sense, then, is not yet to do or believe anything specifically Buddhist. It is merely – to use a term from modern ethical writing[6] – to have a general 'pro-attitude' towards ideas of *karma* and *saṃsāra*, and to the services of those religious practitioners with whom the ideas are associated. In Weber's terms, these form the intellectual stratum or virtuoso tradition of Buddhist monks, Brahmins, and ascetics generally, to whom are opposed the 'popular' or mass traditions of magicians, soothsayers, and the like, whose ideas and practices have always been, and will doubtless for a long time remain, ubiquitous in the religious life of any South Asian village.

3.1.2. As acquaintance with Buddhist doctrine

A more specifically Buddhist sense of the term *sammādiṭṭhi* is found in its use as the first 'limb' of the Noble Eight-fold Path, which summarises and symbolises the ideal Buddhist life. Originally, without doubt, this Path was supposed to be trodden by monks alone, the layman's practice being restricted to alms-giving, and the like. In the course of time, however, as we shall see, this simple dichotomy became blurred so that on the one hand, all 'Buddhists' whether laymen or monks were said to be on the Path, in the sense of progressing slowly through many rebirths toward *nibbāna*.[7] On the other hand, when the Path was restricted to the sense of having *nibbāna* as one's immediate aim, either in this life or very soon thereafter, it came to be thought the concern only of an elite group even among monks. For the moment, however, I shall ignore these sociological ambiguities, and take 'being on the Path' to have the simple, global sense of 'being a Buddhist'. The eight limbs of the Path are shown in the list on p. 90.

In this context, right view is explained as knowledge of certain basic points of doctrine: of the Four Noble Truths,* or of the sequence of

* That life is suffering; that desire is the cause of suffering; that ending desire is ending suffering; that the way to the ending of suffering is the Noble Eight-fold Path.

sammā – diṭṭhi	Right View	*paññā* – Wisdom
saṅkappa	Resolve	
vācā	Speech	*sīla* – Morality
kammanta	Action	
ājīva	Livelihood	
vāyāma	Effort	*samādhi* – Meditation
sati	Mindfulness	
samādhi	Concentration	

Dependent Origination.*[8] In the *Sammādiṭṭhi Sutta*[9] right view is explained in a number of such ways: as knowledge of which states (of mind) are good and bad (literally 'skilful' or 'unskilful' *kusala, akusala*), as knowledge of the Four Noble Truths, as knowledge of the doctrine of the Four Foods,† and finally as knowledge of the whole series of Dependent Origination, in reverse order. This second sense of right view, which one might paraphrase as 'acquaintance with Buddhist doctrine', involves only an initial knowledge of Buddhist teaching, an ability to identify correctly certain key doctrines. It is in this sense that right view can be placed at the very beginning of the Path.

3.1.3. As liberating insight

As I have shown in the list above, the eight limbs of the Path are arranged (in the Canon and frequently in the later literature)[10] into the three categories of Wisdom, Morality, and Meditation (literally 'collectedness' or 'concentration'). When these are taken as a linear sequence, Wisdom occurs twice. At the beginning, it involves simply knowledge of basic doctrine and the motivation – if only in theory – to apply it to oneself. When this application is in fact undertaken, it is said to lead to perception of the phenomenological truth of Buddhist doctrine, and so Wisdom recurs at the end of the Path as liberating 'insight' or 'understanding'. This recurrence of Wisdom is sometimes recognised by the addition of a further two limbs to the Path, *sammāñāṇa* 'right knowledge' and *sammāvimutti* 'right release'. This is said to be the ten-fold Path of the 'adept', in contrast with the eight-fold Path of the 'learner'.[11] In this light, right view as part of Wisdom means 'liberating insight', the three-fold sequence is arranged as a progress from Morality and Meditation as the basis, through the Wisdom or Insight thus acquired to the state of *vimutti* – Release itself.[12]

The *Mahācattārīsaka Sutta*[13] explains how right view can be used to refer to such a wide range of intellectual and spiritual achievements. *Sammādiṭṭhi* is said to be two-fold: firstly there is that

* See Chapter 3.2.5 below.

† On which see Chapter 7.1.4.

right view which 'has corruptions, is connected with (the acquisition of) merit, and ripens to rebirth'. The content of this view is that refrain concerning the results of gifts, sacrifice, service to parents, and so on, whose denial I quoted in Chapter 3.1.1. The *Sutta* comments that 'when one knows that (a) right view is "right view", then that is [also] one's right view'. I take this to mean that not only does a man have the correct pro-attitude to *karma* and *saṃsāra*, but that he perceives this attitude under a Buddhist rubric. That is to say, he is conscious that as a type of right view, it forms part of the Buddhist Path. (The context of this remark, in the *Sutta* as a whole, is an explanation by the Buddha of how 'one-pointedness of mind', which is a psychological state claimed by all forms of Indian virtuoso religion, becomes 'Noble, Right Concentration'. It does so by being accompanied by the other seven limbs of the Path, of which, as the *Sutta* continually reminds us, right view 'comes first'. Thus, both these Indian phenomena, the ordinary man's attitude to *karma* and *saṃsāra* and the 'one-pointedness' of the religious specialist, become Buddhist phenomena by being regarded as parts of the Path.)

The second type of right view given by the *Sutta* is 'that view which is Noble, without corruptions, supermundane, a constituent of the Path'. 'The Path' here does not refer to all Buddhists but only those who are engaged actively on a Buddhist specialist's life, which includes the practice of meditation. Thus it concerns that elite group of monks who are 'on the Path' in the restricted sense of having *nibbāna* as their immediate aim. This higher type of right view is said to be that which is called, 'in one who is on the Noble Path, and is developing the Noble Path, wisdom, the faculty of wisdom, the power of wisdom, the constituent of enlightenment (called) investigation of phenomena'.[14] Within the 'faculty of wisdom', we learn elsewhere,[15] there are different degrees of attainment, of which the highest is the status of *Arhat*, that is, liberation. It is clear that a kind of wisdom, or a view, which admits differences of degree cannot be a simple knowledge *that* something is the case, but rather refers to the possession of a more or less ineffable level of 'insight' or 'intuition', produced by the practice of Buddhist meditation. 'Investigation of phenomena' here also refers to meditation, being the application of the lists of impersonal elements (*dhammā*) by a monk to his own experience – those lists which in Buddhist doctrine replace the idea of a self.

The idea that there can be a gradual progress in right view, from the simple acceptance of Buddhist ideas and practices to liberating insight, is captured by the phrase 'that view which is Noble, leading onward, which leads, for the man who acts on it, to the complete destruction of suffering'.[16] When a monk arrives at the end of suffering, the attainment of Arhatship, he has right view in the third and last sense, of 'seeing things as they really are'.[17] He is the highest of those who are 'endowed with view', or who have 'achieved view'. The *Arhat* who has 'crossed the flood, in his last life, knows things with the highest view'.[18]

3.1.4. Differences between and within the individuals who hold 'right view'

There are, then, three overlapping but distinguishable senses in which Buddhism uses the term right view: firstly, that of a general and pan-Indian pro-attitude to the belief system of *karma* and *saṃsāra*; secondly, that of knowledge of Buddhist doctrine and the motivation to accept and introject it; and thirdly, that of progress towards, and attainment of, liberating insight. These three senses correspond to a classification of people into three groups which is found in the later parts of the Canon and in the commentaries. These are the 'ordinary man' (*puthujjano*), the 'learner' (*sekho*), and the 'adept' (*asekho*); there are three types of Wisdom appropriate to these three types of person.[19] The commentary to the *Sammādiṭṭhi Sutta* quoted above tells us that right view is of two sorts, 'worldly' (*lokiyā*) and 'super-worldly' (*lokuttarā*), in much the same way as the *Mahācattarīsaka Sutta* distinguished two such senses, which we have just seen. These two sorts of right view are held, according to the commentary, by the three types of person, in the following way: worldly right view is held both by the 'ordinary man outside' Buddhism and the 'learner within the teaching'. They are differentiated by the fact that although the outsider is a 'believer in *karma*', he is 'not in accordance with the truth' because he has the 'perversion of self-view' (*attādiṭṭhiparāmāsa*), whereas the learner does not. Super-worldly right view is held by the 'adept' who has attained the level of insight appropriate to one or another stage of the Path. These 'stages of the Path' are the same as the degrees of attainment within the 'faculty of wisdom' mentioned above: they are the wisdom of the 'stream-winner' who is certain to reach *nibbāna* after a limited number of rebirths; of the 'once-returner' who will be reborn as a man only once more; of the 'non-returner' who will not be reborn as a man again, but will attain *nibbāna* during a life in a heaven; and of the *Arhat*, who has attained *nibbāna* in this life, and who will not be reborn again in any form.[20]

As I have mentioned, the idea of being a person on the Path, and therefore at least a stream-winner, must originally have meant no more than being a monk. In the course of history, however, as the immediate attainment of *nibbāna* became less universally a goal of monks, so these four types of person, and the associated sense of 'the Path', came to refer to an elite group of holy men within the monkhood, while the 'ordinary' monk was simply a village priest, whose soteriological aims and expectations were no greater than those of the pious laity. As part of this development, the term *puthujjano*, 'ordinary man', which must originally have referred to any householder in contrast to the ascetic virtuoso, comes to be used not only to refer to the lay Buddhist, but also to the 'ordinary' monk without specialist aspirations.[21] Instead of the act of becoming a monk being the criterion for following the Buddha's teaching, a new criterion arises for 'being a Buddhist' in the wider sense; this is the act of 'going for refuge', which is pledging or confirming one's allegiance to the Three Jewels of Buddhism: the Buddha, his teaching, and the monkhood. The triple repetition of this 'going for refuge' precedes any Buddhist ceremony, however mundane or exalted. Already early in the commentarial tradition, the act of going for refuge is understood to cover a variety of religious needs and aspirations. There are, we are told, two ways of going for refuge: first, the worldly way of the 'ordinary man' who has as his object only the good qualities of the Three Jewels, and who has the 'right view which is based on faith'. This right view stands on the borderline between the first and second senses of the term which I have distinguished. The commentary classifies the holding of this view as one of the Ten Good Deeds. (This is a list of ways of earning merit, and subsequent good rebirth, and as a positive ethical basis for the religious practice of the ordinary man, replaces the negative code of prohibitions which is the canonical standard of ethics, the Five Precepts, and which we might call the 'layman's asceticism'.)[22] The second, super-worldly, way of going for refuge, according to this commentarial passage, occurs when someone becomes a stream-winner, and sees for himself that the Three Jewels are merely an instrument, a means for attaining the real goal, *nibbāna*.[23]

The idea that there is a social and psychological range in the appreciation of doctrine refers not only to a difference *between* individual persons (*puggala-vemattatā*), to which much attention was devoted, but also to differences of insight *within* each individual as he progresses along the Path. Insight into the teaching of *anattā* is held to have two major loci in the intellectual and spiritual education of an individual. In the first place, there is doctrinal acceptance of the teaching, such that the sense of an 'I' which is gained from introspection and the fact of physical individuality is not converted into a theoretical belief in a self. Such a belief is called *sakkāyadiṭṭhi*, conventionally translated as 'Personality Belief'. Literally it means 'belief in a (really) existing body' (though 'body' here does not denote solely the physical body but all five 'constituents of personality' (*khandhā*))[24] and refers not to the phenomenological sense of being a self – which everyone must have until they are enlightened – but to the use of this sense of 'I' as evidence for a metaphysical or psychological theory. This false belief is the first of the Ten Fetters[25] which are gradually lost during one's progress through the ranks of the Four Noble Persons. Losing Personality Belief constitutes the attainment of stream-winner status.

Secondly, there is psychological 'realisation' of *anattā*, which is the loss of pride or 'conceit': this constitutes the attainment of Arhatship. This fetter is explained as the conceit of 'I am', *asmimāna*; 'conceit' here is a particularly appropriate translation, since it suggests both the sense of something 'constructed' or 'made up' by a conceptual act, and also the pride with which this artificial mental object (the supposedly permanent 'I') is regarded. What this 'conceit' refers to is the fact that for the unenlightened man, all experience and action must necessarily appear phenomenologically as happening to or originating from an 'I'. The more enlightened, the less is this phenomenological datum converted into a theoretical belief, in *sakkāyadiṭṭhi*; and the final attainment of enlightenment is the disappearance of this automatic but illusory 'I'. This change in character and psychological condition is brought about by a variety of educational means, both behavioural and verbal, bringing changes in all levels of mental life, affective and cognitive. It is this *gradual* change which allows the notion of a 'gradual' change in right view, from the second to the third senses I distinguished above.

For the *Theravāda* tradition, this personal, introjected application of *anattā* has always been thought to be possible only for the specialist, the practising monk. While the idea of 'the conceit "I am"', and its destruction, symbolises a general orientation for the ordinary man in his self-analysis and religious aspirations, the concrete practice of continuous character change in terms of such teachings has always been said to require the individual gifts, and social circumstances, of the specialist. It is for this reason that the tradition has insisted fiercely on *anattā* as a doctrinal position (so that it can function as a right view in the second of my three senses), but at the same time in practice, as western commentators have always suspected, this abstruse and psychologically difficult doctrine has played a very small part in the daily religious life of almost all Buddhists.*

The *Sutta Piṭaka* contains many examples of religious specialists (including the Buddha) discussing this process of psychological change.

* Nevertheless, there are some striking practical consequences of the specialist doctrine: for example, 'this doctrine understood only by the few has permeated the [Sinhalese] language. [It] has no word for soul, in the sense of an immortal part or adjunct of a human being.' (Gombrich (1971) p. 71.)

One particularly informative instance is the story of the elder Khemaka.[26] On hearing that 'he does not consider there to be a self or anything belonging to a self' in the five *khandhā*, the constituents of personality, some other monks exclaim 'is he not then an *Arhat*?' Khemaka replies that he is not, because, 'with regard to the five *khandhā* I have a *sense* of "I am", but I do not see "*this* is what I am"'. He explains this by analogy with the scent of a flower: the smell is there, but it is impossible to say exactly from where it originates (from petals, or colour, or pollen, etc.). 'Although, friends, a noble disciple has put away the five lower fetters,* still there is a residue in the *khandhā* of the conceit of "I am", of the desire for "I am", the underlying tendency to "I am" which is not fully destroyed.' By practising a life of meditation, however, these things finally disappear. This is explained with the help of another analogy: a piece of clothing, after being cleaned, still retains the smell of the substances used to clean it; but after lying in a sweetly scented box for a certain time, the smell disappears. So, after becoming a monk and then living the religious life to the full, a man's 'conceit of "I am"' comes to be destroyed.[27]

This, then, is the way in which the Buddhist tradition uses the idea of right and wrong views, and the picture of society and psychology which it sees as the background to the operation of this doctrinal opposition. I will now turn more closely to the precise nature of the right view which is the concern of this study: the denial of self.

3.2. Arguments in support of *anattā*

3.2.1. Linguistic forms in which the doctrine is presented

The denial of self is presented in the Suttas in three main linguistic forms. The first is the use of the term *anattā* itself as a description applied to all phenomena and objects of thought. In all cases where the grammatical form of the term can be decided definitely it is used as a noun, placed in apposition to the subject of the sentence, and is to be translated literally as 'a not-self'.[1] As we shall see presently, in Buddhism the concept of a self, *attā*, is taken to postulate something wholly free from phenomenal determination, an entity independent of the process of karmic conditioning. Hence, when it is argued that because both the body and consciousness depend on previous conditions for their existence and so: *kāyo anattā . . . viññāṇaṃ anattā*; we can translate variously, 'body is not an independent entity, consciousness is a "not-self"'.[2] When the term is applied to a plural subject, particularly in the axiom 'all things are

* This is the stage of the non-returner.

not-self' (*sabbe dhammā anattā*), the form is ambiguous, and could be interpreted as an adjective, 'without self'.[3] Since the Buddhist tradition has not placed any emphasis on the grammatical interpretation of *anattā*, I will translate it simply and literally as 'not-self'. In any case, the term applies to any and every item of the Buddhist conceptual universe (*dhamma*), whether parts of the karmic conditioning process or the unconditioned *nibbāna*: 'impermanent are all conditioned things, unsatisfactory, not-self, and constructed; and certainly *nibbāna* also is a description meaning not-self'.[4]

A second, and less frequent form of the denial of self is the quotation in direct speech of certain mistaken ways of regarding phenomena. The most widespread is the group of three 'this is mine, this I am, this is my self' (*etaṃ mama, eso 'haṃ asmi eso me attā ti*). (These three are explained in the commentaries as 'grasping' through desire, conceit (*māna*), and 'view' (*diṭṭhi*) respectively.) Equally the first person singular of the verb 'to be', *asmi*, with the particle *ti* (equivalent to our inverted commas) appears as a mistaken idea: 'I am'. We met 'the conceit of "I am"' (*asmīti māna*, or usually simply *asmi-māna*) (in Chapter 3.1.4) above, and we shall meet a similar use of direct speech in the third argument for *anattā* (Chapter 3.2.4 below).

The third, and least frequent form is the use of the terms *attato* and *anattato*. These are formed by adding the ablative suffix *-to* to the nominal stem, and mean 'as' or 'in terms of' 'self' and 'not-self'. Thus, while it is possible for the 'ordinary man' to 'regard anything as self', it is impossible for the man 'endowed with view', who always sees things 'as not-self'.[5] A synonym for *anattato* is *parato* 'as other';[6] and the same idea is given a dramatic tone in the injunction to renounce what is 'not yours' (*na tuṃhākam*)[7] (that is, everything). As Norman has pointed out, this use of *parato* gives us the linguistic justification for translating *attā* as 'self', and not as 'soul', as has sometimes been done:

> There seems to be no other way of translating *parato* than 'as other', and we must therefore translate *attato* as 'as self' since English recognises the opposition between 'self' and 'other' but not between 'soul' and 'other'. If we have to translate *attā* as 'self' in these contexts, then for the sake of consistency we must do the same elsewhere.[8]

The first and second of the arguments I will discuss below (Chapter 3.2.2–3) take the form of characterising things as *anattā*; while the third and fourth (Chapter 3.2.4–5) argue that the concept of a self outside what can be characterised in this way is pointless, and that a sufficient account of all events is given by the teaching of Dependent Origination. Many misinterpretations of Buddhist thought have arisen through these two sides of the argument not being taken as a whole. If any one part is taken by itself – especially either of the first two – it is then easy to claim that it does not represent a complete doctrine, that the Buddha remained silent on the question of 'a transcendent self' and so on. As will become clear, however, when the arguments are seen as parts of a whole, they form a complete and coherent doctrinal representation of the Buddha's soteriological strategy.

3.2.2. The argument from lack of control

As we saw in Chapter 1, a major motive for world-renouncing asceticism in Brahmanical thought was the desire for universal power, attained through knowledge of, and control over, the self (*ātman*) as microcosmic reflection of the macrocosmic force of the universe (*brahman*). The first way in which the Buddha attempted to deny the existence of such a self was, accordingly, to claim that no such control existed. It is found at the beginning of the 'Discourse on the [fact of things having the] Characteristic of Not-self' (*Anattalakkhaṇa Sutta*),[9] traditionally the Buddha's second discourse. Here he speaks of all five 'constituents of personality' – I take body as an example: 'body, monks is not-self. Were it self, the body would suffer affliction, and one could have of body (what one wished, saying) "let my body be this, let my body be that".' Elsewhere, the Buddha asks an interlocutor 'do you have power [*vaso*] over this body' to change it at will?[10] Usually, it is argued, 'the ordinary man regards (his) body as a self, and is obsessed by the ideas "I am body" or "body is mine"; then the body changes and becomes otherwise, owing to the inherently changeable nature of body, and (he feels) distress, grief, suffering, sorrow, and unrest'. The idea of helplessness in the face of change and the consequent suffering is pictured as 'being prey to' the constituents of the personality as 'murderers'.[11] In the commentaries, things are regularly said to be not-self because there is 'no exercising of mastery' over them. The five constituents of phenomenal personality, the *khandhā*, are not-self because they have no 'leader', no 'guide', no 'inner controller' as the *Upaniṣads* had put it.[12]

Of course, in a general sense this argument can form part of homiletic wisdom in whatsoever theological context. Christ told his audience that no-one was able by his own will to add a cubit to his stature. No doubt in Buddhist preaching to the laity this argument has come to have only a general, aphoristic sense, as a reminder that disease, old age, and death are unavoidable. For the Buddha, however, who was teaching monks as religious specialists, the argument had a specific force. I have mentioned the importance of the idea of control in Brahmanical thought, and I will show in Chapter 3.3.2 below how change and lack of control was to be seen as an immediate and personal 'fact' in Buddhist meditation practice.

3.2.3. What is impermanent, unsatisfactory, and subject to change is 'not fit' to be regarded as self

The *Anattalakkhaṇa Sutta*, whose first argument I have just discussed, continues as follows: in dialogue (of the Socratic kind) with the monks, the Buddha asks 'what do you think monks, is body permanent or impermanent?'

> Impermanent, sir.
> Is what is impermanent satisfactory or unsatisfactory?
> Unsatisfactory, sir.
> Is it fitting to regard [*kallaṃ samanupassituṃ*] what is impermanent, unsatisfactory, and subject to change (in this way) 'this is mine, this I am, this is my self?'
> No, sir.
> So, monks, whatever body has come to be, whether past, future, or present, gross or fine, in oneself or without . . . must be seen as it really is, with right insight, thus 'this is not mine, this I am not, this is not my self'.

In some places, the inter-relation between what are called the 'three marks' of all conditioned things is more succinctly expressed: every phenomenon, whether in oneself or in the external world 'is impermanent; what is impermanent is unsatisfactory; what is unsatisfactory is not-self'.[13] To see in what is impermanent, unsatisfactory, impure, and 'not-self' something permanent, satisfactory, and pure, which is 'self' constitutes four 'perversions of perception, mind, and view'.[14] Sometimes, the idea of the causally conditioned nature of all phenomena is included in the argument: 'how can what comes into existence through what is impermanent, unsatisfactory, and not-self be permanent, satisfactory, and a self?'[15]

Statistically, a very high proportion of the discussions of not-self in the Suttas consists in various versions of this argument. It is this fact, and the fact that it is this argument which most of all requires the other arguments in the teaching to complete its sense, which has led to so many mistaken interpretations, to the effect that the Buddha left open the question of whether there was a self outside the elements of existence which have the three marks. On the plane of spiritual education, the seeming 'incompleteness' of the argument might have certain uses (as a 'direction arrow', as in Chapters 2.3.2 and 4.2.3). On the plane of conceptual analysis, however, it is crucially important not to draw the inference that if the constituents of the personality are 'not-self' and 'not yours' then something else is. This point is made by the third argument.

3.2.4. It is pointless to speak of a self apart from experience[16]

In the *Mahānidāna Sutta*,[17] after a long exposition of the teaching of Dependent Origination, and a brusque dismissal of various ways in which men think to define a self, as 'having form' or 'formless', 'small' or 'infinitely large', the Buddha asks 'how many ways are there in which (a man can) regard self?'. His interlocutor, the monk Ānanda, answers that there are three: feeling is regarded as identical with self, in the words 'feeling is my self'; or the self is regarded as without feeling, 'my self is insentient'; or neither of these things is the case but 'my self feels, my self has the attribute of feeling'.

The Buddha declares that it is 'not fitting' (*na kkhamati*) to regard the matter in any of these ways, for the following reasons. In the first case, where self and feeling are identical, he says that feeling is of three types, pleasant, painful, and neutral. With which is the self to be identified, since only one type can occur at any given time? All three types of feeling are impermanent, causally conditioned phenomena, so that in any case the self would have to be the same, subject to arising and decay. This is an idea so manifestly untenable for the Buddha as to receive no comment. In the second place, where the self was held to be insentient, the Buddha asks, 'where there is no feeling at all, is it possible that one might say "I am"?' Since this is not possible, the view is again 'not fitting'. In the third place, where the self is held to feel, or have the attribute of feeling, he asks a similar question: 'where feeling is completely absent . . . might one be able to say "this (is what) I am"?' Here also, since this is not possible, the view is 'not fitting'.

The idea of a self as separate from the process of phenomenal experience was widespread among contemporary religious thinkers. We have seen, for example, that in certain *Upaniṣads* the conception of *ātman* changed from that of breath as the life-force to that of an inconceivable agent and subject behind all psycho-physical functions. Since it is a matter of undeniable experience that some kind of individuality and personality* is an inherent part of ordinary psycho-physical functioning, there naturally arose a distinction between two 'selves' – one a part of ordinary 'illusory' experience, the other 'real' and transcending that experience. The attitude of Buddhism to this separation of two 'selves' is clarified by considering the phraseology in which this third argument is expressed, and the illuminating contrast with the *Sāṃkhya* system which this phraseology displays.

The Buddha does not speak of a self and the possible relations it might have with feeling, considered abstractly. He asks can the utterance 'I am'

* I presuppose no systematic explanatory framework, whether psychological, philosophical or sociological, in using these terms. By 'individuality' I mean merely the fact of single bodies and the attribution of a plurality of actions and experiences to them; by 'personality', I mean the minimal sense of psychological continuity required for even the shortest sequence of coherent behaviour.

be made when feelings are absent? Although it is true that both Sanskrit and Pali lack the syntactic form of *oratio obliqua*, and so frequently use *oratio recta* where no special significance is intended, here I think there is a particular point to the use of *asmīti* – 'I am'. On a stylistic level, perhaps the use of direct speech here helps to suggest the automatic, spontaneous way in which the sense of self appears in the psychology of the unenlightened man. Certainly, on a more theoretical level, the use of direct speech in this context is connected with the idea that the phenomenological datum of an 'I' is in fact the result of an act of utterance. To assert that the sense of 'I', and its phenomenological reality, is created by an act of self-expression, Buddhism makes use of the terms *ahaṃkāra** and *mamankara* (from *aham*, 'I', and *mama*, 'mine'). *Ahaṃkāra* is a concept of great importance to much Indian religious thinking, and I shall discuss briefly its possible meanings generally, before analysing the particular use Buddhism makes of it.

There are three main ways in which the word *ahaṃkāra* can be understood, ways which are not necessarily mutually exclusive. First, it can be seen as resembling words like *kumbha-kāra*, 'pot-maker'. This is the traditional Indian rendering, as 'I-maker', and is the sense of the term in the cosmic evolution theory of classical *Sāṃkhya* in which, as an element of the material world (*prakṛti*), it creates both the phenomenal individual and his world of sense and sense-objects. (As is usual in *Sāṃkhya* thought this creation conflates what we would separate as cosmogony and psychology.) Secondly, it can be taken as resembling *puruṣa-kāra*, 'the action of man' (which opposes *daiva*, 'fate', 'action of the gods'): thus it would mean 'action of (an) I'. One Pali passage supports this interpretation: 'beings are given over to the idea "I am the agent" . . . for one who looks (at the matter) carefully there is not the idea "(it is) I (who) act"'.[18]

The third, and for Buddhism most illuminating, way of taking *ahaṃkāra* was first suggested by van Buitenen. In this interpretation, the word resembles *omkāra, svākākāra*, and the like, which mean 'the utterance (of) "*om*", "*svāhā*"'. (One might also mention the use of *-kāra* as a suffix for letters and particles: *a-kāra*, 'the letter "a"'; *eva-kāra* 'the word "eva"'. Similarly, there is a word *phutkāra* (and a verb *phutkṛ*), from the onomatopoeic *phut*, used to express the hissing sound made by a snake.) Accordingly, *ahaṃkāra* could mean here 'the utterance "I"'. This seems to me convincing; it not only makes good psychological sense,

* The word is often translated 'ego'. Since this term lacks any systematic meaning in general English usage, and the particular schools of psychology which make use of it in a systematic way differ widely among themselves, I think it is unhelpful either as a translation of Sanskrit or Pali technical terms, or as a term of discussion.

but is also congruent with a frequent motif in cosmogony, which explains the creation of the world as the cry 'I' by 'Being' (*sat*) or *brahman*. For example, the name 'I' (*ahaṃ-nāma*) was the first act in the creation of the world; in the beginning self (*ātmā*) was alone, saw that it was alone, and cried 'Here I am' (or 'This is I', *so 'ham asmi*).[19] (As we have seen, this last phrase is one of those regularly used in Buddhism as a mistaken way of regarding phenomena as being or belonging to a self.) This emphasis on *aham* as an utterance accords well with the use in Buddhism of words or phrases 'in quotation marks' to denote the mistaken way in which the unenlightened man regards phenomena as self. In connexion with 'the conceit "I am"' (*asmi-māna*), seen earlier in Chapter 3.1.4, I mentioned the two analogies of the smell of a flower and that of newly washed linen, which pictured the relationship of the idea 'I am' to the impersonal elements which make up a human being, and its destruction. In this connexion there is a third analogy, which is as informative as it is striking. A king, enticed by the sound of a lute, asks his servants to bring him the sound. They bring the lute, but the king exclaims 'away with the lute. I want the sound.' The servants try to explain: 'this thing called a lute is made up of a great number of parts . . . it makes a sound [literally "speaks", *vadati*] because it is made up of a number of parts, that is box, strings [etc.]'. The king then takes the lute, breaks it up into smaller and smaller pieces, and throws it away. The moral is drawn: 'in this way, monks, a monk investigates the constituents of personality . . . but for him there is no "I", "mine", or "I am"'.[20]

It is of course not only the overt verbal or mental utterance of 'I am', or the explicit belief in a self, which is pointed to by the term *ahaṃkāra*. We saw that when the overt fetter of belief in a self (*sakkāyadiṭṭhi*) is given up, the focus of attention then becomes the selfishness inherent in the affective structure of experience, which is the fetter of *asmi-māna*. We might call this latter the 'unconscious' utterance 'I am'. Using the modern concept of the unconscious to elucidate Buddhist thought is, like all such attempts at cross-cultural parallels in psychology, fraught with potential misapprehensions; but there is, I think, some point to it here.* The majority of occurrences of the words *ahaṃ-* and *mamaṉ-kāra* in the Suttas are as part of a compound *ahaṃkāramamaṉkāra-mānānusaya*: 'the underlying tendency to the conceits "I" and "mine"'. *Māna*, 'conceit', we are already familiar with; *anusaya* 'underlying tendency' is a concept whose complexities were to engage the scholastic tradition in much discussion.[21] There are seven such 'tendencies' which like the

* I shall later have cause to distinguish sharply between something which for *Theravāda* is mental but not conscious, and the unconscious of modern psychoanalytic theory – that is, the *bhavaṅga*-mind. See Chapter 8.3.2 Excursus.

'fetters' include both *diṭṭhi* 'view' and *māna* 'conceit'. They are classed as 'mental formations' (*saṃkhārā*), which must have a mental object, but they are not conscious: 'a young baby lying on his back', although without any cognitive faculties (*manda*, literally 'stupid'), still has an underlying tendency to the five lower fetters.[22] When in a grown person these tendencies become conscious, they are called 'obsessions'. The way to get rid of the 'underlying tendency to the conceits "I" and "mine"', as ever, is to become a monk and lead a life of meditation.[23] The later commentarial work, the *Visuddhimagga*, says that though the conscious 'obsessions' can be removed by the practice of mental concentration (*samādhi*), the 'underlying tendencies', which 'by reason of their persistence' become repeatedly the cause for the arising of greed, conceit, and so on, require the practice of 'insight' (*paññā*). The final eradication of these tendencies is 'liberation without remainder'.[24]

The concepts of *ahaṃkāra . . . anusaya* and *asmi-māna*, then, refer to the automatic reaction to experience in terms of 'I' or 'I am', whether this reaction is manifested consciously or 'unconsciously'; and it is this utterance of 'I' or 'I am' which creates – perhaps better said, which continually re-creates – the 'person' of phenomenological introspection. When I introduced these ideas, I spoke of a contrast with the *Sāṃkhya* system. It is now possible to describe this contrast with clarity and precision.

There are, of course, a number of general metaphysical differences between the two systems; one of the aspects of *ahaṃkāra* in the *Sāṃkhya* system, for example, is its part in the transformation of matter from its undifferentiated state to its final state of differentiation into twenty-four categories, which include the material elements earth, water, fire, air, and ether. Leaving aside, however, such wider differences, there is a particular parallel and contrast in the use of *ahaṃkāra* in the psychological sphere. Like Buddhism, *Sāṃkhya* sees *ahaṃkāra* as an act of pride (*abhimāna*). It is also called *asmitā*, 'the fact of "I am"', or 'I am-ness'.[25] Beyond this 'I'-creating act of pride, however, there is another, 'real' individual, the *puruṣa*, 'person', whose release from engagement with *saṃsāra* is the focus and criterion of religious behaviour. Buddhism, contrastingly, sees any use of a concept of individuality beyond the 'self-expression' of *asmi-māna* and *ahaṃkāra* as a pointlessly speculative view, which is a product of the mundane conditioning factors of craving and ignorance.

At this point in the discussion of Buddhist thinking, one would naturally be led to the general denigration of views; but this side of the denial of self is so widespread and important that I will devote the whole of Chapter 4 to it. For the moment, I think enough has been said of the ideas *asmi-māna* and *ahaṃkāra* as a part of right view; that is to say, the positive psychological system which Buddhism constructs to explain the process of experience and continuity without the supposition of a continuing self.

The discussion of the relations between a postulated self and feelings with which I introduced this third argument for *anattā*, and which led on to the analysis of *ahaṃkāra*, forms part of the *Mahānidāna Sutta*, the 'Great Discourse on Causation'. Similarly, in the *Poṭṭhapāda Sutta*, there is a connexion between this argument and the Buddhist view of causality. The discussion concerns different ways of explaining 'the cessation of experience'. Some hold that the presence and absence of experience is a matter of chance, or the result of magicians' infusing and withdrawing it from a person; or that experience is a man's self, and as the self comes and goes, so a man is conscious or not. Against all these ideas, the Buddha sets his own way of explaining the cessation of experience: a gradual course of training, in which meditative states follow each other in a regular causal sequence.[26] In the same way, in the discussion of psychology generally, the idea of self as an explanation of the continuity of experience and the ideas that experience is a matter of chance or magical influence are all replaced in Buddhist thought by the idea of a causal series. This teaching is that of Dependent Origination, and it is to this that I now turn, as the fourth and last argument in support of *anattā*.

3.2.5. The continuity of experience is explained by Dependent Origination (*paṭicca-samuppāda*)

In the *Mahātaṇhāsaṃkhāya Sutta*[27] a monk is said to have interpreted the Buddha's teaching on continuity thus: '*one and the same* consciousness continues and is reborn, *unchanged*'. He explains consciousness as 'that which speaks and feels, and which experiences at different times the result of good or bad deeds'. The Buddha reproves him strongly, calling his interpretation an 'evil opinion' (*diṭṭhigataṃ*), and asks has he not taught many times that consciousness is generated by causal conditions? 'Consciousness is defined', he continues, 'according to the condition through which it arises . . . if it is conditioned by eye and material objects, it is called eye-consciousness . . . if through mind and mental objects, mind-consciousness.' This is compared to naming different varieties of fire 'grass-fire', 'stick-fire', and so on, depending on whether grass, sticks, or whatever, provides the fuel. The Buddha goes on to teach the need for 'food' to sustain beings, giving the doctrine of the Four Foods,* and then gives the formula for the causal series (in the

* They are: physical food, sense-impressions, mental volitions, and consciousness. See Chapter 7.1.4.

twelve-part form we shall presently meet) no less than six times, as if to ensure that he is not similarly misinterpreted again.

The point here is not to deny that consciousness is in any way the vehicle of rebirth,* but only to deny that it is a *changeless* subject of experience and action. It is a changing, conditioned phenomenon like any other. The Buddha teaches elsewhere that

> consciousness comes into existence because of two things: what are these two? Eye-consciousness comes into existence because of eye and material objects . . . mind-consciousness comes into existence because of mind and mental objects . . . (all these causal factors are) impermanent, subject to change, having the nature of becoming otherwise; eye- . . . mind-consciousness come into existence because of an impermanent cause – how could (they) be permanent?[28]

The same attitude is revealed elsewhere, in a number of different ways. The questions 'who is conscious [literally "who eats the consciousness food?"], experiences contact, feels, craves, grasps?', and 'whose is this consciousness [etc.]?' are rejected as 'not fit questions', and are replied to obliquely by the simple enumeration of the elements of the causal series. That nothing should be superimposed on the lists of impersonal, conditioned elements which are said to make up the human being is also the point of the Buddha's reproach to a monk that he is 'going beyond the teaching' by asking, if the elements of personality are 'not-self', then 'what self do deeds done by a not-self affect?'[29]

For Buddhist thought, the idea that at any given moment of experience there is a self beyond whatever particular bodily or mental phenomena are occurring, is equivalent to the idea that there is a permanent self which endures changelessly. We have seen this in the Buddha's answer to the monk Sāti's 'evil opinion' concerning consciousness, and the connexion is made explicitly elsewhere: the view that 'that which is my self, which speaks, feels, and which experiences at different times the result of good or bad deeds, this self of mine is permanent, stable, eternal, changeless' is a wrong view which arises in the unwise ordinary man. This is called eternalism (*sassatavāda*), and is contrasted with annihilationism (*ucchedavāda*),[30] which is the view that a self exists, and is destroyed at the death of the body – a view which is associated with the denial of *karma*. These two views are seen together in the example of a man who formerly held an eternalist view of self, and who then hears the Buddhist teaching denying self; he thinks 'I will be annihilated, destroyed – I will surely not exist!'[31] Just as in the Buddha's first sermon the Eight-fold Path was the Middle Way between the extremes of sensual indulgence and ascetic self-torture, so here in the conceptual sphere, the

* Indeed, as I will show later (Chapter 7.2.1) it is the most important category of Buddhist psychology for the explanation of continuity and rebirth.

teaching of Dependent Origination is a middle way between the two extremes of eternalism and annihilationism. 'The same man acts and experiences the result – this is eternalism. One man acts, another experiences the result – this is annihilationism. Avoiding these two extremes, the Enlightened One gives a teaching by the Middle Way' – that is to say, Dependent Origination. In another place, the two extremes are said to be 'existence' and 'non-existence' – an idea which engendered much discussion in later Buddhist philosophy. The Buddha firmly rejects the idea that he teaches 'the destruction, annihilation or cessation of a really existent being'. (The point is, of course, that since no such being exists in the first place, nothing can happen to it, whether 'annihilation' or anything else.) He is an 'annihilationist' in that he teaches 'the annihilation of greed, hatred, and delusion'.[32]

Behind all these mistaken views and 'unfit questions' lies the assumption that there is an entity which is denoted by the grammatical subject of verbs, while the Buddha's reply asserts the existence of an event described by the verbal notion, but denies that it is legitimate to infer the existence of a real subject from the verbal form. This difference in linguistic matters is vitally important for understanding the mutual relations between Buddhism and the 'orthodox' systems of Indian thought, which were articulated in Sanskrit; since in Sanskrit linguistic theory, such an inference is necessarily to be made – *kriyā* 'doing' therefore *kartṛ* 'doer'. This is not solely a linguistic matter, though Buddhism does deny the linguistic inference directly – as the *Visuddhimagga* informs us, 'action exists but no doer'.[33] According to the realist theory of the sacred Sanskrit language, the actual Sanskrit word used to refer to something was, in its sound and form, a part of the thing itself. On a conceptual level, this idea had its roots in the old notion that knowledge of a name gave the knower power over the thing named, which we saw in connexion with the Brahmanical idea of knowledge as power (which the Buddha's first argument for *anattā* was concerned to deny). A more sophisticated development of the idea, the conception of *śabda-brahman*, '*brahman* as sound', remained ubiquitously influential in Indian thought, underlying such diverse phenomena as Bhartṛhari's philosophical linguistics, and the use of *mantras*, sacred formulas, in the tantric tradition.

On a social level, acceptance of the idea of Sanskrit as a privileged, sacred language naturally reflected status and power on the Brahmins, as the guardians and transmitters of Sanskritic learning. Although Buddhism was never in outright opposition to the caste system as such, Buddhist monks, as religious specialists needing the support of the laity, were certainly opposed to the pre-eminent position of the Brahmins within caste society. Accordingly, in its very earliest history, Buddhist teaching was carried out in the dialect of each region,[34] the *Mahāyāna* tradition coming to employ Sanskrit only at a much later date.

In considering the teaching of Dependent Origination, which Buddhism used to oppose Brahmanism on the conceptual level, it is crucially important to distinguish between the general idea of conditionality, and the twelve-fold series which has come to be the traditional way in which the teaching is expressed. According to legend, the monk Sāriputta, who was to become the Buddha's disciple 'foremost in learning', first joined the order after having asked for the 'essential point' rather than the 'details' of the Buddha's teaching. He was told 'those things which arise from a cause, of these the *Tathāgata** has told the cause; and that which is their cessation, the great ascetic has such a teaching'. At this the 'eye of truth' arose in him, and in a formula which frequently expresses the content of the liberating realisation of converts to Buddhism in the Suttas, he saw 'all that which has the nature of coming into existence, has also the nature of cessation'.[35] There is a similar short formula which summarises and frequently introduces the fuller list of causal factors. This is (in Rāhula's 'modern version') 'when A is, B is; A arising, B arises. When A is not, B is not; A ceasing, B ceases'.[36] According to Rhys Davids, who analysed the content of the 'Grouped Sayings on Cause', no less than thirty-six of those ninety-three Suttas 'emphasise the importance of mastering the principle of *paṭicca-samuppāda*'.[37] This general principle is *idappaccayatā*, 'the fact of things having a specific cause', which is said always to be the case, even when there is no Buddha to penetrate it in depth and teach the full sequence.[38] The traditional list of twelve factors is given opposite.

Frequently, however, the list of factors exemplifying the idea of conditionality varies from this twelve-fold list; either by omission, as in the *Mahānidāna Sutta* itself, where the first two elements are missing, or by addition, as in the *Sammādiṭṭhi Sutta* I mentioned above, where ignorance and the 'corruptions' (*āsavā*) mutually interact. Sometimes, there are differences within the list, as when consciousness and name-and-form are said to be mutually conditioning (again in the *Mahānidāna Sutta* itself), or when the elements are given in a different order.[39] Given the existence of various forms of the series, and a certain lack of parsimony in the elements of the traditional twelve-fold list, it seems likely that the traditional list is a later schematisation – though not necessarily later than the Buddha's lifetime – of a comprehensive selection of the elements used in Buddhist psychological and eschatological thinking. This selection was then arranged into a list which is supposed,

* A title for the Buddha. See Chapter 4.2.

avijjā-paccayā	*saṃkhārā*	With ignorance as condition there arise	mental formations
saṃkhāra	*viññāṇaṃ*	formations	consciousness
viññāṇa	*nāma-rūpaṃ*	consciousness	name-and-form
nāma-rūpa	*saḷāyatanaṃ*	name-and-form	the six senses
saḷāyatana	*phasso*	the six senses	sense-contact
phasso	*vedanā*	sense-contact	feeling
vedanā	*taṇhā*	feeling	craving
taṇhā	*upādānaṃ*	craving	grasping
upādāna	*bhavo*	grasping	becoming
bhava	*jāti*	becoming	birth
jāti	*jarā-maraṇaṃ soka-parideva-dukkha-domanass-ūpāyāsā sambhavanti*	birth	old age and death, distress, grief, suffering, sorrow and unrest

evam etassa dukkha-kkhandhassa samudayo hoti. Such is the arising of this whole mass of suffering.

more or less exhaustively, to apply the principle of conditionality to the problem of continuity and rebirth. We have then to ask how this schematisation came about, and what the function of the completed list was.

There have been a number of attempts to explain the origin of the twelve-fold series; I will mention two. Frauwallner[40] sees it as a combination of two earlier sequences. The first, starting from craving, was a simple extension and elaboration of the second Noble Truth of the first sermon: that 'the origin of suffering is craving'. Subsequently, the thought of ignorance as a major cause of entanglement in rebirth – an idea, as we have seen, not unique to the Buddha in the religious thought of his time – was added to the crucial concept of *saṃkhāra** as an explanation of the process. Frauwallner's idea is that these two sequences were then combined, with the result that the two births of 'consciousness' and 'birth', originally referring to the same event in their respective sequences, came to be seen as two consecutive events. The series as a whole then comes to represent three lives. This latter is, indeed, the traditional *Theravāda* explanation.† La Vallée Poussin[41] offers a different approach, taking his cue from a poem of the collection called the *Sutta Nipāta*. In this poem there are mentioned each of the elements of the traditional list, with others, as part of a series of dyads with 'suffering', such that each thing causes suffering, and when it ceases suffering ceases. Poussin suggests that this series of pairs was then arranged in a sequence so that instead of each pair being an example of suffering and its causation, the sequence as a whole was taken as an explanation of suffering en bloc.

These two attempts at accounting for the growth of the traditional twelve-fold list are neither mutually exclusive, nor together necessarily a sufficient explanation. They do, nevertheless, give a sufficiently clear idea of what sort of process it must have been, and accordingly, of the nature of the traditional list which was the result of such a process. The list was not an exhaustive analysis of continuity produced *ex nihilo*; rather, it was a selection of items from the pre-existent, or at least separately existent, Buddhist psychological and eschatological universe, a selection which when put together fulfilled two functions. First, it exemplified the basic idea of conditionality, which as we have seen was the 'essential point' of the teaching; secondly, when taken as a whole, it expressed, symbolically, the idea of 'the round of rebirth' without the reincarnating self or person which Brahmanical thinking had postulated.

* This has both active and passive meaning: actively, as a karmic cause, it 'constructs' and 'forms' future life; passively, as karmic result, it is a 'construct' or 'formation'.

† See further, Chapter 7.1.2.

There are two main spheres of religious activity in which this dual function of the twelve-fold list can be seen to work; in both of these spheres, the list of *paṭicca-samuppāda* is only one example of the more widespread use of categorised lists in Buddhist doctrine. On one hand, in meditation practice, such lists represent, both by exemplification and symbolically, the strategies to be adopted by the monk in analysing and evaluating his own experience. I shall return to this presently. On the other hand, for the purposes of preaching, these lists are easily memorable systematisations of the elements and principles of Buddhist doctrinal thinking. In a general sense, it is not surprising in a predominantly oral culture that a system of thought which depends as highly as does Buddhism on intellectual analyses should come to preserve the content of its doctrine by accurate transmission of categorised lists, easily susceptible to rote-learning.

In addition to this general aspect of mnemonic ease, there is a particular reason for Buddhism's adoption of such lists in missionary activity. It was the special nature and genius of the Brahmanical great tradition to proselytise not so much by doctrinal persuasion as by the imposition of certain social mores – most obviously patterns of behaviour towards Brahmins themselves – arranged according only to the very general 'doctrinal' dimension of ritual purity and impurity. Buddhism, by contrast – and this applies especially to the *Theravāda* tradition – as a socially unorthodox missionary great tradition maintained its identity throughout the ubiquitous and essential interaction with the little tradition beliefs and practices of its potential converts by means of a fairly rigid base of doctrinal accuracy. It was this, perhaps, which caused the intense concern with potential schism within the tradition to which the *Abhidhamma* work 'The Points of Controversy' (*Kathāvatthu*) bears witness. Anyone who has listened to a number of sermons in the *Theravāda* tradition will be familiar with the continuing influence of these lists even today. Regularly, a preaching monk will take a particular list as his theme, and while running through its items will make reference to all the motifs of Buddhist thinking. We can see this style of exposition already in the earliest parts of the Canon, from the First Sermon, with its Eight-fold Path and Four Noble Truths, onwards.

That the twelve-fold list of Dependent Origination is designed to be used in preaching is explicitly recognised in the *Theravāda* tradition as early as the *Visuddhimagga*. There, it is said that expositions can start from the beginning, middle, or end, in reverse or forward order – this is called understanding the causal series in terms of the 'different ways of teaching'. The series is 'profound in teaching' because, apart from the fact of being taught in various ways as I have just mentioned, 'in some places . . . it is taught in four sections and three links, in some places in three sections and two links, and in some in two sections and one link'.[42]

There is an interesting development of this function of the twelve-fold causal series, allied with its nature as a symbolic representation of the 'essential point' of the Buddha's teaching. This is in its portrayal as a wheel. The *Visuddhimagga* and the commentaries describe the series as the 'wheel of becoming'; in one place, this is said to have ignorance and craving as its hub, old age and death as its rim.[43] The Indian *Sarvāstivāda* school, and particularly the Tibetan *Mahāyāna* schools, developed the diagrammatic representation of Dependent Origination as a wheel, especially in iconography. While the *Theravāda* tradition lacks such a widespread use of the wheel-image in iconography, it is familiar enough with the wheel as a symbol of Buddhist teaching and its propagation. 'The Setting in Motion of the Wheel of the Law' is the traditional title of the Buddha's first sermon; and the 'Wheel-Jewel' is one of the characteristic marks of the Universal Monarch, who on the level of legend is the secular counterpart of the Universal Saviour, the Buddha. On the social and political level, such a Buddhist king, and his religious counterpart the monk-advisor, are supposed in Buddhist thinking to act together for the maintenance and propagation of Buddhism,[44] in a relationship which is clearly meant to replace the position of the Brahmin priest as the most important of the religieux in the political sphere.

Let me summarise what I have said about the teaching of *paṭicca-samuppāda*, the fourth argument in support of *anattā*. In the first place, any idea of a permanent subject of experience and agent behind action, whether this is a global concept of individuality such as 'self' or 'person', or a particular element of human beings such as consciousness, is replaced in Buddhist thinking by the idea of a congeries of impersonal, conditioned elements. It is the combination of these particular elements in the process of Dependent Origination which explains the fact of human life and experience, and its continuity. The fundamental idea of conditionality is then exemplified by a series of twelve items taken from psychology and eschatology. This twelve-fold sequence, taken as a whole, embodies the idea of a succession of events and lives in the 'round of rebirth', without the supposition of a reincarnating individual; and finally, seen en bloc (especially in its representation as a wheel), the series comes to symbolise in its entirety Buddhist doctrine and its social propagation. On all these levels, the teaching of Dependent Origination is designed to oppose Brahmanical thinking, as right view (*sammādiṭṭhi*) opposes wrong view (*micchādiṭṭhi*).

3.3. The denial of self as a strategy in 'mental culture'

The four arguments which constitute the denial of self form part of right view, or wisdom. As I showed in the first section of this chapter, these are terms which are used to refer to a number of different levels in the appreciation and use of doctrine. In the second sense of right view – the 'acquaintance with Buddhist doctrine' of laymen and non-practising monks – this doctrine remains a relatively static matter of external belief, with little attempt at continuous, increasing introjection of it. The third sense of right view, however, does involve such introjection, and is said to be a gradually deepening 'insight' into the truth of the doctrine, produced by an active life of 'mental culture' (*bhāvanā*).[1] In this sense of right view, Wisdom recurs at the end of the Path, as the 'right knowledge' which produces 'right liberation'. During the life of mental culture which leads a monk to this end, Concentration (*samādhi*) and Wisdom progress together, and correspond to two different types of meditation practice. These are, respectively, the methods of *samatha*, 'tranquillity' or 'absorption', and *vipassanā*, 'insight'.[2] *Samatha* meditation is the practice of those techniques of concentration which lead to the 'one-pointedness' of mind, which forms part of almost all Indian virtuoso religious practice. These techniques, and the psychological states achieved by them, although the object of much development by Buddhism, are not claimed by the tradition to be specifically Buddhist phenomena. *Vipassanā* meditation, on the other hand, which is the application of Buddhist psychology to the personal experience of the monk, is claimed to be particular to the Buddhist tradition. In most cases, these two techniques are practised together, though one reads of the 'dry-visioned' saints, who dispense with the attainment of refined states of concentration – those states which constitute what is usually designated 'mystical experience' – and attain liberation through the introjected understanding of Buddhist psychological 'truth'.[3]

In this section, I will deal with the place of the arguments in support of *anattā*, as examples of right view, in this active life of mental culture. Just as one cannot appreciate Buddhist thinking generally without knowing something of the Indian cultural universe in which it was articulated, so in the case of particular doctrines, such as the denial of self, one cannot appreciate their meaning and function without considering the practical religious life of which they have always – from their very earliest beginnings – formed a part.

3.3.1. 'Purity of View'

The basis of Buddhist monastic life is morality, *sīla*. In detail, this means keeping to all of the two hundred and twenty-seven rules of discipline in the monastic code, the *Pātimokkha*. These include not only the five precepts observed by all Buddhists, but a host of other observances, some of which seem to be very minor, relating to matters of personal deportment and etiquette.* The usual explanation given by the tradition is that the observance of morality gives the mind calm: a calm which is a necessary preliminary to the 'higher' practices of Concentration and Wisdom (or Insight).[4] Modern psychological and anthropological writing gives *us* further insight here. Following William James and Mary Douglas, Carrithers holds that Buddhist notions of purity

> stem from what are, in the final analysis, intellectual needs: that what is pure is what falls within ordered categories . . .; for *Theravāda* monks, moral purity fulfils the same necessity. The insistence on observing the two hundred and twenty-seven rules of the monastic code in detail fosters an unshakeable sense of certainty: the monks can identify their proper role and attitude in every situation.[5]

Right view for a monk has a similar function of providing the monk with a sense of purity and certainty. In the Canon one finds together as a pair *sīla-* and *diṭṭhi-visuddhi* 'purity of behaviour and view'. There is a seven-fold list as follows: 'Purity of behaviour, Mind, View, Crossing over doubt, Knowledge and Vision of what is the Path and what is not, and of what is the Way, and Knowledge and Vision' (*tout court*).[6] This sequence is followed by Buddhaghosa throughout the *Visuddhimagga* – translated by Ñāṇamoli as the 'Path of Purification'.[7] The chapter of this work entitled 'Purification of View' contains an extended analysis of human personality into those ordered categories with which we have begun to be familiar. The most important of these categories are the five *khandhā*, which I have translated as 'the constituents of the personality', or 'the categories'; these are body, perception, feeling, mental formations, and consciousness; the twelve *āyatana*, 'bases', which are the five senses (plus mind) and their objects; and the eighteen elements (*dhātu*) which are the senses, their objects, and the resultant sense-consciousness. These lists are those which, according to the Suttas, were used by the Buddha himself. Later Buddhist tradition extended this style of analysis in the *Abhidhamma*, 'with the creation of a schedule [*mātikā*] consisting of triple [*tika*] and double [*duka*] classifications for sorting these states [of mind – *dhamma*], and the enumeration of twenty-four kinds of conditioning relation'.[8] The dénouement of this development are the lists of twenty-four kinds of (derived) materiality, the fifty kinds of 'mental formation', and the eighty-nine possible states of consciousness.[9]

* I am speaking here, naturally, at the level of theory. Historically, Buddhist monasticism has been as much subject to human weakness as has anything else.

Just as the strict control of behaviour in terms of the two hundred and twenty-seven monastic rules gave the monk certainty in any situation, so here the strict analysis of experience in terms of these ordered categories gives him certainty and 'purity' in mental life. This is not, one should add immediately, simply a matter of dogmatic concern for doctrinal accuracy. The analysis of experience in these ways has a particular point as a strategy of spiritual education. In order to understand what this strategy is, I must retrace my steps a little, to gain perspective on the place of these lists in Buddhist thought.

3.3.2. The 'point' of meditation

We saw in Chapter 2 that the analysis of personality in the religious milieu of the Buddha's time had developed certain motifs from earlier Vedic eschatological speculation into a dichotomy: on one side, the phenomenal individual, seen as a composite of non-valued, impersonal constituent parts; on the other, an indescribable self, venerated as that from which all value proceeds. The Buddha, as we saw, followed the first side of this dichotomy, but refused to consider any central self, leaving the direction of value away from the constituents of the personality simply as a 'direction arrow'. The new criterion for value-judgements and religious behaviour generally was to be *nirvāṇa*, which was 'empty' of self and all conceptual content. Accordingly, within the development of Buddhist thought there arose a dichotomy. Anything with conceptual or experiential content was to be assimilated to the impersonal, non-valued side of the dichotomy; since in this sphere everything was dominated by desire and grasping, anything with conceptual content became potentially graspable. Against this stood the empty unconditioned *nibbāna*, susceptible neither to conceptualising nor grasping.[10] One approach to the attainment of the 'emptiness' of *nibbāna*, naturally, was a direct assault on any form of conceptualisation, any view whatsoever – I shall deal with this in Chapter 4. The other approach, with which I am concerned here, was to proceed through an analysis of what does have conceptual content, in order to classify it into known categories; the ability to classify any experience or concept into a known, non-valued impersonal category was held to be a technique for avoiding desire for the object thus classified. This technique is what lies behind the privileging of certain types of conceptualisation as right view.

In considering the use of all the lists I have mentioned in meditation, one must bear in mind the distinction we met with in connexion with the teaching of Dependent Origination; that is, between the 'essential point' and the 'details'. The elaboration by the scholastic side of the monkhood of the categories and lists used by the Buddha is reasonably seen as the details of Buddhist doctrine. The monk in actual meditation practice, however, is of course trying to understand the point. It is not all eighty-nine possible states of consciousness he applies to himself, but the principle that whatever is recognisably contentful is to be seen as impersonal and not to be desired. It is not all twelve causal factors and twenty-four conditioning relations which he has to see at work in himself, but the fact of conditionality. Thus here a monk who has gone to the forest, the root of a tree, or an empty place, considers 'eye is a not-self, as are material objects, the ear and sounds, the nose and smells, the body and what is tangible, the mind and mental objects'.[11] Using the four-fold analysis of the Four Foundations of Mindfulness (*satipaṭṭhānā*), which is the most frequently used system of classification followed in meditation, the Buddha teaches the monks to reflect thus:

> what is the origin of body? It originates from nourishment, and comes to an end with the cessation of nourishment. What is the origin of feelings? They originate from sense-contact, and end with its cessation – [similarly] . . . Mind originates from name-and-form, and ends with its cessation . . . Mental objects originate from attention, and end with its cessation.[12]

The monk is to think 'the ideas of "I" and "mine" will be destroyed in me . . . I will have the right view [*sudiṭṭho*] of cause and things which come about through causes'.[13]

The second argument for *anattā*, which stressed the connexion between the three marks, in denying that any phenomenon was a self, is to be put to use in meditative reflection:

> when a monk lives with a mind familiar with the practice of seeing impermanence . . . familiar with the practice of seeing unsatisfactoriness in what is impermanent . . . familiar with the practice of seeing not-self in what is unsatisfactory, in his body, his consciousness, and all external objects, with a mind which has turned away from the conceits "I" and "mine", he quickly reaches liberation.[14] The perception of impermanence, when developed and increased . . . wears down and destroys the conceit 'I am'.[15]

The truth of the first argument (from control) is to be perceived in meditation in this way: whether the 'Noble disciple' is contemplating his body, perception, feelings, mental formations, or his consciousness,

> there is alteration and change; but his consciousness is not occupied with this alteration and change (in any of the *khandhā*), no disturbance arises in him through being occupied with such change. Objects of thought arise, but do not remain to obsess his mind; he is without any fear, annoyance, longing or grasping because of such an obsession.[16]

3.3.3. *Dhammā* as both elements of the normative system and objects of experience in meditation

The things, then, which a monk 'sees' in meditation clearly follow the patterns laid down by Buddhist doctrinal thinking. *Dhammā* here are both elements of the normative system to be applied, and 'objects' of experience in insight meditation. For the *Theravāda* tradition, the 'ultimate' psychological reality of these *dhammā* has never been a matter of question. For other Buddhist schools, however, particularly in the literature of the *Prajñāpāramitā* and *Madhyamaka*, who extended the style of teaching I shall discuss in Chapter 4, these categories are as much products of thought as the idea of self, and equally empty. There are some passages of the *Visuddhimagga* which suggest that the value of these patterns of self-analysis lies *only* in their strategic function as instruments of mental culture. 'Why does the monk see conditioned things as impermanent, unsatisfactory, and not-self? To contrive a means to deliverance.' The situation is compared to that of a fisherman catching hold of a snake, thinking it at first to be a fish. He 'contrives a means to free himself' from the snake by swinging it around in the air to weaken it, and then throws it away. So a meditator, thinking conditioned things to be a self at first, 'contrives a means to free himself' from them by weakening their hold over him 'by means of the attribution of the three marks'.[17] Elsewhere, the same work says that the Buddha taught the doctrine of the eighteen elements 'for the purpose of abolishing the perception of a soul [*jīva*]'. The monk is to carry out a detailed investigation of the teaching concerning *nāma-rūpa* 'in order to abandon more thoroughly the worldly designation of a "being" [*satto*] or a "person" [*puggala*], to surmount confusion and establish himself on a plane of non-confusion'. After doing this, 'when each component is examined, (he sees) there is no being as a basis for the assumptions "I am" or "I". The view of one who sees in this way is called "seeing things as they really are" [*yathābhūta-dassana*].'[18]

As the last quotation shows, the difference between what I have called the instrumental function of analysing experience in terms of impersonal categories, and the view that such an analysis represents reality 'in ultimate truth' was easily glossed over by the *Theravāda* tradition. In order to appreciate how other Buddhist schools came to make such a distinction, we must look at the style of teaching in the early Suttas from which these schools took their cue.

4 Views, attachment, and 'emptiness'

The Apostle tells us that in the beginning was the Word. He gives us no assurance as to the end.

It is appropriate that he should have used the Greek language to express the Hellenistic conception of the *Logos*, for it is to the fact of its Graeco-Judaic inheritance that Western civilisation owes its essentially verbal character. We take this character for granted. It is the root and bark of our experience and we cannot readily transpose our imaginings outside it. We live inside the act of discourse, but we should not assume that a verbal matrix is the only one in which the articulations and conduct of the mind are conceivable.

In certain Oriental metaphysics, in Buddhism and Taoism, the soul is envisioned as ascending from the gross impediments of the material, through domains of insight that can be rendered by lofty and precise language, towards ever deepening silence. The highest, purest reach of the contemplative act is that which has learned to leave language behind it. The ineffable lies beyond the frontiers of the word. It is only by breaking through the walls of language that visionary observance can enter the world of total and immediate understanding. Where such understanding is attained, the truth need no longer suffer the impurities and fragmentation that speech necessarily entails.

George Steiner, 'The Retreat from the Word' (1967) reprinted in Steiner (1979) pp. 31ff

In this chapter, I will deal with a different aspect of the doctrine of *anattā*. It is a form of the denial of self which in the *Theravāda* tradition has been of most importance in the ethical and psychological dynamics of spiritual education, while in other traditions, especially *Mahāyāna* schools, it has been much developed as a topic of epistemology and ontology, under the general name of 'Emptiness' (*śūnyatā*). In thus completing and deepening our understanding of the denial of self, we shall enter more and more into the concerns, theoretical and practical, of the specialist or virtuoso Buddhist. It is vital to do this, however, if we are to appreciate, correctly and sympathetically, the soteriological strategy of *anattā*; and it is this strategy which provides the cultural ambience, both behavioural and psychological, which the *Theravāda* tradition itself has seen as the (no doubt idealised) milieu in which its representations of the person, of identity and continuity, have been elaborated.

In the *Theravāda* version of this form of *anattā* it is not the case, as it was in Chapter 3, that arguments in support of *anattā* are offered with the aim of persuading the listener to accept the doctrine (or at least to confirm his acceptance). Rather, the doctrine is here taken as given, and the Buddhist notions of 'desire', 'attachment', and 'conditioning' are applied to the conceptual realm of views, in a particular way. One can best appreciate this aspect of *anattā* by regarding Buddhism here as judging all views in relation to the single affective dimension of 'attachment'. The dichotomy between right and wrong views is replaced, one might say, by a continuum, along which all conceptual standpoints and cognitive acts are graded according to the degree to which they are held or performed with attachment. At the lowest point on the continuum, there is the conditioned, ignorant view-point of the 'ordinary man', or those of opposing views, in which view is seen as simply a manifestation of desire; at the highest point (strictly speaking not on the continuum at all), there is the unconditioned freedom from view of the enlightened, desireless, and silent sage. I will separate three stages of the continuum: first, explicit ideas and theories of a self; second, the right view of Buddhism, which will only lead to *nibbāna* if it is not itself made the object of desire and attachment; and thirdly, the silent wisdom of the sage.

It will become abundantly clear that this approach rests on two types of argument which are traditionally classified in western logic as 'fallacies in discourse': that of the *argumentum ad hominem*, in which 'we reject what someone says on the irrelevant grounds that *he* is in no position to say it', and that of the *argumentum ad verecundiam*, which is an 'appeal to authority or to feelings of reverence or respect'.[1] It will become equally clear, however, that what might be counted as a fallacy in the discourse of such logicians is for an Indian religious teacher merely one of the tools of his trade. The Buddha did not see himself as a philosopher constructing an ethic of argumentation but as a healer concerned to cure the suffering of mankind, from which he himself had recovered. The tumour of desire and attachment was diagnosed as causing the sickness, and it was to be excised by all possible means.[2]

4.1. Views and attachment

4.1.1. Ideas of 'self' as conditioned phenomena

I mentioned in Chapter 3 that one linguistic form of presenting the *anattā* doctrine involved the words *attato* and *anattato*, meaning 'as' or 'in terms of' self and not-self. This form is frequently found as part of a group of four possible ways of regarding the relationship between self and the constituents of personality, all of them, naturally, mistaken.

Taking 'body' as an example, a man regards 'body as self [*rūpam attato*], self as having the body [*rūpavantaṃ vā attānaṃ*], the body as in the self [*attani vā rūpaṃ*], or the self as in the body [*rūpasmiṃ vā attānaṃ*]'.[3] Elsewhere, these four 'ways of regarding', along with other views such as the Upaniṣadic 'this is the self, this (same thing) is the world; after death I shall become permanent, lasting, eternal, not subject to change' are said to be 'constructions' or 'mental formations' (*saṃkhāra*).[4] That is, they are not simply denied on a conceptual level, but their very existence as conceptual phenomena is classified along with other karmic events, in the category *saṃkhāra* – fourth of the five *khandhā*, the constituents of personality, and second in the chain of Dependent Origination. The text I have just cited continues, asking about such a view of self: 'This construction, what is its cause, its arising, its ancestry, its origin? . . . Desire, monks, arises in the ignorant ordinary man, influenced by feeling born of sense-contact; from that there is this construction. Thus, monks, this construction is called impermanent, causally arisen.' The four ways of seeing a relation between *khandhā* and a self are elsewhere said to be '(ways of) regarding which lead to the arising of suffering', which contrasts with their opposites, which are the 'path leading to the cessation of (false) Personality* . . . a (way of) regarding which leads to the cessation of suffering'.[5] (The terminology here is strongly reminiscent of the Four Noble Truths, of which the second, third, and fourth deal with the 'arising', 'cessation', and 'way (or "path") leading to the cessation of suffering'.)

The *Pañcattaya Sutta* speaks of those who 'have views about the future', saying 'that an existing being is destroyed (at death)', that on the contrary 'after death the self is existent'; that then the self is either conscious or not; that it has form or is formless; or that 'the self and the world are eternal'; and many other such opinions. On all these views, the Buddha comments tersely: 'knowing that what is composite is gross, but also that there is the cessation of what is composite and seeing an escape from it, the *Tathāgata* has gone beyond it'.[6]

'The Discourse on all the Corruptions' (*Sabbāsava Sutta*) speaks in a similar vein, with more psychological detail.[7] An 'ordinary man, ignorant of the Noble Teaching', does not pay 'careful attention'. This is explained as the kind of attention which allows the 'corruptions' of sensuality, (craving for continued) existence, and ignorance to arise and increase. When these 'corruptions' are allowed to arise and increase, a certain type of thinking occurs; this type of thinking is illustrated by the following phrases (amongst others): 'Did I exist (or not) in the past? What was I in

* *Sakkāya*: as in *sakkāyadiṭṭhi*, Personality Belief, discussed in Chapter 3.1.4.

the past? Will I exist (or not) in the future? What will I be in the future?' The text continues:

to someone who does not pay careful attention in these ways, one of six views arises – 'I have a self' . . . 'I do not have a self', . . . 'By self I know the self'* . . . 'By the self I know the not-self', . . . 'By the not-self I know the self', . . . 'That which is my self here, which speaks, feels, and which experiences at different times the results of good and bad deeds, will become permanent, constant, eternal, not subject to change.'

All these views are summarily dismissed as examples of '(mere) viewpoint [*diṭṭhigataṃ*], a jungle of view, a wilderness of view, a disorder of view, a quivering of view, a fetter of view. Fettered by the fetter of view, monks, the ignorant ordinary man is not freed from birth, old age and death, distress, grief, suffering.' I explained the fetter of Personality Belief above (Chapter 3.1.4) as the conversion into a metaphysical or psychological theory of the automatic feeling of 'I', which is necessarily part of psychological functioning before enlightenment, when the 'conceit of "I am"' disappears. In this *Sutta*, we see depicted both the stages of this supposed process of conversion, and their alleged connexion with, and causal dependence on the 'corruptions'.

In two long sections of the *Saṃyutta Nikaya*, the 'Section on View' and the 'Collected Sayings on View',[8] various views on the self, the world, the 'Personality Belief', and so on, are all said to arise causally. The causes are the existence of the *khandhā*, and attachment to them. On each occasion this point is followed by the refrain from the second argument for *anattā* (as in Chapter 3.2.3). Elsewhere, it is said that 'all ascetics and Brahmins who regard self in different ways have in mind the five *khandhā* of grasping, or one of them'. Here again, an 'ordinary man' regards the *khandhā* in one or other of the four relations with self, and there comes to be the 'feeling "I am"'. From this feeling arise various speculations concerning this 'I', in the present and the future. Just as overt views of self arise causally, so it is said that the sense of 'I am' arises through a cause;† the cause is the existence of the *khandhā*, and the analogy is given of someone 'fond of adornment' gazing at the image of his own face in a mirror.[9]

Views of self, then, are not merely castigated because they rest on supposedly untenable intellectual foundations; rather they are conceptual manifestations of desire and attachment, and as such need not so much philosophical refutation as a change of character in those who hold them. This change of character will issue ultimately in the attainment of

* The phrase discussed in Chapter 2.2.2.
† *Upādāya*. This can also mean 'through attachment'.

enlightened status; the enlightened sage holds no views of self, as we shall see, because he is beyond conditioning. In the intermediary stage between the status of 'ignorant ordinary man' and that of sage, the right view of Buddhist teaching is to be held against other wrong views. This right view, however, must not itself become an object of attachment. Similarly, the states of mind attained through Buddhist meditation are 'constructions', not to be grasped at with desire.

4.1.2. The need to avoid attachment even to 'right view'

In Chapter 3 I distinguished three senses of right view, as pro-attitude, acquaintance with Buddhist doctrine, and as liberating insight. For simplicity here I will conflate the second and third senses, and will take them jointly to denote 'Buddhist doctrine' or 'attitudes and states of mind approved by Buddhism'.

Right view in my first sense – what I described as a 'general pro-attitude towards ideas of *karma* and *saṃsāra* and to the services of those religious practitioners with whom the ideas are associated' – is frequently said to result in good rebirth, not in *nibbāna*, the ultimately important goal. In Chapter 3 I mentioned a distinction between two types of right view, of which the first, and inferior, sort is said to 'have corruptions, be connected with (the acquisition of) merit, ripening to rebirth'. The phrase 'having corruptions' here means that the layman who holds it still is concerned, amongst other things, with *kāma* – usually translated 'sensuality' but connoting anything 'worldly' – and *bhava*, '(craving for continued) existence'. The adoption, by laity,* of Buddhist beliefs and practices is thus seen as a good thing, bringing merit and good rebirth (in heaven, or usually nowadays as a human being in the time of the coming Buddha, Metteyya); but it is still within the sphere of *karma*, from which it is the specialist's aim to escape. One of the achievements consequent on such an escape is the 'divine eye', which enables the enlightened man to see other beings going from birth to death in the process of *saṃsāra*, according to their *karma*. This 'divine eye' sees that while wrong view leads to hell, 'those who respect the Aryans,† are of right view, and acquire *kamma* through their right view' go to heaven.[10] In the 'Great Discourse on the Analysis of *Kamma*' (*Mahākammavibhaṅga Sutta*),[11] one of the causal agents in the process of *kamma* is this same possession of right or wrong view. There is 'nothing so apt', we read, to cause rebirth in heaven or hell as right or wrong view. 'Lower, middling, or

* I speak of 'laity' purely out of sympathy with Buddhist theory; historically, of course, perhaps the majority of monks should be included in this category.

† A term used to refer mainly to Buddhist monks, though also to any religieux of whose conduct the Buddha approves.

excellent ideas, view and thought' lead to an appropriate lower, middling, or excellent rebirth.[12]

The 'lower' sense of right view, then, is straightforwardly said to be a matter of the lesser goal of good *karma*. In the 'higher' sense of right view, which is acquaintance with Buddhist doctrine and its active, introjected application by the monk 'on the Path', there is held to be an ever-present danger of growing complacent, attaching the highest value to doctrine and allegiance to it as an end in itself, without using it to progress further and further in the practice of 'mental culture'. When I spoke of this mental culture in the previous chapter, I emphasised the aspect of purity in conceptual and mental life, quoting a seven-fold sequence of 'purities'. If we look at the context in which this sequence occurs, we will see it in a particular light: in brief, it is a means to an end, not an end in itself. The *Sutta* in which the sequence is found is called the 'Discourse on the Relay of Chariots' (*Rathāvinīta Sutta*).[13] A monk is asked whether the religious life is led for any of these purities, in turn. He replies that it is not, but that it is lived for 'final *nibbāna* without attachment'. He is then asked if this final *nibbāna* is equivalent to any of the purities, in turn. Again he replies that it is not, explaining the matter in the following way: just as a king might use a relay of chariots to reach a city, dismissing each chariot in the sequence and mounting the next, so a monk uses each purity to attain the next, and uses the last to attain 'final *nibbāna*'.

A very similar, but much more widely known simile is that of the raft. In the *Sutta* in which it occurs,[14] the Buddha says that just as a man who has crossed a river would not be doing 'what should be done' with his raft, if he were to put it on his back and carry it with him, so his teaching is 'for the purpose of crossing over, not for clinging to . . . You should let go even right teaching [or "states of mind", *dhammā*], how much more wrong!' In a poem of the *Sutta Nipāta*, in which the Buddha tells a householder of all the advantages he (the Buddha) has won by his homeless life, he says 'the raft was bound, well-made, (with which) I crossed the flood and reached the further shore; (now) there is no need for a raft'.[15] In the *Mahātaṇhāsaṃkhāya Sutta*, where as we have seen (Chapter 3.2.5) the Buddha tells the monk Sāti in no uncertain terms that he must not misinterpret his teaching, he declares the need to understand 'with right wisdom, as it really is' certain items of doctrine. He continues: 'but monks, this view, thus purified and cleansed, if you clung to it, took pride in it, cherished it, would you then, monks, have understood that the simile of the Raft is a teaching taught for crossing over, not for clinging to?'[16]

It is not only the conceptual formulations of doctrine which are thought to be potential objects of mistaken and harmful attachment. Both the general attitude of renunciation necessary for a monk, and the states of mind produced in him by the practice of Buddhist meditation, are only of value as instruments, and must not themselves replace *nibbāna* as the final goal.

An interesting, but somewhat difficult *Sutta* which follows this pattern is the *Dīghanakha*.[17] The eponymous wanderer is said to hold the view 'all is not pleasing to me'. The Buddha asks 'this view of yours, does it not please you?' Dīghanakha, realising the paradox, says uncomfortably 'if it were, then this would just be such, that would just be such'. I take this to mean that if the view itself were pleasing, there would be no reason not to be pleased by one thing or another in the world in the first place. The Buddha explains that most people in Dīghanakha's paradoxical plight would not give up their former view, but would take another – that is, would be caught in a self-contradictory 'disorder of view'; wise men, however, give up the first view without taking another. He says that although Dīghanakha's view is 'close to detachment . . . and lack of grasping', wise men see that 'obstinately holding to it and adhering to it' would involve them in quarrels and disputes with others who do not share the view, and so they give it up without substituting another. This is the 'casting out and renouncing of views'. The point here is that the attitude of renunciation and dislike of worldly pleasures which is vital to the homeless life of the monk must not itself become an object of dogmatic attachment.

Earlier in this chapter (4.1.1 and n. 6) I quoted the *Pañcattaya Sutta* in connexion with the conditioned nature of ideas of 'self'; in the present context it is instructive to follow this *Sutta* further. It goes on to say that even if someone casts out all those troublesome speculations and enters on the practice of Buddhist meditation, attaining the peace and happiness of various meditative states, still if he holds any such state as 'real' and 'excellent', he will be distressed when it comes to an end. The Buddha likens the alternation between meditative peace and its cessation to that between sun and shade. Again, even when a person passes beyond these states of meditative success, still he must not think 'Tranquil am I, at peace am I, beyond grasping am I.' Such a person, who 'declares that what is only a beneficial path is *nibbāna*' has still not reached that final goal. The reason is that even this last claim by the monk 'is shown to be an (act of) attachment'. It is a form of attachment, we can see, because the claim is still phrased in terms of 'I' (*aham asmi*). After each and every one of these stages, the meditative successes, the claim to be 'tranquil', and so on, the Buddha makes the same comment, which I quoted in connexion with the ideas of 'self': 'Knowing that what is composite [or "constructured", *saṃkhataṃ*] is gross, but also that there is the cessation of what is composite, and seeing an escape from it, the *Tathāgata* has gone beyond it.'[18]

The meditative states which the *Sutta* mentions are called the first four *jhāna* 'Meditative levels'; the second four are also said, elsewhere, to be 'composite' or 'constructed' (*saṃkhata*).[19] The 'Lesser Discourse on Emptiness' (*Cūlasuññatā Sutta*)[20] speaks of these states also, in a wide behavioural and psychological context. A monk must gradually reduce all 'disturbances' from both without and within. First, he goes to the forest, and reflects that 'there is only this amount of disturbance, that is the solitude dependent on the perception of forest'. This perception (of the forest) is said to be 'empty of the perception of village and of people'. 'With regard to what is left, he knows that it is existent, (saying) "this is".' I take this last phrase to mean that, in the true spirit of 'insight' meditation, which 'sees things as they really are' – that is, as conditioned elements – the monk is clearly aware, first, that the particular state or event of mind which he experiences at each moment is what it is (according to Buddhist *dhamma*-analysis), and second, that it is a conditioned, 'constructed' phenomenon. This interpretation is supported by what follows. Going through from the fifth to the eighth meditative level the monk knows that each level is empty of that which preceded it, and that the level presently occurring 'is existent, (saying) "it is"'. Going beyond even the eighth *jhāna*, the monk reaches 'the concentration of mind that is signless', where he knows that even this exalted state 'is constructed, thought out' (*abhisaṃkhato*, *abhisañcetayito*).[21] At this stage, the only amount of 'disturbance' left is the mere existence of the six sense-spheres, which are 'dependent on the body, with life as condition'. (These six senses, we read elsewhere, are themselves naturally 'empty of self and what belongs to self'.)[22]

Thus, we can see that right view in its first sense is simply a karmic agent, which will not lead the monk closer to *nibbāna*; there are higher senses of right view which do lead him closer to it, but even in relation to these attachment is mistaken, since they themselves as doctrines are meant to have only an instrumental status as means of psychological change; and the attitudes adopted by, and states of mind attained by the monk, as he lives the meditative life which produces that change, are themselves merely conditioned phenomena; their value lies not in themselves but in their usefulness in helping the monk attain the unconditioned state, *nibbāna*.

4.1.3. The 'selflessness of things' in *Theravāda* and *Mahāyāna*

Before I discuss the third point on the continuum of views and attachment – or rather, as I said, the point at which the continuum is abandoned – I should like to investigate those passages in *Theravāda* texts which bear a (more or less superficial) resemblance to the ideas of *Mahāyāna* Buddhist schools on emptiness and 'the selflessness of things' (*dharmanairātmya*). *Mahāyāna* texts themselves do quote passages from the *Theravāda* texts as evidence of these ideas in what they called the 'Lesser Vehicle' (*Hīnayāna*).[23]

We find in *Mahāyāna* thought, in addition to and encompassing the three marks of impermanence, suffering, and not-self, a fourth, 'emptiness', which had two forms: the selflessness of persons (*pudgalanairātmya*), and that of things. This latter has, I think, itself two main aspects. In the first place, there is an increased emphasis on the plain fact that nowhere in experience is to be found a substantial self, either as the knower or as the 'own-being' (*svabhāva*) of the known objects of thought and perception. 'Own-being' is a term of great complexity in Buddhist philosophical discourse;[24] in a psychological perspective, it denotes the alleged tendency to see the categories of Buddhist thinking – *dhammā* (Sanskrit *dharmāḥ*) – as in some way real existents, and hence as stable, reliable objects of knowledge. The second aspect of the 'selflessness of things' is precisely an increased emphasis on the idea that *dhammā* should be seen not as stable, reliable objects of knowledge, but rather as instrumental means of categorising the contents of mental life in such a way as to reduce and eventually destroy 'selfish' desire and attachment. According to this mode of thinking, to see *dhammā* as having 'own-being' is already to begin to feel dogmatic attachment for them.

Of course, in *Mahāyāna* texts, the 'selflessness of things' is not reducible simply to a soteriological attitude, though it certainly includes that. Not only have the texts known as the 'Perfection of Wisdom Discourses' produced, by their sheer volume and repetitiveness, a different aesthetic feeling for the pervasive truth of selfless 'emptiness'; but also in the epistemological and ontological discussions of *Mahāyāna* schools – particularly the *Madhyamaka* – the 'ultimate' non-existence of *dhammā* led to an entirely different philosophical orientation from that of the *Theravāda Abhidhamma*. We can, however, point to a number of similarities, both in letter and in spirit. As to the letter, one can remark the very phrase *sabbe dhammā anattā*, which denies selfhood to all phenomena. *Dhammā* are the objects of the sixth sense, mind, and we have seen frequently enough that these are said to be impermanent, not-self, and so on, and specifically 'empty of self and what belongs to self'. In the *Abhidhamma* work 'Enumeration of Phenomena' (*dhammāsaṅgaṇi*) it is said that 'all *dhammā* are means of [literally "pathways of"] verbal designation, of expression, of (conceptual) description'.[25] As we shall see in Chapter 4.1.4, the status of an enlightened man is such that he has gone beyond 'verbal designation, expression, and description'.

The argument that Buddhist categories and modes of analysis are not themselves objects of value, but merely the chariots which take the monk to the city of *nibbāna*, or the raft which ferries him to the further shore, is found explicitly in the Suttas, as I have shown. The 'spirit' of the denial of value to *dhammā*, the aesthetic feeling for emptiness is also found: 'body is like a heap of foam, feeling like a bubble; perception is like a mirage, mental formations like a banana tree, and consciousness like an illusion'. The monk who knows that both the body and the world (*loka*) are like foam, or a mirage, will be free from the passions and is 'not seen by the King of Death'. The *khandhā* are like sand-castles, to be knocked down and abandoned when no longer desired. Phenomenal elements, such as 'feeling' and 'name-and-form' are described as 'having the nature of falsehood' whereas only *nibbāna* 'has the nature of genuine truth'. A frequently recommended way of regarding the *khandhā* is as 'impermanent, unsatisfactory, a disease, a boil, . . . as empty, as not-self'.[26]

The notion of 'emptiness' is also recognised. We have seen the phrase 'empty of self and what belongs to self' used in relation to the six senses, their objects, and appropriate forms of consciousness; this remark is made as a reply to the question 'what does the phrase "the world is empty" mean?' This same phrase 'empty of self . . .' is a form of reflection which a monk 'in the forest, at the root of a tree or in an empty place', is recommended to apply to himself. The Buddha says 'see the world is empty by removing the view of self'.[27]

The *Visuddhimagga*, which systematises *Theravāda* doctrine and practice, extends and explains these ideas. I have already quoted passages from this text which regard the analyses of Buddhist psychology as strategic instruments of mental culture. In the chapter on 'Seeing what is, and what is not the Path', there is an extended discussion of the dangers which ensnare a 'beginner with tender insight'. These are such things as 'illumination', 'knowledge', 'rapture', 'tranquillity', and the like. When any one of these things occurs, 'desire arises in him which is subtle and peaceful in form, and he is not able to discern it as a defilement . . . (he thinks) "surely I have reached the Path, surely I have reached fruition" . . . Thus he takes what is not the Path to be the Path.' When any of these dangerous occasions for attachment arise, the monk is to reflect, as always 'this is not mine, this is not I, this is not my self'.[28]

The passages I quoted as giving the 'spirit', or aesthetic feeling for emptiness, are further elaborated here:

body is like a heap of foam because it cannot endure being pounded, feeling is like a bubble on water because it is enjoyed for a moment, perception is like a mirage because it is illusory, mental formations are like a banana tree because they have no core, and consciousness is like an illusion because it deceives.[29]

Similarly, the *khandhā* are to be regarded as

impermanent because of non-eternality and having a beginning and end; unsatisfactory because of being oppressed by growth and decay, and through being a cause of suffering; a disease because of being maintained by causal conditions and through being the root of disease; a boil because of resulting from the sword of suffering, oozing with the filth of the defilements, swelling with growth, ripening with ageing and bursting with dissolution; . . . empty because of the absence of an owner, a tenant,* a doer or feeler, or a superintendent; and not-self because themselves without owner, etc.[30]

The later *Theravāda* certainly thought that 'emptiness' and 'not-self' represented the same thing. The *Visuddhimagga* declares: 'the contemplation of emptiness is the contemplation of not-self. By it, the attachment to (the idea) "there is a self" is abandoned.' The two contemplations are said to be 'one in meaning, different only in the letter'. It is by 'paying attention to not-self, [that] formations appear as empty'. In one text, there are said to be various 'gateways to liberation', each of which is appropriate to individuals of different temperaments. The contemplation of emptiness is the gateway suited to those whose temperament is dominated by the conceptual failing of 'delusion' (rather than the affective failings of 'greed' or 'hatred'), since it concerns 'the category of understanding' (or 'insight'). A similar connexion between emptiness and the place of conceptual change in progressing along the Buddhist Path may be seen in the remark that it is specifically when 'a *learned man* pays attention to (constructions as) not-self, [that] he attains the liberation through emptiness'.[31]

This last idea might remind the Buddhist scholar of the *Mahāyāna* idea that seeing the 'selflessness of persons' could remove the moral 'obstacle of defilements', while it requires seeing the 'selflessness of things' to remove the conceptual 'obstacle of knowledge'. We cannot make an easy assimilation of the *Theravāda* and *Mahāyāna* ideas, however, since it was precisely the *Mahāyāna* contention that the Lesser Vehicle could only lead to the destruction of the obstacle of defilements, not to that of knowledge.

A full comparison between *Theravāda* and *Mahāyāna* ideas is neither possible nor necessary here. Suffice it to say that it was the aspect of the teaching of not-self at present under discussion – the dimension in which views, whether right or wrong, are set against the psychological fact of attachment, which provided the possibility for the radical development

* The image of the body as a house is a very pregnant one – see Chapter 5.3.1 below.

of the ideas of 'emptiness' and 'the selflessness of things' which I have mentioned. The *Theravāda* tradition has chosen to emphasise conceptually the kind of approach to *anattā* which I discussed in Chapter 3; but we will misconstrue *Theravāda* doctrine as an ideal religious attitude if we fail to see that the approach I am discussing at present was equally important, albeit emphasised more in the practical sphere of spiritual training.

4.1.4. The transcendence of views by the sage

In the Suttas, the contemporary religious and philosophical milieu is often characterised as a great variety of teachers and systems. I mentioned earlier the Six Heretics, who symbolise teachings other than those of Buddhism, and that one of the functions of this symbolisation is to delineate an image of the Buddha and the Buddhist sage as above pointless speculation and argument, having trodden a sure, tranquil path to release. The monk Kaccāna explains that whereas householders quarrel because of 'their attachment, bondage, greed, obsession, and cleaving to the lust for sensuality' ascetics and Brahmins quarrel because of 'attachment [*et al.*] to the lust for view'. The questioner asks if there is anyone who has overcome the two forms of attachment, and is told of the Buddha, living in a nearby village; he promptly bows in that direction and asks to be accepted as a lay follower.[32] One of the most frequent terms for an enlightened sage like the Buddha is *khīṇâsava* – 'with corruptions destroyed'. These 'corruptions' are in the first instance a list of three: *kāma* 'sensuality', *bhava* '(craving for continued) existence', and *avijjā* 'ignorance'. To this list of three was added a fourth, *diṭṭhi* 'view'. They are also called 'bonds' (*yogā*), and the 'bond of view' is explained thus:

> here someone does not understand as it really is the rise and fall of view, the satisfaction and danger in view, and the escape from view; not knowing (all this) he is obsessed by the lust for view, the delight in it, the love, infatuation, thirst, and fever for it, the cleaving to it, and the craving for it.[33]

The term 'corruption of view' is then used directly, and without explanation, to refer to a hindrance to the religious life. In a similar way, the bare word *diṭṭhigataṃ* is used to condemn or dismiss certain views or ideas. The past participle *-gata* means literally 'gone (to)', but in both Pali and Sanskrit, it 'is often used at the end of a compound to mean "(being) in" without any sense of prior motion'.[34] One might then translate, as I have already done, 'opinion' or 'viewpoint'; in order to bring out the pejorative connotations 'prejudice' could be used; a good translation is the French '*parti pris*'.

The *Theravāda* commentarial tradition has usually explained the 'corruption of view', or '*parti pris*' as referring to wrong, or 'speculative' views. If this were the only explanation, one might reasonably wonder why 'view' should have been singled out for special mention, particularly as 'ignorance' is already a cardinal sin in many Buddhist contexts. The present aspect of the teaching, where dichotomy of right and wrong view is replaced by a continuum on which all views are seen against the psychological fact of attachment, shows us that when 'view' is seen as something bad, or detrimental to the monk's religious practice, in fact what is denoted is *any* view which is held 'with attachment'. It is because the Buddha and the enlightened sage are beyond attachment that they are beyond 'view' in this sense.

The *locus classicus* for this point is the *Brahmajāla Sutta*.[35] In general, the *Sutta* tells of the many ways in which the Buddha excels other 'ascetics and Brahmins'. At first, only 'trifling inferior matters of mere morality' are discussed. They are said to be the sort of thing that might impress the 'ordinary man', but not to be those on which the real excellence of the Buddha is based.

There are, monks, other teachings, deep, difficult to see and understand, peaceful, excellent, not accessible to reasoning, subtle, to be experienced by the wise, which the *Tathāgata* himself has experienced, realising them by super-knowledge. Speaking of these things, someone would speak right praise of the *Tathāgata*, in accordance with the truth.

Although this *Sutta* is frequently quoted in the secondary literature, it is seldom emphasised just what the precise grounds for the Buddha's superiority are. This superiority is not a matter of the conceptual content of any views, wrong or right, but is because the views of all others, including the 'eel-wrigglers' whose lack of positive assertion has a verbal resemblance to the Buddha's own in certain other contexts,* are conditioned products of their individual experience, which is explained by the teaching of Dependent Origination. Each view is merely 'something experienced by these ascetics and Brahmins, who neither know nor see, and are subject to craving'. All of these thinkers 'have their experience as a result of sense-contact in [any or all of] the six senses'; and in them 'with (this) feeling as condition there arises craving, with craving as condition there arises grasping, . . . becoming, . . . birth, . . . old age and death, distress, grief, suffering, sorrow and unrest'. This, it will be recognised, is word for word the second half of the 'Dependent Origination' list. Throughout the list of views, on the self and the world, their eternity, infinity or otherwise, and so on, there is the same reference to causation which we met earlier in the chapter. After each set of views,

* In connexion with the Unanswered Questions, see 4.2 below.

the refrain is repeated that the Buddha knows how they have arisen, what karmic result they will lead to: but he also knows things 'far beyond'. It is by seeing arising and decay in the six sense-spheres that a monk can come to see things 'far beyond'.

It is important to realise that the alleged fact of others' views being conditioned is the *only* point on which the inferiority of the sixty-four types of view, and the superiority of the Buddha, are based. It is here, par excellence, that the *argumentum ad hominem*, the denigration of others' views on the ground of the character of those 'others', and the *argumentum ad verecundiam*, the appeal to feelings of reverence and respect (for the Buddha), can be seen in Buddhist thinking. 'Faith', or 'confidence' (*saddhā*) is certainly the appropriate virtue here.

The status beyond conditioning and views is forcefully depicted in the last two parts of the *Sutta Nipāta* – the 'Chapter of Eights' and the 'Chapter on the Ideal'. These poems have a rather different flavour from the Suttas, which I have been quoting up until now. There is scant mention in the whole *Sutta Nipāta* of the stereotyped lists whose part in Buddhist doctrine I have so much emphasised; there are no *khandhā*, no Eight-fold Path – and hence no right view – recurring on almost every page, as there are in the Suttas. This fact, and the linguistic peculiarities and difficulties in which the text abounds have made scholars see the *Sutta Nipāta* as representing a very early stage of Buddhist literature, before the 'scholastic' list-making tendency came to pervade the whole corpus of the Canon. Whether or not this historical argument is true, it is certainly the case that we are in a different aesthetic and spiritual milieu here. Briefly, one can say that these poems represent the summation, in *Theravāda* literature, of the style of teaching which is concerned less with the content of views and theories than with the psychological state of those who hold them.[36]

I have mentioned the importance of purity in Buddhist thought, but also the importance of not taking purity itself to be the goal. These ideas are expressed here forcefully:

> Those who hold rules* to be the highest thing,
> thinking purity comes from (practice of) self-restraint
> take up rites* and observe them (dutifully),
> (thinking) 'if we learn this, then we'll learn purity'
> – (these) self-proclaimed experts are (just) bound for rebirth.
>
> When someone is deficient in rule and ritual,*
> having failed to perform some act, he trembles,

* *Sīla*, 'rule(s)'; *vata*, 'rites', 'ritual': 'attachment to rule and ritual' is one of the first fetters, lost at the attainment of stream-winner status.

he yearns and longs for purity here,
like one who has left home (but) lost the caravan.

So renounce rule and ritual,
all action which brings praise and blame;
without yearning (for) 'Purity, Impurity!'
(a man) should live free, not grasping at peace.

The importance of not 'grasping' at views is equally important:

When a man in the world, abiding in views,
esteems something especially (as) 'the highest',
then he says that all others are inferior;
in this way he is not beyond disputes.

The man who holds opinions, defining (things) for himself,
comes to further quarrels in the world;
(only) when a man renounces all opinions,
does he make no quarrel with the world.

One is reminded here of the Buddha's claim that it is not he who quarrels with the world, but the world which quarrels with him![37] At the end of the *Dīghanakha Sutta*, which I quoted to illustrate the necessity of renouncing all views, the Buddha says 'The monk whose mind is freed thus . . . agrees with no-one, disputes with no-one; he makes use of conventional terms without being led astray.'[38] Elsewhere the Buddha is said to be able to speak of the various different means of 'acquisition of personality' without being led astray by 'worldly forms of speech and expression and conventional descriptions'. To say the words 'I speak', or '(others) speak to me' is only a 'conventional usage' which the enlightened man uses without 'resorting to conceit'.[39] Thus,

The (true) Brahmin who has considered (things correctly) does not
submit to figments of the imagination;
following no view, he is a kinsman not even of knowledge.*
Knowing the conventions of ordinary men,
he remains indifferent, where others grasp.

Attachment to teachings leads to (verbal) discussion.
How, by what means to discuss the man without attachment?
He takes up and rejects nothing –
he has washed away all views here.

Just as a flame put out by a gust of wind
goes down† and is beyond reckoning,

* *ñāṇabandhu*. To become a monk, one abandons ordinary family ties; to reach enlightenment, one must abandon all 'family' ties to knowledge.

† A phrase meaning literally 'sets', like the sun. To be able to appreciate the full flavour of the phrase, one must bear in mind the fact that since Vedic times, the movement of the sun had been a major motif in representations of time and temporality.

so the sage freed from name-and-form goes down
and is beyond reckoning.

There is no definition (by which to measure) the man 'gone down',
there is nothing in terms of which he might be discussed:
when all attributes (of human existence) are removed*
so have all ways of speech been removed.

Of the enlightened *Tathāgata* elsewhere we read:

Whatever the various ways of speech,
on which ascetics and Brahmins rely,
they are all inappropriate
when reaching the *Tathāgata*, who is beyond all ways of speech.[40]

With the sentiments expressed in these verses, we have come to the last and highest point on the continuum of views and attachment. Many of the points I have made about this continuum – especially about the last and highest stage, of the *Tathāgata* and the possibility of linguistic description of such status – are amply exemplified by the unfortunately notorious Unanswered Questions. By way of summing up and re-affirming the theme of this chapter, I will turn to these questions, which are really quite straightforward, despite the many misinterpretations they have suffered in the interpretative literature. I shall deal with the questions at some length, as they represent an area in which the *anattā* doctrine can very easily be misconstrued.

4.2. The Unanswered Questions

The questions which are consistently refused an answer are:[1]

1. *sassato attā ca loko ca*	Are self and world eternal?
2. *asassato attā ca loko ca*	Are self and world not eternal?
3. *antavā attā ca loko ca*	Do self and world have an end?
4. *anantavā attā ca loko ca*	Do self and world not have an end?
5. *taṃ jīvaṃ taṃ sarīraṃ*	Are soul and body identical?
6. *aññaṃ jīvaṃ aññaṃ sarīraṃ*	Are soul and body not identical?
7. *hoti tathāgato paraṃ maraṇā*	Does the *Tathāgata* exist after death?
8. *na hoti tathāgato paraṃ maraṇā*	Does the *Tathāgata* not exist after death?

* *Dhammā*. All those conceptual means by which saṃsāric existence is described.

9. *hoti ca na ca hoti tathāgato paraṃ maraṇā* — Does the *Tathāgata* both exist and not exist after death?
10. *neva hoti na na hoti tathāgato paraṃ maraṇā* — Does the *Tathāgata* neither exist nor not exist after death?

4.2.1. The questions are linguistically ill-formed

The first four questions are similar to a standard type of 'pointless speculation' which we have already met. The fifth and sixth are found once alone, where they are classed as 'unfit questions'.[2] Commentarial passages dealing with the last four questions frequently gloss *Tathāgata* as 'being' (*satto*), once as 'self' (*attā*).[3] This should give us a clue as to the correct interpretation: all the questions have to do with referring terms, such as '*Tathāgata*', 'self', 'being' and so on. According to the analysis we met in Chapter 3, for Buddhism there is no real referent for these terms. What appears as an individual, through the combination of a single body and the conceit of 'I am', is the '(phenomenal) person' (*puggala*), the 'personality' (*sakkāya*, or *attabhāva*);* in fact, all phenomena, both material and immaterial, 'form' and 'name', are composites made up out of impersonal elements.

I mentioned in Chapter 3 the comparison between the *khandhā*, producing the sound 'I', and a lute producing a note. In a similar, and better-known analogy, the nun Vajirā answers a question from the god of death concerning the destiny of a 'being' thus:

> 'being'? Why do you rely on that? This is a prejudice [*diṭṭhigataṃ*] on your part; there is no being here, purely a heap of conditioned elements. Just as when there is a collection of parts, there is (use for) the word 'chariot', so when the *khandhā* are there, there is the conventional term 'being'.

In a similar vein, the nun Selā explains that the human 'puppet' comes together and is destroyed through the existence and destruction of its cause; the cause is the existence of the *khandhā*, senses and 'elements'. There is a recurring line 'See the painted puppet, a mass of sores, a composite thing.'[4] The *Visuddhimagga* explains:

> just as a puppet is empty, soulless (*nijjīvaṃ*) and without curiosity, and while it walks and stands merely through the combination of strings and wood, yet it seems as if it had curiosity and interestedness; so too this [human] 'name-and-form' is empty, soulless and without curiosity, and while it walks and stands merely through the combination of the two together, yet it seems as if it had

* See Chapter 5.2. Briefly, the *attabhāva* is the 'individuality' referred to by the ordinary-language use of 'I'. It is an illusory individual produced by the 'conceit "I am"', from a collection of impersonal, separate elements.

curiosity and interestedness. This is how it should be regarded; hence the Ancients said:

> 'The mental and the material are really here,
> But here there is no human being to be found.
> For it is void and merely fashioned like a doll,
> Just suffering piled up like grass and sticks.'[5]

The sense of 'personality' when hardened into a theoretical position, or at least the working assumption of continuing individuality on which the 'ordinary man' bases his thinking and religious action, is called *sakkāyadiṭṭhi*, Personality Belief, a term which we have already met. This arises through regarding self and *khandhā* in one of the four mistaken ways (as in Chapter 4.1.1 above).[6] The monk Sāriputta explains that 'when Personality Belief exists, these (four) views [on the unanswered questions and the sixty-four views of the *Brahmajāla Sutta*] exist; when it does not, these views do not'. The words here clearly recall those of the short formula for Dependent Origination we met in Chapter 3.2.5. The Buddha also explains that views on the Unanswered Questions are caused by regarding self and *khandhā* in one of the four ways.[7]

In this light, it is clear that the most important reason for not answering the questions is that they are linguistically ill-formed. They use personal referring terms, which according to Buddhist thinking have no real referent; hence, any answer given directly to them would necessarily confirm the misleading presupposition that such terms do refer to some real and permanent individual. Smart has remarked[8] that asking these questions, for Buddhist thinking, is like asking nowadays whether the present king of France is bald; with the crucial difference that while it is for us a contingent truth that no king of France exists, it is for Buddhism a necessary truth that no 'self' exists to be denoted by such terms.

4.2.2. Those who ask them do so because they are conditioned by 'attachment'

We have just seen that views on the Unanswered Questions are simply forms of Personality Belief; a theoretical error caused by seeing a relation, of one sort or another, between a 'self' and the *khandhā*. The seeing of a relation in this way is caused by wrongly drawing a conceptual inference from the phenomenological existence of 'the conceit of "I am"'. The enlightened man no longer has this sense of 'I', and so although he can use first person singular verbs, names, personal pronouns, and so on, he is not – as we saw – 'led astray' by them. He does not draw any conceptual conclusions about the status after death of the non-existent referent of such verbal forms. The Buddha tells Ānanda that an enlightened man will not hold a view on the Unanswered Questions, because

> whatever verbal designation or means of verbal designation there is, whatever expression or means thereof, whatever description or means thereof, whatever knowledge or realm of knowledge, whatever rebirth or experience of rebirth – by knowing these with superknowledge the monk is freed. But it is not fitting to have the view that 'the freed monk does not know or see'.[9]

Ānanda himself, having refused to answer the questions, is charged with agnosticism, in the words 'Then your reverence is one who neither knows nor sees!' He replies that he does 'know and see', but that having a view on the questions is 'a prejudice [*diṭṭhigataṃ*]; whatever prejudice there is, whatever fixing on a view, insisting on it, being obsessed by it, whatever origin and cessation of view – all this I know and see'.[10] The content of this 'knowing and seeing' is precisely the linguistic point I have made. The Buddha says that ordinary men know only what can be named, whereas the enlightened man 'has no conceits'. He tells the wandering ascetic Vacchagotta that 'the *Tathāgata* is freed from denotation by the *khandhā*' and so it is not the case that one might describe him in terms of them. It would show an almost wilfully obsessive perversity in interpretation if one were to take the subject-noun and object-pronoun in these last two phrases, and ask 'if the *Tathāgata* cannot be described in those terms, how is one to describe him?' The Buddha explains there is 'no mind' which might describe the Buddhas of past ages, who attained final *nibbāna*. The young monk Sabhīya Kaccāna explains that nothing can be said about a *Tathāgata* after death, since 'any reason or grounds for description have been completely destroyed'. Sāriputta tells a monk who regards the *Tathāgata* after death as 'broken up and perished', that since 'the *Tathāgata* cannot be found in truth and reality even in this life' so neither can 'he' be regarded as suffering dissolution (or anything else) at death.[11]

We saw earlier that any ideas of 'self' are regarded as conditioned products of desire; not surprisingly, the same point is made here. Sāriputta teaches that views on the questions are a result of not seeing the *khandhā* as they really are, and that this lack of vision arises through not giving up craving for them. Moggallāna tells Vacchagotta that other teachers hold views on the matter through regarding the *khandhā* as 'this is mine, this I am, this is my self'. To hold a view here is to be under the sway of Māra – the god of death, whose realm is co-extensive with that of desire. The householder Anāthapiṇḍika explains that views on the questions arise either through a man's own lack of 'careful attention', or from his relying on the (mistaken) words of another. Such a view is 'constructed, thought up, causally produced'. Elsewhere, a view on the matter is said to be 'a prejudice, (resorting to) craving, ideas, and grasping, a conception, an imagining, an occasion for remorse'. While the ordinary man does not understand the rise and fall of such views, as conditioned phenomena, the wise man does, and so 'is not perturbed, nor has any doubt' concerning the Unanswered Questions.[12]

4.2.3. Reasons for their misinterpretation

As, I hope, can be seen from all these examples, the status of these Unanswered Questions is quite clear. Conceptually they rest on the mistaken assumption that a real entity exists as a referent for terms such as '*Tathāgata*', 'being', and the like; psychologically, the fact of making such an assumption, and therefore asking the questions, is a conditioned result of ignorance and craving. What has perhaps caused the confusion regarding the questions is the fact that they are often presented in the texts in a manner which is less clear than is the explanation I have given. But then, one can hardly expect a body of sacred texts, consisting of normative, exhortatory narratives, to give at the same time a logical, meta-linguistic account of its own doctrines. There are at least three reasons which might lead to misinterpretation.

Firstly, there is the fact that such terms continue to be used in so many contexts – including those dealing with these questions – despite Buddhism's view that personal terms have no real referent. This is partly, but not wholly, for narrative convenience. A language has yet to be discovered which does not use a 'subject–predicate' structure. Moreover, Buddhist teaching is intended to be of use to the 'ordinary', unenlightened man, who must by definition think in terms of 'selves' and 'I', and by whom ordinary language is taken at face value. It was doubtless the difficulty of expressing in ordinary language, to ordinary people, the teaching that ordinary language and psychology is based on an illusion, that caused so many later *Mahāyāna* Buddhist teachers to take refuge in silence.

Secondly, the denial of self is not a nihilism. Despite every refusal of 'self' on the conceptual and verbal level, the Buddha taught a way to salvation which he very forcefully distinguished from nihilism or 'annihilationism'. I have suggested that the scholar cannot try himself to resolve the paradox, to supply his own verbal account of the 'ultimate reality' to which the Buddha is held to have referred, but must simply elucidate the logic and function of particular forms of words. Accordingly, when we find certain positive-looking descriptions of the *Tathāgata*, it is pointless to take this as evidence for a 'hidden', and more acceptably non-nihilist doctrine which we as interpreters can then put into words. For example, it is said that the gods cannot find the mind of a *Tathāgata*, since it is 'untraceable'. Similarly, Māra cannot find the consciousness of the *Arhat* Godhika after his suicide, since, as the Buddha explains, he has attained final *nibbāna*, 'with consciousness unestablished'.[13] The nun Khemā, and the Buddha after her, declare that the Buddha both before and after death is 'immeasurable like the vast ocean'. Elsewhere the *Tathāgata* is compared to an ocean, as the mind of a monk in a particular meditative state is compared to the 'immeasurable' waters of the Ganges.[14] The use of ocean-imagery in the expression of 'mystical' feeling is widespread and well-known, but it is not my purpose to investigate the possible ways of concretising (and distorting) the resonances of this kind of poetic feeling. Suffice it to say that the existence of this kind of attitude toward *nibbāna* and the state of the enlightened man after death precludes the nihilistic psychological inferences which one might be tempted to draw from the conceptual refusal to speak of a 'self', or *nibbāna* – what I have called the 'linguistic taboo' of *anattā*.

Both these two points are important in considering the third reason for misinterpretations of the Unanswered Questions. Since the Buddha was questioned by 'ordinary' men, who necessarily, according to his teaching, thought in terms of individuals, and 'self', and since it was necessary that these deluded petitioners should not mistake the denial of self for nihilism, sometimes the questions are refused because they are said to be irrelevant to the practice of the religious life. Certain passages of this sort are regularly quoted, and used to suggest that the Buddha's attitude to 'metaphysical problems' [sic] was agnostic;[15] or even that he retained at heart an Upaniṣadic view of a positive, cosmic 'Self', and merely intended his *anattā* teaching to deny the 'small' self, the phenomenological 'I'. It is vital to see here that this reason for refusing the questions is subsidiary, and only given in narrative contexts where it has a particular connexion with the practical, strategic aspects of religious education.[16]

Rāhula[17] has elegantly demonstrated the necessity of seeing the Buddha's remarks in their narrative context in relation to his well-known refusal to answer Vacchagotta's question 'is there (or is there not) a self?' I will illustrate it with two passages concerning the refusal to answer the Unanswered Questions. In the first, a 'reasoning of mind' arises in the monk Mālunkyāputta in meditation[18] – already his views are seen as a hindrance to his religious practice. He goes to the Buddha and belligerently demands that the questions be answered, or he will renounce the monkhood. In this context, it is reasonable for the Buddha to reply, as he does, that he never promised to answer such questions when he accepted Mālunkyāputta as a monk. He gives the analogy of a man pierced by an arrow, who does not wait to find out the name, family, skin colour, and so on, of the man who shot it, before taking it out. In the same way, a man pierced by the arrow of suffering should aim to get rid of it before asking questions about the nature of the universe which caused such a state. Within the narrative, this analogy, and the Buddha's insistence that the religious life does not depend on an answer to such questions, are clearly intended to get Mālunkyāputta back to his meditation training, leaving useless questions behind. The preservation of such a narrative in the Canon is equally clearly intended to provide – by contrast – a model for monks to evaluate the relative importance of practical religious training and sophisticated conceptual analysis. It does not mean that such an analysis is not possible, nor that Buddhism as a whole rejects all speculation because it is harmful to the attempt at salvation. What is rejected is harmful speculation based on mistaken premises.

Similarly, there is the story of Poṭṭhapāda.[19] He is able to ask the Buddha questions about refined states of meditation, but still after that conversation, he is said to 'rely on' a conception of self as an explanatory scheme. He regards it, successively, as 'gross-material, having form, built up of the four elements, feeding on solid food', then as 'made of mind, with all parts great and small, not deficient in any (sense-)organ', and finally as 'immaterial . . . made of awareness'. He says that he finds it impossible to do without some such assumption, and so the Buddha remarks that it will be difficult for him to understand Buddhist teaching. At the start of the Discourse he had been characterised as mixing with contentious and undignified ascetics, but being unlike them in acknowledging (though not understanding) the Buddha's special eminence. The other ascetics laugh at him, not merely because he does not understand the teaching, but because he admires the Buddha nonetheless. It is in *this* psychological context that the Buddha is depicted as telling him that the questions are not conducive to spiritual progress. As the narrative continues, free from the gaze of the contemptuous ascetics, the Buddha praises Poṭṭhapāda for 'having eyes to see', unlike the others, and proceeds to give him a more personal instruction. All the other thinkers who talk about the self after death, in various ways, do so 'without any good ground': for example, those who say the self is perfectly happy do so without ever having been continuously happy even for half a day, do not know a method for the attainment of such a state of happiness, nor have ever even heard gods reborn in a happy heaven speak of their state. The obvious inference is that Poṭṭhapāda should give up his groundless speculations, and concentrate on what he can know for himself, namely the Buddhist Path. Again, this is not a universal recommendation to an 'empiricism' or practical, anti-metaphysical agnosticism, but a piece of advice given to an enthusiastic but easily misled admirer.

The Buddha goes on to explain that there are three 'modes of personality',[20] corresponding to the 'gross-material', 'mind-made', and 'formless' selves which Poṭṭhapāda had imagined, and that his teaching is designed to 'get rid of' each one. It is wrong, he says, to assume that the personality currently in existence is 'real', while the others are 'false'; he illustrates this by an analogy with milk, butter, and ghee, which develop naturally from each other, but which are 'defined differently' at different stages. 'Just so, . . . when any one of the three modes of personality is occurring, it does not receive the designation appropriate to another. These are worldly forms of speech, worldly expressions, worldly conventions, worldly descriptions; the *Tathāgata* makes use of them without being led astray.'

In this way, the dialogue builds up from a group of gossiping mendicants, arguing over 'perception' and the 'self'; leads through a delicate handling by the Buddha of the 'learner' Poṭṭhapāda; and ends with a clear statement of Buddhist doctrine. At the end of the Discourse, Poṭṭhapāda becomes a lay follower only, while his companion Citta becomes a monk. Clearly Poṭṭhapāda is still impressed, but still without deep understanding. It is in *this* narrative context that the Buddha is depicted as refusing to answer the questions when put by Poṭṭhapāda, because they are not conducive to progress.

In almost all other cases where the questions are refused for this practical reason, if one looks at the context, it is possible to see an explicit connexion with the facts of training. For example, when the Buddha says that the questions are 'unprofitable reasonings', which are not conducive to the religious life, it is in a long series of talks concerning what is useful for practice and what is not. When he makes the same remark to the novice Cuṇḍa, it is as one of the many ways in which he describes himself as a good and benevolent teacher. When Sāriputta tells Kassapa the questions are fruitless, the passage occurs in the 'Sayings on Kassapa', all of which have to do with matters internal to the monastic life of the *Saṅgha*.[21]

So, one of the points to be made about the Unanswered Questions is that – like many other things – they are irrelevant to the practice of the Path. As we have seen, this is a subsidiary aspect, dependent on the linguistic analysis which shows them to be ill-formed, and to contain presuppositions which do not allow a direct answer.

4.3. Quietism and careful attention

In Chapter 3, I argued that our understanding of the arguments in support of *anattā* was complete only if it took into account the way in which the right view approach was put to use in the actual practice of the (ideal) monk. In the approach I have been considering in the present chapter, it is equally important to see a concern with practical matters of spiritual education. I will discuss only one aspect of this, which might be called 'Quietism'. In using this term, I do not mean to refer to the seventeenth-century Christian movement of that name, nor indeed to any technical sense it might have in Christianity. I use it simply as a shorthand reference to an attitude which emphasises passivity in religious practice, and which seeks to attain as its final goal a state of beatific 'inner quiet'.*

We have seen, in the 'Lesser Discourse on Emptiness' (in Chapter 4.1.2 above) that the monk is recommended to seek solitude, and to avoid 'disturbances', both without and within. In the same way, attachment to views is held to lead to harmful results both externally, through quarrelling and hostility to opposing views, and internally by the confusion and needless diversification of experience caused by 'imaginings' (*papañcā*), which are held to be imposed on the simple contents of awareness – contents, of course, defined and perceived in terms of Buddhist *dhamma* theory.

4.3.1. Disturbances without

I quoted earlier a passage which declared that while householders quarrel because of their lust for sensuality, ascetics do so through lust for views. The concern to avoid disputes within the Buddhist monkhood is apparent in many places in the Suttas.[1] The Buddha says that it is unpleasant for him even to think of a place where monks are arguing, let alone go there, and he teaches that 'when, in a dispute, words are bandied back and forth, with views held maliciously, angry minds, sulkiness, and discontent, there is lack of internal peace . . . (and) it is to be expected that this will lead to protracted troubles and distress, and the monks will not live at ease'.[2] In the sections of the *Sutta Nipāta* I mentioned in connexion with the sage's transcendence of view, many verses decry the use of fixed views and 'truths' to denigrate opponents and gain praise (or blame) for oneself. For example,

> (Questioner) Those who abide in views,
> And quarrel, (saying) Only this is the truth;
> Do they all bring blame on themselves,
> Or do they gain praise in this way?

* I intend to refer to a reasonably homogeneous range of attitudes and practices found, in varying degrees, in different religious traditions. I do *not* intend to suggest that there is necessarily any similarity, whether psychological, or still less ontological, in the supposed results of the quietistic search.

(The Buddha) These are trifling matters, not enough to bring calm.

They are both the results of quarrelling, I say.
Seeing this, do not quarrel,
Know that tranquillity is no basis for disputes.

Just as the Buddha recommended non-violence (*ahiṃsā*) in the behavioural sphere, so too in the verbal:

Just as a knight, fed on royal food,
goes shouting after an opponent,
go, knight, to where he [the opponent] is,
for me the time for fighting is past.*

Those who take up a view and argue,
saying 'only this is the truth!'
to them say 'there is no-one here
to oppose you in a war of words'.

To those who live having lain down the sword
who do not counter view with views,
what will you gain from them, Pasūra,
by whom nothing more is grasped here?[3]

The word *visenikatvā*, which I have interpreted here as 'having lain down the sword' is difficult to translate accurately and exactly; but it occurs elsewhere in a similar doctrinal ambience, as does the word *visenibhūto*, literally 'having become armyless'.[4] The idea of 'waging warfare in talk' (*vadaṃ . . . paṭiseniyati*) is found elsewhere, and is explained as a monk cursing someone who has cursed him, angering one who has angered him, or quarrelling with someone who has quarrelled with him.[5] There is a common form of words, used to introduce stories of strife and discord both among ascetics generally and within the Buddhist monkhood, in which the participants are described as 'quarrelsome, wrangling, living wounding one another with weapons of the tongue'.[6]

This assimilation of verbal argument to physical contest and warfare could be illustrated by the English terminology of debate: one 'defends' one's own, and 'attacks' another's position, by 'marshalling evidence', 'advancing arguments' and so on. That this verbal similarity should conceal, or lead to, a real hostility in argumentation is an accidental and – optimistically – rare occurrence. For Buddhism, in this quietistic mode of thinking, the connexion is more natural and immediate.

* Literally 'already there is nothing (here) to fight about'.
In the words 'knight' (*sūra*) and 'opponent' (*patisūra*) there is a play on the name of the Buddha's interlocutor, Pasūra.

4.3.2. Disturbance within

The external sources of disturbance, then, are seeking praise or blaming others, waging verbal warfare, and so on. Internally the main sources of disturbance are the 'imaginings' and 'ideas' which 'assail' a man. The *Madhupiṇḍika Sutta*[7] explains this clearly: the Buddha is asked 'what is your doctrine, what do you teach?' He replies that according to his teaching 'there is no quarrelling with anyone in the world', and that in this way 'ideas [or "perceptions", *saññā*] do not obsess' the monk practising rightly. He explains how this comes about:

> from whatever cause, monks, imaginings, ideas and estimations assail a man, if there is nothing in that in which to find pleasure, nothing to welcome or to become attached to, this itself is an end to the underlying tendency to lust, to repugnance, to views, perplexity, conceit . . .; this itself is an end to taking the stick,* taking a weapon, disputing, quarrelling, arguing, accusations, slander, lying speech.

Subsequently, the monk Kaccāna continues with this theme. In a sequence which has strong resemblances to that of Dependent Origination, in the items mentioned, in their order, and in the use of *paṭicca*, 'dependent on', *paccaya*, 'condition', and *nidānam*, 'cause', he says that:

> eye-, ear-, . . . and mind-consciousness arise dependent on eye, ear, . . . mind (and their objects); the meeting of the three is sense-contact; with contact as condition there is feeling; what one feels, one has ideas about; what one has ideas about one reasons about; what one reasons about one has (vain) imaginings about. When one (vainly) imagines, from that as cause there occur the imaginings, ideas and estimations which assail a man.

The word *papañca* (Sanskrut *prapañca*) and its derivatives are widespread in Indian religious thought, denoting mental objects and events which hinder spiritual progress. From a root *pra-pañc*, meaning to extend or spread out, the term connotes diffuseness, manifoldness, in contrast to the 'one-pointed' attention and wisdom of the sage. According to Ñāṇānanda's illuminating work on the subject 'the tendency toward proliferation in the realm of concepts may be described in any one of those terms (diffuseness, etc.) and this is probably the primary meaning of *papañca*'.[8] Elsewhere, *papañcā* are said to have ideas (or perception) as their cause; the 'root of imaginings and estimations' is said to be the idea 'I am the thinker' (or, simply, 'the thought "I am"', *mantā asmīti*) an idea described as an 'internal craving'.[9] We have encountered

* *daṇḍa*. A great deal of Buddhist talk about non-violence uses phrases which speak of 'not having' or 'giving up the stick'.

the thought, or 'the conceit "I am"' many times in these pages. One passage describes it in a number of ways: it is 'something conceived', 'something shaken' and 'caused to quiver' – images which remind one of the comparison we met earlier between the utterance 'I' and the sound of a plucked lute-string – and finally 'something (vainly) imagined'.[10] All these terms are past passive participles, a grammatical form which embodies the point that the *Madhupiṇḍika Sutta* was concerned to stress, that the 'imaginings' which 'assail' a man are causally produced, the result of particular (though perhaps unconscious) actions on the part of the unenlightened man.

4.3.3. The practice of careful attention

The form of meditative reflection appropriate here is naturally the attempt to avoid producing these 'imaginings'. In the 'Discourse on the Synopsis of Fundamentals' (*Mūlapariyāya Sutta*)[11] all possible objects of perception and thought – 'earth, liquid, heat, . . . the plane of infinite space, . . . what is seen, heard, felt, cognised, . . . *nibbāna*' – are said to be seen by the ignorant ordinary man in terms of some relation to himself (much as in the four-fold relation between self and *khandhā* above). Both the learner and the *Arhat*, on the other hand, do not do this, but see 'earth as earth, liquid as liquid . . .' (and so on). The group of things 'seen, heard, felt, cognised' is one of the earliest forms of category into which the impersonal elements of the personality were sorted.[12] In all of them (taking what is seen as an example), the enlightened man 'sees what is to be seen, but has no conceits about what is seen, what is not seen, what is to be seen, and the seer'.[13] The way to destroy all 'conceits' is not to see a relation to a 'self' in any of the senses, their objects, or the corresponding sense-consciousnesses; that is, it is necessary that 'in the seen [etc.] there will be only the seen'. In what is seen, heard, felt, or cognised, 'the sage lives (with) clear (mind)'.[14]

We saw earlier that the practice of this kind of 'careful attention' (*yoniso manasikāra*) was to be applied throughout the attainment of states of mind approved of in Buddhist training. A good example of the right way of seeing these states – as conditioned, and not the possession of an 'I' – is that of 'the cessation of perception and feeling', the highest state of meditative trance possible in Buddhism. The monk does not think '*I* will emerge from it . . . *I* am emerging from it . . . *I* have emerged from it'; rather, he knows that there comes to be emergence from that state simply because 'the mind has previously been prepared in such a way as to lead to such a state (of emergence)'.[15]

The monk, then, is to see every state of mind, from everyday sense-perception to the most refined levels of Buddhist meditation, as conditioned, 'constructed', empty of an 'I', empty of anything worth being attached to. When this is achieved, when the 'conceit "I am"' is destroyed, the monk will be able to say, in the standard and suitably impersonalistic phrases '(re)birth is destroyed, the holy life has been lived, what had to be done has been done, there will be no more of this [saṃsāric] life'.[16]

Part III

Personality and rebirth

5 The individual of 'conventional truth'

It is self-evident that every historical study is to a large extent dependent on the condition of the tradition with which it has to work.

Erich Frauwallner (1953) p. 30

On whatever theoretical horizon we examine it, the house image would appear to have become the topography of our intimate being.

Gaston Bachelard (1957) p. 18, English translation (1964a) p. xxxii

5.1. 'Conventional' and 'ultimate truth'

5.1.1. The argument so far, and what follows

I said in the Introduction that the form of this book results from my approach to two classic problems in the study of Buddhism. Of the first, the doctrine of *anattā*, I have now completed my account. In discussing it, I have had occasion to refer, at many times and at crucial moments, to the second problem, 'Buddhism and Society' – conceived in terms of my particular concern, of how the dimension of social and individual differentiation within Buddhist culture is perceived by, and how it affects, the intellectual products of its textual tradition. This problem will now become increasingly important in the second half of the book, Parts III and IV, in which I shall discuss the *Theravāda* conception of the person, of personal identity and continuity (both in its general form and in the particular case of rebirth).

The dimension of 'Buddhism and Society' will enter into my account in various ways, as elements both of the *Theravāda* material and of my interpretative grasp of it. In the first place, there is the meta-linguistic dichotomy between 'conventional' truth (*sammuti-sacca*, Sanskrit *saṃvṛti-satya*) and 'ultimate' truth (*paramattha-sacca*, Sanskrit *paramārtha-satya*). This has been the main means by which Buddhist intellectualism has oriented itself in society and culture, as a conceptual parallel of the opposition between the great tradition, of Pali texts and virtuoso scholarship and meditation, and the various little traditions of vernacular preaching and ritual, both 'Buddhist' and non-Buddhist, which are found throughout the areas of South Asia to which *Theravāda* has spread. Secondly, as I said in the Introduction, at the same time as presenting *Theravāda* ideas of personality and continuity in terms of these indigenous categories, and as parts of the conscious and rational structure of its belief system, I shall develop an analysis of them in terms of certain unconscious and non-rational patterns of imagery. I shall try by this means to connect the philosophical and psychological doctrines I shall be dealing with to wider patterns of cultural perception, to quite simple and unsophisticated imaginative pictures of society, psychology, and cosmology.

These are the two major ways in which 'Buddhism and Society' will condition the following account. There are two other important ways in which we shall see that the wider cultural milieu informs and determines the doctrinal content of *Theravāda*, two other threads from which – in addition to its own particular and unique concerns – the fabric of its intellectual cloth is woven. In the first place there are themes and projects taken from the previous and 'hegemonous' Brahmanical tradition. We have already seen how the general form of the *saṃsāra-karma-nirvāṇa* system had been developed in the pre-Buddhist sacrificial culture of the Brahmins, and how Buddhism adopted and adapted it. We shall see also that in the details of its psychology and philosophy *Theravāda* makes use of motifs taken from Brahmanical thought. Secondly, we shall see that ideas which derive from the wider and more 'popular' culture of what we call 'Buddhist societies' intrude themselves into the doctrinal accounts of personality and continuity, both as elements which remain more or less unchanged, and as stimuli which provoke reactions from the intellectual form of *Theravāda*, reactions which themselves then form fundamental parts of the doctrinal edifice. (In connexion with this latter, I am thinking mainly of the need felt to systematise and hierarchise ideas of 'individuality'.)

In order to introduce both the general themes of the rest of the book, and the particular idea of the two forms of 'truth' with which I shall be immediately concerned in this chapter, I shall summarise briefly the argument so far. Chapter 1 drew an outline picture of Indian religion at the time of the Buddha, and emphasised how, in the gradual permeation of the sub-continent by the Sanskritic culture of the invading Aryans, there arose the great tradition of Brahmanical belief and practice, distinct from, and culturally hegemonous in relation to, the various little traditions of each locality and tribe. Within this Brahmanical tradition, certain crucial changes came about in eschatological ideas, changes which centred on an increasing emphasis on the sacrificial ritual. The final picture of the world which resulted from this, and from the

Brahmanical interpretation of the institution of world-renouncing asceticism, had as its main structural outline a dichotomy between the idea of *saṃsāra*, the world of time, the 'round of rebirth', and that of *mokṣa*, final and timeless release from *saṃsāra*. As both a cause and an expression of this developing world-view, there arose a certain picture of society: on one hand the world of caste-relations, in which the man-in-the-world was committed to a pre-determined and ever-recurring pattern of rights and obligations; on the other, the world-renouncer, released from such a social position and progressing towards a truly individual liberation. These two pictures, the metaphysical and the social, are but two sides to the same historical coin.

Chapter 2 dealt with the great tradition of Buddhism, in which the opposition between man-in-the-world and world-renouncer became even more clearly institutionalised, in the figures of the layman and Buddhist monk. After sketching something of the variety in 'Buddhist' culture, it showed how the teaching of the Buddha, and of the Buddhist intellectual tradition, developed some of the motifs of Brahmanical thinking, while leaving some very overt and symbolic gaps in the treatment of final release, *nibbāna*. Briefly, the idea was that collections of impersonal elements, pushed on by the force of action, *karma*, created personality and continuity. With the later *Upaniṣads* Buddhism shared a negative and deprecatory attitude to this process, thus reversing the positive attitude of the *Vedas, Brāhmaṇas* and early *Upaniṣads*. In connexion with the most significant difference in the treatment of final release, a discussion of the use of personal terms in Buddhist texts showed that its central teaching, the denial of self, consisted in fact in what I called a 'linguistic taboo'[1] in certain technical areas of discourse. In many types of narrative – ethical, exhortatory, behavioural – the use of terms like *attā*, 'self', and *puggala*, 'person', was accepted as useful and meaningful; only in explicitly theoretical contexts, where the discourse contained or openly presupposed a definite system of psychology and metaphysics, were personal terms rigorously excluded.

Chapters 3 and 4 took up this matter of theories, or views, and showed what part they play in the intellectual and meditative life of the Buddhist virtuoso. The right view approach emphasised the idea of impersonal elements arranged in categories, and put this to a particular use in meditative self-analysis. The no-view approach, on the other hand, deprecated the activity of theorising *per se*; it emphasised the 'attachment' with which fixed theoretical positions are supposed to be held, claiming this to be a more spiritually important factor than the content of the views themselves.

5.1.2. 'Conventional' perception of self and other

In the present chapter, and the next, I will turn to the analyses of personality and continuity which, though obviously made by intellectuals, scholastic specialists, nevertheless result from and reflect the relatively non-specialist areas of discourse, in which personal terms denoting unitary 'individuals' are found. It is true that Buddhist specialist thought – in which both meditative virtuosity and scholastic conceptualisation have shared a common intellectual programme – has always been accorded the highest value, and has been the final arbiter of 'truth' for the Buddhist tradition as a whole. Nevertheless, most Buddhists, whether monks or laity, have not advanced far in either scholarship or meditation, and so have themselves not had any immediate personal involvement with the kinds of discourse, thinking, and practice which the last two chapters have described. Anthropological accounts of Buddhist societies have furnished us with numerous examples of beliefs and practices which depend on the assumption of unitary and enduring 'persons'. To take Gombrich's conclusions from Ceylon as an example:

> Despite the doctrine that we are but a series of groups connected by actions, people do in fact think of themselves as having a more or less stable and concrete existence. From this it is a short step to conceiving this existence as extending beyond death . . . *prārthanā* [a religious aspiration or wish, 'prayer'] for happy rebirths and the transfer of merit to dead relatives show that the *anattā* doctrine has no more affective immediacy with regard to the next life than with regard to this, and that belief in personal survival is a fundamental feature of Sinhalese Buddhism in practice.[2]

Most Buddhists, therefore, have had a simpler view of personality and continuity than that which I have so far discussed, and which we will see elaborated in Part IV. Roughly, one might say that this simpler view is the naive westerner's view of reincarnation, in which a series of lifetimes, each containing a unitary 'individual', is somehow connected together as the successive lives of one 'person'. It is such an idea, or other more or less sophisticated versions of it, on which the religious practice of most Buddhists has depended, and which has been the main conceptual tool with which their view of psychology and ethics has operated.

I will choose two examples of the practice of the ordinary man, in the 'conventional' world, which throw light on attitudes toward personality and continuity. Firstly, there is the self-interest inherent in the activity on which is based all Buddhist non-meditative practice, merit-making.* The main hope which lies behind the acquisition of merit – all those practices which Spiro summarises as 'kammatic' Buddhism – is that after death the

* Indeed, from very early in the tradition, meditation itself has been one of the Ten Good Deeds which earn merit and good rebirth.

'owner' of the merit will be reborn in heaven as a god, or as a man on earth in happy circumstances. In Gombrich's terms, there is a 'cognitive' interpretation of this in line with orthodox Buddhist sentiments: it is a process of gradual self-perfection which continues until the force of merit is enough to allow a direct assault on the selflessness of *nibbāna*. Indeed, perhaps the most widespread Buddhist goal nowadays can be seen in this light; one hopes for rebirth as a man in the time of the coming Buddha Metteyya specifically because at that time, it is thought, the attainment of *nibbāna* – generally thought impossible now because of the corruption of the age – will once again become a feasible religious aim. 'Affectively' of course the desire for birth as a god or as a rich man may have little to do with such orthodox sentiments. Gombrich tells the story of an old layman, devout in practice and preaching, whose main preoccupation could be gathered from his glowing accounts of the female inhabitants of heaven, where he clearly hoped to be reborn.[3] There is a story recorded in the textual tradition which closely parallels this: the monk Nanda was being lured back to the lay life by the charms of his ex-wife. The Buddha took him to a heaven where the female spirits were infinitely more attractive, and promised that if he practised the religious life assiduously, he would be reborn in that heaven. Nanda's practice was so assiduous that he came to see the truth of the Buddha's teachings in their entirety, and attained *nibbāna*, after which naturally he had no more desire for females, human or heavenly.[4]

Indeed, a Buddhist who hopes that 'he' will be reborn in happier circumstances, and will eventually attain *nibbāna*, can point to a very good parallel in the textual tradition – the Buddha himself. The *Jātaka* stories tell how through incalculable ages, in all manner of lives divine, human, and animal, 'the' *Bodhisatta* (future Buddha), from the time of 'his' decision as Sumedha to attempt to attain supreme enlightenment, gradually acquired all the 'ten perfections' before becoming the Buddha in 'his' life as Siddhattha Gotama. The narrative context for these stories is always given as some occasion in the Buddha's life: the context is given, the reason for the tale, and at the end the Buddha identifies himself with the leading character, and usually some of his other better-known monks with the lesser characters. For example, the first story in the collection ends:

> Having delivered his lesson and his teaching, and having told the two stories, . . . the master concluded by identifying the birth as follows: 'Devadatta was the foolish young merchant of those days; his followers were the followers of that merchant; the followers of the Buddha were the followers of the wise merchant, who was myself.'[5]

As I remarked earlier, these stories (many of which incorporate folk-tales which have little or nothing to do with Buddhist doctrine – some are simple morality fables like those of Aesop or the Sanskrit *Pañcatantra* collection) form the major part of the literary and ethical experience of the ordinary Buddhist peasant. An interesting story recorded in the commentaries shows the relation between this type of discourse and that of Buddhist doctrine in its strictest form: the monk Sāti, whose mistaken ideas about the transmigration of consciousness we met earlier (Chapter 3.2.5), is said by the commentary to have been one of the monks whose task it was to commit the *Jātakas* to memory, and to be otherwise unlearned. Hearing the words 'at that time, monks, I was [e.g.] Vessantara', he wrongly inferred that though all the other constituents of personality were destroyed at death, consciousness (the presumed referent of the pronoun and verb) continued.[6]

The following point is crucial if we are correctly to appreciate the place of Buddhist doctrine in the real life of Buddhists and of Buddhist society: *just as it was a narrative necessity, in the dialogue between the Buddha and Sāti, that there should be a wrong view of consciousness in order for there to be an occasion for the Buddha's right view, so socially and psychologically it was and is necessary that there be both affective and cognitive selfishness in order that the doctrine of* anattā *can act, or be thought to act, as an agent of spiritual change. For Buddhist thought, the existence of (for example) enthusiastically self-interested merit-making is socially, psychologically, and indeed logically necessary as the raw material which is to be shaped by* anattā.

The second example of ordinary Buddhist practice which illustrates attitudes toward personality and continuity is that of interaction with others who are considered to be stable and persisting individuals. Apart from the obvious fact of ordinary human interpersonal action and perception, there is a wide variety of such 'others' in the religious life of ordinary Buddhists, from major and well-known gods to local deities and spirits; one important type of spirit is the *peta*, 'the departed'.* These may be malevolent or dangerous spirits, or may simply be dead members of one's own family. An especially common practice is the transference of merit gained from performance of religious rituals to such departed relatives, in order to help their karmic progress through *saṃsāra*. As with the former example, there are many references to the *petā* and to

* There are clear historical links between this type of spirit and the 'Fathers' (*pitaras*) whom we met in Chapter 1. Both are closely connected with the whole range of supernatural beings (such as *holman* in Ceylon, *nats* in Burma, and *phii* in Thailand) whose cultural position in South Asian societies does not depend on the belief system of *saṃsāra-karma-mokṣa*; indeed they doubtless existed long before the intellectual tradition came to formulate those ideas.

practices associated with them in the textual tradition. There is a whole collection of 'Stories of the Departed' (*Petavatthu*) in the Canon,[7] and indeed many passages incorporated into the main collections of Suttas dealing with the life and teachings of the Buddha himself.[8] As before, a 'cognitive' interpretation is possible which will accommodate these ideas to more orthodox Buddhism. For example, ethically, the idea of transferring merit can be interpreted not as a straightforward gift from one person to another, but as the donor giving the recipient the chance to rejoice at his (the donor's) acquisition of merit, and thus to acquire some himself.[9] Conceptually, the idea of others' continued life after death is no more problematic than one's own; as we saw in Chapter 3, according to the strictest doctrinal accounts of psychology, the unenlightened man must by definition have a sense of 'I', must find a 'person' within when he introspects: this sense of self, manifested simply as a reaction-pattern, is called *asmi-māna*, 'the conceit "I am"'. Naturally, in this context, 'I am' implies also that 'you are'. For *Theravāda* doctrine, unreflective religious practice of the sort I have exemplified, and the perception of self and other which it involves – whether as a reaction pattern or an explicitly formulated Personality Belief – involves one or other of these two types of 'selfishness'. They are both fetters on the Path – *but without fetters there would be no liberation.*

5.1.3. The two truths

The distinction which Spiro makes between 'kammatic' Buddhism, in which the aim is good rebirth, and 'nibbanic' Buddhism, in which the aim is the cessation of rebirth, should not (as Spiro himself points out) be seen as denoting two entirely separate systems of belief and practice.[10] Rather, we might see these interpretative categories as representing two ends of a continuum, two poles to which Buddhist thought and practice can be oriented. Within the Buddhist textual tradition, it is this distinction in orientation, this dichotomy in patterns of thinking and types of discourse which is referred to as that between conventional and ultimate truth. As I suggested in Chapter 2, the simple ideological categories of Buddhist thought do not correspond directly to all observable social realities, any more than do the categories of western anthropologists. Accordingly, the sharp distinction between the two types of truth is not to be taken as being supposed to correspond to any sharp distinction between classes of individuals, or texts. We have seen that the difference between layman and monk, despite its being a clear difference in social status, with extensive ritual marking the transition, and clear differences in behaviour and appearance marking an individual as one or the other, nevertheless does not immediately confer a difference in soteriological status. In the same way, although the difference between the two types of truth can – as we shall see presently – be given a clear logical outline, it should not be thought that this in fact marks an absolutely clear division between areas of thought and particular texts, such that specific ideas and passages can be always and unambiguously assigned to either side of the division.

The idea that there might be 'higher' or 'lower' truth, or knowledge, is found in the *Upaniṣads*, and in other systems of Indian thought besides Buddhism.[11] Its earliest appearance in the *Theravāda* tradition is in a *Sutta* which refers to different kinds of *Sutta*, those 'whose meaning is literal' and those whose 'meaning is to be interpreted' (*nītattha*, *neyyattha*).[12] The commentary explains that a *Sutta* is one whose meaning is to be interpreted if, for example, it speaks of 'persons' (*puggala*); this is because 'in an absolute sense no person exists' (*paramatthato pana puggalo nāma n'atthi*). A *Sutta* whose meaning is literal is one which 'speaks of (the) "impermanent, unsatisfactory, not-self"'.[13]

In the same way, in the later two truths, conventional truth is that which speaks of selves, persons, spirits, gods, and so on; ultimate truth is that which speaks in terms of the analytical categories of Buddhist doctrine, the 'categories', 'sense-bases' (*āyatana*), 'elements' (*dhātu*) and so on.* The commentary to a *Sutta* which speaks of an 'ignorant person'† in connexion with rebirth and conditioning, explains:

> [The Buddha] uses conventional language in both these terms [i.e. *purisa*, *puggala*]; Buddhas have two types of speech, conventional and ultimate. Thus 'being', 'man', 'person', [the proper names] 'Tissa', 'Nāga', are used as conventional speech. 'Categories', 'elements', 'sense-bases' are used as ultimate speech. . . . The fully enlightened one, the best of those who speak, declared two truths, the conventional and the ultimate; there is no third. Words (used by) mutual agreement are true because of worldly convention; words of ultimate meaning are true because of the existence of elements.[14]

Sometimes the words which are classed as ultimate truth are more general technical terms of doctrine. Commenting on the compound 'the one person' (*eka-puggala*), used of the Buddha, there is the following:

* In *Mahāyāna* Buddhist thought, consonant with the approach called 'the selflessness of things' (*dharma-nairātmya*), of which I spoke earlier (Chapter 4.1.3), the analytic categories of Buddhist thinking are themselves said to be only 'conventionally' true, while the ultimate truth is that of emptiness. Problems arose, however, concerning the treatment of the twelve-fold list of Dependent Origination, on which all Buddhist doctrine, including that of emptiness, is based. Sometimes it was classed as conventional, sometimes as ultimate. These difficulties need not concern us here, however, as for *Theravāda* thought ultimate truth simply and unambiguously refers to the categories of impersonal elements found in Buddhist doctrine.

† Mentioned in Chapter 2.2.1.

'Conventional' and 'ultimate truth'

The Blessed One, the Buddha, has a two-fold teaching – conventional teaching and ultimate teaching. Thus 'person', 'being', 'woman', 'man', '*kṣatriya*', '*brahmin*', 'god', 'Māra' [the god of death] – such is conventional teaching. 'Impermanent', 'unsatisfactory', 'not-self', 'categories', 'elements', 'sense-bases', 'the foundations of mindfulness' – such is ultimate teaching.[15]

The *Abhidhamma* text, 'Points of Controversy', contains a long discussion on the existence or non-existence of the person;* the *Theravāda* argument throughout is that 'there is no person in real and ultimate fact'.[16] The commentary explains how the word 'person' can be used, in phrases clearly intended to echo those used in the formula for Dependent Origination: 'When the constituents of personality exist, there exists the worldly usage "such and such a name, such and such a family".'[17] It continues by quoting the *Sutta* passage in which the Buddha makes use of 'worldly forms of speech' without being 'led astray', which we met in Chapter 4. It was a constant theme of that chapter that linguistic usage – especially in the case of 'the *Tathāgata*' – was likely to confuse and pre-judge difficult questions of doctrine. It is clear that these later ideas of two types of truth are simply generalising the point about the *Tathāgata* to all persons (we saw that the commentaries to the *Tathāgata* passages frequently glossed *tathāgata* as *satta*, 'being'), and making it explicit by the two-fold codification of linguistic usage.

In Chapters 3 and 4 we have often looked to the *Visuddhimagga* for explicit accounts of ideas and attitudes implicit in the earlier teachings of the Suttas. Here also, the following passages, taken from Chapter 17 of that work, clarify the matter. A man is said to be able to be 'confused', and to incur (bad) *karma* by his wrong grasp of things, in three ways. Firstly, 'confused about death, not understanding death as "everywhere dying is the breaking up of the constituents of personality", he describes it as "a being's transmigration from one body to another", (thinking that) "a being dies"'. Secondly, in the case of birth, instead of realising that it is merely the appearance of a new group of *khandhā*, he thinks 'a being is reborn', or that it is 'a being's reappearance in a new body'. Thirdly, in the case of *saṃsāra* as a whole, instead of realising that 'the succession of constituents of personality, of elements and sense-bases, carrying on without a break, is what is referred to as "*saṃsāra*"', such a person thinks that 'a being comes and goes from world to world'.[18] Similarly, in reply to the question 'whose is the result [literally "fruit"] of action, if there is no experiencer?', there is the reply:

'Experiencer' is a convention, for the mere occurrence of the result; as one says 'it fruits' as a convention, when fruit appears on a tree. Just as it is simply owing to the occurrence of fruit on a tree, which are one part of the phenomena [*dhammā*,

* For this discussion see Chapter 6.1 below.

plural] called a tree, that it is said 'the tree fruits', or 'the tree has fruited', so it is simply owing to the arising of the result of action [the 'fruit'] consisting of the pleasure and pain called experience [*upabhoga*], which is one of the constituents of personality, which [together] are called 'deities' and 'human beings', that it is said 'a deity or a human being experiences or feels pleasure or pain'. There is therefore no need at all here for a superfluous experiencer. [Literally: 'another experiencer'.][19]

It would, of course, be possible to say a great deal in interpretation and evaluation of these two truths – most obviously in relation to homiletic discourse, almost all of which, even for the virtuoso, must needs be carried on in conventional terms. For my purpose, which is the exposition rather than the evaluation of Buddhist doctrine, it is enough to remark that this is how the *Theravāda* tradition has schematised the relationship between the different areas of thinking and discourse which its textual tradition contains; and to point out the congruence of this meta-linguistic schematisation with the social and psychological picture of human nature which Buddhism presents. Both types of discourse are seen as containing truths, for two main reasons. In the first place, since the phenomenological reality of the 'ordinary man' and of the 'learner' on the Path is necessarily patterned according to 'the conceit "I am"', for them discourse containing talk of unitary individuals will be – *pro tempore* – 'true'; secondly, as I hope to have shown in Chapters 3 and 4, for the most refined type of virtuoso Buddhism, doctrines which can be given verbal expression are in the last analysis simply instruments, tools for a spiritual culture which culminates by abandoning them in the 'silent wisdom' of the sage.

In the next section I will discuss the two most important concepts with which the intellectual, scholastic tradition has systematised the conventional view of personality and rebirth. These are *attabhāva*, literally 'self-state', which I will translate as 'individuality' to retain the Pali word's flavour as a technical term; and *puggala*, for which I will use the normal translation of 'person', meaning by that to imply the sense of 'personality' or 'character'.

5.2. *Attabhāva* 'individuality', *puggala* 'person'

5.2.1. *Attabhāva:* the word and its denotation

The *attabhāva* is a compound formed from *attā*, 'self', and the ending *-bhāva*; this latter, in both Pali and Sanskrit, is used in a similar way to the English '-hood' or '-ness', and means 'the state' or 'condition' of being something. For example, from *atthika*, 'needy', comes *atthikabhāva*, 'the condition of being needy', 'destitution'; from *asaraṇa*, 'not remembering', *asaraṇabhāva*, 'amnesia'. With some nouns, the sense is that of having a certain status: from *samaṇa*, 'ascetic', *samaṇabhāva*, 'the status of ascetic'; *bhikkhubhāva*, 'the status of monk', '(full) monkhood', is a term used to denote the status of monkhood after the ordination ceremony, which follows a period of probation.[1] *Attabhāva*, then, refers to the fact, condition or status of being a 'self' – a 'self', that is, in the sense in which the unenlightened man feels himself to be a separate individual, confronting real others.

According to Buddhist thought, as we have seen, this sense of self arises through mistakenly taking one or all of the five 'constituents of the personality' as a self. *Attabhāva* is explained in the same way: 'Through either the body's or the five categories' being taken in the sense "this is my self", they are called *attabhāva*.' There are four 'grounds for individuality', which are the same as the four ways of conceiving a relationship between 'self' and *khandhā* which we met in Chapter 4. According to the *Visuddhimagga*, '*attabhāva* is what the body is called, or else the five-fold *khandhā*, since its real being is only as a concept derived from (grasping) them'.[2] Although 'only a concept' for the most sophisticated level of Buddhist intellectual and doctrinal analysis, this sense of self, as we have seen, is held to be necessarily a phenomenological reality for the unenlightened: and so in discourse which is not phrased in terms of the category-analytic, Abhidhammic style, the word *attabhāva* can be used to pick out this (ultimately illusory) phenomenon for description and comment.

5.2.2. Various forms of individuality

There are a number of different ways in which this individuality can be seen. First, there is the sense of individuality as defined by social status. The Buddha teaches the Brahmin Esukāri:

> On recollecting his ancient family lineage on his maternal and paternal sides, wherever there is the production of an individuality, it is reckoned accordingly. So, if there is the production of an individuality in a noble family, it is reckoned as a noble. If there is the production of an individuality in a *brahman* family, it is reckoned as a *brahman*. If there is the production of an individuality in a merchant family . . . [or] in a worker family, it is reckoned as a merchant . . . [or] a worker.* As a fire, *brahman*, no matter on account of what condition it burns, is reckoned precisely as that: if the fire burns because of dry sticks it is reckoned as a dry stick fire; if the fire burns because of chips . . . grass . . . cowdung, it is reckoned as a fire of chips . . . grass . . . cowdung – even so, *brahman*, . . .[3]

* These are, of course, the four *varnas*, 'estates' of Brahmanical social theory, arranged as typically in Buddhist texts with the kingly or noble 'estate' *preceding* that of the Brahmins.

Elsewhere, it is said that 'in whatever individuality (a being) previously existed' it is possible to remember his former lives, in the following standard phrases: 'there I had such-and-such a name, was of such-and-such a family, such-and-such a caste'.* In the *Visuddhimagga*, the idea of 'male' and 'female faculties' is used to explain why a particular individuality 'is reckoned as a man or a woman'.[4]

It is, of course, part of the usual explanation of the caste system that birth in a high or low caste, as man or woman, represents both the karmic result of good or bad actions, and the potential for karmic advance in the future – the better the caste, the better the chances for religious success.† In this sense, social distinctions are of the same order as distinctions between the various types of being in the cosmological hierarchy – gods, spirits, men, and animals are all potential karmic destinies. Accordingly, the word *attabhāva* is used to designate particular beings as gods, spirits, men, and animals.[5]

Attabhāva can also be used to draw attention to the material or immaterial nature of individuals. Frequently, it simply means 'body'.[6] For example, the ocean is said to contain many marvellous beings, including various sea-creatures with *attabhāvā* of different lengths. In a simile explaining the dangers involved in undertaking the life of meditative solitude in the forest, the Buddha says that someone embarking on that life will either 'sink or float', just as different animals (elephants, bulls, cats) will either sink or float in water depending on the size of their *attabhāva*. The years of a human being's life from sixty to seventy are called 'the stooping decade', and those from seventy to eighty 'the bent decade', because in such old age the *attabhāva* stoops and becomes bent like a plough. Gods and monks with magic powers are said to create *attabhāva* of various sizes; gods can create 'gross-material' *attabhāva*, so as to be seen more clearly.[7]

Acquiring a 'gross-material' *attabhāva* is the first of the three ways of 'acquiring individuality', or personality (*atta-paṭilābha*, explained as *attabhāva-paṭilābha* by the commentary) which we have already met.[8] The others are the 'mind-made' and the 'formless'. These three types of individuality correspond to the three main levels of Buddhist cosmology – the worlds of physical sensuality, refined materiality, and immateriality. Although, therefore, *attabhāva* can simply refer to a physical body as the basis for individuality, it does not necessarily do so.

* *evaṃ-vaṇṇo*. This is the Pali form of Sanskrit *varṇa*, strictly speaking referring to the four *classes* of castes, rather than particular castes themselves.

† This is, of course, denied by Buddhist theory; in practice most Buddhists share the Brahmanical attitude to caste and religious potential, excepting the particular pre-eminence of Brahmins as such.

We find mention of mind-made *attabhāva*, and of *attabhāva* as either 'material, immaterial, with or without perception [or "consciousness", *saññī*], or as neither with nor without it'. In the 'formless' or 'immaterial' worlds, the *attabhāva* is made up of the four mental 'constituents of personality', without body.[9]

It is not my concern here to go into the details of the *Theravāda* cosmological-soteriological system, but rather to show that a series of lives taking place anywhere in the system is referred to as a series of *attabhāva*. An often-repeated phrase for a series of lives is 'a becoming, a destiny, an abode for beings, a transmigration, a womb, a station-for-consciousness,* an acquisition of individuality'.[10] We read of someone reaping the benefit of a good deed for 'a hundred, a thousand, a hundred thousand individualities'; a phrase meaning 'from birth to (re)birth' is explained by a series of terms, among which is 'the repeated production of individualities'. The motive force for such a series of lives is, of course, *kamma*. Incurring *kamma* through sense-desire, feelings, perception or the 'corruptions', a man 'produces an individuality born from that'. Acts performed from greed, hatred, or delusion will have their fruit 'wherever the individuality is produced'. The *Visuddhimagga*, distinguishing between *kamma* results to be experienced 'here and now' and those 'to be experienced on (subsequent) rebirth' uses the terms 'in the present' and 'in the next individuality'. The 'one-seeder', who is to gain *nibbāna* in the next lifetime, is said by the commentary to 'produce only one (more) individuality'; while the enlightened sage 'does not produce individuality in the future'. A very frequent commentarial gloss on the phrase *diṭṭhe vā dhamme*, 'in the present', 'here and now' (used of *kamma* results, benefits of the religious life, or *nibbāna*) is 'in the present individuality'. A man who cannot understand the Four Noble Truths 'in the present individuality' is said to be foolish.[11]

In this latter sense, *attabhāva* comes to refer to the whole of one lifetime: in a pun on the word *viharati*, 'lives', it is said that the continuity of one life involves a sequence of four postures – standing, sitting, lying, and walking. 'By cutting off [*VIcchinditvā*] the discomfort of one posture (by replacing it) with one of the others, he carries [*HARATI*] the individuality on.' In a phrase which clearly indicates a life-long vocation to monkhood, a monk is said to 'dedicate his individuality' to the Buddha or to a meditation teacher.[12]

The word *attabhāva*, then, has as its denotation the individuality which appears in the consciousness of the unenlightened; its connotations are one or more of the senses I have exemplified. In this way, the

* On the various worlds of *Theravāda* cosmology and the (connected) idea of 'stations of consciousness' see Chapter 7.2 and Table 2 below.

concept is used by the *Theravāda* intellectual tradition as a means by which its non-personal, category-analytic mode of discourse can be made to come half-way to meet the personalised, self-interested style of thinking and perceiving which is held to be characteristic of all ordinary, unenlightened discourse. For Buddhism, conventional thinking presupposes unitary selves or persons who are in some way subject to a series of discrete rebirths. Ultimate thinking refers solely to collections of impersonal elements, the sequence of which provides continuity both within 'one lifetime' and in the process of 'rebirth'. The idea of *attabhāva* forms the bridge between these two.[13]

5.2.3. *Puggalā*: 'persons' as character types

The second concept with which the intellectual tradition has systematised the conventional view of personality and rebirth is *puggala*. Where *attabhāva* was more oriented towards expressing, in a suitably impersonal way, the structure of individuals and rebirth as particular forms of existence, *puggala* is more oriented toward description of those individuals and reborn 'persons' as character-types. In Chapter 2 I said that one of the Buddha's immediate and pressing injunctions was to self-control and self-knowledge; and that although the ultimate discovery of the religious life would be the meditator's 'realisation' of selflessness, nevertheless on the way to that final goal the practitioner would find out much about his character – in Buddhist terms, about the particular arrangements of *kamma*-result which appear to him as a personality. Chapters 3 and 4 have shown the way in which the 'realisation' of selflessness is supposed to proceed; now we shall see in more detail the genre of character-analysis which is supposed to precede the conclusion of that process.

As with *attabhāva*, there are a variety of senses in which *puggala* is used. Generally, they may be summarised as having to do with differences in character, ethical disposition, spiritual aptitude and achievement, and karmic destiny. There are many places in the Canon where these topics are mentioned, but the most extensive treatments are found in the collection of Suttas known as the *Anguttara Nikāya* and in a work of the *Abhidhamma* entirely devoted to the subject, the *Puggala-paññatti*, 'Designation of Persons'.

Examples of the most general, and not intrinsically religious sense of *puggala* are when some people are said to reply to the point, others diffusely; or when one person is said to be like a carving on a rock, because his anger is quick to arise and long-lasting, another like a carving in the earth because although his anger is quick to arise it does not last long, and another is like a carving in water because 'though he be harshly spoken to, rudely spoken to, yet he is easily reconciled, he becomes agreeable and friendly'. This kind of description gains an ethical dimension in such passages as the following: some persons are 'self-tormentors', like ascetics bent on a life of self-mortification; some, like butchers, bandits, or executioners, torment others; some, like nobles or Brahmins who indulge in ascetic practices and perform large animal-sacrifices, torment both themselves and others; and some, like Buddhist saints, torment neither themselves nor others.[14] These kinds of difference between 'persons', of which there are well over a hundred in the *Sutta Piṭaka* alone, to say nothing of the entire work called the 'Designation of Persons', naturally become significant in the practical matter of religious training. The 'difference between persons' (*puggala-vemattatā*) is an important consideration brought to bear on the length of the probationary period required before acceptance into full monkhood.[15] Once accepted as a full monk, differences in temperament will necessitate different types of meditation practice. The three basic categories in terms of which these differences are depicted are the three 'roots' of greed, hatred, and delusion, and their opposites. When these are combined in various ways – a temperament may be predominantly greedy/hating, for example – we have the six 'roots of the person'. The *Visuddhimagga* explains that the source of different temperaments are the previous (karmic) habits, or the 'elements' and 'humours'. The elements here are earth, water, fire, and wind; the humours are phlegm, bile, and wind. Thus for example, a person is of predominantly deluded temperament because the earth and fire elements, and the phlegm humour are in excess.[16] I mentioned in Chapter 2 that the system of Ayur-Vedic medicine, from which these ideas of elements and humours are derived, is one of the types of explanation for human nature and experience which co-exist with that of *karma* in the actual practice of Buddhist societies. Here we can see this symbiosis reaching into the domain of Buddhist intellectual analysis.

The examples of the different senses of *puggala* which I have given so far have concerned synchronic differences between character-types. The word is also used to indicate diachronic differences in karmic destiny. For example, these are 'four persons found in the world', one who acts immorally and is reborn in a hell; one who acts immorally and is reborn in a heaven; one who acts morally and is reborn in a hell; and finally, one who acts morally and is reborn in a heaven. (The differences are due to *kamma* from previous lifetimes, and the point of the passage as a whole is that the results of action may be either immediate or delayed.) Similarly, 'there are ten persons found in the world', with different behaviour and knowledge, and different resultant rebirth. For example, 'a certain person is immoral'; at death he [sic] decreases in status (literally 'goes to degradation'). An often-repeated schematisation of these ideas is expressed in a four-fold pattern of 'darkness' and 'light'. 'There are four persons; one is dark and destined for darkness; one dark and destined for light; one light destined for darkness; one light destined for light.' One particular and very important categorisation of persons in this way is the list of Four Noble Persons (*ariya-puggala*): stream-winner, once-returner, non-returner, and the enlightened man. By distinguishing in each case between being on the path towards attaining a status, and actually having attained it, these are often referred to as the 'four pairs', or 'eight persons'. With the addition of the ordinary man (*puthujjana*), these become the 'nine persons'.[17]

There are many other ways in which 'persons' are classified in terms of rebirth and *kamma*. All of them share with those I have quoted the fact of being expressed linguistically by a single subject (noun or pronoun) and two verbs, each of which refers to actions or states in different lifetimes. In terms of the *anattā* doctrine, a strict interpretation of such phraseology would lead to a view of an enduring self or person, and as such would be unacceptable in Buddhist doctrinal eyes. To the charge that such usage contradicts the *anattā* doctrine, Buddhism has two answers. The first is simply to reiterate the distinction between conventional and ultimate truth, and to relegate all discourse of the present sort to the lesser category. The second, and more striking idea, is that the reborn person is 'neither the same nor different' (*na ca so, na ca añño*) from the one that died.* It is certainly true that the Buddhist tradition as a whole has not been always and everywhere agreed on all the details of this matter: one very numerous school called the *Puggalavāda* (Sanskrit *Pudgalavāda*) 'Personalists', accorded a special status to the concept of the person. I will deal with the discussion between this school and the *Theravāda*, as recorded in the *Theravāda* work the *Kathāvatthu*, in Chapter 6. Here, I will discuss the *Theravāda* attitude to two of the topics which were much discussed in debates between the *Puggalavāda* and other Buddhist schools: the memory of former lives, and the *Bhārahāra Sutta*, the '*Sutta* on the Bearing of the Burden'.

5.2.4. The memory of former lives; and 'bearing the burden'

We saw, in connexion with the use of *attabhāva* to designate a particular social status, something of the standard phraseology in which the memory of former lives is expressed (Chapter 5.2.2 above). The full description is as follows, in Rhys Davids' translation:[18]

* I will explore some of the ramifications of this idea in Chapter 6.

(The monk) recalls to mind his various temporary states in days gone by – one birth, or two or three or four or five births, or ten or twenty or thirty or forty or fifty or a hundred or a thousand or a hundred thousand births, through many an aeon of dissolution, many an aeon of evolution, many an aeon of both dissolution and evolution. In such a place such was my name, such my family, such my caste, such my food, such my experience of discomfort or of ease, and such the limits of my life. When I passed away from that state I took form again in such a place. There I had such and such a name . . .

Just as one particular *attabhāva*, 'with such and such a name, . . .' is only a conventional reality for the unenlightened, so the newly enlightened monk, having reached *nibbāna* during his lifetime – and so still having a 'body-self' as the referent of the pronoun and verb – can look back over a series of such unenlightened 'individualities' and identify the social and experiential details of each. The fact that the conceptual and psychological status of each *attabhāva* should also be the status of the remembered 'lives' (*nivāsa* – literally 'abodes' or 'dwelling-places', an image which we shall presently see to be very significant) is shown by another passage which explicitly puts the two together.[19] The verb *anussarati*, which is here translated as 'remember', or 'recall to mind', also means to 'know' or 'be aware of' in the present. (A cognate word, *sati*, is the technical Buddhist term for that mindfulness or self-awareness, the inculcation of which through meditation practice as a continuous psychological skill leads to enlightenment.) The wanderer Udāyin says to the Buddha: 'I, lord, even insofar as I have had experience of this (present) individuality, am not able to recollect it in all its qualities and details. How, then, should I recollect a variety of former abodes, thus: one birth, two, . . .' We can see from this that two alleged results of Buddhist religious practice which appear to be different, are in fact part of the same process. First, the practice of the meditative life of mindfulness is held to teach the monk 'self-knowledge' in two senses: both in that he will come to have a general awareness of the individual character which is his karmic inheritance, its faults, merits, and spiritual potential;* and also in that he will become conscious, moment to moment, of what actually occurs in the experience of that individual character. Secondly, this intensified self-awareness may lead – should a monk choose to attempt the practice – to a backward-moving light of recollection which first illumines the past experience of the present 'individuality', and then an increasing number of past 'individualities'.

The criteria according to which each of these lives, both present and past, is individuated consist in large measure, as we have seen, in matters

* As I remarked in Chapter 2.2.2 it is better to say that someone *is* a particular character, rather than that 'he' *has* one – there is no transcendent self behind the one which appears in everyday life.

of social status: 'such and such a name, such and such a family'. It is this aspect, I think, which allows us to empathise more fully with the Buddhist attitude to individuality as conventional. It has become a commonplace of western psychology to see personality and identity as in part, if not entirely, a product of social role, interpersonal perception, and so on. Equally, it is common in anthropology to find that the social definition of individuals is a major part of what many different cultures see as 'persons'.[20] There is, however, in the Buddhist case an even stronger bridge for our understanding, thanks to the work of Dumont, to which I have already had frequent recourse. We saw in Chapter 1 that the complementary opposites of 'man-in-the-world' and 'world-renouncer' formed the picture of social reality, of which the soteriological picture of *saṃsāra* and *mokṣa*, rebirth and release, was but the metaphysical transcription. Dumont suggests that the man within caste society is not an individual in our western sense, but that the renouncer is the only Indian figure who is comparable as an autonomous social and spiritual agent. In his words 'the unreality of caste and the individual in the world is given immediately. Transmigration does not therefore create it, it only represents or explains it.'[21] If, then, the man-in-*saṃsāra* (at the present level of ideological abstraction all those on this side of *nibbāna* are 'men-in-the-world') is the very paradigm of 'unreality', it is clear that the memory of a sequence of such lives does not give experience of a real reincarnating individual self or soul. Indeed, the only time in the Buddhist scriptures in which the memory of former lives is explicitly connected with any theoretical conceptions of individuality and continuity is precisely when certain non-Buddhist religieux are said to have such a memory, and *wrongly* to conclude that there *is* an eternal, transmigrating self.[22] In Dumont's words again, 'Buddhism truly expresses the place of the individual in Indian society.'[23]

With these remarks in mind, let me turn to the other topic I mentioned in connexion with the 'Personalist' school, the *Bhārahāra Sutta*.[24] In this discourse, the Buddha speaks of 'the burden, the bearing of the burden, its being picked up, and set down'. These are explained as follows: the burden is the five *khandhā*; picking up the burden is desire; setting it down is the cessation of desire. The word *bhārahāra* 'the bearing of the burden' is explained thus: '"the person" is what should be said; that venerable one, of such and such a name, of such and such a family'. Here we have the same words which denoted the 'individuality' in the memory of former lives – clearly the 'person' here is equally a matter of conventional truth.* The commentary, after giving examples of personal names

* The emphasis on social status is increased here by the use of the honorific *āyasmā*, 'venerable one'. This is an etiquette term for monks, and not householders, but as I

and lineages, to explain 'of such and such a name, . . . family', says 'in this way, in using the phrase "bearing of the burden", he [the Buddha] shows the person to be a matter of mere convention'. I have translated the word *bhārahāra* here as 'the bearing of the burden', although many others (including some very influential scholars)[25] have translated it as if it were an agent noun, 'the bearer of the burden'. The word *hāra*, however, in both Pali and Sanskrit, can only be either an adjective used of someone 'carrying' something; or a noun, meaning 'the act of carrying' something. Here, the compound *bhārahāra* is almost certainly a noun, since it appears in a list of three compounds of which the first two are definitely neuter nouns.[26] The idea, then, is that the 'person' is a state created by the act of 'picking up' the burden of the *khandhā*, through desire, a state which simply consists in the act of 'bearing the burden'.

I have tried in this section to thread my way through some of the complexities and paradoxes which result from the existence of different types of discourse in the *Theravāda* tradition. I have tried to show how the apparent contradiction between the strict *anattā* doctrine and those many passages which speak of unitary individuals has been explained by Buddhist intellectual thought: first, by the distinction between conventional and ultimate truth; and second, by the systematisation of conventional truth in terms of the two concepts of *attabhāva* and *puggala*. Two things will be glaringly obvious: the vast majority of actual Buddhists will have had neither the interest nor the intellectual sophistication to have bothered with the scholastic texts which contain these ideas. For them, talk of 'persons' who are reborn will simply and directly relate to their religious feelings and ideas. In the second place, although these meta-linguistic doctrines do succeed – given Buddhist presuppositions – in making a coherent whole of Buddhist teaching, it can scarcely be denied that they have the flavour of rationalisations after the event, rather than an original and determining influence on the development of Buddhistic culture. I wish now to turn to something which I think *has* been such a determining influence, to a pattern of thinking and imagination which has united scholarly analysis and 'popular' culture into one 'collective representation'.

5.3. House imagery

So far in my study of Buddhist thought, I have made use of two kinds of interpretation. First and foremost, by means of a logical and linguistic

remarked, at this level of ideological abstraction all the unenlightened are equally 'men-in-*saṃsāra*'.

analysis of certain Buddhist doctrines, I have tried to show the internal structure and coherence which, to Buddhist eyes, they possess. Second, I have given some very general outlines of the social setting in which these doctrines arose, and in which they function. Moreover, I have tried in some measure to relate the results of these two types of interpretation to each other. In this section I will introduce a kind of analysis which will recur throughout the rest of this study: that is, I will try to depict a certain pattern of imagery contained in the texts. I will argue that such patterns of imagery give us access to fundamental and unconscious structures of the imagination in Buddhist culture; and that these structures unite all Buddhists, from the meditators and scholastics to the ordinary peasant, into one cultural world. They do this by providing the possibility of shared patterns of self-perception, and by placing this self-perception in a single social and psychological universe. The uses of imagery which I will quote and discuss are taken solely from the textual tradition of *Theravāda*; but I think it will be clear that they reflect modes of perception which are much more widely distributed throughout Buddhist societies.

The type of imagery I will investigate in the present context is that of the house. Speculation on the psychological and religious significance of the house has not been lacking in the west. For Freudian psychoanalysis, the symbolic representation in dreams and neurotic fantasy of the body by images of a house is common.[1] For Martin Buber's religious and poetic imagination 'there is a cosmos for man only when the universe becomes a home for him with a holy hearth where he sacrifices'.[2] Mircea Eliade – typically perhaps with more synthetic enthusiasm than analytical precision – suggests that: 'having a body and taking up residence in a house are equivalent to assuming an existential situation in the cosmos . . . passing beyond the human condition finds figural expression in the destruction of the "house", that is, of the personal cosmos that one has chosen to inhabit'.[3] In the patient but daring reconstructions of western scientific and literary imagination made by the French critic Gaston Bachelard, 'a house constitutes a body of images that give mankind proofs or illusions of stability. We are constantly re-imagining its reality: to distinguish all these images would be to describe the soul of the house; it would mean developing a veritable psychology of the house.'[4]

It is not at all my intention to suggest by this mention of western ideas any simple and premature conclusions for the comparative study of psychology and religion. Rather, I will take Bachelard's words as programmatic, and attempt to distinguish the place of house-imagery in the *Theravāda* Buddhist imagination. This place is coherent and complete as a manifestation of Indian culture; only when we have many more detailed studies of particular traditions will any attempt at general conclusions be possible. Using the *Theravāda* material, I shall, in the first of the following two sections, describe the entire soteriological scheme of Buddhism in terms of various aspects of the image of 'leaving home for homelessness'; in the second I shall recapitulate this scheme, using the tradition's own idea of the three 'seclusions' (*viveka*).

5.3.1. Leaving home for homelessness

The idea of the physical body as a house is easily exemplified: 'Just as when a space is enclosed by timbers, creepers, grass and clay, it is called a "house", so when a space is enclosed by bones, sinews, flesh and skin, it comes to be called "body".'[5] Just as many different types of people – Brahmins, merchants, and so on – come from all the four quarters to stay in a guest-house, so many different types of feeling come to arise in the body. A monk is recommended to accept alms-food for the maintenance of his body, just as the owner of a decaying house uses props for its maintenance.[6]

Similarly, the mind is regarded as a house. When a house has an ill-thatched roof, rain enters and soaks the roof-beams and walls; in the same way, it is said, when a mind is 'undeveloped' or 'unguarded', desire enters, to penetrate and saturate all actions, whether of body, speech, or mind.[7] The commentary to one of these passages, which tells the story of the monk Nanda (in Chapter 5.1.2 above), makes the Buddha remark that formerly, when Nanda was inclined to return to the lay life, his 'individuality' was like an ill-thatched house, but that now he has attained *nibbāna*, it is well-thatched.[8] Many passages which speak of houses or 'huts' (*kuṭī* – a term both for a monk's cell within a monastery, and a hermitage retreat) are explained by the commentaries as referring metaphorically to the *attabhāva*, which may be closed or open to the rain of the 'defilements'.[9] The *attabhāva*, as we have seen, is the sense of individuality which appears to the unenlightened man, through the physical fact of the body, and the psychological fact of *asmi-māna*; what it 'really' (in 'ultimate' terms) refers to is the group of five *khandhā* in existence at any given moment in time. Accordingly, we find the *khandhā* spoken of as a house. Just as children play with houses made of earth (*paṃsvāgāra* – perhaps 'sandcastles') only so long as they retain desire and affection for them, and afterwards break them up and cease to play with them, so a monk should break up and abandon the five *khandhā* by destroying desire for them. Just as an old house thatched with dry, inflammable grass allows easy access to a fire, so a man who has desire for any of the objects of the six senses (including mind) allows easy access to Māra (the god of death). A man who grasps the *khandhā* as 'I' or 'mine' and then sees the terrible danger in this when he begins to practise the Buddhist Path is said to be like a sleeping house-owner who awakens to see his house on fire. The foolish man prey to fears and misfortunes (without the certainty which comes from wise practice of the Buddhist Path) is like an ill-thatched house prey to fire.* [10]

Traditionally in South Asian society, to speak of life as a householder is to speak of life in a village. We saw that as early as the *Upaniṣads*, the picture of the renouncer is of one who leaves the village for the forest. Accordingly, images of the village are used to express ideas of the individual and his psychology in the same way as images of a house. The six sense-bases are to be seen as an empty village, because they have no inhabiting self; and their corresponding external objects are like village-robbers who oppress and plunder the village. Birth, old age, and death 'afflict' the *khandhā* as village-robbers do a village. The body with its thirty-two parts (as defined in the meditation on the foulness of the body) is like a village with thirty-two families.[11]

Given that the individual is seen as a house or a village in this way, it is not surprising to find that the *locus classicus* for the memory of former lives, and the 'divine eye' which sees the death and rebirth of other beings, incorporates these images. When a monk remembers his past 'abodes', in the standard phrases we have met, it is said to be like a man going from one village to another; he knows with regard to each village 'there I stood in such and such a way, sat, spoke, and remained silent in such and such a way'. Similarly, when a monk sees the death and rebirth of other beings, it is like a man watching people come out of one house and enter another. The Buddha says that he sees people being reborn in a heaven just as one might watch a man walking towards, and entering a palatial house. Desire is the 'house-builder' who causes rebirth in *saṃsāra*. The commentaries here explain the 'house' as *attabhāva*; similarly, to the verse 'This was your old hut [*kuṭī*], you desire a new one. Discard the hope of a hut; a new hut will be painful again', the commentary explains the series of huts as a series of rebirths, a series of *attabhāva*. The word *niketa*, which can mean simply 'a house', is used in a series of terms designating a series of lives: 'in whatever former birth, former becoming, former dwelling-place [*niketa*]'.[12]

To live any one life in *saṃsāra*, then, is to live like a householder in a village, in the house of each 'individuality'. The association of ideas between the household life and rebirth, of course, is not limited to such figurative representations. Not to renounce desire by leaving home for the life of monkhood is par excellence the condition for further rebirth. It is

* The idea of ordinary life as being 'on fire' with the flames of desire is a common one, as we have seen.

said that just as an elephant trainer ties an elephant to a post to 'subdue his forest habits', so a monk is tied to the post of the Four Foundations of Mindfulness to subdue his 'householders' ways'. The commentary here explains 'householders' ways' as dependence on the 'five strands of sense-pleasure' (*pañca-kāma-guṇa*); and this connexion is frequent. Both the Buddha and the previous Buddha Vipassi left their lives as princes – symbolically leaving the epitome of the householder's life for that of the renouncer – and in doing so renounced a life of dependence on the 'five strands of sense-pleasure'. This connexion is so obvious to Buddhist eyes as to follow automatically: 'giving up the five strands of sense-pleasure, . . . leaving your home!' urges the Buddha. 'Living homeless' is explained by the commentary as 'not making a home in the five strands of sense-pleasure'; a monk is to reflect that it is unseemly for him to pursue the passions, since he has 'forsaken the passions, going forth from home to homelessness'. Leaving a home in the village is to leave family and kin: 'Leaving father and mother, sisters, kinsmen and brothers, abandoning the five strands of sense-pleasure Anuruddha indeed meditates.' The connexion of ideas is expressed in the comic evolution myth of the *Aggañña Sutta*, which satirises Brahmanical cosmogony. When first the characteristics distinguishing male and female appeared, sensual passion for each others' bodies arose in some beings, and because of this they began to indulge in sexual intercourse; other beings, disgusted, stoned them and forced them to build houses to conceal their immorality.[13]

We can see the way in which the literal and metaphorical senses of 'home' and 'homelessness' are blended immediately and naturally in *Theravāda* thought by two exegeses of a verse from the *Sutta Nipāta*. It occurs in the 'Chapter of Eights', from which I quoted a number of verses in Chapter 4, and pictures the 'ideal type' of the homeless wandering sage:

> Leaving home, wandering homeless,
> a sage makes no ties with the village.
> Empty of sense-desire, putting nothing before him
> he has no quarrel to make with anyone.[14]

The verse is explained both by its commentary, and by the *Haliddikāni Sutta* of the *Saṃyutta Nikāya*.[15] In the *Sutta*, the monk Mahākaccāna explains as follows: in 'leaving home' (*okaṃ pahāya*), the 'home' is each of the first four *khandhā* (body, feeling, sensation, mental formations), in which consciousness 'frequents the home' by being 'tied there through lust'. One 'does not frequent the home' by abandoning such lust. 'Wandering homeless' (*aniketa-sāri*) is explained metaphorically also, as not being bound to the impressions of the six senses. 'Making no ties in the village' and 'empty of sense-desire' are both explained literally. The word *apurekkharāno*, which I have translated literally as 'putting nothing before him', usually has the sense of not 'honouring' or 'choosing'; here it is taken as having more the sense of not 'anticipating' anything.[16] It is explained as not thinking 'may I have such-and-such a body [and the other *khandhā*] in the future'. The sage's having no quarrel with anyone has, of course, all the resonances which I described in Chapter 4.

The *Sutta Nipāta's* own commentary[17] explains 'leaving home' as 'rejecting (any) occasion [*okāsa*] for [the continuance of] consciousness based on (the other four *khandhā*),* by abandoning lust and desire'; 'wandering homeless' is explained as 'not frequenting the home(s) of the sense-objects, on account of desire'. 'Making no ties in the village' and 'empty of sense-desire' are again taken literally; while 'putting nothing before him' is explained as 'producing no future individuality'.

It is through this association of ideas that *oko* and *anoko*, originally 'home' and 'homeless(ness)' come to have the direct meanings 'attachment' and 'non-attachment'.[18] We can see exactly the same thing with the word *ālaya*. It has a simple meaning as 'home' or 'abode' in a quite literal sense; the extended meaning of 'attachment' is very frequent, and is found in a well-known passage where the Buddha hesitates to preach, immediately after his enlightenment. He thinks that no-one will understand his message, because 'beings are devoted to attachment, take pleasure in it, delight in it'.[19] The standard commentarial explanation of these phrases is that beings 'cling' (*ālayanti*) to the five strands of sense-pleasure. We have seen how closely the idea of these five strands is associated with the household life: if we follow the commentary to three of the hesitation-passages a little further, the connexion is put beyond doubt.[20] It is just like a king, we are told – again the king is taken as the epitome of the householder – who retires to his private pleasure garden, happily to enjoy its pleasures, and who 'is not willing to leave'. The verb used here, *nikkhamati*, can also refer as a technical term to the act of 'leaving home' to become a monk, and I think there are resonances of that sense here. The commentaries continue by likening to such a king all beings who 'take pleasure in their homes of [attachment to] sense-pleasure and desire', and so 'dwell in the round of *saṃsāra*'.

That the metaphor implicit in the use of *ālaya* to mean 'attachment' is not dead is shown by a conscious pun on it in the *Milinda Pañha*.[21] The king Milinda asks the monk Nāgasena a question: did not the Buddha say two contradictory things? He said both that 'danger is born from intimacy, dust is born of a house; the sage's vision is to be homeless and

* The sense of this phrase will be explained in Chapter 7.2.2.

without intimacy', and that 'one should build charming dwelling-places and lodge the learned (monks) therein'. Nāgasena explains that dwelling-places should be built in two cases: for nuns, and in the case of their being given to the order by pious laymen; but that 'a son of the Buddha' – that is, a monk who has left his home and family for the 'family' of the monkhood – 'should not feel attachment [or, "make a home"] out of his dwelling place' (*na . . . ālayo karaṇīyo nikete ti*).

The negative term *anālayo*, 'without *ālaya*', in both its literal and metaphorical senses, becomes a regular epithet for the enlightened sage;[22] *ālaya-samugghāta*, 'the destruction of "home-attachment"' becomes a regular epithet for *nibbāna*,[23] while the man who abandons all *ālayāni* is no longer subject to rebirth.[24]

Now that I have reconstructed the social and psychological resonances of house-imagery, we can see that the act of 'leaving home' has three stages: first, one must leave home physically by abandoning household life for the monkhood. Then, one must abandon home psychologically, by destroying desire for and attachment to the present 'individuality'. Third and last, one must – at the death of the 'body-house' – leave home ontologically by abandoning forever the village of *saṃsāra*.

5.3.2. Three forms of 'seclusion'

The division of 'leaving home' into three stages which I have just made follows a similar division into three of the concept of *viveka*, 'seclusion', contained in the *Theravāda* texts themselves. The three stages are 'seclusion of body, of mind, and of substrate'.[25] These three seclusions are given technical meanings in Buddhist specialist discourse, which I will explain in due course; I will also use them as pegs on which to hang an imaginative picture of the progress from ordinary man to enlightened saint, seen in terms of the gradual change from 'home' to 'homelessness'.

In the first place, one must leave home to become a monk: the standard term is *pabbajjā*, 'going forth', and the standard phrase is *agārasmā anagāriyaṃ pabbajjā*, 'going forth from home to homelessness'.[26] The standard scene is depicted as follows:

> A householder, or householder's son, or one reborn into another family hears [Buddhist teaching]. Through hearing that teaching, he acquires faith in the *Tathāgata*. Endowed with this faith that he has acquired, he reflects: the household life is confined, full of dust;* going forth is in the open. It is not easy for one who inhabits a house to live the holy life, wholly fulfilled and purified, polished like a conch-shell. Suppose now that I cut off hair and beard, put on the saffron robes, and go forth from home into homelessness?[27]

* The commentaries often explain this as 'the dust of the passions'; the image is clearly connected with the idea of religious progress as 'cleansing' or 'purification'.

In the earliest texts, this act of 'going forth' is sufficient basis for an individual to be thought directly and actively on the Path to *nibbāna*. Later, when matters had become more complex, and the distinction between village- and forest-dwelling monks had become a socially and symbolically accepted fact, the term 'seclusion of body' came to refer, in a technical sense, to the forest life as the ideal type of active renunciation.[28]

Becoming a monk, even as a forest ascetic, is not enough, of course: the Buddha tells a monk who 'lives alone and proclaims the virtues of living alone' that he (the Buddha) does not consider simple physical seclusion to be enough. There is another way, he says, of 'perfecting the solitary life'; 'when what is past is renounced; what is future is given up; when with regard to the individuality presently existing desire and lust are thoroughly subdued'. 'Living alone' is elsewhere explained as not having desire as a companion (literally 'as a second'); although a monk might dwell in forest hermitages, free from the noise and commotion of human society, still if he feels desire for the senses and their objects, he dwells 'with a companion'. The *Visuddhimagga* contains a story of two monks, one living in the forest, one in a large city temple. The forest-dweller visits the city-dweller, and surprised at his lack of possessions, his simple life free from material comforts, says 'For those like you, venerable sir, everywhere is a forest-dwelling.'[29]

The second stage, seclusion of mind, is given in the later literature a technical sense, referring to successive purifications of the mind through increased meditative absorption, or through the progressive abandoning of the fetters on the gradual path to enlightenment. In a larger perspective, this seclusion of mind can be seen as a metaphor for the entire orientation of Buddhist religious practice. We have seen that 'household life' is equated with the psychological fact of attachment to sense-pleasure; and that body and mind, both separately and together as an 'individuality' are expressed imaginatively as a house. 'Leaving home' in this sense simply means to undergo the appropriate behavioural and psychological changes which are held to lead to the cessation of rebirth. There is, however, a particular use to which the image is put, which expresses the experience and aims of someone *during the process of 'mental cultivation'*. Although an individual may have left home to become a monk, and although he may have begun on the specialist meditative life, still – according to Buddhist psychology – he will find that to his unenlightened mind there is an 'I', a 'self within'. Given the – temporary – reality of this 'inhabiting self', the image of the mind as a house, village, and so on, can be used to express this state of affairs. The modern *Theravāda* monk Nyanaponika, himself quoting from an older text, provides an illuminating example. I spoke in Chapter 3 of the process of 'insight' meditation, by which the process of experience is analysed in terms of the various categories of Buddhist psychology: 'the ability to classify any experience or concept into a known, non-valued impersonal category was held to be a technique for avoiding desire for the object thus classified' (Chapter 3.3.2). It was this technique which led to the simplification and ordering of experience called Purity of View. William James, writing of the appetite for purity in religion, remarked that: 'The saintly person becomes exceedingly sensitive to inner inconsistency, or discord, and mixture and confusion grow intolerable. All the mind's objects must be ordered with reference to the special spiritual excitement which is its keynote.' In relation to the 'retiring pietist', who resembles the 'quietistic Buddhist' whom I described in Chapter 4, he continues by suggesting that such a person avoids 'variety and confusion' by 'leaving disorder in the world at large, but making a smaller world in which he dwells himself and from which he eliminates it altogether'.[30]

Nyanaponika, in his pamphlet *The Power of Mindfulness*,[31] speaks of the practice of insight meditation as having 'The Functions of "Tidying" and "Naming"', and as being a process of 'tidying up the mental household' by identifying the elements of mental and physical activity in terms of Buddhist category analysis. He predicts that the meditator

> will everywhere be faced with a tangled mass of perceptions, thoughts, feelings, casual bodily movements, etc., showing a disorderliness which he certainly would not tolerate, for instance, in his living room. . . . It is the little daily negligence in thoughts, words, and deeds, going on for many years of our life (and as the Buddha teaches, for many existences) that is chiefly responsible for creating and tolerating that untidiness and confusion in our minds which we have described. The old Buddhist Teachers said 'Negligence produces a lot of dirt and dust, even a whole heap of refuse. It is as if in a house only a very little dirt collects in a day or two; but if this goes on for many years, it will grow into a vast heap of refuse.'*

The commentarial passage quoted here makes these remarks in explanation of the ideas that 'negligence is dust'. (We have seen the idea that the household life is 'dusty'.) The point is made that a young monk should not think that he can wait till he is older before he comes to 'understanding' through the practice of the Path.

The image of such an unenlightened 'self' living in a body-house is then used in Buddhism in a way which is common to other Indian systems. The senses are seen as 'doors' to the body-house; the paramount virtue of Buddhist practice, mindfulness (*sati*), is then expressed as 'being guarded

* Using a modern English phrase, we might say that the unenlightened meditator might be condemned to living in the house of his 'individuality', but he should not 'make a home' out of it.

as to the sense-doors'.[32] We have seen that in many ways village-imagery replicates house-imagery: an extended simile tells us of a 'border town' whose six gates are well guarded by a wise door-keeper, who only allows certain messengers through to the 'lord of the town'. 'The town is a metaphor [*adhivacanam*] for the body . . . the six gates a metaphor for the six senses . . . the door-keeper mindfulness . . . the lord of the town consciousness.'[33]

This sort of imagery, as I have said, is specific to a particular stage of practice and experience, according to Buddhist psychology, and should not be mistaken for representation of a theoretical idea of a 'self within'. This is shown clearly by a passage in the *Milinda Pañha*.[34] The king asks Nāgasena whether 'an experiencer' (*vedagu*) exists; the monk asks what he means by this, and the king explains it as an 'inner soul' (*abbhantare jīva*). This soul sees with the eye, hears with the ear, smells with the nose, . . . and is conscious of objects of thought with the mind. In just the way, he says, that they are sitting in the palace and can look out of any window they wish, so the 'inner soul' can look out of any sense-door it wishes. Nāgasena refuses to accept this picture, stressing the need for all the appropriate conditions to be present in order that any particular sensory or mental experience can take place. For instance, one cannot see a material object with the ear, hear a sound with the eye, and so on. His most important argument, for my present purposes, is this: if the latticed windows of the palace were removed, then they would be able to see material objects outside more easily; but if the eye were removed, it would be impossible to see any objects in 'the great space' which would remain.[35] From these and other considerations, he argues for the Buddhist explanation of sense-experience, 'in a talk connected with *Abhidhamma*' (that is, in terms of 'ultimately true' elements): 'Dependent on eye and material objects arises visual consciousness; co-nascent with it are sensory contact, feeling, perception, volition, one-pointedness [i.e. attention] and the life-principle.* Thus all these things arise through conditions, and no experiencer exists.'[36]

I showed earlier that Buddhism sees any talk of a self or an 'I' beyond the process of experience as a 'conceit'; here again, the causal account of experience is given, and the complementary lack of any use for the concept of an 'I' beyond it. In most other Indian systems which use the imagery of a self within the body-house – particularly those influenced by the *Sāṃkhya* conceptions I earlier contrasted with those of Buddhism – there is a soul or self within which is the 'owner of the body' (*dehin, śarīrin*) and 'the knower of the (sense-) field' (*kṣetra-jña*). It is

* On the 'life-principle', see Chapter 8.1.2.

because this is *not* the case for Buddhism that the following lines can be given as one of a list of wrong views which include the basic heresy of denying the validity of *karma*: 'Just as someone leaves one village and enters another, . . . just as someone leaves a house and enters another, so the soul enters another body.'[37]

When an individual comes to 'realise' the truth of the *anattā* doctrine which invalidates, 'ultimately', the use of such imagery, he reaches the third stage of 'leaving home', the third type of seclusion, seclusion from substrate.[38] The term 'substrate' refers to any and all of the things which form the basis of rebirth – desire, attachment, *karma*, the five *khandhā*; and the 'rejection' or 'absence' of substrate is a synonym for *nibbāna*.[39] Seclusion from substrate is thus explained in one place as follows: 'Defilement, the *khandhā*, and accumulation of *karma*, [*abhisaṃkhāra*]* are called substrate. Deathless *nibbāna*, the coming to rest of all conditioned things, is called "seclusion from substrate".'[40] The 'condition of seclusion' is said by a commentary to be 'the state of *nibbāna*, secluded from all conditioned things'.[41] This, then, is the final act of 'leaving home'. In a famous verse, the Buddha exclaims, on reaching enlightenment: 'I have wandered through many births in *saṃsāra*, seeking but not finding the housebuilder; repeated birth is full of suffering. Housebuilder! You are seen, you will not build a house again. All your rafters are broken, your ridge-pole is shattered. My mind is beyond conditioning, and has reached the end of desire.'[42]

I hope that all these pages of examples will have made evident the ubiquity and regularity of house-imagery in *Theravāda* thinking. I said earlier that this pattern of imagery represents a fundamental structure of the imagination, which unites all Buddhists, whatever their conceptual sophistication, into a single cultural world. Moreover, where Dumont's analysis of renunciation in India, and its metaphysical transcription as *saṃsāra/mokṣa*, was able to connect together the indigenous perception of the social system of Indian society with the soteriological ideas of its religious thought as a structural correspondence, our present immersion in the world of *Theravāda* imagination gives this formal connexion greater psychological content and depth. It is, perhaps, a misleading reification to speak in terms of 'vehicles' of thought. Nevertheless, we can, I think, differentiate thinking according to whether it is connected with more or less concrete images, whether it is more or less accompanied by immediate and unquestioned affective connotations and inferences, and whether it can more or less easily be appropriated consciously

* On this term, and its important use in connexion with consciousness as the vehicle of rebirth, see Chapter 7.1.1 and 7.1.3.

in an 'abstract' theoretical discourse. For the sociology of knowledge this differentiation would be made according to the relative distance of cognitive representations from their social basis, from their immersion in everyday behaviour and perception. In Chapter 5.1, we saw something of the everyday religious practices and assumptions of the ordinary Buddhist. In Chapter 5.2, we saw two concepts with which the intellectual tradition has systematised these 'conventional' practices and assumptions, and has related them to the 'ultimate' doctrine of *anattā*, and the complex analyses of personality and continuity which it entails. The discussion of house-imagery in the present section has, I hope, shown how this assimilation and hierarchisation of ideas into two 'truths' is possible; and how the thought of different individuals, or of one individual in moments of different reflective abstraction, can at one and the same time be characterised by great differences in the surface level of conceptual content and sophistication, and also represent manifestations of a *single* Indian and Buddhist cultural tradition.

6 'Neither the same nor different'

> Another occasion the mind often takes of comparing, is the very being of things; when, considering anything as existing at any determined time and place, we compare it with itself existing at another time, and thereon form the ideas of *identity* and *diversity*.
>
> John Locke, *An Essay concerning Human Understanding*, Book 2, Chapter 27

> If I say 'It will not be me, but one of my future selves', I do not imply that I will be that future self. He is one of my later selves, and I am one of his earlier selves. There is no underlying person who we both are . . .
>
> It is sometimes thought to be especially rational to act in our own best interests. But I suggest that the principle of self-interest has no force. There are only two genuine competitors in this particular field. One is the principle of biased rationality: do what will best achieve what you actually want. The other is the principle of impartiality: do what is in the best interests of everyone concerned.
>
> Derek Parfit (1971)*

At this point in my study of Buddhist thought, I will turn to some of those questions which I mentioned in the Introduction as arising from the denial of self. I will try to show where in Buddhist thinking we should look for an answer to them, and thus how the taboo on speaking of 'self' or 'person' in 'ultimate' discourse is integrated into a psychological and moral attitude of greater coherence than that which the doctrinal rigidity of the denial of self might seem to imply. In particular, I will deal with the problems of identity and difference in personality (with special reference to the sequence of lives in rebirth), and with the resulting attitude toward action and moral responsibility. In the first section of this chapter, I will discuss the doctrine of *anattā* in its later *Theravāda* application to the 'person', and will show how the rigorous insistence on the taboo against speaking of 'self' or 'person' is maintained. In the second section, I will deal with a style of Buddhist thinking which is less rigid, and which admits certain imagistic representations of continuity and rebirth as a

* In a note appended to a reprint of the paper in Burnyeat and Honderich (1979), entitled 'Postscript 1976', Parfit adds that 'talk about "successive selves" is only a *façon de parler*: taken as anything more it can be misleading'. Given that the conventional truth of Buddhism which speaks of a series of 'persons' is equally a *façon de parler*, the quotation is all the more apt to illustrate Buddhist ideas here.

means of explaining identity and difference. In both these sections I will be, for the most part, content simply to represent in more or less as many words the ideas and arguments which are found on the surface level of discourse in three theoretical texts of the *Theravāda* tradition, the *Kathāvatthu*, *Milinda Pañha* and *Visuddhimagga*. In the third section I will try to go beneath this surface level, to discover (using, loosely, the Chomskyan metaphor) the 'deep structure' of Buddhist thought about action, 'self' and 'other'. I will try to show how at this level moral responsibility for 'oneself' and compassionate concern for 'others' in *saṃsāra* are coalesced into a single underlying attitude; an attitude which then 'generates the surface syntax' of ideas about personality, rebirth, and moral action.

6.1. 'A person is not found'

The three texts from which I shall draw my material here all continue that style of Buddhist thinking which I described in Chapter 3 under the heading of 'right view'; that is, where a specific contentful theory is held to be correct, and is set against an opposing position which is represented as 'wrong view'. The *Kathāvatthu*, 'Points of Controversy', is a compilation of scholastic problems looked at from the *Theravāda* point of view. Traditionally it is a record of the different opinions expressed at the third Buddhist Council.[1] The 'dialogues' between the Theravādin and his opponents are markedly Socratic in character; their rigid logical pattern is of interest to the historian of Indian logic, but in my account I will replace the complex dialectics of the exchanges for a more discursive presentation of the *Theravāda* view. The *Milinda Pañha* is traditionally held to be the record of a meeting – perhaps based on some real event – between the Bactrian king Milinda (Menander) and the Indian monk Nāgasena. The king puts a series of beginners' or outsiders' questions to the monk, which allows the monk both to re-state and to develop certain basic Buddhist ideas. Although the monk's answers are phrased in such a way as to give an impression of logical argumentation and persuasion, the text equally bears something of the flavour of a Buddhist 'catechism'. The *Visuddhimagga*, finally, is as we have seen a masterpiece of scholarship, both as a summary of *Theravāda* doctrine and, as Ñāṇamoli has suggested,[2] 'a detailed manual for meditation masters'.

6.1.1. Four arguments

The relevant sections of the *Kathāvatthu* contain a debate between representatives of the *Theravāda* and the 'Personalist' school, which I mentioned in Chapter 5. We have very little evidence on which to base a reconstruction of their doctrine, and most of what we have, like the *Kathāvatthu*, is written from an opposing, and probably distorting, point of view.[3] I will restrict myself to presenting the *Theravāda* position. This can be organised as four main arguments: all of them are linguistic, the last explicitly so, and rest on the distinction between 'ultimate' and 'conventional' truth.

(i) The first point concerns the epistemological and ontological status of the 'person'. We have already met the basic argument: the impersonal elements of existence (*dhammā*) are the contents of ultimate truth, while the 'person', the sense of 'I' which appears in the thought and discourse of the unenlightened, is only conventionally true. The *Kathāvatthu* merely expresses this in abstract form. The elements of existence – by this time numbering fifty-seven* – are 'found' or 'known in real and ultimate fact' whereas the 'person' cannot be said to exist or be known in this way.[4] Moreover, the fifty-seven 'ultimate existents' are all necessarily separate from one another, and so the 'person' – if it exists – must be equally separate from any or all of them; but, in this case, any relation between (for example) the element 'body' (*rūpa*) and the 'person' will be the same as any relation between body and 'soul', which the entire Buddhist tradition rejects as the fifth and sixth of the Unanswered Questions. The same point is then put in a different way in the claim that any relationship between the 'person' and the 'ultimate existents' must be the same as one of the four possible relationships between a 'self' and the *khandhā* – as identical, self 'having' the *khandhā*, self 'in' the *khandhā*, or *khandhā* 'in' the self – which, as we have seen, are the kinds of assumption which are alleged to lie behind any Personality Belief, any mistaken view on the Unanswered Questions, and the phenomenological reality of the *attabhāva*, 'individuality'.[5]

(ii) The second argument concerns the description of rebirth in terms of a 'person': is it 'the same' or 'different'? To allege that 'a person transmigrates' is impossible, because the 'person' involved in the process cannot be said to remain the same, different, both or neither. (This is the standard four-fold disjunction of Indian logic.)[6] It is clear that this argument develops the fourth argument for *anattā*, which replaced the idea of a self as agent and experiencer with the lists of causally connected impersonal elements. The 'Collected Sayings on Cause' of the *Sutta-Piṭaka* had asked whether 'one person acts' and 'the same' or 'another experiences (the result)'; and whether the factors of Dependent Origina-

* Five *khandhā*, twelve 'sense-bases' (*āyatana*), eighteen 'elements' (*dhātu*), twenty-two 'controlling powers', or 'faculties' (*indriya*).

tion are caused by (the same) 'self' or (a different) 'other'. In both cases all four possible alternatives are rejected.[7] It is important to notice here that the fourth alternative, 'neither the same nor different', is explicitly rejected both by the *Sutta* and *Kathāvatthu* passages. This is because in these contexts we are in the realm of ultimate truth, in which the theory of impersonal elements is simply asserted categorically, as a denial of the opposed 'self-theory'. As we shall soon see, when more 'conventional' matters of moral agency and continuity are confronted (rather than ignored), it is this fourth alternative which is chosen to represent the relationship between the 'person' who acts and the one who is reborn to experience the consequences.

The *Kathāvatthu* continues by arguing that the straightforward idea that one and the same 'person' is subject to rebirth is unacceptable, because in a change of state from man to that of god, spirit, animal, from Brahmin to noble (or whatever), there must be some definite change, since otherwise there would be nothing to describe as 'death', nor could there be a series of different karmic results, good and bad states arising in sequence from good and bad actions.[8] The whole argument is summarised in the following way: since the impersonal elements are accepted by all Buddhist schools to be impermanent and subject to destruction, to speak of a 'person' here involves the inescapable dilemma between annihilationism and eternalism. 'If (one says that) when the *khandhā* disintegrate a person disintegrates, this is the view of annihilation, which the Buddha avoided; if (one says that) when the *khandhā* disintegrate the person does not disintegrate, the person is then eternal, just like *nibbāna*.'[9]

(iii) The third *Theravāda* argument concerns the allegedly needless superimposition of a 'person' on top of the impersonal elements as a description of action and experience. This takes up certain of the ideas in the third argument for *anattā* of the Suttas. In that argument, the 'self' could not be identical with feelings, since feelings must be pleasant, painful, or neutral; in all three cases they are impermanent, causally conditioned phenomena, none of which descriptions could apply to a 'self'. Here the *Kathāvatthu* argues that if the 'person' is 'a concept derived from the *khandhā*' it must be subject to the same types of description as they are.[10] That is, for example, if derived from a material form of a particular colour, the 'person' would have to be that colour; if derived from 'good feeling', 'bad feeling', or 'neutral feeling', it would have to be good, bad, or neutral. The point here is that ordinary experience always contains all three types of feeling (and many other mutually exclusive phenomena) in constantly changing succession; the 'person', as a concept derived from these phenomena, would have also to change constantly – an idea taken to be evidently repugnant. Moreover, since the elements of existence always appear at any moment in conjunction, why does one not derive the concept of a number of 'persons' equal to the number of elements in any given conjunction?[11] The fact of reflexivity in consciousness, the fact of 'self-awareness' does not prove there is a 'person' above and beyond any particular experience, since experience can, it is argued, occur without such awareness, and in that case does the 'person' not exist? In any case, whether one speaks of 'he who feels', the 'contemplator', or the one who 'looks on', there always remains the problem of the relation of this 'spectator-self' to the elements – is it the same or different?[12]

Just as the description of experience in terms of the impersonal elements is deemed to be sufficient, and the postulation of a 'person' beyond them pointless, so in the description of *karma* there is no need for any additional agent: if there is a 'doer' or 'instigator' (literally 'causer to be done') of action, who causes or instigates the 'doer/instigator'? Equally, if there is a 'person' who experiences the karmic result, separate from that result, why is there no 'experiencer of the person' and so on, according to the commentary, in an endless 'series of persons'? Putting the two together, there is the inevitable question 'are "doer" and "experiencer of the result" the same or different?' No answer is possible, since the four possible explanations for the causation of happiness and suffering – by self, other, both or neither – are all untenable.[13]

(iv) The first three arguments are all implicitly linguistic: they rest on the doctrine that ultimate truth in conceptual description and analysis consists *solely* of the separate, mutually discriminable impersonal elements of existence (*dhamma*), and that therefore any use of personal terms, like 'self' or 'person', in such discourse must necessarily violate the logical rules which determine the possible relationships of identity and difference between the various elements. The fourth and last argument explicitly confronts the citation by the 'Personalist' opponent of various passages in the Suttas in which the Buddha uses personal terms. Examples given include: 'there is the person who works for his own good'; 'that person (who attains *nibbāna*) after being reborn seven times at most'; the Four Pairs of Men and the Eight Persons.[14] To these and other examples, the Theravādin counters first by citing passages from the Suttas which state the doctrine of *anattā* clearly: 'all things are not-self', a 'being' is composite, like a chariot, everything should be looked on as empty,[15] and so on, in the manner to which Chapters 3 and 4 have accustomed us. There are three types of teacher in the world, we are then told: one who teaches the existence of a self 'in real and established fact' both in this life and in the next – this is eternalism; the second teaches a self in this life but not after death – this is annihilationism; the third teaches neither – this is the Supreme Buddha.[16] This re-statement of the original *anattā* position is accommodated to the use of personal terms cited by the opponent by an implicit appeal (made explicit by the commentary) to the two levels of truth. Did not the Buddha also speak of a 'butter-jar' and 'a constant supply of milk-rice', when it is impossible to make a jar out of butter, and there is no milk-rice which is 'permanent, fixed, eternal, not subject to change'? The commentary explains that 'the meaning of teachings is not always to be grasped according to the form of the verbal expression'. A 'butter-jar' or 'oil-jar' is not made out of butter or oil, but out of gold; it merely contains butter or oil. The phrase 'constant supply of milk-rice' refers simply to a guaranteed daily supply of rice. In the same way, 'person' is a conventional usage, dependent on the existence of the *khandhā*; Buddhas make use of two kinds of teaching, the conventional and the ultimate (as in Chapter 5.1.3 above).[17]

The *Visuddhimagga* makes the same point:

> In all becomings, births, destinies, stations and abodes, there appears only name-and-form,* occurring by means of the connexion between cause and effect. So (the wise man) sees no doer beyond the doing, no experiencer of the result beyond the occurrence of the result. He sees clearly, with right insight, that the wise use conventional forms of speech, (such that) when there is a doing, they speak of a 'doer', when the result occurs, they speak of 'one who experiences the result'. Here the Ancients said 'there is no doer of the deed, no experiencer of the result. Elements alone occur, that is right vision.'[18]

6.1.2. Acceptance of a taboo

It does not, I think, require an unusually developed critical curiosity to feel that this kind of argumentation in the later *Theravāda* texts perhaps still leaves some further questions to be asked, and perhaps does not in itself suggest how an individual Buddhist aspirant might situate himself in a moral universe – a universe which, while not necessarily peopled by Kantian subjects, all citizens in a 'Kingdom of Ends', still might offer a more recognisably human face to action and responsibility than does the theory of impersonal elements bound together by the automatic laws of *karma*. Before we see how such a moral universe comes to be built in *Theravāda* thought and imagination, we must be clear what precise function the relentless assertion of the ultimate truth of the *anattā* teaching has in the dynamics of Buddhist belief.

A forthright declaration that 'no person is to be found' occurs in the *Milinda Pañha*. At the beginning of their conversation the king politely

* The most simple, two-fold classification, which subsumes all the rest.

asks the monk his name, and receives the following reply: 'Sir, I am known as "Nāgasena"; my fellows in the religious life address me as "Nāgasena". Although my parents gave (me) the name "Nāgasena", . . . it is just an appellation, a form of speech, a description, a conventional usage; "Nāgasena" is only a name, for no person is found here.'[19] The king, not surprisingly perhaps rather taken aback, expostulates that if this is the case, who gives and receives alms, who keeps or breaks Buddhist precepts as a moral agent? These questions are left unanswered, however, as the king changes his approach and asks a different question (obviously intended by the Buddhist author(s) of the text to lead simply and directly into a Buddhist mode of explanation): if the monk is addressed as 'Nāgasena', what is the referent of this name? He enumerates the parts of the body, in the standard thirty-two phrases of Buddhist tradition, and the five *khandhā*, and is told that none of these is Nāgasena, nor does Nāgasena exist apart from them. He complains that 'Nāgasena' is then only a sound, and that the monk is not telling the truth. His interlocutor then turns the tables on him, asking whether the chariot in which he (the king) came can be identified as the pole, axle, or any of the parts which make it up. The king explains that because of the existence of the parts, the word 'chariot' exists 'as an appellation, a form of speech' and so on, using exactly the same words as had Nāgasena about his own name. The monk then quotes the comparison between a 'being' and a 'chariot' which we met earlier. This is how 'ultimately', he says 'no person is found'.[20]

I have argued that the doctrine of *anattā* is, in the last analysis, a linguistic taboo in technical discourse; and that this taboo functions as a soteriological strategy, in two ways: in detail it forms part of a particular style of meditative self-analysis within the practice of Buddhist specialists; in general, acceptance of the linguistic taboo preserves the identity and integrity of Buddhism as an Indian system separate from Brahmanism. The fashion in which the text of the *Milinda Pañha* places the categorical, not to say dogmatic, assertion of this taboo in the face of the king's understandable and reasonable questions shows how the doctrine here has, in the conceptual sphere, that air of ineluctable and incontestable necessity which is associated with the idea of *taboo* as a general category in the determination of behaviour; that is, where the term is taken to denote 'all those mechanisms of obedience which have ritual significance'.[21] We are here seeing how the linguistic taboo of *anattā* functions as an agent of what we might call 'Buddhicisation', through what Steiner calls 'the classification and identification of transgressions (which is associated with . . . processes of social learning)'.[22] Certainly, there *is* a Buddhist account of morality and responsibility which would answer the king's questions – the second and third sections of this chapter will approach it from the point of view of the apparent 'agent's' psychology, and Chapters 7 and 8 will approach it in terms of the general theory of continuity. The crucial point is, however, that any intellectual or personal dealings with such an account must be preceded by an assertion and acceptance of the *anattā* teaching as a right view, and a submission (or at least theoretical allegiance) to the soteriological strategy of which it forms the basis.

I can illustrate what I mean here by quoting another passage from the *Milinda*. It follows immediately after the one I have just mentioned: the conversation between monk and king has been broken off, to be resumed at the palace on the next day. On the way to it, one of the king's servants, who is accompanying the monk, takes up the thread of the previous conversation. He asks 'Sir, what is it which I address as "Nāgasena"?' The monk asks him what he thinks it is, and he replies 'the soul, the inner wind, which enters and comes out [as, or with the breath], that I conceive as "Nāgasena"'. We saw in Chapters 1 and 2 how a major part of the Brahmanical idea of *ātman* had to do with the idea of a 'life-breath', which developed into that of an enlivening self behind all bodily and mental functions, including breath. The reply put in the servant's mouth clearly partakes of that style of thinking. The monk, however, refuses to consider any of the subtler nuances of that sort of 'breath-mysticism', and proceeds matter-of-factly with a Buddhist approach. If this 'wind-breath' were to enter the body without leaving again, or leave without re-entering, would a man remain alive? At the servant's negative reply, Nāgasena proceeds by adducing the examples of conch-, bamboo-pipe-, and horn-blowers, whose expelled breath does not return, without their dying because of it. The servant declares himself incompetent to continue the conversation, and asks for an explanation. Nāgasena concludes 'this is not a soul; in-breathing and out-breathing are just activities set in motion by the body'.[23] He then gives the servant 'a talk on *Abhidhamma*' – that is, no doubt, a discussion in which all human phenomena are exhaustively explained by categories of impersonal elements. My point here is this: the text of the *Milinda* places this seemingly inconclusive episode in a prominent position at the start of the work, immediately after the assertion that 'a person is not found'. The servant's idea contains an oblique, but obvious reference to that whole strain of Indian religious thinking exemplified and symbolised by the *Upaniṣads*. Just as the episode is bracketed from the main narrative of the conversation between the king and the monk, so at the level of allusion and presupposition, the Brahmanical, Upaniṣadic, style of thinking is referred to in an aside, and dismissed. Within the narrative, the servant becomes a lay-follower. Taken as a whole, I would argue, the episode is an example of the way in which Buddhism – when adopting the right view stance – insists that all who are on the Path, lay-followers and beginning monks, accept *en bloc* the 'correct', Buddhist approach to psychological and spiritual conceptualisation, and equally reject all others.

6.2. Images of identity and difference

For Buddhism categorically to assert the distinction between conventional and ultimate truth is, of course, not enough. The questions which arise from its acceptance of the *saṃsāra/karma* belief system, and its simultaneous denial of a permanent self or person are legion, and King Milinda asks many of them, for example 'Who is reborn?' Nāgasena replies 'name-and-form'; not in the sense that it is reborn unchanged, but in the sense that 'one does a good or evil deed with (one) name-and-form, and because [or "by means"] of this deed [instrumental case] another name-and-form is reborn'.[1] If any 'individual' needs to be identified as the subject of the first verb here, it is the illusory and impermanent 'I' of each lifetime, the *attabhāva*. Each lifetime, delimited by the birth and death of the physical element, is a collection of impersonal elements – summarised here as 'name-and-form'. From this collection, with the help of 'the conceit "I am"', arises the phenomenological *sense* of personal agency which, in Buddhist eyes, is the only truth corresponding to the linguistic usage of active verbs with an implied subject. The monk continues by adducing a number of comparisons: a man who has stolen some mangoes claims himself to be innocent of theft, on the grounds that the mangoes he stole were different from the mangoes the owner had planted. A man lit a fire to warm himself, and left it alight when he went away; it burned a neighbour's field, but the man claims himself to be innocent on the grounds that the fire he failed to put out was different from the fire which burned the field. Similar defences are given by a man whose lamp set fire first to a house then to a whole village; and by a man who married a girl who had previously, as a child, been betrothed to another (along with the bride-price). Finally, a man who bought some milk from a herdsman left it for a day, during which time it turned to curds; on returning the next day, he demanded the milk he had bought, claiming that he had bought milk, not curds. In all these cases, the king is made to agree that the arguments are not to be accepted, as the phenomena in sequence are connected, the latter being 'produced from' the former. In the same way, the monk argues, 'however much one name-and-form ends with death, at rebirth there is another name-and-form produced from the former'.[2]

I argued in Chapter 5 that the ubiquity of house-imagery in the imagination of the *Theravāda* tradition enables us to connect together, as parts of a single cultural whole, the abstract constructions of Buddhist theory and the vivid 'perceptions' of psychology and ethics in everyday Buddhist life. In a similar way, in the present context, we can see that both at the ultimate level of Buddhist thinking about the continuity of impersonal phenomena, and at the conventional level at which the unenlightened 'I' needs to use concrete images to relate 'himself' to past and future births, use is made of regular and standard patterns of simile and imagery.

In the *Milinda Pañha*, the king asks another of the questions which Buddhism has had to face in connexion with its ideas of rebirth: 'is he who is reborn the same or different?' (from the one who died).[3] Nāgasena, accepting the conventional use of the personal pronoun, gives the answer which has become so common in the *Theravāda* tradition, both ancient and modern: 'neither the same nor different' (*na ca so na ca añño*). He argues this by a comparison with the connexion between youth and old age. When the king, in answer to the monk's question, declares that 'the young boy, tender, lying on his back, was one thing, I who am now full-grown am another', Nāgasena argues that in this case, 'you can have no mother or father, . . . nor be one of moral habit or of wisdom . . . Can it be that one (person) trains in a craft, another becomes proficient, (or) . . . that one (person) does an evil deed and they cut off the hands of another?' The king replies that this is not so, but asks for the explanation (since, of course, the previous discussion in which he was told that 'a person is not found' has warned him away from the idea that 'the same' person is young, old, and reborn). The monk explains '*I* was a young boy, . . . and *I* am now full-grown; all these [plural] are held together as one in dependence on the same body.' Two similes are given: a lamp burning all night long, which has different flames at different times, all held together in dependence on the same lamp; and milk, turning to curds, then to butter, then to ghee. 'Even so, a continuity of elements runs on; one arises, another ceases.' We have just met versions of both these similes, in the list of comparisons Nāgasena gave to the question 'who is reborn?' The image of milk-into-ghee we met in a previous chapter (4.2.3) in connexion with the different 'acquisitions of individuality'. The use of flame-imagery as a means of picturing continuity naturally gains breadth and resonance from its use in general psychology and ethics, most obviously as the flame of desire, and of 'life-as-suffering'. When the king asks how 'that which does not transmigrate, nevertheless is reborn'[4] the monk offers the famous image of one lamp's flame being lit from another. The *Visuddhimagga* explains:

while the flame of a lamp does not move over from one wick to another, yet the flame does not because of that fail to be produced, so too, while nothing whatever moves over from the past life to this life, nevertheless aggregates, bases and elements do not fail to be produced here, with aggregates, bases and elements in the past life as their condition, or in the future life with [those] here as their condition.[5]

On the ultimate level, then, the image of a sequence of flames expresses the idea of continuity without absolute identity; on the conventional level, the unenlightened individual can picture 'himself' and 'his' part in such a sequence as one flame – an image which, as I have suggested, will impress its suitability on a Buddhist mind for psychological and ethical reasons more general than that of its conceptual fitness to express identity and difference in continuity.

The same thing is true of the other main means of picturing continuity – the image of seeds and fruit. This also has many other ramifications in the imaginative self-perception of Buddhist psychology.* When king Milinda asks if there is any 'being' which 'passes over' from one body to another, and receives a negative reply, he concludes that moral responsibility is therefore abrogated (literally 'one is freed from evil deeds'). The monk argues that this is not so, and repeats the argument about stolen mangoes we have just met. Just as the stolen fruit exist 'in (causal) dependence' on the seeds planted by the owner, so 'because of deeds done by one name-and-form, another name-and-form is reborn', and so moral responsibility is not abrogated. The king next asks where deeds done by one name-and-form remain; the monk explains that it is not possible to point to a place where they remain, just as one cannot point to the fruit of a tree which has not yet borne fruit. 'As long as a continuity is not broken off', it is not possible to locate the 'storing' of karmic responsibility. The king next asks whether one who is reborn knows that he is to be reborn; the monk answers that he does, in the same way that 'a householder-farmer who casts seed on the earth, when it rains well (knows) "crops will be produced"'.[6]

On being asked the very general question 'what is *saṃsāra*?' Nāgasena replies:

Sir, what is born here dies here; having died here it uprises elsewhere; being born there, there it dies; having died there it uprises elsewhere . . . Suppose, sir, some man, having eaten a ripe mango, should plant the stone and a large mango-tree should grow from it and yield fruit; and that the man, having eaten a ripe mango from it too, should plant the stone and a large mango-tree should grow from it

* Which I shall explore in Chapter 7.3 below.

and yield fruit. In this way no end to those trees can be seen. Even so, sir, what is born here dies here . . .[7]

Exactly the same image had previously been used to express the idea that no 'earliest point' of *saṃsāra* could be found.[8] We have seen that the *Visuddhimagga* answers the question 'whose is the result [*phala*, also literally 'fruit'] of action, if there is no experiencer?' by an appeal to the imagery of fruit appearing on trees.[9] In the verses immediately following the categorical assertion that there is no 'doer' or 'experiencer' (cited in Chapter 6.1.1 above), it is said 'and so, while *kamma* and result thus causally maintain their round, as seed and tree succeed in turn, no first beginning can be shown'.[10]

These two types of imagery, of flames and seeds-and-fruit, are not the only means used to picture identity and difference between lives in the process of rebirth. Others include the transmission of learning from teacher to pupil and a person's reflection in a mirror.[11] The *Visuddhimagga* clearly summarises the point of them all. Explaining how rebirth does not involve consciousness moving from one place to another, nor its coming into existence without karmic conditions, it says:

Let [the similes of] an echo and so on [others given here include a lamp, the impression made by a seal, and a mirror-image] be the illustration here: there is neither identity nor difference in a sequence of continuity . . . If there were complete identity in a sequence of continuity there would be no curds (formed) from milk; if there were complete difference, the owner of the milk would not be (entitled to) the curds. This is the case with all conditioned things . . .[12]

6.3. Self and other: compassion

6.3.1. The perception of self and other in memory and anticipation

These, then, are some of the main images which Buddhism has used to picture identity and difference in karmic continuity. A fundamental question still remains: granted that a Buddhist might accept these images as giving an adequate account of rebirth on the cognitive level, and granted that he is prepared to see 'himself' as one flame of a continuously burning fire, or as one part of a sequence from seed to fruit, what motivation can the theory provide for one 'I' both to accept the karmic inheritance from past 'selves', and to work for the benefit of those in the future?* Put very simply, if someone is told by Buddhism that he is an unenlightened, illusory, and impermanent phenomenon, destined to

* I am not concerned with what the actual motives of Buddhists may have been, or may be, as they are discovered by empirical psychology and sociology. I am concerned with the inner logic of Buddhist ideas, with what their 'deep structure' is empowered to generate.

come to an end at the death of the body, but leaving a karmic inheritance for a future 'I' who is 'neither the same nor different' – why should he not reply 'what do I care?' The Buddhist answer to this, as we shall see, will never be without a moral exhortation, but it will be seen to be a religious prescription for action whose appeal rests on a far wider psychological basis than that provided by the question of moral retribution alone.

Let us look at the process of rebirth from the point of view of an unenlightened Buddhist, necessarily conceiving an 'I' as the subject of experience and agent of karmic action, but convinced by Buddhist theory that this 'conceit' is the most basic reason for his continuing lack of enlightenment. How is this 'I' to be related to past and future 'selves'? In the first place, as we saw in Chapter 4.1.1, concern for the past and future in the manner 'what was I', 'what will I be' and so on, is specifically castigated as a form of 'not paying careful attention' and as a manifestation of 'the conceit "I am"' in the past and future tenses.[1] This fact helps to explain the marked lack of emphasis on memory of former lives in Buddhist thought.[2] In western philosophical and psychological thinking, memory has always had a crucial role in the problem of personal identity and continuity; whether or not some other *criterion* of identity – such as the numerical identity of a space-occupying body or the possession of experiences by a pure Ego, for example – is thought more important theoretically, it has always been accepted that on the phenomenological level, a major part of the *sense* of continuity consists in a given relation of experiences in different times and places to a more or less unitary central nexus of self-interest, to what William James called the 'particular feeling of warmth and intimacy' which characterises subjectivity and memory alike.[3] It should be clear by now, I hope, that this 'central self-interest' is the prime target of Buddhist religious action, and so its extension into the past by memory is hardly likely to receive much emphasis. We have also seen that when the memory of past lives does take place, it gives access only to a series of *attabhāvā*, to a collection of 'individualities' determined as such by, amongst other things, social position and status. Again, since the whole burden of Buddhist soteriology – in the actual practice of virtuosos, and in the symbolic, orienting sense in which non-specialists appropriate the conceptual products of asceticism – is to destroy any position in the social system of *saṃsāra*, it is not surprising that such a memory plays little active part in religious life. Although the memory-of-former-lives forms part of one of the standard versions of the Buddha's enlightenment, it is by no means necessary for every person's enlightenment.[4] According to a text of the Indian *Sarvāstivāda* school,[5] the purpose of the attainment is not verification of *karma*, rebirth, and so on, but the increase of disgust for *saṃsāra*.

If any individual attains to such a memory, what is to be the relation between the present, remembering 'self', and the 'individualities' of past lives which are remembered?[6] If the 'person' who is reborn from one life to the next is 'neither the same nor different' from the one that died, it seems obvious that the balance will shift towards the 'different' pole the further from any given life memory goes. To be sure, there is some 'sameness' preserved through the impersonal connexion of *karma*, through the objective fact that the collections of impersonal elements in past lives happen to be connected in temporal extension with those of the present. But subjectively, as far as any '"I"-conceiving individual' is concerned, the 'persons' are as much, if not more, like 'others' as 'selves'. As Demieville has shown,[7] the attainment of memory-of-past-lives is always accompanied in Buddhist texts by other 'special attainments', especially by that of the 'divine eye' which sees the death and rebirth of other beings in *saṃsāra*. While these two attainments can be differentiated *cognitively* – there is obviously a theoretical distinction to be drawn between one line or one series of rebirths and all other such lines or series – nevertheless, *affectively* the past 'selves' seen in the memory-of-former-lives and the 'others' seen with the 'divine eye' are *equidistant* from the present, observing 'I'.

The idea that self and other have the same epistemological and soteriological status can be seen in a large number of different contexts in Buddhist thought. We saw in Chapter 5 that the phrase 'in this individuality' was used to distinguish the present life from those of past and future in a sequence of rebirths. The very same phrase is also used to differentiate a present 'self' from contemporary 'others' in matters of meditation practice and ethics.[8] We have encountered 'the conceit "I am"' many times, in many contexts, but so far only in relation to the psychology of an individual, considered in itself. It is, however, often referred to in connexion with a comparison between self and others: there are three forms, that one is 'better', 'equal', or 'worse' than others.[9] When these three forms of 'conceit' are lost by a monk at the attainment of Arhatship, it is said – very significantly – that as well as being indifferent to sense-pleasures and 'having nothing' he remains 'engaged in the practice of mercy and compassion for (all) living things'.[10] We can begin now to connect the ethical and psychological relation between lives in one continuity with the mainstream of Buddhist ethics and psychology generally. In the meditation practice of the Divine Abidings (which is recommended for all character-types)[11] the practice of the first, 'loving-kindness', takes as its objects 'beings', 'persons', 'those endowed with individuality'. The object of the practice is 'breaking down the barriers' between self, and others, whether these be dear friends, neutral persons, or enemies. The monk is to see the equality of all beings to himself – not in the sense that he is to have the 'conceit' of equality between real selves, but in the sense of 'not making the distinction "this is another being"'. The end result of this practice, as of the second and third – 'compassion' and 'sympathetic joy' – is the attainment of the fourth Abiding, 'equanimity', which 'sees the equality of (all) beings'. That is, it regards the *attabhāvā* of 'self' and 'others' with the same serene, impartial eye, since the objects of all the Abidings are but 'mental objects consisting in concepts'.[12]

6.3.2. What is suffering?

A detailed analysis of the concept of *dukkha*, variously translatable as 'suffering', 'pain', 'unhappiness', 'unsatisfactoriness', and so on, leads to the same conclusion. For the monk, it is both diagnosis of and homeopathic treatment for life-in-*saṃsāra*. Interpreters of Buddhism have often been puzzled by the idea of *dukkha* – it is clearly wrong to suggest that life is experienced as continuous suffering, and Buddhism has been thought a little over-pessimistic and peevish to suggest that what suffering there is overshadows any pleasure. Two things lead one to a correct understanding. First, *dukkha* is most precisely translated as 'frustration' or 'unsatisfactoriness' – and this is a judgement passed not as a description of life but as a reflective conclusion drawn from soteriologically oriented premises. Second, the suffering, or 'unsatisfactoriness' is not purely personal, but includes the experience of all beings, as a characterisation of saṃsāric life as a whole, when considered in contrast to the state of *nibbāna*. There are, we are told,[13] three kinds of *dukkha*. 'Ordinary suffering' is everyday physical and mental pain, contrasted with ordinary happiness, or indifferent feelings. 'Suffering through change' is the unsatisfactoriness alleged to be inherent in the fact that all feelings, all mental and physical states are impermanent and subject to change. This sort of suffering can be registered phenomenologically as 'ordinary suffering' through distress at the cessation of pleasant feeling; but more generally, it is not so much an actual state of distress as a proper seriousness in the face of impermanence and death: 'When it is seen that that which is impermanent is unsatisfactory, there can be no occurrence of blissful feeling.'[14] It was the reflection, arrived at in meditative solitude, that 'indeed this world is in distress: one is born, grows old, dies and is reborn. No-one knows the escape from this suffering, this growing old and dying', which led the previous Buddha Vipassī to leave his life of ease as a prince and seek release.[15]

The third form of *dukkha* is 'suffering through (the fact of) conditioned existence'. In part, this is connected with the previous idea of suffering through change and impermanence. The Buddha declares: 'When I said "whatever is experienced is (a case of) suffering", it was spoken in connexion with the nature of constructed things to decay, waste away, fade away and cease, and change.'[16] Generally, the idea that what is 'constructed' or 'conditioned' is in itself a form of suffering depends on the whole of Buddhist doctrine, on the disjunction between what is causally conditioned and the unconditioned *nibbāna*, and on the system of value-judgements which is entailed by it.* Thus *dukkha* in Buddhist thought represents not a life-denying pessimism, but (part of) a specific soteriological project. Earlier I used the medical metaphor of describing *dukkha* as homeopathic treatment of saṃsāric life diagnosed as 'unsatisfactory'. Robinson,[17] who rightly draws attention to the positive descriptions of life, both as a man and as a god, in Buddhist texts, uses an idea from comparative religion to make a similar point. Arguing from the observation that in many cultures initiation into a warrior brotherhood or shamanistic guild takes the form of an ordeal by suffering – perhaps ritualised – before the transformation into the new status, he says that concentration on *dukkha* in Buddhism is thus 'a state of prolonged initiation, lasting until *nirvāṇa* is attained. The Buddha rejected physical mortification, but in its place he put mental mortification, the contemplation of universal suffering.' This comparison should certainly not be taken too far, but I think its basic point is sound. That is, to see life as 'suffering' represents not an empirically derived judgement on life, but a goal-oriented soteriological project. It is an attitude which devalues ordinary life in comparison with *nibbāna*; an attitude in which any individual experience, however fortunate (like that of the Buddhas Vipassī and Gotama before they renounced the life of privileged royalty for that of a mendicant), is submerged in a wider reflection on the impermanence and conditionality of saṃsāric existence as a whole.

The most important and fundamental practice of the *Theravāda* life which aims to put an end to suffering is that of insight meditation, in which what appears to be 'personal experience' is broken down into its constituent, impersonal elements and their impermanence seen as a form of 'unsatisfactoriness'. When I discussed this practice in Chapter 3, I spoke of it only as a form of self-perception. In fact, it is always said that the analyses must be carried out both 'internally' and 'externally' – that is, as the commentaries[18] gloss, with regard to the groups of *khandhā* of both 'self' and 'others'. The 'Great Discourse on the Foundations of

* Rāhula's modern exposition ((1967) pp. 20–6) of this type of *dukkha* has to interpolate several pages of doctrine in order to make explicit why it is 'suffering'.

Mindfulness'[19] repeats this injunction in every paragraph. While of course it will be far easier, more vivid and compelling to apply any sort of meditative reflection to one's own experience, the conclusions drawn from it, according to Buddhism, are to be applied to all 'beings'.

6.3.3. Compassion and the rationality of Buddhist action

If we recognise the close connexions between the perception of universal *dukkha*, 'self' and 'other' seen as *attabhāvā* of equal significance, and the sequence of rebirths as containing 'persons' who are 'neither the same nor different' from one another, we will be able to appreciate the insight behind Poussin's words: 'if a Buddhist undergoes the discipline which leads to *nirvāṇa* – that is, the discipline owing to which no new being is to be born in his stead – it is in order to diminish by one the number of living and suffering beings'.[20] Dumont has also seen the connexion: 'Again, it is not one man with a particular existence who is liberated, a whole string of existences comes to an end, having previously become condensed in the renouncing individual: he is not only himself; there is here a necessary link with what has been called Buddhist charity.'[21] We might express the point of view of any given, individual 'I' in the following way. The world of *saṃsāra* represents, as it were, a four-dimensional throng of 'individualities': some of these happen to be connected with 'him' in a linear temporal series, and so represent past and future 'selves'; some are not thus connected, and so remain for ever 'others'. The crucial point is this: unless he is an omniscient Buddha, or a monk who has acquired the memory of former lives (that is to say, for Buddhist theory itself practically no-one) *any given individual cannot know which of these are which.* Accordingly, the rationale for action which acceptance of Buddhism furnishes provides neither for simple self-interest nor for self-denying altruism. The attitude to all 'individualities', whether past and future 'selves', past, future, or contemporary 'others' is the same – loving-kindness, compassion, sympathetic joy, and equanimity.

Those familiar with contemporary discussions of personal identity in English-language philosophy will see how the Buddhist attitude fits in with what is called the qualitative notion of identity; and, since inheritances from the past and – especially – anticipations of the future are crucial to notions of rationality in moral thought and assessment, how, through the idea that moral agency in *karma* provides at one and the same time for the future benefit of descendant 'selves' (who are 'neither the same (as) nor different (from)' the agent) and 'others' (which two categories, indeed, a present 'self' cannot distinguish from each other), Buddhism conceives as part of such a qualitative identity a version of rational action which includes necessarily the dimension of altruism.[22]

Equally, those familiar with *Mahāyāna* Buddhist thought will have been struck immediately by the similarity between the 'deep structure' I have claimed for *Theravāda* ideas, and the image of the ideal religious agent of *Mahāyāna*: the *Bodhisattva*, who combines deep insight into the selflessness of persons and things with universal compassion for suffering beings, and who takes as his motto for action 'the equality of self and other'.[23] One could say that the appearance on the surface level of *Mahāyāna* discourse of such an idea represents not a new departure in Buddhist thought, but a bringing to consciousness of what remains in *Theravāda* at an unconscious, 'deep structure' level.

Many parallels to the ideal conduct of a *Bodhisattva* can be adduced from *Theravāda* sources. In an earlier life as Sumedha, Gotama – the Buddha of our era – made the vow to become a 'Supreme Buddha', to help all beings cross to the 'other shore' of *nibbāna*, rather than attain Arhatship, enlightenment in and for itself. The birth of a Buddha is the birth of the 'one person' who conduces to 'the good of the many, the happiness of the many, (who is born) out of compassion for the world, for the welfare, good and happiness of gods and men'. His decision to preach the Buddhist *Dhamma*, having reached enlightenment, but then hesitating to do so, was taken 'out of compassion for beings'. Towards the end of his life he told his followers more than once that 'whatever is to be done by a teacher seeking the welfare of his disciples, that has been done by me out of compassion for you', and he was begged to stay alive for the same reason. He tells his first disciples to go and preach 'for the good of the many, the happiness of the many, out of compassion'; the released man teaches because his mind is moved by 'mercy and compassion' and the same compassion is said to be the reason for monks teaching generally. As we have seen, in *Theravāda* history there has come to be recognised a distinction between two types of monk, the village-dwelling 'priest', ministering to the needs of ordinary people, and the forest-dwelling 'hermit', whose life is oriented towards meditative seclusion. One of the earliest and most prestigious practitioners of the hermit life recognised by the tradition is Mahākassapa, who is made to say that the purpose of such a life is one's own present happiness, and one's compassion for others in the future who may be inspired to imitate the example.[24]

It is not my concern here to discuss why the *Theravāda* tradition has chosen to emphasise the ideals of renunciation and ascetic self-restraint rather than compassion and involvement. One hopes that nowadays we have superseded the simplistic *a priori* ethnography which seeks to deduce cultural traits such as 'life-affirmation', 'life-denial', 'world-acceptance', or 'world-rejection', from the apparent logic of the ideals pictured in the textual tradition. Certainly, we possess ethnographic accounts which have stressed the positive, 'loving' aspects of modern *Theravāda*, and the negative 'individualistic' aspects of *Mahāyāna* societies.[25] In any case, my point here is neither ethnographic nor historical. Because of the inner logic of its ideas, Buddhism has been able to achieve a number of things which *prima facie* acquaintance with the doctrine of *anattā* would seem to render impossible. On the social level, it has been able to legitimate a full and positive involvement with the 'conventional' world of society, providing a rubric for those who appear to themselves as individuals under which they might feel both a justifiable moral concern for themselves, and also a non-ascetic, 'non-heroic' altruistic concern for others (at least in aspiration). On the individual level, the fact that moral action of any sort involves compassion avoids the cold, nihilistic aloofness which has seemed inherent in the denial of self.* This underlying and unconscious structure of ideas provides the possibility of individual feeling for moral responsibility. The patterns of imagery which we met in the second section of this chapter provide the concrete, conscious means of karmic self-perception in a doctrine of rebirth without reincarnation. It is against this background of Buddhism as practised and experienced, that the intellectual tradition of *Theravāda* – in verbal contest with Brahmanical thought and with scholastic opponents within the Buddhist fold – has been able to insist so fiercely and rigidly, as we saw in the first section, that 'in ultimate truth' no permanent 'self' or 'person is found'.

* As it seemed, influentially, to Weber and Schweitzer, by whom the terms 'cold', 'aloof', 'world-denying' and so on were first used.

Part IV

Continuity

7 Conditioning and consciousness

> It is around the verb *saṃskṛ* – the activity which shapes, arranges together, consolidates, and brings to completion – that the reflections of the Buddha are concentrated, as were concentrated those of the *Brāhmaṇas* before him, for it is in it that one finds the key to these two systems which posit a certain kind of action as the source of reality.
>
> Lilian Silburn (1955) p. 200

> Man, to be sure, merits and earns much in his dwelling. For he cultivates the growing things of the earth and takes care of his increase.
>
> Martin Heidegger (1971) p. 217*

Chapters 5 and 6 have dealt with 'conventional' matters of personality and rebirth, and with the form of self-perception and the attitude to action in Buddhism, which result from this *Weltanschauung*. In this chapter, and the next, I will turn to the *Theravāda*'s 'ultimate' account of continuity (in any form, whether within one life or across 'lifetimes' in rebirth). My discussion of this account will have two main levels. On one hand, I will simply present the facts of *Theravāda* thought on the matter, and show the ways in which it has manipulated the lists of impersonal element-categories in which alone ultimate doctrine consists, in order to provide an answer to the problem. On the other hand, along with this presentation of *Theravāda* thinking, I shall be concerned to relate it to its cultural and social context; that is, to its Brahmanical cultural heritage and to its continuing place in the peasant society of South Asia. It is possible to regard *Theravāda* doctrine here simply as an inter-related conceptual whole, as an ensemble addressed to, and designed to provide a coherent account of, the more or less single issue of continuity in time. Naturally, modern *Theravāda* authors tend to take this approach.[1] While not denying that this is a possible and valid approach to doctrine, I shall wish rather to examine the various steps of the *Theravāda* conceptual dance separately, and to derive their choreographed unity not from the essential logical nexus of a philosophical position, but from the various historical realities of Indian and Buddhist culture, from the various conceptual needs and projects which have arisen in the particular circumstances of the Buddhist tradition.

* From a discussion of a poem by Hölderlin, entitled *Poetically, man dwells.*

In this chapter, I shall be concerned with the overall Buddhist account of temporality, with its attitude to continuity in time as the result of a 'constructive activity' which produces and conditions the existence and nature of further life, and with the 'constructed' nature of consciousness in the life thus produced. In the first two sections, I will present these ideas, setting them firmly in their specific cultural context. In the third section, I will continue the study of Buddhist imagery which I began in Chapter 5. Here I will explore the use of vegetation imagery in representing the ideas of 'construction', consciousness, and time. I will, as in the case of house imagery, try to use this pattern of imagistic representation as a means both to understand the 'deep structure' of Buddhist thought, and to appreciate the relation of this specialist, intellectual thinking to certain general features of life in Buddhist society.

7.1. The construction(s) of temporal existence

7.1.1. *Abhisaṃkhāra*: 'constructing' and 'constructed'

The two fundamental themes in the Buddhist attitude to the continuity of life and time, its creation and cessation, are both derived from the previous Brahmanical tradition, in slightly different ways. The first of these is the idea of constructing future existence by action; and the second is the focus on the consciousness of the religious virtuoso as the theatre of religious achievement, and the criterion of religious value. It is in this consciousness that it is possible for the process of constructing future existence in *saṃsāra* gradually to cease.

We saw in Chapter 1 how, in the *Brāhmaṇas*, the Brahmin priesthood urged their clients – actual and potential – to concentrate on sacrificial ritual as the only means by which they could 'produce and order a sequence of time in which to live'. 'Time and continuity', I said, 'were not simply and deterministically given to man; rather, they are the result of a constant effort at prolongation, a constant pushing forward of life supported by the magical power of the sacrifice.' This constructive activity of the ritual produced both the ordering and continuation of the cosmic cycle as a whole, and a new life after death for the particular person who had performed the sacrifice. We saw also, in connexion with the evolution of the idea of *karma* as the generalisation to all action of motifs previously associated with sacrificial ritual, that words derived from the verbs *kṛ*, or *saṃs-kṛ*, to 'do, perform, make, form, construct', were ubiquitous. For example, the word *karma* itself, the term for the 'world of what is well-performed' (*sukṛtāṃ/sukṛtasya loka*), and the idea of constructing a self or person by sacrifice (*aiṣṭikam ātmānaṃ saṃskaroti*).

Buddhism adopted both the attitude and the terminology, making constructions, or 'formations' (*saṃkhāra*) basic to its account of *karma* and rebirth. Perhaps Buddhism's most important contribution to this development of the concept of *karma* was to have made the crucial act a mental one, a 'volition' or 'intention' (*cetanā*) such that it was the presence of this, rather than the external act alone, which became the karmically significant force. It was the French scholar Silburn who first drew detailed attention to the complex of ideas in Brahmanical thought relating sacrificial activity to the construction of temporal existence, and who stressed that it is this intellectual heritage which informs Buddhist thinking: speaking of the Buddhist idea of *abhisaṃskāra* (Pali *abhisaṃkhāra*), which she translates as 'intention and organisation', she writes

> in order that (an) act should have a temporal consequence, it must be brought to completion and taken on [as one's own]. This bringing to completion is expressed by the verb *abhisaṃskṛ* – and is not unconnected with the bringing to completion of the sacrificial activity in which the sacrificer 'takes on the sacrifice as a whole to make of it his enduring person'.[1]

We saw also in Chapter 1 that the final version of the *saṃsāra-karma-mokṣa* belief system incorporated the Brahmanical interpretation of – perhaps one should say also its reaction to – the institution of world-renunciatory asceticism. In this interpretation, apart from the simple parallel between the social polarity of life-in-society and world-renunciation and the metaphysical polarity of *saṃsāra* and *mokṣa*, the crucial development for my present purpose was that in which the motifs of earlier Brahmanical thought – including that of the construction of future life in time through activity – were changed from being descriptions of a system of external ritual to being parts of an interiorised pattern of self-perception. In this development there took place the crucial reversal of values, which I have mentioned; that is, whereas in earlier Brahmanical thought, the construction, by sacrifice, of a sequence of time and of a new life for the reborn person had been claimed as a possible, desirable, but by no means inevitable eventuality, now it came to be accepted as the *inevitable* result of all such action. This fate was consigned to the ordinary man as a lesser goal, while the highest religious aim, that of the renouncer, became precisely the opposite – escape from the inevitable sequence of action and rebirth altogether, by the manipulation of conscious self-perception in order to attain 'saving knowledge'.

There are, then, two ways in which Buddhist thought organised psychological space in a manner derived from its Indian cultural heritage. In the first place, it accepted the general perception of the cosmos in terms of *saṃsāra*, *karma* and *mokṣa* as a conceptual background. In the second place, as the important figure against this background, it placed the consciousness of the religious virtuoso as focus and criterion of soteriological activity, and in opposition to the acquisition by the specialist (in this case the Buddhist virtuoso monk) of 'saving knowledge' (here 'insight' or 'wisdom'), it set the inevitable prolongation of life-in-*saṃsāra* by the 'ignorant' action of the ordinary man. It is in this light, I think, that we can understand the position of the concepts of *saṃkhāra* and *abhisaṃkhāra* in Buddhist psychological thought, and how it is that these concepts were seen in conjunction with that of *viññāṇa*, 'consciousness', as the basis of the ultimate Buddhist account of temporality and continuity.

The concept of (*abhi*)*saṃkhāra* contains within it both active and passive meanings: using the distinction between the Latin indicative present for 'he makes' and the past passive participle for '(is) made', Poussin writes '*saṃskāra* can mean equally "that which *conficit*" as "that which is *confectus*"'.[2] Frauwallner, making a similar distinction in German, translates *saṃkhāra* as *Gestaltung*, 'formation', and remarks that it can refer not only to what 'is formed' (*gestaltet*), but also, because 'it means that something is put into a state of readiness, which will continue to take effect in the future', to 'impulses of will' or 'intentions' (*Willensregungen*).[3] Both the activity which constructs temporal reality, and the temporal reality thus constructed, are *saṃkhāra*. In the taxonomy of phenomena in Buddhist thought, *saṃkhāra* is the fourth of the five 'categories' (*khandhā*) which make up the human person. It is a mental category ('name' as opposed to 'form') and is thus normally translated 'mental formations'; 'inherited forces'[4] is a good alternative, as it suggests both the dynamic, forward-looking ideas of volition, desire, and so on, and also the fact that these saṃsaric phenomena are themselves held to be conditioned by and arise out of former *karma*.

In the following quotations, words derived from the roots *saṃ-kṛ* and *abhisaṃ-kṛ* are ubiquitous and are held to be mutually defining: the technical term 'formation' (*saṃkhāra*) is explained as '(people) form a construction, thus they are "formations"' (*saṃkhatam abhisaṃkharotīti tasmā saṃkhārā*). Similarly, those who 'take delight in formations' are said to 'construct (further) formations which conduce to rebirth'. Happiness and suffering are said not to arise out of the activity of a self, another, and so on, but 'have as their cause the intention behind (acts of) body, . . . speech, . . . (and) mind'. 'If an ignorant person performs (such) a meritorious, demeritorious or neutral act, (his) consciousness is on its way to merit, demerit (or) neither.*[5] The body is not to be seen

* I have deliberately translated the words *saṃkhatam*/*saṃkhāram abhisaṃkharoti* in three ways, as 'form a construction', 'construct a formation', and 'perform an act'. This is very inelegant as English translation, but it is meant to convey something of the different

as belonging to any self – it is neither 'yours' nor 'others' – but as '(a product of) previous *karma*, (as) something constructed and willed (into existence)'. 'Whatever a man wills, intends, and is obsessed by,* that becomes an object for the persistence of consciousness . . .; consciousness thus persisting, thus having grown, there comes to be the appearance of future rebirth.' It is only when 'consciousness is not persisting, not growing, not forming constructions', that there comes to be release.[6]

7.1.2. Different versions of the Dependent Origination list

The technical term *saṃkhāra*, as well as being the fourth of the five *khandhā*, is also found as the second of the twelve elements of the Dependent Origination list, connecting the first, 'ignorance', and the third, 'consciousness'. It is clear that the passages I have just quoted which use words derived from *(abhi)saṃs-kṛ* are equivalent to these first steps of Dependent Origination, expressed in an expanded prose style, instead of the simple formulae 'conditioned by ignorance there arise formations, conditioned by formations there arises consciousness'. When I discussed Dependent Origination in Chapter 3, I mentioned that one of the difficulties in its interpretation arises from the presence in it of two 'births', that of consciousness/name-and-form (numbers three and four) and of 'birth' itself (number eleven). The *Theravāda* tradition has resolved this difficulty by taking the twelve-fold sequence as a whole to refer to three lives, as shown by the left-hand column of Table 1.

The list can also be taken in other ways: for example, in two sections ((i) and (ii)), from ignorance to sense-contact (numbers one to six) as the past into the present, and from feeling to old age and death (numbers seven to twelve) as the present into the future. The idea thrown into relief by this temporal perspective is that present experience (sense-contact and feeling together as the presently occurring moment) exist as the result of previous *karma*; while desire for that experience sets the karmic wheel spinning onwards again into the future.[7] Yet another interpretation, in four sections, starts from this idea of desire or craving as the cause of karmic continuity. (The list, of course, includes both the 'original sins' of Indian religion – desire and ignorance.) In the four-fold interpretation shown in the right-hand column of Table 1, the elements numbered eight to ten (*karma*-process A) are taken as 'past causes'; numbers eleven and twelve (rebirth-process B) as 'present effects'; numbers one and two

senses of the words, as technical Buddhist terms with the cultural history I have described in the text, but which refer also to a straightforward idea of moral agency.

* This last verb is from the same root as *anusaya*, the 'latent tendencies' which, though unconscious, condition character and behaviour as seen in Chapter 3.2.4.

Table 1

past life	1 ignorance	(i)	*karma*-process	C
	2 formations			
present life	3 consciousness		rebirth-process	D
	4 name-and-form			
	5 the six senses			
	6 sense-contact			
	7 feeling			
	8 craving	(ii)	*karma*-process	A
	9 grasping			
	10 becoming			
future life	11 birth		rebirth-process	B
	12 old age and death			

(*karma*-process C) as present causes; and numbers three to seven (rebirth-process D) as future effects. Hence the linear sequence A–D runs from numbers eight to twelve, and one to seven.[8]

There are, then, various ways of interpreting the list, of which the division into three lives is but one. The existence of mutually compatible interpretations both bears witness to the ingenuity of Buddhist scholasticism, and also suggests the nature of the criteria according to which the twelve elements were arranged into their final form. In this final form, ethical concerns and eschatological theory are woven together as warp and woof of a single cloth. The pattern of this cloth expresses, exhaustively and consistently, the entirety of basic Buddhist doctrine, in such a way as to allow any one focal point of teaching – needed for preaching, commentarial explanation, and so on – to be extracted, while at the same time allowing a means to connect this focal point with Buddhist doctrine as a whole. The fundamental function of the Dependent Origination list, both in these interpretative details and *en masse* as a symbol, is to express the Buddhist idea of the 'Wheel of Life' turning continuously without any self as a causal agent or persisting subject of *karma*. The particular interpretation of the sequence as referring to three lives certainly makes good sense, representing in a certain perspective one segment of the continuously turning wheel. Nevertheless it cannot be doubted, I think, that this sort of presentation of the Dependent Origination list demonstrates a surface rationalisation and organisation of symbols and technical terms of the system once generated, rather than a determining influence on the generation of the system in itself. One such original determinant, I would argue, is precisely the connexion of ideas I have been tracing between (*abhi-*)*saṃkhāra* and *viññāṇa*, 'constructions' and 'consciousness'. So far, I have outlined the early history of this connexion of ideas in Brahmanical thought and early Buddhist psychology. I will now continue by following its further elaboration in the commentarial literature.

7.1.3. 'Construction-consciousness'; and its cessation

The word *abhisaṃkhāra* is used in the Suttas outside the eschatological context to express the idea of a previously determined or arranged force. A monk who arranges in advance that his absorption in a certain meditative state will last a particular length of time, is said to make a 'previous determination' (*pubbe abhisaṃkhāra*) to that effect.[9] A wheel will roll along as long as lasts 'the impulse which set it moving' (*yāvatikā abhisaṃkhārassa gati*).[10] When used in the eschatological context, then, the term *abhisaṃkhāra* denotes a karmically forceful, 'constructive' act, which determines a specific length of *saṃsāric* continuity. There are said to be three types of such acts, as we have already seen: meritorious, demeritorious, and neutral.[11] It is this 'basis of constructions' which 'determines the suffering experienced through rebirth'.[12] The idea of such constructions, such acts, as being conditions for the future occurrence of an appropriate form of consciousness, which is itself the 'dependently originated' condition for psycho-physical individuality ('name-and-form') and so on, is expressed also by the use of the term 'construction-consciousness' (*abhisaṃkhāra-viññāna*); a term which simply omits the sense of temporal-causal sequence from the use of its two component words in conjunction. A poem of the *Sutta Nipāta* consists of a dialogue between a householder and the Buddha on the respective merits of household and homeless life. Both the poem and its commentary are full of allusions to, and resonances of, that whole strain of house-imagery which I depicted in Chapter 5. When the Buddha tells the householder that he has no cow, no bull as 'leader of the herd', and so on, the commentary explains that the herd of cows are various types of *saṃkhāra* and *abhisaṃkhāra*, while the 'leader of the herd' is 'construction-consciousness'.[13] In a similar vein, as an explanation of the idea that a sage lives 'homeless', we read that this is because 'he makes no occasion for consciousness associated with constructions'. The other commentary on the same passage explains 'there is for him no occasion for construction-consciousness and the like'.[14]

The creation of continued life in time through this construction-consciousness, then, expresses in a technical sense the basic Buddhist idea of conditioning, itself derived from the previous Brahmanical ideas on the creation and maintenance of temporality. Now that the cessation of this process is the desired goal, a corresponding way of *not* creating future life (seen as inevitable, rather than desirable but not inevitable) has to be incorporated into the elucidation of construction-consciousness.

This was done, in the following way. Just as in the pattern of house-imagery, the first, physical act of leaving home to become a monk is the first step of a gradual process of psychological and ontological 'leaving home', so in the case of construction-consciousness, the path from household life-in-*saṃsāra* to release in *nirvāṇa* involves a *gradual* lessening of the karmic construction of future life. This is expressed in the texts, as usual, as a progression through the four stages of the stream-winner, once-returner, non-returner, and *Arhat*. In the case of the first of these, 'through the destruction of construction-consciousness (consequent on) the insight belonging to the path of stream-winning, whatever name-and-form might arise in beginningless *saṃsāra* – apart from the seven lives [which are left] – is destroyed, calmed, sets (like the sun), and subsides'.[15] The same thing is true of the once-returner and non-returner, who have ended saṃsāric existence, apart from the two lives and one life they have left respectively. In the case of the *Arhat*, all name-and-form whatever are destroyed.

In considering the detailed nature of the destruction of construction-consciousness, especially when it applies to the released man, the *Arhat*, we must bear in mind two things. First, that 'the attainment of *nibbāna*' can be spoken of in two ways, general/imprecise and specific/precise; that is, in the general sense in which *nibbāna* simply reverses or ends all those processes which engender life-in-*saṃsāra*, and the particular sense in which *nibbāna* has two stages. These two stages are *nibbāna*-in-life, or '*nibbāna*-with-substrate', where the monk is released from desire and suffering, but still has a psycho-physical name-and-form as the basis of continued life; and '*nibbāna*-without-substrate', final *nibbāna*, when he dies. The second thing to be borne in mind is the difference between the active and passive senses of (*abhi*)*saṃkhāra*, as 'that which *conficit*' and 'that which is *confectus*'. The texts which speak of the destruction or cessation of construction-consciousness sometimes do so in the general sense, in which the process of conditioning, as I have described it, is simply imagined or stated to be stopped. In the exposition of the Dependent Origination list, corresponding to the form 'conditioned by A there is B', there is a negative form 'through the cessation of A there is the cessation of B' (A-*nirodhā* B-*nirodho*). In one of the versions of the list, it is said that suffering arises conditioned by (*inter alia*) 'formations' and 'consciousness', and ceases with their cessation. The commentary explains 'formations' as the three types of construction, and consciousness as 'construction-consciousness born together with *karma*'.[16] Similarly, when the Buddha explains that for a sage who is not caught in sense-pleasure, consciousness 'is not fixed in (the round of) rebirth' and 'is destroyed', the commentaries explain this consciousness as construction-consciousness.[17] In these kinds of context, the idea of 'destroying construction-consciousness' is to be understood only in the general way in which *nibbāna* as reversal and cessation of *saṃsāra* is understood.

It is in connexion with the precise, two-stage sense of *nibbāna* that we can use the distinction between active and passive senses of (*abhi*)-*saṃkhāra* to elucidate the texts which speak in this context of the cessation of construction-consciousness. Corresponding to the active and passive senses here, we might translate *abhisaṃkhāra-viññāṇa* as either *constructive*-consciousness or as *constructed*-consciousness. Thus, when the preliminary *nibbāna*-with-substrate occurs, then *constructive*-consciousness is completely destroyed and no further life will be constructed. However, there is still a *constructed*-consciousness which exists as a 'karmically-resultant-consciousness' (*vipāka-viññāṇa*). In general, enlightened men are said to be still affected by the results of their past bad *karma*, although they create no new *karma*: the most famous example is of Moggallāna, one of the Buddha's chief disciples, who – though enlightened – died a violent death as a result of having killed his parents in a former life. Each released saint preserves a particular character, an individual personality, thanks to the presence of the 'traces' or 'impregnations' of his particular karmic heritage.[18] Of course, the very fact that there *is* a psycho-physical substrate during the remainder of a released saint's lifetime shows the continuing effect of *karma*.

Although an enlightened man's consciousness is a karmic result, it is not limited by usual saṃsāric constraints. It is 'indescribable, infinite, radiant on every side'.[19] We should not misinterpret this kind of consciousness as a 'cosmic consciousness', in the manner of the *Vedānta* picture of ultimate reality as *sat-cit-ānanda*, 'Being-Consciousness-Bliss'. Rather, like the 'widespread, far-reaching, immeasurable' mind with which the monk experiencing the Divine Abidings is endowed, and like the 'immeasurable mind' of a monk in the fourth meditative stage,[20] and like the Sphere of Infinite Consciousness attained as the seventh stage, this consciousness will cease, at final *nibbāna*. When final *nibbāna* is attained, everything ceases, even those states and virtues which Buddhism itself holds dear. The passage I quoted earlier which spoke of the destruction of construction-consciousness by a stream-winner, says in the case of the *Arhat*: 'through the cessation of the last consciousness of an *Arhat* who is dying into final *nibbāna*-without-substrate, wisdom, mindfulness, and (all) name-and-form cease'.[21] This 'last consciousness' is said to be a *constructed*-consciousness, and it is through the 'cessation by non-arising, in virtue of the non-arising' of this *constructed*-consciousness that *nibbāna* becomes final.[22] It is in this way that in final *nibbāna* the cessation of *constructed*-consciousness succeeds that of *constructive*-consciousness which took place at the attainment of *nibbāna*-in-life.

The concept of *abhisaṃkhāra-viññāṇa*, then, refers to that consciousness which continues throughout *saṃsāra*, both constructing future temporal existence, and itself constituting the medium for the temporal reality thus constructed. One should not think that this construction-consciousness refers to some special type or level of consciousness which is different from the ordinary element *viññāṇa*. It is, rather, a means of describing that ordinary element, a way of depicting it as an unenlightened constructed phenomenon, which produces continuity and rebirth for the 'persons' who appear in it. It does not refer to the elongation of a personalised consciousness through time, but to the creation of time by the accumulation of instances – or as we shall see in the next chapter, of 'moments' – of the impersonal element-category consciousness; on to this consciousness, as on to a screen, are projected a series of lives, a sequence of 'individualities'.

7.1.4. Food and the 'descending spirit'

In the introduction to this chapter, I said I would present Buddhist ultimate ideas in terms of their Brahmanical antecedents, and their continuing cultural depth. We have now seen how the idea of the construction of temporal existence by sacrifice in Brahmanical thought, and the project of internalising sacrificial motifs which was initiated by the institution of world-renunciation, issued finally in Buddhism in the complexities of the scholastic commentarial idea of a construction-consciousness. Let me now turn to two other ideas, which are found in the Buddhist textual tradition at all levels of intellectual sophistication, but which also reflect modes and patterns of thinking more accessible to the ordinary man. Often, this kind of connexion is phrased as a 'popularisation', or even 'distortion' of 'real' Buddhist thought. Rather, let us say that Buddhist ultimate doctrine systematises, from a virtuoso point of view, structures of thought which existed previously, and which continue to exist, in a wider cultural dispersion. The two such ideas I will examine here are those of consciousness as a 'food' for the sustenance of future life; and of the 'descent' of consciousness, seen as a *gandhabba*-spirit, as an explanation of rebirth.

We met in Chapter 1 the idea that the inhabitants of other worlds, or of the next life, needed food to sustain their existence: the sacrifice was the food of the gods, the Fathers needed food to continue their shadowy existence, and the 'store' of good deeds was seen as a kind of nourishment for the next life, equivalent to food in this world. This theme was taken up again in the *Upaniṣads*, in a variety of speculative elaborations:

'from food arise all beings . . . verily, they obtain all food, who worship *Brahman* as food'. If we remember the complex of ideas about fire, as the 'soul within', which was the microcosmic correlate of the Sun as symbol of the vivifying warmth of the universe, we will understand the following:

The sun takes food (to itself) by means of its rays; by this means it gives out heat. Supplied with food, living beings here digest [*pacanti*, literally 'cook']; fire burns by means of food. Food is the source of this whole (universe); the source of food is time; the source of time is the sun . . . The oblation which is offered in the fire, that it leads to the sun. The sun rains it down with its rays; from that there is food, and from food there is the arising of beings.

As in earlier Brahmanical sacrificial speculation, then, the revolutions of the sun in a sequence of days and nights produce the possibility of life and continuity in time for living beings; and this process is maintained by the sacrificial fire. In the new developments of the *Upaniṣads*, however, it is not surprising to read that 'there is something else to be known. There is a further development of the Self-sacrifice, namely food and the eater of food . . . The conscious person is within material nature; he is the eater who eats the food of the material world.'[23] One can see here, I think, an Indian correlate of the pattern of ideas described by Bachelard, in his investigation of the western imaginative picture of fire in past centuries: 'it is perhaps the idea that fire feeds itself like a living creature which is foremost in the opinions developed about fire by our unconscious'. Proceeding by an analysis of the idea that the stars and sun feed themselves by consuming 'terrestrial exhalations', he concludes) 'Were it not for the myth of digestion, were it not for this entirely stomachal rhythm of the Greater Being that is the Universe, a Being who sleeps and eats, adjusting his diet to the day and to the night, many prescientific or poetic intuitions would be inexplicable.'[24]

The development of this strain of speculative thought in virtuoso Indian religion took place against a general cultural background – not, indeed, confined to India – in which offerings of food to spirits, gods, dead ancestors, and the like, formed the major instrument of magico-religious practice and aspiration.[25] Throughout the development of Buddhist virtuoso ideas, equally, these 'magical-animistic' ideas and practices, as Ames called them, have held sway over 'popular' Buddhism.[26]

It is in this light that one should see the use of the idea of food (*āhāra*) in Buddhist eschatology. The Buddha teaches that 'all beings subsist on food'.[27] There is much emphasis in Buddhist teaching on the physical facts of food – its necessity for the creation and maintenance of the body (it is regularly said to be 'originated from food'), the moral need to avoid delight and over-indulgence in it (for what are ultimately, of course, eschatological reasons), and so on. The idea of particular importance here, however, is that of the Four Foods – 'solid (physical) food', 'sense-impressions', 'mental volitions', and 'consciousness'.[28] These four foods are instruments of continuity, 'for the maintenance of beings that exist or are seeking to exist', in two connected senses. First, existence and experience in any one lifetime will last as long as there is physical and mental material for it, just as a lamp will burn for as long as it has 'nourishing fuel' (*āhāra*), but will go out when without such nourishment. Secondly, it is desire for all four forms of nourishment which conditions future life: 'these four foods have desire as their cause, arise from it, are born from it, and originate from it'. 'Desire' in this passage is then traced back through the normal Dependent Origination sequence, through feeling, sense-contact, the six senses, name-and-form, consciousness, to formations and ignorance. If we take this sequence in its forward direction, *āhāra* will be seen to stand for number nine, 'grasping' (*upādāna*),[29] and to imply the future process of rebirth ('becoming, birth, old age and death') *en masse*. Elsewhere we read that 'what is born, become, arisen, made, constructed, is impermanent, formed of decay and death, a seat of disease, perishable, originated from food . . .; the escape from this is peace, . . . the coming to rest of (all) formations, bliss'.[30]

We have seen how closely the idea of 'volition' or 'intention' is tied to that of 'forming constructions' which condition consciousness in the process of *karma*. In the doctrine of the Four Foods, the third and fourth, 'mental volitions' and 'consciousness', clearly represent that same process. In the commentarial tradition, the consciousness-food is often explained technically as the first 'moment' of consciousness at rebirth ('re-linking', *paṭisandhi*), and also at least once as construction-consciousness.[31] The 'ultimate' Buddhist attitude here is well demonstrated by the following passage: a monk asks the Buddha 'who eats consciousness-food?' The Buddha reproves him strongly for asking an 'unfit question', and replaces it with the more correct formulation 'of what is consciousness the food?' The answer is that 'consciousness-food is the cause of the appearance of rebirth in the future'. In a similar vein, we read that when there is desire for any of the Four Foods, 'consciousness is established and grows; (when this is so) there is descent of name-and-form, . . . increase in constructions, . . . the appearance of rebirth in the future'.[32]

In this last passage we find mention of the second theme from 'popular' religion which is adapted in Buddhist virtuoso thought. This is the idea of name-and-form, consciousness, or a *gandhabba*-spirit 'descending' at the moment of (re)birth. Already early in the present century, Poussin,[33] speaking of the distinction between Buddhism as a 'discipline of salvation' and the 'religions' with which it combines in social and historical actuality, had remarked on a regular pattern of ideas, which he expressed as follows (using somewhat outmoded terminology): 'we know that the aborigines [of India], as is the case with many savages, believed in reincarnations; they explained conception by the descent of some disincarnated spirit who had previously inhabited a human or an animal body, or even a tree'. We can see a version of this idea in the use of the *gandhabba* (Sanskrit *gandharva*) in Buddhism. In Indian mythology from earliest Vedic times, the *gandharva* was a celestial spirit, particularly a musician, who lived in a city in the clouds. We saw earlier how in the *Upaniṣads*, the vitalising cycle of water from clouds to earth was used to represent the saṃsāric life-cycle. Moreover, the *gandharva* was associated also in mythology with the 'cosmic waters' which existed before the creation of the world. From both these ideas, the *gandharva* came to be linked with the ideas of generation of life, of birth from the womb.[34] In Buddhist texts, the *gandhabba* appears ordinarily as one of the many types of spirit; but also in the following way: 'Monks, it is on conjunction of three things that there is conception . . . If there is coitus of the parents, and it is the mother's season, and the *gandhabba* is present, . . . there is conception.' The idea is repeated in the *Milinda Pañha*, where a further element from mythology is added. The king quotes this passage concerning the need for three things in conjunction if conception is to take place, and then adduces certain apparently contradictory cases of miraculous births where no coitus occurred. This is explained by the monk as resulting from the entreaty by Sakka, king of the gods, to various *devas* in the heavens, that when their lifespan there is exhausted they should 'descend' into an earthly womb, out of compassion for the needs of the 'parents'. (One example is the need of two elderly ascetics, who cannot have children in the normal way because of their vows of asceticism, for an attendant in their old age.) This application of the idea obviously shares a common mythopoeic origin with the legendary birth of the Buddha, who descends consciously and out of choice from the *Tuṣita* heaven into his mother's womb.[35]

The term 'descent' is also used in connexion with certain of the elements of ultimate Buddhist theory to denote birth.[36] It is found by itself as a regular synonym of birth: 'birth, origin, descent, appearance'. We read that for a man who lives seeing enjoyment in the 'fetters', 'there is descent of consciousness. Conditioned by consciousness there is name-and-form' (and so on in the usual list). Similarly, 'there is descent of consciousness; when there is descent, there is name-and-form' (and so on). The Buddha asks 'were consciousness not to descend into the mother's womb, would there arise therein name-and-form?' and 'were consciousness, once descended, to become extinguished, would name-and-form appear in this world?' (He receives, naturally, negative replies.)[37]

The relationship between consciousness and name-and-form in the Dependent Origination list is very close; indeed they are on occasion said to be mutually conditioning, like two bundles of reeds which lean against one another for support. Accordingly, we read also of the 'descent of name-and-form'. A man who lives seeing enjoyment in the fetters brings about future 'descent of name-and-form'. 'Whatever a man wills, . . . becomes an object for the persistence of consciousness [as in Chapter 7.1.1 above] . . . Consciousness thus persisting and having grown, there is descent of name-and-form.' When there is desire for the Four Foods, it is said, then consciousness 'persists and grows' and there is 'descent of name-and-form'. The *Visuddhimagga* explains consciousness in the Dependent Origination lists as 're-linking', and name-and-form as 'descent'.[38]

For the sake of formal clarity, we can distinguish these two uses of the term 'descent', in connexion with the two ultimate elements of consciousness and name-and-form, in the following way: in the former case, the first 'moment' of consciousness, when it is about to join with the material causes of an embryo, is the descent. In technical terms this is 're-linking consciousness', in 'popular' language it is the *gandhabba*, or the 'being seeking rebirth', or 'the being about to enter the womb'.[39] In the latter case, it is at the moment when these elements have already been conjoined, and the psycho-physical unity of the embryo ('name-and-form') is thus formed, that there is said to be descent.

In this first section, I have described the development in which certain ideas from Brahmanical sacrificial thought previous to the Buddha, and from the continuing thought and practice of the ordinary Buddhist, have been taken up in Buddhist philosophy. We can thus understand how Buddhism represents a single, though internally differentiated cultural field. At one extreme of this range, there is the peasant, for whom the life of constant agricultural toil, repeatedly engaged on the same tasks and in the same social hierarchy, is the concrete form in which *saṃsāra* exists. Drawing on millennia of cultural history, in which such a life has been set against the ideal renouncer-monk's escape from such toil and suffering, it will be easy for him (should he bother with matters of such abstractedness) to imagine the truth of the Buddhist doctrine he hears preached, that the construction of continuity in time consists in the continual and repeated creation of the necessary nourishment. Similarly, understanding birth as the descent of a (doubtless ill-defined) spirit, he will be able more or less easily to construe the transformation of this idea in Buddhist doctrine, that consciousness descends into the mother's body, to form a being constructed out of the *karma* resulting from previous lives-in-*saṃsāra*.

At the other extreme of the cultural field of Buddhism, there is (for example) the modern western intellectual monk Nyanatiloka. In a suitably modern 'scientific' spirit, he replaces the idea of karmic 'formations' or 'constructions' with that of '*karma*-energy', in explaining rebirth as follows:

> According to Buddhism, there are three factors necessary for the rebirth of a human being, that is, for the formation of the embryo in the mother's womb. They are: the female ovum, the male sperm, and the *karma*-energy, *kamma-vega*, which in the *Suttas* is metaphorically called the *gandhabba*, i.e. 'ghost'. This *karma*-energy is sent forth by a dying individual at the moment of his death. Father and mother only provide the necessary physical material for the formation of the embryonic body. With regard to the characteristic features, the tendencies and faculties lying latent in the embryo, the Buddha's teaching may be explained in the following way: The dying individual, with his whole being convulsively clinging to life, at the very moment of his death, sends forth *karmic* energies which, like a flash of lightning, hit at a new mother's womb ready for conception. Thus, through the impinging of the *karma*-energies on the ovum and the sperm, there arises, just as a precipitate, the so-called primary cell.[40]

7.2. The stations of evolving consciousness

We have seen that the thought of certain very influential religious specialists in India at the time of the Buddha took as a fundamental project the internalising and psychologising of Brahmanical sacrificial ideas. In the previous section I identified as one result of this project the Buddhist idea of a construction-consciousness, which was the agentive element, and medium, of continuity in time. In the present section, I will pursue further the role of consciousness in continuity; and we shall see how certain elements from Buddhist ethical theory, and from the supposed meditative experience of monks, were transformed into a system of temporal and cosmological extension.

7.2.1. Consciousness transmigrates

We have seen that the Buddha vigorously repudiated the idea that it was consciousness which transmigrated *unchanged*.[1] It is quite clear, nevertheless, that consciousness is the element whose appearance in a new life constitutes birth (as we have seen, this is its 'descent'); and it is its departure which signifies death. When a man dies, his body 'with consciousness gone' lies like a lump of wood, abandoned by disgusted relatives. When 'vitality, heat and consciousness' leave the body at death, it lies like a 'senseless' (or 'mindless') lump of wood. Although the good disciple's body at death will be scattered and devoured by dogs, still his mind (*citta*) will 'rise up and reach the heights'. In answer to the general question 'what part of (a man) transmigrates?' we read 'mind'.[2] (Although for some purposes the terms *viññāṇa*, 'consciousness', and *citta*, 'mind' are differentiated in Buddhist thought, here they amount to the same thing. Indeed, they are explicitly said to be synonyms: 'that which is called "mind", "thought" [*manas*], "consciousness"'.)[3] The solution to the apparent paradox here of course is to see consciousness or mind as a *constantly changing* continuant; ultimately, this solution evolved into the theory of the momentariness, which I shall treat at length in Chapter 8. Here I want to stress that although consciousness is said to change constantly, and is not thought of as a unitary or personal 'soul', still it is the element whose evolution is the thread on which continuity and the series of lives-in-*saṃsāra* are woven.

Consciousness is not only the agentive element of rebirth, but of continuity in time in any sense. The concept which Buddhism employs here is that of the 'stations' of consciousness (*viññāṇa-ṭṭhiti*). When consciousness is 'stationed' in any of these, it produces and continues the phenomenal world. The Pali Text Society's Dictionary translates *viññāṇa-ṭṭhiti* as '*viññāṇa*-duration, phase of mental life', and comments that 'the emphasis is on duration or *continuation* rather than place, which would be *ṭhāna*'.[4] We shall see, however, that there is a considerable ambiguity and homogeneity between this idea of the stations of consciousness and the static places of heaven and hell in Buddhist cosmology.

In order to understand the way in which Buddhist thought uses this concept to cover two rather different groups of stations – as we shall see, the 'four' and the 'seven' – and the way in which the idea is transformed into a system of cosmology, we must remember the fundamental ambiguity in the Brahmanical idea of *loka*, on which I remarked earlier, in Chapter 1.2.5. That is, in the speculations of Brahmanical sacrificial thought, a *loka* was both a sphere to which sacrificial action gave temporary, 'sacred', access in this life, and also a destiny which might be attained continuously after death. In the *Brāhmaṇas*, as Gonda says

> that these states of existence in which one is ritually reborn are made by oneself and that in the future one will receive that form of existence and those circumstances in life which one has gained or brought on oneself before that future birth may be understood from . . . [the phrase] 'man (or the personal principle in him) is born into the existence made (by him)'.[5]

In the *Upaniṣads*, where sacrificial action is replaced by psychological practices, 'spiritual growth culminating in mental identification with provinces or aspects of material or immaterial reality leads to participation in the respective *lokas*'.[6] Thus, in the *Upaniṣads* we read 'he who meditates on mind [*citta*] as *Brahman*, he obtains the mind-worlds; himself fixed, stationed, imperturbable, he obtains worlds that are fixed, stationed, imperturbable. As far as mind extends, so far he has freedom of movement.'[7]

7.2.2. The four and the seven 'stations'

The ambiguity and homogeneity between states of mind which may be attained temporarily through religious practice and destinies to be attained continuously after death, can be seen also in the Buddhist idea of an 'evolving consciousness' (*saṃvattanika-viññāṇa*). We have already met the simple term *saṃvattanika*, 'evolve', 'leads to', etc., in the phrase 'constructions which lead to (re)birth'. It is also used to speak of 'beings coming to (rebirth in) the Radiant World', of meritorious acts which 'lead to heaven', of bad deeds which 'lead to hell, an animal's womb, or the *Peta*-realm', and of ways of thinking which do or do not 'lead to *nibbāna*'.[8] In the *Sutta* which speaks of 'evolving consciousness', and the commentary to it, the terms used to denote the places or spheres to which consciousness evolves display the two senses of the word *loka*.[9] In the first place, there are three types of meditative reflection through which 'at the break-up of the body, after death, it is possible that (the monk's) evolving consciousness might reach imperturbability'. We have seen that through meritorious, demeritorious or 'neutral' ('imperturbable') constructions, consciousness attains to these three types of existence. The commentary here mentions this idea, saying that the 'imperturbable' types here lead to the fourth, fifth and sixth meditative states (the fourth *jhāna*, the plane of 'infinite space', and that of 'infinite consciousness'). These remarks were doubtless made in order to accord with the text of the *Sutta*, which goes on to show types of meditative reflection which lead to the seventh and eighth stages, the planes of 'nothing' and 'neither perception nor non-perception'. On all these occasions, it is possible for 'evolving consciousness' *after death* to attain each particular stage. Elsewhere, of course, these stages are attained before death, temporarily, during the course of meditation.

With a similar ambiguity and homogeneity, the concept of stations of consciousness covers both meditative states and ethical attitudes of mind in the present life, and also destinies for it after death. We have already met the general idea of consciousness being stationed, or 'persisting': 'whatever a man wills, intends, . . . becomes an object for the persistence [or stationing] of consciousness; consciousness thus persisting [stationed]' (and so on).[10] Similarly, we learnt that 'all beings subsist on (or "persist through") (the four) foods', while the foods function 'for the maintenance (or "persistence") of beings'. (All words here for 'stationing', 'persistence', 'maintenance' are connected with *ṭhiti.*) It is, then, the persistence, maintenance or stationing of consciousness which is fundamental to continuity. In the first place, this stationing comes about through the moral (or rather, immoral) event of attachment, and the constructions which are thereby created. When a poem declares that the Buddha 'knows all stations of consciousness', the commentary explains that there are two sorts: four stations 'by virtue of constructions', and seven stations 'by virtue of rebirth'.[11] In the former case, the four stations are the four other *khandhā*, the constituents of personality; and it is by becoming attached to these four that consciousness 'is maintained and persists'.[12] The commentaries here explain consciousness as construction-consciousness, or *karma*-consciousness. We saw in a previous chapter that consciousness 'makes a home' for itself in the four other *khandhā*.[13] The commentary to this passage speaks of the four *khandhā* as objects for 'the stationing of construction-consciousness'. In this first case, then, the four stations of consciousness are derived from a this-worldly, ethical idea of psychological attachment or non-attachment to the phenomenal personality.

The seven stations are derived from a mélange of virtuoso meditative analysis and ordinary Buddhist cosmology. They are four types of heaven, of which three correspond to the first, second, and third meditation stages (*jhāna*); and then in addition the fifth, sixth, and seventh stages. The fourth and eighth stages are said elsewhere to be two additional 'spheres' (*āyatanāni*). All of these stations and spheres are said by the commentaries to be 'places for rebirth-consciousness'.[14] Similarly, there are said to be nine Abodes for Beings* which also correspond to meditative stages.[15] Both of these enumerations, the seven stations and the nine Abodes, are found in the *Visuddhimagga*, where death (in the memory of former lives) is also explained in the words 'having passed away from one becoming, womb, destiny, station for consciousness, Abode of Beings, class of Beings'.[16] It is, accordingly, only when consciousness is not thus stationed, does not have such an Abode, that rebirth does not take place and the monk is not released; in this case, however much Māra (the god of death) or the gods generally may search, they will not be able to trace the man who, 'with consciousness not stationed, has reached final *nibbāna*'.[17]

* The commentaries explain this often as 'places to dwell'. There are obvious resonances here of the pattern of house-imagery I emphasised in Chapter 5.3.

The stations of evolving consciousness

In the case of the seven stages of consciousness, the hierarchical arrangement clearly began from the attempt to distinguish a hierarchy of states of mind attained through meditation. It is through the collocation of these meditative levels with the various heavens and hells of Buddhist mythology that a full cosmology is achieved. Table 2 gives the final *Theravāda* schematisation of all these levels and heavens.[18]

Table 2. *Buddhist psychological cosmology*

Meditation level/Destiny at rebirth		Length of life
Formless Worlds		
8 Plane of neither perception nor non-perception		80,000 Great Aeons
7 Plane of nothingness		60,000 Great Aeons
6 Plane of Infinite Consciousness		40,000 Great Aeons
5 Plane of Infinite Space		20,000 Great Aeons
Worlds of (refined) Material Form		
4 Fourth Meditation level, with six heavens		From 16,000 down to 500 Great Aeons
3 Third Meditation level, with three heavens		64, 32, 16 Great Aeons
2 Second Meditation level, with three heavens		8, 4, 2 Great Aeons
1 First Meditation level, with three heavens		One, a half or one-third 'incalculable' aeons
Worlds of Desire		
Six divine worlds	good	From 16,000 down to 500 celestial years
Human World	good	No determined length
World of demons	bad	No determined length
World of spirits	bad	No determined length
World of animals	bad	No determined length
Hell	bad	No determined length

It seems clear that a number of different elements have gone to make up the final more or less organised doctrine of the stations of consciousness. In the first place, there is the Buddhist ethical and psychological teaching – which can be taken without any temporal reference – that when consciousness becomes attached to any part of ordinary phenomenal experience (symbolised as the four other *khandhā*), it constitutes an unenlightened, saṃsāric phenomenon. When this idea is connected with the idea of *karma* – and taken with temporal reference – there results the concept of a karmically active construction-consciousness, which 'evolves' through the constant repetition of such occasions of attachment in the four stations of consciousness. In the second place, the emphasis among virtuoso Buddhist practitioners on internal meditative experience naturally produced the idea of an inner universe of states of mind held to be brought about by meditation. Taken in their immediate context, this range of states of mind represents simply an attempt to describe, and prescribe, a common inner world which the practitioners of Buddhist 'mental culture' might share. Thanks to the general pattern of Indian specialist thinking, however, this shared inner world was also seen as a shared cosmological universe, a system of shared destinies in the seven stations of consciousness.

I said earlier that the place of consciousness as focus and criterion of soteriological activity was one of the means by which Buddhist thought organised psychological space in ways derived from its Indian cultural heritage. Buddhist psychology, along with the *Upaniṣads* and the earlier Brahmanical sacrificial thought, all see the different worlds or realms of the universe as both spheres or aspects of reality to which access can be gained in the present life (by meditation or sacrifice respectively), and also as destinies which can be attained more permanently in a new life after death. Without this double nature of the concept of *loka*, Buddhist thinking about continuity could not have combined, as it has, ideas taken from ethico-psychological analysis and meditative self-perception with those of general cosmology in order to produce finally the concept of consciousness continuing in time by means of the activity of stationing itself, both within the human personality and in the various heavens and 'planes' which make up the cosmos.

7.3. Vegetation imagery

In this section, I will continue the style of analysis I began in Chapter 5 when investigating the place of house imagery in the *Theravāda* imagination. Here I will concentrate on vegetation imagery, in relation to the themes of the chapter as a whole: conditioning, consciousness, and time. It will be clear throughout that these two patterns of imagery are closely linked parts of the same form of cultural perception (a point to which I shall return in the Conclusion). I have, indeed, already adumbrated this imaginative world, in speaking of 'popular' ideas earlier in this chapter (at the end of 7.1.4). We saw in Chapter 6 how the imagery of seeds and fruit was used to represent the Buddhist attitude to identity and difference in a psychological continuum, and to the various 'persons' reborn in it. Indeed, this pattern of imagery is also enshrined in the pan-Indian terms for causation (or, as Buddhism prefers, 'conditioning'). For example, *mūla*, 'root', and *bīja*, 'seed', are frequent terms for a cause; while *phala*, 'fruit', and *vipāka*, 'ripening', are standard terms for the effect. Of course, in most instances these are dead metaphors; I hope to show that in *Theravāda* thought the metaphor is only recently deceased, and always liable to resuscitation.

7.3.1. Continuity through the *karma* of agriculture

It is not surprising perhaps that the overwhelmingly agricultural peasant society of South Asia should picture human activity and its causal efficacy as a process of husbandry, whether in the natural or religious spheres. To take but one example at random from Brahmanical literature, it is said that 'the objects given to Brahmins become treasures in the next world, and there is no end to the fruits produced by the seed-like gifts sown in the land-like Brahmins and cultivated with the plough of the *Vedas*'.[1] Similarly, for the lay Buddhist activity of acquiring 'merit' (*puñña*) 'like fields are the *Arhats*; the givers are like farmers. The gift is like the seed, (and) from this arises the fruit.' For '(lay)men "offering sacrifice",* . . . doing good deeds which bring rebirth, what is given to the monkhood is rich in fruit'.[2] 'Gifts to those who in this world are worthy of gifts [i.e. monks] bring great fruit, just like seeds sown in a good field.' Accordingly, the Buddha, individual accomplished monks, and the monkhood as a whole are said to be the 'unsurpassable field of merit' for the other-worldly aspirations of the peasant Buddhist.[3]

The image of monkhood as a field is elaborated in other ways: for example, it is a good field for the 'seed of the Teaching' (*dhamma*), whereas laymen are only a middling field, and those of opposing views a bad field. In a connected and rather charming figure, young monks who do not see the Buddha in person and who are not thus encouraged to practise, are compared to seedlings which wither away for lack of water. In a less charming figure, it is said that just as when mildew falls on a field, its crops will not last long, so wherever women are admitted to the order, the *dhamma* will not last long.[4]

In these, and in other ways, the institution of the monkhood is seen as providing a means of religious action which parallels the agricultural activity which characterises secular life. In this perspective, we can see that imaginatively, for the lay Buddhist, activity of any sort will be described as a process of inculcating the growth of seeds into fruit. Certainly, lay life is uncompromisingly described in these terms in the texts: when two young men discuss the possibility of becoming monks, one of them describes 'what belongs to the household life'. It is constant application to the tasks of agriculture, to ploughing, sowing, irrigation,

* The use of inverted commas here is meant to indicate that, of course, the verb *yajati* does not mean literally 'to sacrifice' in the Brahmanic sense, but generally to perform religious practices, and in particular to give food to monks.

reaping, and so on, year after year. 'These activities never stop, there is no end to them' ('activities' here translates *kamma* in the plural). It is impossible therefore that householders, 'possessed of, provided with the five strands of sense-pleasure', should ever know unconcerned happiness.[5] We have seen that at the level of ideological abstraction household life constrained within the 'five strands of sense-pleasure', and 'going forth from home to homelessness', represent the two realms of *saṃsāra* and *nirvāṇa*. Moreover, we have seen that the succession of lives in *saṃsāra* is like the ever-recurring cycle of the production of seeds and fruit. We can then understand the symbolic dichotomy further by seeing that *saṃsāra* is a life of constant agriculture, planting seeds and reaping their fruit, while *nirvāṇa* is the abandonment of such a life. Of course, it is only at the simplest level of ideological abstraction that such a dichotomy operates: in fact, as we saw, 'leaving home' comes in gradual stages, of which the physical and social act of becoming a monk is but the first, to be followed by the psychological and ontological forms of 'going forth'. Accordingly, the agricultural life of *saṃsāra* is not restricted to the material husbandry of the layman; it includes all the metaphorical agriculture of *karma*, in which the unenlightened monk participates as much as the lay believer.

In general it is said that 'like the seed that is sown, so is the fruit that is harvested. The doer of good (plants and reaps) good, the doer of bad, bad. When the seed is sown and planted, you shall experience the (appropriate) fruit.' Actions performed with greed, hatred, and delusion come to fruition through rebirth, like seeds planted in fertile soil with abundant rain; actions performed without these faults, like seeds burnt and thrown away, do not come to such fruition. These three faults are called the 'roots' of what is bad (and their reverse, of what is good), and they are weeds in the field of mankind. When 'the roots of good and evil' are not cut off in a person, then he will experience future happiness or suffering as surely as seeds thrown on a fertile or stony field do or do not come to fruition. Actions performed by men of good or bad view conduce to happiness or suffering as bitter or sweet seeds grow to bitter or sweet plants. A man who offers a traditional Brahmanical sacrifice, involving the killing of animals, and who has wrong views, intentions, and so on, will not gain any good result, like a man planting bad seed in unfavourable soil.[6]

In a connected image, continuity is seen as the growth of a tree: just as when the roots of a tree are watered, it grows and 'with such nourishment, such fuel, it may stand for a long time to come', so when a man lives 'seeing enjoyment in things which can be grasped' there comes to be growth of craving, 'descent' of consciousness and name-and-form, and so on. When a man does not live in this way he is like a man who cuts the roots of the tree, with the result that he becomes 'like a palm-tree stump, cut off at the roots, coming to no further existence and unable to arise again in the future'. (This last phrase is often used in speaking of a released man, in contexts where no explicit vegetation imagery is found.) Similarly, it is said that 'just as a tree, whose roots are undamaged and firm, may be cut and still grow again, so when the underlying tendency to craving is not destroyed, this suffering appears again and again'. Just as when someone cuts a living tree with an axe, sap flows, so when objects of sense or mind come into the range of a man with greed, hatred, and delusion, they 'obsess the mind'.[7]

7.3.2. Seeds of good *karma*

Once this pattern of imagery is regularly used to represent action and its results, the underlying idea – that all growth of *karma*-seeds is eventually to be stopped – can be lain aside in particular contexts, and the image used more positively. That is, good karmic action and its results can be pictured as a desirable form of agriculture. We find many examples of this type of imagery being used in relation to the practice of the Buddhist religious life. In a famous passage found twice in the Canon[8] a farmer, having been approached by the Buddha for alms, exclaims that while he (the farmer) works in the fields, ploughing and sowing, and after that eats his food, mendicants like the Buddha do no such work. The Buddha replies that he too ploughs and sows, and explains as follows: 'My seed is faith, austerity the rain; insight is my yoke and plough, my pole modesty, mind the strap; mindfulness my plough-share and goad; . . . energy is for me the ox which bears the yoke, drawing on towards rest from work [*yogakkhema* – a frequent synonym for *nibbāna*].' The image is used for the practice of the Path, with its three component parts of Morality, Concentration (Meditation), and Insight (Wisdom). Thus, 'two qualities of a seed are to be adopted'.[9] These are, first, that though a seed may be small, still when sown in a good field with sufficient rain it will yield abundant fruit: similarly, morality will yield the whole fruit of renunciation if the religious life is practised properly. Secondly, a seed planted in a well-cleared field germinates quickly; equally, the mind of a practising monk, if 'purified in an empty place, planted in the excellent field of the Foundations of Mindfulness', will develop quickly. In general, growth in the religious life is said to depend on morality, just as all seeds and vegetation depend on the earth. The right or wrong attitude of the disciple determining the effect of his hearing or practising the Buddhist *dhamma* is likened to good or bad seeds growing (or not growing) in a field; while good and bad preaching of the *dhamma*, and those who practise in accordance with both kinds, are likened to good and bad fields and seeds, respectively. Just as a tree without branches and leaves does not put forth shoots, nor come to fruition, so a man without morality and concentration will not come to insight in the life of 'mental culture'.[10]

We can, I think, gain empathy into the psychological attitude recommended here from one particularly ingenious application of the image.[11] There are three 'urgent duties' of a householding farmer. He must plough and harrow his field quickly, he must plant the seed quickly, and he must be quick to water it. Although he has these three urgent duties to perform, he cannot hasten the growth of his crops by saying 'let the crops spring up today . . . ear tomorrow . . . ripen on the next day!' It is, rather, a natural process of seasonal change which brings the crops to ripening. In the same way, although a monk has the three urgent duties of the 'higher training in morality, concentration, and insight', he has no 'magic powers or influence' to hasten their development. In a psychological perspective, this depiction of Buddhist training suggests the feeling of inculcating a natural process of personal growth, rather than the magical or 'occult' production of spiritual states. Seeds work slowly, beneath the ground, as the process of character development in Buddhist training is meant to work slowly, beneath the level of conscious perception. In a social perspective, this kind of attitude toward religious practice is perhaps intended to separate Buddhism from the ubiquitous magicians, astrologers, and the like, with whom at the village level Buddhist monks have had to share the role of religious specialist.*

7.3.3. Imagery and doctrine

In all these examples of the use of vegetation imagery, we have seen a progression from the idea that the activity of the layman is always agricultural, in both material and religious spheres, to the idea that the entire 'lay-life of *saṃsāra*' demands and is constituted by the cultivation of 'seeds', 'fruit', 'fields', and so on – both in the general sense referring to any action, *karma*, of laymen and unenlightened monks alike, and in the particular sense that the practice of the renouncer-monk's life of 'mental culture' operates in the same agricultural manner as the husbandry of the householding peasant. Given this range over which vegetation

* A similar intention may be seen to lie behind the inclusion of 'false claims to magical powers' in the four most serious offences in the monks' code of discipline (*pārājika* – the others being sexual intercourse, theft, and murder). Even truthful claims to such powers have been classed as a minor offence. The point here is that by dissociating itself from the attitudes and claims of magicians and their ilk (at least in doctrinal ideal), Buddhism attempts to characterise itself as a serious, sober, tradition of religious exertion.

imagery is applicable, it is not surprising to find it applied further to more specific matters of doctrine. In the *Visuddhimagga*, the 'non-interruptedness of continuity' through the successive elements of the Dependent Origination list is said to be like 'a seed's reaching the stage of being a tree, through the stage of being a shoot [and so on]'; and

> The six-fold sense-base planted in name-and-form reaches growth, increase and fulfilment, as a forest thicket does when planted in good soil; . . . when there is becoming there is birth, as when there is a seed there is a shoot, and death is inevitable for one who is born, as falling down is for a tree that has grown up.

Formations are 'like the seeds of a poison-tree, because they are the cause of the continuity of the *khandhā*'. Birth, old age, and death grow in the *khandhā* as weeds, creepers, and so on, grow in the ground, and as sprouts, flowers and fruits grow on trees. The continued occurrence of *khandhā* in successive lives is likened to a great tree, growing on the earth's surface, and 'continuing the tree's lineage through the succession of seeds up to the end of the aeon'. A man who feels revulsion for the process and practises the Buddhist Path is like a man who poisons the tree and prevents its further growth.[12]

A sequence of 'individualities', *attabhāva*, also is a process of vegetative growth: the 'human puppet' arises neither through the agency of self nor other, but 'by reason of a cause', just as a seed grows in a field nourished by moisture. Different persons (*puggalā*) are produced, with different physical and psychological attributes, through differences in *karma*, just as different trees are produced by different seeds. The once-returner, who is to produce but one more 'individuality' before attaining *nibbāna*, is called a 'one-seeder' while the released *Arhat* has 'rendered consciousness seedless'.[13]

This idea of consciousness as 'seeded' or 'seedless' is very important in all Buddhist thought, not only in the *Theravāda* tradition; and it enables us to summarise and conclude the 'ultimate' ideas of this chapter. We have seen how Buddhism drew on Brahmanical ideas of 'constructive activity' as the producer of temporal continuity, and on the renouncers' introjection of sacrificial motifs into individual consciousness, to elaborate its doctrine of constructions and construction-consciousness as the agents and vehicles of *karma*. Accordingly, when men have 'a mind with no desire for future existence', and have 'no desire for growth', then their 'seeds are destroyed', just as they have destroyed rebirth. When a verse tells us that the sage who 'examines the ground and destroys the seed . . . sees the end of birth and death', the commentary explains that the seed here is construction-consciousness. Similarly, when it is said that consciousness becomes 'established' (or 'stationed') as a seed in the field of *karma*, with desire as the moisture (as an explanation of how there comes to be future rebirth), the commentary explains that consciousness here is construction-consciousness. It is said that all types of seed depend on earth and water for their successful growth: 'The four stations of consciousness should be seen as the earth [that is, as the *Sutta* explains, the four other *khandhā*] . . . lust and desire as the water . . . and consciousness and its food as the seed.'[14]

In other schools of Buddhism, the imagery of seeds and their fruit in relation to consciousness was even further developed. For example, the *Mahāsāṃghika* school spoke of a 'root-consciousness' which was the basis of continuity in *saṃsāra*; similarly, the *Vijñānavāda* tradition's 'home-consciousness' (*ālaya-vijñāna*) which has the same role, is regularly said to 'contain all the seeds' of *karma*. In these ideas, the original metaphor inherent in the use of such imagery becomes deadened, and the words take on the character of dry technical terms. In *Theravāda*, on the other hand, the imagery of seeds and fruit is never regularised to the extent of becoming technical terminology built into the ultimate account of continuity; correspondingly, the metaphor remains more alive. *Theravāda* tradition does speak of a type of mental phenomenon which assures continuity – the *bhavaṅga*-mind; and it does have a preferred metaphor to represent it – the image of a stream or river. To understand these ideas, however, requires considerable background preparation: it is to this task that I turn in Chapter 8.

8 Momentariness and the *bhavaṅga*-mind

Scholasticism. 2. Servile adherence to the methods and teaching of the schools; narrow or unenlightened insistence on traditional doctrines and forms of exposition.

Oxford English Dictionary

Nothing is more dangerous to reason than flights of the imagination, and nothing has been the occasion of more mistakes among philosophers.

David Hume, *A Treatise of Human Nature*, Book I, Part IV, Section 7

. . the power of imagination, a blind but indispensable function of the soul, without which we should have no knowledge whatsoever, but of which we are scarcely ever conscious.*

Immanuel Kant, *Critique of Pure Reason*, Transcendental Analytic, Book I, Chapter I, Section 3 (A78, B103)

In Chapter 7, I discussed the fundamental attitude to, and some crucial ideas about, temporality and continuity in *Theravāda* thought; and I connected these with certain broad themes in socio-cultural perception in the peasant, agricultural life of Buddhist societies. In the present chapter, I shall continue and complete the 'ultimate' account of continuity in *Theravāda* thought, in the ideas (found largely in the commentarial tradition and thereafter) of 'momentariness' and of 'the *bhavaṅga*'. This latter is a term usually suffixed by *-citta*, or *-manas*, '-mind', or *-sota*, 'stream'. I shall continue with the method of studying patterns of imagery – here those of a chariot, and of rivers or streams, and water generally – but I shall not be concerned to trace any direct connexion between the use of such images in the philosophy and psychology of Buddhism and wider structures of social perception. I shall, rather, trace a connexion between this imagery and certain wider and simpler patterns of thinking within Buddhist doctrine, in its ethics and psychology; and, secondarily in the case of river imagery I shall attempt firmly to disengage these patterns of thinking from certain themes in western thought, which have often been alleged to be similar: that is, specifically, from western ideas of a 'stream of consciousness' and of a (Heraclitean) Doctrine of Flux. In this way, I shall argue, the study of imagery can reveal not only

* Kemp Smith translation, p. 112.

the wider imaginative world in which religious or philosophical ideas are embedded, but also how unanalysed and unconscious metaphors can be built into modern interpretative thinking.

The image of the *bhavaṅga* as a stream is certainly built into much of the writing of modern *Theravāda* thinkers, for whom, indeed, the concept is basic to any 'ultimately true' account of personal continuity:

> The existence of the sub-conscious life-stream, or *bhavaṅga-sota*, is a necessary postulate of our thinking . . . whatever constitutes the true and innermost nature of man or any other being is this subconscious life-stream . . . [It is] the *sine qua non* of life, having the nature of a process, lit. a flux or stream (*sota*).[1]

> The stream of being, then, is an indispensable condition or factor, the *sine qua non* of present conscious existence; it is the *raison d'être* of individual life; it is the life-continuum; it is, as it were, the background on which thought-pictures are drawn.[2]

It is the concept of *bhavaṅga* which can 'give a satisfactory theory of personality and survival without introducing a permanent and unchanging entity like a soul'.[3] It explains continuity generally, as well as rebirth; thus we read not only that 'this law of rebirth can be made comprehensible only by the subconscious "life-stream" in Pali *bhavaṅga-sota*',[4] and that 'the *karma* of a human being who has died produces another form, appropriate to its particular realm, to carry on the world-line of cause and effect belonging to that specific current of existence',[5] but also that

> the 'dying and being reborn' process is actually continuous throughout life, for consciousness consists of a succession of thought-moments or *citta-vīthi* (Courses of Cognition), which are like beads strung on the connecting thread of *bhavaṅga*, or the unconscious life-continuum. Each conscious moment in its arising and passing away is a little birth and a little death.[6]

Apart from the imagery of rivers or streams, the major source of the development of the *bhavaṅga* concept in *Theravāda* thinking is the theory of momentariness; that is, the developed Buddhist idea that all continuity, whether psychological or material, is produced by a sequence of 'moments' (*khaṇa*), of minute, temporally 'atomic', particles of matter, consciousness (and in the case of *bhavaṅga*, 'un-consciousness'). In tracing the origin of this theory from its more general parent idea of impermanence, I shall have occasion to discuss a number of other Buddhist concepts, such as the 'life-faculty', which also have a role to play in accounts of continuity.

8.1. 'Impermanent are conditioned things'

In Buddhist legend, the very first convert to Buddhism obtained release at the thought, occurring to him during the Buddha's first sermon, that 'whatever is subject to origination, all that is subject to cessation'.[1] Similarly, the Buddha's dying injunction was to remember that 'subject to decay are conditioned things'.[2] It is this perception of impermanence and death which,

> when developed and made much of, destroys all sense-desire, all desire for body and existence [*bhava*], and destroys all ignorance, all conceit 'I am'. Just as a farmer in the autumn, ploughing with his ploughshare cuts through all spreading roots, so the perception of impermanence, . . . destroys sense-desire, . . . all conceit of 'I am' . . . In what way? . . . By seeing 'such is body (feeling, perception, mental formations and consciousness), such their arising, such their cessation'.[3]

As Nyanatiloka says, 'It is from the fact of impermanence that, in most texts, the other two Characteristics, suffering [*dukkha*] and not-self [*anattā*] are derived.'[4] This emphasis on impermanence is developed a great deal in ethics, and (as we shall see) in meditative reflection. Its extension into theoretical psychology was to lead finally to the radical shortening of the life of all existents to the duration of an infinitesimal 'moment'. Such a theoretical account, however, had also to deal with the intermediary problem of accounting for the fact of a human lifetime as 'conventionally' understood, howsoever short and doomed to death it might be. What provides its temporary stability? How is it that the interim between the moments called (in 'conventional' terms) 'birth' and 'death' is generated in the process of *karma* as a meaningful unit?

8.1.1. What constitutes a lifetime?

We saw in Chapter 7 that the overall answer to the question is that the energy and impetus of time, and life within it, are provided by the 'construction(s)' of renewed consciousness in *saṃsāra*. More specifically, to answer the sorts of problem to which the questions I posed above refer, there arose the concept of particular constructions, called variously, 'life-formations' (*āyu-saṃkhārā*), 'life' (*āyu*) *simpliciter*, or the 'life-faculty' (*jīvitindriya*), whose function it is to condition the temporary unity and stability of a lifetime.

Certain passages in the Canon speak of the differences between life and death as being due to the presence or absence of 'life, heat, and consciousness'.[5] Just as a ball of iron is lighter, softer, and more pliable when hot than when cold, as it has heat and air, so a human being is lighter, softer, and more pliable when possessing life, heat, and consciousness; just as a conch-shell is capable of producing sound if there is a man (to blow it), if the man makes an effort to do so, and if he actually succeeds in producing breath, so the body is capable of experience through the six senses if there are present life, heat, and consciousness. Elsewhere it is argued that the sense-organs 'continue to exist dependent on life', while this life depends on heat; heat, in its turn, depends on life. The relationship of mutual dependence here is explained by an analogy with light and a flame: it is the flame which produces light, but it is visible only by means of the light which it has produced. The text goes on to say that these 'life-formations' are not 'phenomena which can be experienced', since although a monk might have attained to the meditative state of the 'cessation of experience' (literally of 'perception and feeling'), still his 'life is not spent, (his) heat not allayed, (his) sense-faculties are purified'. In death, on the other hand, 'life is spent, heat is allayed', and 'the sense-faculties are broken apart'.[6]

The life, heat, and 'faculties' (purified or not) which are necessary for any kind of existence, even that minimal subsistence which is the state of 'cessation', are of course 'formations', 'constructed' out of *karma*. Such 'life-formations' are equally obviously impermanent: they are said to pass away with greater speed than that shown by anything imaginable. It is impossible for anyone to avoid the final passing away of life formations, although the Buddha, when afflicted by a grievous illness, by an act of will suppressed his disease, 'took control of his life-formations and lived on'. Indeed, he might have prolonged his 'life-formations' until the end of the present cosmic aeon, had not his attendant monk Ānanda omitted to request him to do so. Any monk who attains Arhatship by the practice of certain meditations can come to know exactly how long his life-formations will last, and thus how long will be his 'life-term'.[7]

8.1.2. The life-faculty

The fundamental idea we have been considering, that the difference between life and death is due to the presence of – amongst other things – 'life', shares the same logical peculiarities as that of Molière's young doctor, who derived the power of opium to induce sleep from its *virtus dormitiva*.[8] Much the same thing might also be said of the use of the idea of an hypostatised entity called the 'life-faculty' (*jīvitindriya*) as an explanation of stability and unity in one lifetime. The commentaries to two of the passages I quoted as speaking of 'life, heat, and consciousness', gloss the term 'life' by the term 'life-faculty'.[9] The standard definition of the term is given in a series of synonyms, as follows: 'the life, persistence, going on, keeping going, progress, continuance, preservation, existence of phenomena'.[10] In a list of 'most important factors' (literally, 'heads'), the 'most important factor of continuity' is said to be the life-faculty. It is known as 'a real and ultimate fact'. Where conventional truth speaks of the life and death of 'beings', or 'breathing things',* ultimate truth speaks of the existence and cessation of the life-faculty.[11]

The life-faculty is of two kinds: bodily and mental (or 'material' and 'immaterial'). (The same general definition I quoted above is given separately in the case of both bodily and mental life-faculties.) The former is counted as part of the 'category of body', the latter as part of the 'category of mental formations'. The latter mental phenomenon is later said to be one of the seven 'concomitants of consciousness accompanying all mental events'.[12] The function of both kinds of life-faculty is said to be that of maintaining the (conventional) unity called a person, formed, as it is in fact, of a plurality of groups of simultaneous impersonal elements: 'the function of the life-faculty is to maintain elements which arise together'. It is this function which makes it 'the controlling factor in a continuing process'. It is said to 'watch over' or 'preserve' the groups of elements as a wet-nurse does a child; but at the same time it is not itself independent of the elements which are to be maintained together, as a pilot cannot exist without a boat.[13]

We might describe the part played by the concept of the life-faculty in an overall Buddhist account of personality and continuity in the following way: what is conventionally called a human being, or a person, is in fact a series of groups of impersonal elements (*dhammā*); these elements are, paradigmatically, grouped for the purposes of analysis into five categories (*khandhā*). The general, overriding force which moves and preserves the sequence is *karma*; in particular, within the group of constructed elements which exist at any given moment of the sequence, there are two karmically resultant formations (that is, within the body-category the material life-faculty, and within the mental-formations-category the immaterial life-faculty) whose function it is to maintain together, as a temporary unity, that collection of elements of which they are members. As we shall see presently, both forms of life-faculty are, like the other elements which they maintain together, only momentarily existent. When the 'moment' arrives in which neither form of life-faculty is 're-constructed' or 're-formed' by *karma*, then the unity of the psycho-physical elements with which they were formerly associated in one name-and-form is dissipated, and the 'individual' 'dies'.

Theravāda needs to divide the life-faculty into two forms, for a number of different reasons. In Buddhist cosmology, there are 'worlds' without matter, where a purely immaterial life-faculty is required; and there are equally 'unconscious beings', and states of complete unconsciousness during human life, which require a material life-faculty.[14] The most

* *Pāṇā*, as in the first of the Five Precepts, against 'the killing of living beings', *pāṇātipāta*'.

important state of unconsciousness here is the meditative state, to which I have already referred, of the 'cessation of perception and feeling'. For other Buddhist schools, it was, amongst other things, the problem of maintaining individual continuity through periods where no conscious activity was thought to occur – most obviously in 'cessation' and dreamless sleep – which led to the postulation of a 'deeper' level or type of consciousness, which guaranteed continuity.[15] For *Theravāda* it is the material life-faculty which continues to exist during cessation. We saw that a monk who has attained to the state still has 'life': the commentary explains that by this is meant the material life-faculty. The process is likened to the damping down and re-kindling of a fire: a monk becomes weary of mental activity, and enters cessation, just as a man might weary of 'the occurrence of a fire', and so put it out and cover it with ashes. He then sits quietly until he wants fire again, when he takes away the ashes and re-kindles the flames. The coals covered with ashes correspond to the material life-faculty during cessation, while the uncovering of the ashes and the re-appearance of flames correspond to the emergence from the state and the re-appearance of immaterial mental phenomena.[16]

8.1.3. Chariot imagery

The use of fire-imagery here fits neatly into the general pattern of Buddhism: life-in-*saṃsāra* and temporally extended experience seen as a flame burning in the fire of desire, whose 'going out' when temporary is cessation, when permanent *nibbāna*. There is another pattern of imagery which will illuminate the particular problem of unity and continuity within one lifetime with which we are immediately concerned. The image is that of a moving chariot, or cart. In order to give a full idea of the flavour of this image, let me first mention another idea relevant to continuity here: life as a sequence of the four 'postures' (*iriyā-pathā*), standing, sitting, lying down and walking. 'This life is weak and frail, . . . it is tied up with the (four) postures . . .; it continues only when they are occurring evenly; when any one of them prevails (unchangingly), the life-formations are stopped.' 'Breaking the (sequence of the) postures' is equivalent to 'cutting off the life-faculty' as a description of the danger avoided by the possession of 'the livelihood known as lasting-a-long-time'.[17]

The term *iriyā-pathā* means literally 'ways of going'; in the passage just cited, the terms translated as 'livelihood' and 'lasting' (*yātrā*, *gamana*) are equally derived from basic verbal roots meaning 'to go'. The sequence of words I have quoted above as synonymous defining terms for the life-faculty similarly have this flavour. The word *viharati*, which is used to refer to both the temporary 'abiding' in a meditative state and the ordinary, continuous 'living' of life, is defined by a similar sequence of terms, which differ only in that their grammatical form is verbal: 'progresses, continues, preserves, goes, keeps going, moves on, lives'.[18] The commentary explains all these verbs by means of the idea of the sequence of the four postures: for example, the occurrence within the list of synonyms of the verb 'lives' (*viharati*) is explained as referring to 'the carrying on of life through cutting off one posture by another'. We have already met the pun on *viharati* which speaks of 'carrying on the individuality' by means of the sequence of postures. The term *viharati* used for meditative abiding, is explained similarly: 'by abiding in a posture . . . he produces the progress, conduct, preservation, keeping going, moving on, abiding of individuality'.[19]

The *Vibhaṅga* commentary which elaborates the sequence of verbs synonymous with *viharati* in terms of the four postures, explains *vattati* (which I have rendered as 'continues', but which comes from a basic root meaning 'to turn') as 'the continuance of the chariot of the body by the four postures'. As a commentarial explanation of the description of the body as 'four-wheeled' we read that the wheels are the four postures. (The same idea is given somewhat artificially as an explanation of the term *cakka-vatti*, meaning 'wheel-turner' in the sense of 'conquering king', and of the simple idea of 'mounting a chariot' to escape bandits.)[20] The importance of chariot imagery in this area of Buddhist thought is not limited to this simple literary conceit. The use of the image of a chariot for the continuance of the physical body, and the metaphor of chariot-driving in matters of psychology, both connect Buddhist thought with, and differentiate it from, a very general pattern of thinking about time and continuity in Indian culture.*

The standard point made about the monk's use of alms-food has it that such food is not for enjoyment, or personal beautification, but for 'the maintenance, the keeping going of the body'.[21] The *Visuddhimagga* explains that here 'maintenance is a synonym for the life-faculty; thus, "for the maintenance and keeping going of this body" means for the purpose of causing the life-faculty of this body to continue'. The monk is thus to use alms-food in the same way that a charioteer uses axle-grease, not for enjoyment or embellishment, but simply to keep his chariot going.[22] The image of the physical body as a chariot is common elsewhere in the *Visuddhimagga*: the fourteen chest-bones resemble a decaying chariot frame; the heart in the body is like a piece of meat lodged in an old chariot frame; the joints of the body lubricated by synovial fluid are like a well-greased axle.[23] In the Suttas, we are urged to

* I shall speak, for simplicity, of 'chariot'-imagery. The terms so translated can in fact often denote vehicles we should rather term 'carts', 'wagons', and so on.

remember that the body will come to old age and death, just as splendid royal chariots decay. The Buddha compares his old body to a 'worn-out chariot', only kept going by supports, and soon to fall apart. Indeed, one is urged to see the whole world as a painted royal chariot as wise men do, and have no attachment for it. For those without this vision 'the world turns by *karma*, beings move on through *karma*; beings are bound to *karma*, like the lynch-pin of a moving chariot'.[24]

The image is used also psychologically. Where the body was a four-wheeled chariot, it is said that 'the one-wheeled chariot rolls on', with the meaning that the chariot is the monk's body, and the wheel his mindfulness. A monk is to regard mind and mental factors with equanimity, as a charioteer is indifferent to his horses; equally, the monk practising mindfulness over the senses, or concentrating his mind to attain the 'higher powers', is like a driver keeping guard over his horses and chariot.[25]

The fundamental spirit behind the use of the image of a moving chariot to express the Buddhist attitude to continuity in one lifetime is this: I have argued already that 'for Brahmanical thinking, time and continuity were not simply and deterministically given to man; rather, they are the result of a constant effort at prolongation, a constant pushing forward of life'; and that Buddhism took over this attitude, with the value-judgements reversed. The dynamic, forward-moving connotations of the series of synonymous terms which are given in definition of the life-faculty, and of 'living' as a 'sequence of the four postures', bear witness to such an underlying attitude. The unifying spirit behind all these highly technical, ultimate ideas is illustrated by the image of the frail combination of physical and mental states called a 'person', or a 'life', being pushed along by the constant driving force of *karma*, just as a chariot is driven along a road, until it decays and falls apart through age.

Of the wider uses of chariot-imagery in India, a few egregious examples must suffice. In one of the great hymns to time of the *Atharva Veda*, time is said to be like a horse drawing a chariot, 'whose wheels are all beings, . . . whose axle is immortality'; a long hymn of the *Ṛg Veda* speaks of the movement of the sun and time as that of a horse-drawn chariot, with much numerical symbolism – the seven horses (days), the three-axled wheel (the three seasons), the wheel (of the year) with its twelve spokes (months), carrying seven hundred and twenty children (the nights and days of a year).[26] This kind of imaginative thinking is common in early India.[27] Common also in India (and indeed elsewhere) was the use of the metaphor of chariot-driving for individual psychology: in a famous passage of the *Kaṭha Upaniṣad*, the body is compared to a chariot, with the self, its owner, riding in it; 'intellect' (*buddhi*) is the driver, 'mind' (*manas*) the reins, the senses the horses, and the objects of sense the ground over which they range. The man who attains release 'reaches the end of the road'.[28] *

For Buddhism also, the enlightened man is one who 'has reached the end of the road', whereas the man still unreleased is as yet a 'traveller' on 'the long road called the round (of rebirth)'.[29] The image of life as travelling in a chariot has a crucial difference in Buddhism from that of the *Upaniṣad* just quoted. For Buddhism, of course, there is no self riding in the chariot as its 'owner'; we have seen that the *khandhā* have no 'owner'.[30] Despite this crucial doctrinal difference, the idea of a lifetime as a road to be travelled is still strong in Buddhist thought. The terms *addhā* and *addhāna*, derived from Sanskrit *adhvan*, 'road', can mean both 'time' generally, and 'a lifetime' in particular.[31] The phrase *tayo addhā* refers to the three times of past, present, and future, while *addhāyu* means 'a lifespan', and the phrase 'one who has reached the end of his road' (*addhagato*) is synonymous with 'advanced in years, old'. Accordingly, when we read of the man who has not abandoned desire, that for him *dīghaṃ addhānaṃ saṃsāraṃ*, we can translate both as '*saṃsāra* is a long road', and as 'the round of rebirth will last a long time'.[32]

8.1.4. Conclusion

We have seen in this first section a number of related concepts with which Buddhism has sought to solve the problem of the temporary unity and stability of one lifetime, given the all-pervasive truth of impermanence – the life-formations, life-faculty, the sequence of the four postures. I have suggested that the spirit behind these technical formulations can best be grasped by the image of life in time, and a lifetime, as travelling along a road like a chariot. Lest it might be thought that the life-faculty creates a real individual to exist through a lifetime, one must remember that other use of chariot imagery which we met earlier:[33] that is, the argument that just as there is no real, eternal thing in a chariot, but merely a temporary assemblage of parts which receives the conventional designation 'chariot', so there is nothing more to the 'person' but a temporary assemblage of parts. As we saw, the life-faculty is a temporary part, like the others which it is its function to 'maintain together'. If, then, nothing real or ultimate endures for the length of a lifetime, how long does what is real and ultimate endure?

The answer to this question is that all the real elements of a person endure only for a 'moment':

* See also the examples given in Chapter 2.3.1 and nn. 3 and 4.

In the ultimate sense, the life-moment of living beings is extremely short, being only as much as the occurrence of a single conscious moment. Just as a chariot wheel, when it is rolling, rolls [that is, touches the ground] only on one point of [the circumference] of its tyre, and, when it is at rest, rests only on one point, so too, the life of living beings lasts only for a single conscious moment. When that moment is ceased, the being is said to have ceased, according as it is said 'In a past conscious moment he did live', not 'he does live', not 'he will live'. In a future conscious moment not 'he did live', not 'he does live' [but] 'he will live'. In the present conscious moment, not 'he did live', [but] 'he does live', [and] not 'he will live'.[34]

Those texts I quoted earlier, which spoke of the life-faculty and its function of maintaining all the other elements together,[35] continue by asserting that the life-faculty ceases at the end of each moment, along with the other elements which it holds together:

It does not prolong existence beyond the moment of cessation, since neither it itself nor the elements whose existence it was to have prolonged exist (any more). It does not cause [the other elements] to continue after the moment of cessation, as it is itself dying out, like the flame of a lamp when the wick and oil are used up.

There is a reference here to the idea that each existent element lasts for one moment, itself composed of three 'sub-moments': arising, presence, and cessation (*uppāda*, *ṭhiti*, *bhaṅga*). It is this idea to which the early Buddhist teaching of impermanence finally evolved; and it is to this idea that I now turn.

8.2. The 'ultimate' extent of a lifetime: momentariness

Each 'real' and 'ultimate' element lasts for only a 'moment'. This idea became so fundamental to developed Buddhist thinking* that Buddhism came to be referred to as *kṣanikavāda*, The Theory of Moments.[1] The idea of the conversion of such a series of moments, or 'point-instants', into the world of human experience has been compared to that of the conversion of still photographs into a cinematic moving picture;[2] in Stcherbatsky's perhaps more elegant metaphor, the Universe in *kṣanikavāda* is represented as a *staccato* rather than *legato* movement.[3] Various attempts were made by the tradition to compute the actual temporal length of such moments: for example, that each day contains 86,400 seconds, which equal 6,449,099,980 moments – thus 1/74,642 second per moment.[4] Frequently, the idea of a finger-snap is used to designate the smallest perceptible unit of time;[5] and a finger-snap itself is said to contain sixty-four, or even billions of moments.[6] In fact, we read, no simile can illustrate the shortness of the moment;[7] that is to say, what

* The *Madhyamaka* school, however, is a notable exception.

appears in Buddhist theory as a 'moment' is not in itself an object of conscious perception, nor even capable of being illustrated by anything else which is. In dealing with the idea of momentariness therefore, we are in a wholly conceptual, non-empirical realm. Accordingly, when tracing the development of the theory, we must look for logical, or at least natural, extensions of basic Buddhist concepts.

8.2.1. The meditations on impermanence and death

Such natural extensions of Buddhist thinking can be found with regard to the ideas of impermanence and death, as they were developed as subjects for virtuoso meditative reflection. I argued earlier that the emphasis on *dukkha*, 'suffering' or 'unsatisfactoriness', in Buddhist thought was not an empirical observation or judgement on life, but a form of perception undertaken as a soteriological project. The Buddha replaced the physical mortification ubiquitous elsewhere in the ascetic practice of Indian religious virtuosos, with the mental mortification of the contemplation of universal suffering. Equally, in the reflections on impermanence and death, we should see this same project of replacing a physical asceticism by one of the mind.

The idea of the impermanence and transience of life was easily associated with the idea of the omnipresence of change. A frequent synonym for 'impermanent' is 'subject to change' (*vipariṇāma-dhamma*); we saw that the first argument for *anattā* asserts that suffering arises from the inevitable fact that the constituents of personality 'change and become otherwise'. In Buddhist virtuoso reflection, change in large, external, and physical matters is to be replaced by an increased perception of the small-scale changes within consciousness itself: the Buddha asserts that it is easy for the 'ignorant ordinary man' to feel repulsion for the body, since its impermanence, its growth and decay, its 'being taken up and put down' at birth and death, are easy to see. (Clearly he is deliberately classing the physical asceticism of Brahmanical practice (*tapas*) with the ignorance of the ordinary non-religious layman.)[8] Such a person, however, will find it more difficult to feel repulsion for, and so renounce, 'that which is called mind [*citta*], thought [*manas*], consciousness [*viññāṇa*]'; for he is accustomed to think of it (in the usual way) 'this I am, this is mine, this is my self'. The Buddha continues, in ironical vein, by saying that it would be better for such a man to regard the body as a self rather than the mind, since at least the body lasts for anything up to a hundred years or more, whereas the mind 'by night and by day arises as one thing, ceases as another'. He compares this fickleness of the mind, as so often, to a monkey jumping from one branch to another.[9] Indeed, there is no other single thing so 'quick to change' as the mind.[10] It is important to realise here that for Buddhism there is no distinction between change in the content or objects of consciousness (it is such fickleness and inconstancy which the monkey simile usually stresses) and change in consciousness itself. In the sequence of 'moments' of consciousness there is no continuing self as 'knowing subject', to whom the various contents of consciousness might appear as objects – accordingly, change in content here is equivalent to change in form; and change in form is equivalent to change in being (which is to say, to the 'cessation' of the previous moment, and the 'arising' of a new moment as a separate existent).

We can see this clearly expressed, as well as the progression from the perception of physical change to the more refined and valued perception of mental change, in a passage of the *Visuddhimagga*.[11] Here, a monk is to see the three characteristics of impermanence, suffering, and not-self as applying to the body, first over a period of a hundred years (as we have seen, the traditional length of a lifetime, from the Vedic period on), and then in gradually decreasing lengths of time: in three periods of thirty-three years, in each of the ten decades, and so on, until he reaches the seasons of the year, the waxing and waning of the moon, and then each day. Next he is to reflect that 'the body occurring by night ceases there, without reaching the day'.[12] Finally, in each physical movement, such as lifting the feet in the process of walking, the monk is to see the body as changing constantly: 'thus formations keep breaking up, like crackling sesamum seeds put into a hot pan; wherever they arise, there they cease, stage by stage, section by section, term by term, each without reaching the next part'. Turning from the facts of bodily change to those of mind, the monk is to see the very consciousness which perceived bodily change as itself impermanent, unsatisfactory, and not-self. He does this by a 'further (act of) mind'. Similarly, this second (act of) mind is to be seen as impermanent, unsatisfactory, and not-self, by a third, the third by a fourth, the fourth by a fifth, and so on.[13]

The structure of this gradual process of perception is the application of the characteristics usually attributed to a lifetime as a whole – notably birth, change, and death – to ever decreasing extents of time. In the other meditative reflection which lay behind the growth of the theory of momentariness, that on death, we can see the very same structure, and the very same project of mental mortification (in an etymologically exact sense of the term). The monk is to start from the perception of inevitable 'ordinary' death – defined as 'the cutting off of the life-faculty comprising one lifetime' and finally to reach 'momentary death, reckoned as the dissolution, each moment, of formations'.[14] He is to reflect on life's 'limitedness of extent' beginning from the usual one-hundred-year span, until he realises eventually that the extent of future life is completely uncertain, even for the time it takes to swallow a mouthful of food, or to breathe in and out. He is then to continue by perceiving death 'in terms of the shortness of the moment'. The text then continues with the idea that 'in the ultimate sense, the life-moment of living beings is . . . a single conscious moment', using the image of a chariot wheel's touching the earth only at one point, which I quoted earlier (at the end of Chapter 8.1.4 above).[15] The same passage is given in the commentary to the *Sutta Nipāta*. The phrase being explained is 'life is short', and the commentary glosses 'life' in the usual way, as defined by the sequence of synonyms 'persistence, keeping going, continuance', and gives the image of the chariot wheel to elucidate the idea that life is short 'through the limitation of (its) duration'.[16] In both texts, there follow these verses[17]

> Life, individuality (*attabhāva*), all pleasure and pain
> continue for one short mind-moment . . .
> Even those gods who live for eighty thousand aeons*
> are not identical for two mind (-moment)s.

8.2.2. Life is but a moment

There is, then, developed through the form of mental asceticism which consists in the increasing introjection of meditative reflection on impermanence and death, a formal parallel in Buddhist thought between the ordinary idea of a lifetime, and that of the infinitesimal 'moment' in which 'real' elements exist. The parallel is drawn explicitly by the *Theravāda* tradition: 'Past, future, and present are two-fold, according to the method of the Suttas or the analysis of the *Abhidhamma*. According to the method of the Suttas it is divided by lifetime . . . According to the analysis of the *Abhidhamma* it is divided by moment.' The text explains (using the example of matter (*rūpa*)) that in the former case all matter before birth is past, all that after death is future, while 'the matter occurring between rebirth and death is present'. In the latter case, there are three parts of a moment: 'arising, presence, and cessation'. Matter which has passed through these three sub-moments is past, that which has not yet passed through them is future, while 'matter passing through these three (sub-)moments is present'.[18]

The analogy here may be traced in terminology other than the precise formal parallel of birth-life-death and arising-presence-cessation. We read that formations are characterised by 'arising, change in what persists (or "continuous change"), and old age'.[19] (The commentary here explains old age by 'decay' (*jarā*).) Similarly, we read that an 'occurring moment' has three phases, 'arising, decay, and cessation'.[20] The *Visud-*

* That is, gods in the highest heaven. See Table 2 in Chapter 7.

dhimagga declares that (the idea of) 'continuity is destroyed' by seeing the 'rise and fall' of things, their 'arising, growing old, becoming otherwise'.[21] The 'arising' of elements is described as their 'acquisition of individuality' – the term used, that is, in conventional language, for rebirth in a new life.[22]

Given that the idea of the momentary, perceptually subliminal existence of real and ultimate elements had arisen through such a development of Buddhist thought and practice, there still remained the problem, for Buddhist scholasticism, of producing a comprehensive account of the psycho-physical functioning of such elements. This account had not only to deal with ordinary perception and cognition, with the process of death and rebirth, and so on, but it had to face a specific problem: the elements supposed to be involved in conscious processes could not be imagined to be continuously active, without a break, throughout every infinitesimal 'moment' of life; indeed, there were states of mind such as deep, dreamless sleep and the meditative state of cessation, where no conscious activity was said to take place for some length of time. The key to the answers given to these problems lies in the distinction between the mind in its active state, in which 'mental processes' (*citta-vīthi*) occur, and the mind when inactive, 'process-free' (*vīthi-mutta*). This latter state of mind was termed *bhavaṅga*; though equally momentary, equally subject to the sub-moments of arising, presence, and cessation within each moment, *bhavaṅga*-mind could be assumed to exist on all those occasions when the elements of active consciousness were not.*

8.3. The *bhavaṅga*-mind

8.3.1. Origin and etymology of the term

The details of the concept of *bhavaṅga* are found in the commentarial literature, the *Milinda Pañha*, *Visuddhimagga*, and the twelfth century 'Summary of *Abhidhamma*' (*Abhidhammattha-saṃgaha*); there is a bare mention of some of the terms of its use in the theory of perception and cognition, in what appears to be its final form, in the earlier *Abhidhamma* work, the *Paṭṭhāna*.[1] The earliest occurrence of the word is in the Suttas, where it is by no means the technical term it was to become, but nevertheless is used in a way wholly consonant with the general Buddhist attitude to continuity. There are two sets of four *aṅgas*, 'constituents', 'limbs', or 'parts': first the constituents of morality, concentration, wisdom, and release. (As we saw, these are the parts of the (completed) Path.) Secondly, there are the constituents of body, perception, feeling,

* With the notable exception of cessation. See further below.

and existence or becoming (*bhavaṅgam*). Clearly here the generic term *bhava* is being used in place of the fourth and fifth *khandhā*, mental formations and consciousness, taken together. These two, as we saw in Chapter 7, are the crucial agents of rebirth and continuity generally, and it was their joint function in this regard which led to the idea of construction-consciousness as the agent and medium of rebirth. It is quite natural, then, for these two to be called the 'constituent of existence'.[2]

The term *bhavaṅga*, 'limb', 'factor', or 'constituent of existence', is used also to refer to any and all of the twelve members of the Dependent Origination sequence.*[3] Poussin,[4] reviewing the *Théorie des Douze Causes* in Buddhism, comments here that of all the twelve it is *viññāṇa*, consciousness, which,

> on account of its permeating [all the other parts] and its persistence, receives *par excellence* the name of *bhavaṅga*, chief part of existence. It is the seed and the marrow, as much from the physical point of view as the psychological, of all that development which constitutes an existence (*ātmabhāva*), a 'share' of life between a conception and a death – a development which is not supported by any permanent principle (soul), but which is nevertheless organic, vitalist, governed by an internal force.

When considered in this light, *bhavaṅga* can be seen relatively colourlessly as a 'part', or particular (individual) 'portion' of being.[5] Nyanaponika speculates that '*aṅga* may here have the alternative meaning of "link" as well, and consequently *bhavaṅga* would signify "link of existence"'. As he says, however, 'the word *aṅga* in the compound *bhavaṅga* is usually explained in the Commentaries by *kāraṇa*, "cause"; accordingly the entire term would mean, literally, "cause" (or condition) of (continued) existence'.[6] It is a condition of existence in two senses: first, in the sense of its mere occurrence as a phenomenon of the saṃsāric, temporally extended sphere, as a necessary part of any individual name-and-form. As befits such a formation, it is both a causal, 'construct-ive' and a resultant, 'construct-ed' factor: as the latter, it is said that one of the 'occasions for the occurrence' (literally 'maturation', or 'ripening') of resultant-consciousness is '*bhavaṅga* for the length of a life'.[7] Secondly, it is itself a conditioning factor of existence, in the particular sense of being a necessary condition for any *conscious* experience of life. It is only on the basis of *bhavaṅga* that any mental processes can arise. Thus it is said that while *karma* is the general condition of any 'resultant mind', it is *bhavaṅga* which is the condition for 'active mind'.[8] Any one 'stream' of *bhavaṅga* provides the opportunity for, and links together, a series of mental processes, in one connected and conscious existence. The western

* In the same relatively colourless way as the eight parts of the Path are called its eight 'limbs', *aṭṭhaṅga*.

philosopher J. S. Mill defined matter as a 'permanent possibility of sensation': one might borrow the phraseology here to describe the *bhavaṅga* – the 'subject' of what Mill calls 'sensation' rather than its object – as offering an 'impermanent possibility of experience'.

These, then, are the meanings attributed to the term *bhavaṅga* in *Theravāda*, and its general place in the logic of personal continuity. I will turn now to the function it is held to have in a number of different particular contexts: deep sleep, ordinary perception, and cognition, the process of death and rebirth, and the meditative state of cessation; finally, I will look at the idea, to which scattered references are made in *Theravāda*, of *bhavaṅga-citta* as 'pure and luminous mind'.

8.3.2. Its functions

(i) *In deep sleep*. In a tidy and internally coherent way, the concept of *bhavaṅga* is used to explain the condition of deep sleep, in which no conscious processes, no dreams, occur. In the *Milinda Pañha* Nāgasena explains that

> one who dreams does so neither when (fully) asleep nor when awake, but in the interval state while falling deeply asleep before *bhavaṅga* is reached . . . When someone is deeply asleep, his mind is in the *bhavaṅga* state; a mind in the *bhavaṅga* state does not function . . . whereas one sees dreams with a functioning mind.

The stage of sleep in which dreams occur is called 'monkey-sleep . . . the middle stage of sleep' whereas 'the final stage is in *bhavaṅga*'.[9] The commentary to the *Abhidhamma* work *Vibhaṅga* says that dreams occur neither when one is deeply asleep nor when one is awake. On the one hand, 'one sleeps (deeply) with *bhavaṅga*-mind; this has no perceptual or cognitive object [literally "no object consisting in (material) form, etc."] nor is it associated with desire etc. These sorts of mind occur in one who is dreaming.' Accordingly, to ascribe dreams to this *bhavaṅga* state would involve a 'conflict with *Abhidhamma*'. On the other hand, to count dreaming sleep as a form of being awake would involve a 'conflict with the Code of Discipline', since a man is not to be held morally responsible for what occurs in dreams, as he is when awake. Rather, dreams occur to one in 'monkey-sleep'; 'for just as the sleep of a monkey is quick to change, so is this sleep . . ., which occurs again and again, arising from *bhavaṅga*'.[10] The *Visuddhimagga* explains that '*bhavaṅga*-consciousness occurs . . . as long as no other (state of) mind arises to interrupt its continuity . . . occurring endlessly as in periods of deep, dreamless sleep'.[11]

(ii) *In perception and cognition.** The *Vijñānavāda* school of Buddhism uses a concept of *ālaya-vijñāna*, the 'home-consciousness', which has many similarities with the *Theravāda bhavaṅga*.[12] There are differences, however: in Vasubandhu's version of *Vijñānavāda*, in what is called his 'idealist' system, the objects of normal perception are created out of the *ālaya-vijñāna* in just the same way as are dreams; that is, both are equally 'illusory', equally 'unreal'.[13] In *Theravāda*, on the contrary, although *bhavaṅga*-mind shares the same formal relationship to the arising both of dreams and of normal perception, it is never suggested that the objects of the two forms of 'mental process' are either ontologically or epistemologically equivalent.† The arising of the mental process of perception, as we shall see presently, 'interrupts the continuity of *bhavaṅga*' in the same way that the occurrence of dreams in 'monkey-sleep' does; but the similarity in psychological process should not be thought necessarily to entail any further ontological commitment.

In order to see the details of the mental process of perception in a proper perspective, one should remember two general themes of Buddhist psychological thought. In the first place, it is regularly said that all six sense-consciousnesses arise through, and in dependence on, the internal sense-organ and the external sense-object. Thus in the case of mind, 'mental consciousness arises dependent on mind and mental objects'.[14] The physical senses, when not actively involved in the processes of perceptual consciousness, could be supposed to continue simply as parts of the continuing body. The continued existence of mind when not involved in mental consciousness, on the other hand, presented a problem. The problem was solved in later *Theravāda* by the assertion that mind in this state was *bhavaṅga*-mind.[15] The *Visuddhimagga* says that 'mental consciousness arises dependent on *bhavaṅga*-mind, mental object, and attention'.[16]

In the second place, as we have seen, it is said that the life-formations pass away with unimaginable speed, and that the formations of mind are even quicker to change than those of the body. In the development of the theory of mental processes, this relationship was quantified, so that one moment of matter is equivalent to sixteen or seventeen moments of mind.‡ Thus 'the lifespan of material phenomena is seventeen moments of mind';[17] in a description of 'the short duration of the material

* As mind is considered in Buddhism to be a sixth 'sense-base' (*āyatana*), I will use the simple term 'perception' in the text of this section to refer both to the perceiving of objects of the physical senses, and to the cognising of objects of mind, that is thoughts.

† On this see further section (v) below.

‡ The two figures arise through the inclusion in any one sequence of one moment of *bhavaṅga* before the start of the mental process proper. (That is, whether, in the list given below, moment number one, 'past *bhavaṅga*' is included in the mental process or not.)

life-faculty', we read that 'while (one moment of) matter that has arisen is present, sixteen (moments of) mind arise and break up'. Similarly,

> While (one moment of) matter endures, *bhavaṅga*-mind arises and ceases sixteen times. Mind's (sub-) moments of arising, presence and cessation are equal; but of matter, the arising and cessation (sub-) moments are quick, like those (of mind), whereas the presence (sub-) moment is long – it lasts while sixteen moments of mind arise and cease.[18]

The concomitance of the two is likened to a tall, long-striding man, and a small, short-striding man walking together. For every step that the tall man takes, the small one takes sixteen.[19]

With these two general points in mind, then, I will turn to the details of a mental process in an act of perception* (I will adopt the seventeen-moment version). The stages are given in the list below.

1. *atīta bhavaṅga*	past *bhavaṅga*-moment
2. *bhavaṅga calana*	disturbance of *bhavaṅga*
3. *bhavaṅga upaccheda*	*bhavaṅga* 'cut off'
4. *pañcadvārāvajjana*	'advertence' through the five sense-doors
5. *pañca-viññāṇa*	consciousness (through one) of the five senses
6. *sampaṭicchana*	'reception'
7. *santīraṇa*	'examination'
8. *voṭṭhapana*	'determining'
9–15. *javana*	(karmically-operative) 'impulsions'
16–17. *tadārammaṇa*	'registering'

Since my concern with this seventeen-moment series is with its relevance to the problem of continuity, I think that many details of its account of a perceptual process can safely be ignored.[20] For the present purpose, the series can perhaps be divided into four sections. Firstly, moments one to three represent the initial entry of the perceptual object into the 'subject's' awareness – better said, into the receptive medium of mind, temporarily associated with material elements in one name-and-form. Second, moments four to eight represent a gradually increasing attention to the stimulus, in which its particular nature and qualities are recognised. Third, moments nine to fifteen represent the reaction to the stimulus, in the sense of 'full cognition' or 'apperception' – two equivalents for *javana* often given in modern *Theravāda* works. (It is during these moments that the perceptual process becomes karmically significant, through the operation of desire, 'the conceit "I am"', and so on.

* In the case of an object 'entering through the mind-door' (that is, a thought), the process passes directly from moment number four, 'adverting', to number nine, the first 'impulsion'.

The previous moments one to eight are thought of as results of previous *karma*.) Lastly, moments sixteen and seventeen represent a 'registering' of the perception as a whole, including the *javana* reaction. These two moments occur only if the stimulus is strong. In modern terms, perhaps, one might interpret these two moments as the transition from a perception to the (short-term) memory of it; a transition necessary if the event is to be stored in (long-term) memory. The figure below gives a diagrammatic rendering of the arising of one such mental process in a continuing stream of *bhavaṅga*.

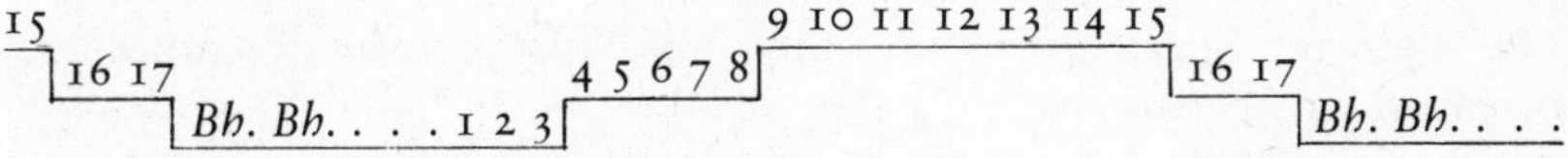

There is an extended simile quoted in many texts, both ancient and modern, which admirably illustrates the process, and connects the present use of the *bhavaṅga* concept with that in connexion with deep sleep, which we have already met.[21] A man is sleeping under a mango tree, with his head covered (past *bhavaṅga*-moments, and moment one); the wind rustles the branches, loosens a mango-fruit, and it falls, striking the sleeping man (moments two and three); he is aroused from sleep (moment four); removes his head covering (moment five); he picks up the fruit (moment six); examines it (moment seven); recognises it as a mango (moment eight); he eats it (moments nine–fifteen); along with the last morsels, or after-taste (moments sixteen–seventeen), he puts back his head covering and goes back to sleep (subsequent *bhavaṅga* moments).

Excursus: *bhavaṅga* and the 'unconscious'. This is perhaps the point to offer some remarks on the use of the modern term 'unconscious' as a translation of *bhavaṅga*. Many modern *Theravāda* writers do so.[22] As a loose translation it will – perhaps – suffice, as will the even looser 'subconscious'. Insofar, however, as the term might be thought to include interpretation as well as simple word-translation, serious difficulties arise. Certainly, the *bhavaṅga* is a mental but not conscious phenomenon; but in following the sense of the term 'unconscious' further into psychoanalytic theory, the similarity ends. For Freud, the word unconscious was used not only in what he called a 'descriptive' sense, but also in a 'systematic' sense.[23] That is, as he writes, apart from the descriptive sense, in which 'we call a psychical process unconscious whose existence we are obliged to assume – for some such reason as that we infer it from its effects – but of which we know nothing', it is also the case that 'we have come to understand the term "unconscious" in a topographical or systematic sense as well . . . and have used the word more and more to denote a mental province rather than a quality of what is mental'.[24] Insofar as the Buddhist concept of *bhavaṅga* might be thought of as being part of a *topographical* account of mind, it is so only in relation to a systematic account of perception, and not of motivation. The motivation of action, of course, is the crucial area of psychology for any psychoanalytic theory. While many aspects of the Buddhist attitude to motivation do resemble some Freudian themes,[25] they are nowhere related systematically to the *bhavaṅga* in the *Theravāda* tradition before modern times. Accordingly, the modern comparison between *bhavaṅga* and the psychoanalytic unconscious must be developed as part of what one might call 'speculative' or 'creative' Buddhist philosophy, rather than by historical scholarship.

(iii) *In death and rebirth.*[26] A modified form of the mental process of perception is held to explain the process of death and rebirth. The stages are given in the list below.

	1.	*atīta bhavaṅga*	past *bhavaṅga*-moment
	2.	*bhavaṅga calana*	disturbance of *bhavaṅga*
Previous	3.	*bhavaṅga upaccheda*	*bhavaṅga* 'cut off'
Life	4.	*manodvārāvajjana*	'advertence through the mind-door'
	5–9.	*javana*	'impulsions'
	10–11.	*tadārammaṇa*	'registering'
	12.	*cuti citta*	death-thought
'Death'			
New	13.	*paṭisandhi-viññāṇa*	rebirth-linking consciousness
Life	14.	*bhavaṅga*	*bhavaṅga*

The process here from moments one to eleven is the same as any process of thought (as opposed to perception) during life. The 'death-thought' of moment twelve is a species of *bhavaṅga*: 'the very last *bhavaṅga*-mind of one life is called the "death(-moment)"'.[27] The next moment, 'rebirth-linking', is part of the mental side of a new name-and-form. This consciousness is usually explained as being that referred to as the third 'limb' of the Dependent Origination series, and in the idea of the 'descent of consciousness' at rebirth. In the next moment the *bhavaṅga* of a new life begins, to continue its 'stream' in the normal way. The content of the last thought, the five 'impulsion' moments, is of a special nature, which allows us, even in the midst of such abstruse intellectual Buddhist concepts, to refer yet again to the ideas of 'popular' Buddhism, indeed to ideas of Indian folklore generally. Here again, we can see that, as I argued earlier, 'Buddhist ultimate doctrine systematises . . . structures of thought which existed, and continue to exist, in a wider cultural dispersion.'

The content of the last thought before death, it is said, can be one of three possible kinds. First, it can be a memory of a significant act done shortly before death, or of an act habitually performed during life. Second, it can be not an actual act, whether recent or habitual, but a symbolic image of acts done during life – for example, a knife in the case of a butcher. Third, it can be an image or symbol of the sphere in which rebirth is to take place.[28] In giving these three possible contents of a last thought, Buddhist theory is incorporating the idea, found throughout India, that the last thought before death, whether a memory of life or an anticipation of rebirth, is of special importance in determining the subsequent rebirth.[29] Many examples of this idea can be found in two works of the *Theravāda* canonical tradition, both of which derive from 'popular' Buddhism: the *Petavatthu* and *Vimānavatthu*, 'Stories of the Departed' and 'Stories of the Mansions [that is to say, Heavens]'. Indeed, in the Suttas, monks visit laymen on their death-bed, to ensure their dying thoughts are wholesome; and the Buddha recommends that lay-followers similarly encourage each other in Buddhist virtues on such occasions.[30]

In the cases of the process of death and rebirth, of the ordinary processes of perception, and of deep sleep, the *bhavaṅga* functions quite literally as a 'stop-gap' in the sequence of moments which constitutes mental continuity. There is, however, another possible gap in mental continuity which the *bhavaṅga* does not 'stop up'.

(iv) *In 'cessation'.* We have already encountered, on a number of occasions, the highest meditative attainment possible in Buddhism, the 'cessation of perception and feeling' (*saññā-vedayita-nirodha*). In so far as this is a state, like deep sleep, in which no conscious activity, no 'mental process' occurs, we might expect that cessation should be thought to consist simply, like deep sleep, in an unbroken sequence of *bhavaṅga*-moments. We saw also that the difference between life and death was due to the presence in the former of 'life, heat, and consciousness'; it might be thought that as a monk in cessation is still alive, his remaining consciousness should be the *bhavaṅga*-mind. Other Buddhist schools which argued for the concept of a type or level of consciousness akin to the *Theravāda's bhavaṅga* did use both deep sleep and cessation together as examples of the need for such a type of consciousness.[31] Indeed, in the *Milinda Pañha* passage I quoted earlier discussing *bhavaṅga* and deep sleep, cessation is given as the other occasion on which there is no 'functioning mind'.[32] However, it is quite clear from a number of different texts that there is in cessation no 'functionless' *bhavaṅga*-mind either. A monk in cessation is 'without mind'; when he enters it his 'mental continuity is suspended'.[33] It is only possible to attain the state in a sphere with all five *khandhā*, 'because of the absence of physical basis' in spheres without body.[34] We have seen that it is the 'material life-faculty' which continues during cessation, while 'immaterial phenomena', in which the *bhavaṅga* must be included, are suspended.[35] It is said that one of the things which a monk intending to attain the state should do is to ascertain whether or not his 'life-formations' will last for the requisite seven days. This is important because cessation 'cannot ward off death' and so the arrival of death during the seven days for which cessation was meant to last, would bring an untimely end to the state, in order that death should occur. The commentary here explains that 'there is no death during cessation because death takes place by means of the final *bhavaṅga*'.[36] In normal circumstances, it is only when the state ceases, and after two moments of active consciousness have passed, that there occurs again a 'subsidence into *bhavaṅga*'.[37]

Personal continuity spanning a period of cessation, then, is guaranteed by the continued existence of the body, or rather the material life-faculty, and not by the continued occurrence of *bhavaṅga*-moments. Certainly the state of cessation is a very rare occurrence, and for practical purposes in every other sphere of psychology *bhavaṅga* can be regarded as the crucial factor in continuity. For theoretical purposes, however, the non-existence of *bhavaṅga* in cessation cannot be ignored, and so it cannot be held to be in every sphere the *sine qua non* of identity and continuity that the modern Theravādins whom I quoted at the beginning of this chapter regard it as being.

(v) *As 'pure' and 'luminous' mind.* Throughout the history of Buddhism, in all parts of Asia, one finds the theme that mind in its 'natural' or 'original' state is 'pure', 'bright', 'luminous', and so on, while its usual state of being 'defiled' or 'dusty', is the result of the individual's perceiving objects and events with desire.[38] While this idea is not developed and systematised in *Theravāda*, as it was in other schools, we do find traces and suggestions of it; and it is mind in its *bhavaṅga* state which is said to be pure and luminous.

The metaphors of 'cleansing' and 'purifying' the mind, and thus making it 'bright', naturally run into each other. When a *Sutta* speaks of the mind being stained and dirty as a cloth might be, the commentary explains that mind is dirtied by 'adventitious defilements' and that 'naturally [or "ordinarily"], when mind is at the stages of rebirth linking and *bhavaṅga*, it is thoroughly pure'. 'Natural mind' is *bhavaṅga*-mind.[39] In a standard sequence of adjectives describing the mind of a monk who has attained the higher stages of the Buddhist Path, and the consequent higher powers, such mind is said to be 'purified and cleansed'; the *Visuddhimagga* glosses the latter as 'bright', or 'luminous'. (The image of the purified, undefiled mind as bright (usually like gold) is common.)[40] A famous passage quoted frequently in the later literature of *Theravāda*, both ancient and modern, has it that 'mind, when freed from adventitious defilements, is luminous'. The commentaries here say that 'mind' means *bhavaṅga*-mind.[41]

Theravāda has not systematised this ethical and psychological metaphor into an epistemological and metaphysical 'idealism', as did other Buddhist schools. For the *Vijñānavāda* for instance, there was no difference between the fact of mental objects' existing at all, and the fact of mental defilement. It is only the ignorant, desiring, unenlightened mind which creates out of itself the separation between subject (*grāhaka*, 'grasper') and object (*grāhya*, 'grasped'). In *Theravāda*, what we might call the 'idealist tendency', which in some contexts is quite pronounced,[42] is confined to the ethical sphere. That is to say, mind is regarded as creating the *desirability* of the objects of perception and thought, not their very existence. Thus there is a distinction to be drawn between the mere fact of mental objects existing, and their being occasions for moral defilement. However, insofar as for any *unenlightened* individual, any mental process is potentially, and indeed usually, an occasion for desire and 'the conceit "I am"', one might argue that the 'idealist' and 'ethical' approaches to the idea of 'pure mind' amount in practice to much the same thing. Accordingly, it is in this sense, perhaps, that when no such mental process occurs, the 'process-free' mind which is left – *bhavaṅga* – is said to be pure and luminous.

8.4. River imagery

The *Theravāda* concept of *bhavaṅga*, then, is this: with the exception of the meditative state of cessation, where personal continuity is carried by bodily continuity, the identity and continuity of one karmic unit – of one 'person' or 'individuality' within a lifetime, and of a single series of them, across a number of rebirths – is guaranteed by the existence of moments of *bhavaṅga*-mind, which occur whenever there are no moments of mental process, of conscious functioning. Each of these *bhavaṅga*-mind moments, of course, is itself a separate, temporally 'atomic' existent; and so, when we read a modern *Theravāda* writer telling us that moments of conscious functioning are 'like beads strung on the connecting thread of *bhavaṅga*',[1] we must realise that in 'ultimate' terms this connecting thread is itself like a series of beads. Indeed, since the 'connecting thread' does not exist when the beads of conscious functioning do – as we saw, it is 'cut off' – the image finally breaks down as a systematic representation.[2] The continuity of one karmic unit is simply a string of beads – some of which are moments of conscious functioning, some of which are 'unconscious' *bhavaṅga*-mind – which have no underlying connecting thread, save the overall force of *karma* which creates them. This example shows a general difficulty in the interpretation of theoretical concepts in Buddhist psychology in terms of inappropriate or misinterpreted imagery; and this is even more forcefully demonstrated by that other image which the *Theravāda* tradition, both ancient and modern, has chosen as its regular description of the *bhavaṅga*-mind: that of a flowing river or stream.

8.4.1. The stream of *bhavaṅga*

It is said that in one lifetime, between what are called in ultimate terms the 're-linking-' and the 'death-moments', 'in the absence of mental processes, a mind called "continuity of *bhavaṅga*", because of its being a part (or "condition") of existence, occurs unbrokenly like a flowing river'.[3] The *Visuddhimagga*, in explaining that *bhavaṅga* occurs in periods such as deep sleep without mental processes, has it that *bhavaṅga* occurs 'like a flowing river'. From this simile derives the more immediate metaphorical term 'stream of *bhavaṅga*'.[4] The image is used in more detailed ways to picture specific ideas: the two moments of 'registering' (numbers sixteen and seventeen in the perceptual process) are said to follow the 'impulsion' moments, as water follows a little after a boat going upstream. The same image occurs elsewhere with the boat going 'across a fierce current'; here 'registering' occurs, and then gives way to *bhavaṅga*, just as a little water follows the boat and then goes 'with the stream' again. The interruption of *bhavaṅga* by a process of perception is likened, in an elaborate simile, to the water of a river being diverted into irrigation channels, and eventually returning to the 'full river', 'the time when the water flows [only] in the river is like that of the proceeding of *bhavaṅga*'.[5]

The idea of a 'stream of consciousness', of course, is common in western thinking, as a term in philosophy, psychology, and literary criticism. The phrase is often used by modern *Theravāda* writers, and by western interpreters, sometimes in conjunction with the idea (apparently but perhaps wrongly derived from Heraclitus)[6] of a Doctrine of Flux, to suggest that in early Buddhism mind was regarded as a pseudo- or semi-continuity, like a river produced from ever-changing waters, such that any two temporal stages of the river are 'both the same' as, and 'different' from each other (or neither), and so on.[7] I would not want to argue that something like this cannot be seen as the general attitude of Buddhism; I would argue, however, that river imagery in the early *Theravāda* texts had an entirely different specific meaning. The uses to which the imagery is put are various, as I shall show presently; but it is never used in *Theravāda* texts to illustrate the fact of change and the connected paradoxes of identity and difference. Rather, the dominant idea is of desire, and life-in-*saṃsāra*, as an uncontrolled forward flow, in which the ignorant unenlightened man is swept away to suffering and death. The use of the river image to illustrate the idea of *bhavaṅga*-mind is to be seen in terms of this underlying attitude.

8.4.2. Negative uses: the stream of desire

The imagery of streams, rivers, and water in general in the *Theravāda* tradition can be divided into two groups, which I will call the 'negative' and 'positive' uses – a distinction which is meant to indicate whether the themes and concepts illustrated by such imagery receive negative or positive evaluation in Buddhist thought.

In the negative use, the fundamental idea is of desire, of the craving for and enjoyment of sense-pleasure as an uncontrollable force, a current by which one is drowned or carried along helplessly in the round of rebirth, *saṃsāra*.[8] We read of 'desire that flows along', of 'attachment and sense-pleasures that flow along', of the 'swift-flowing stream of desire'. In the *Visuddhimagga* desire is called both a stream and a river, and it is said that 'greed, swollen with the river of craving' takes beings to hell as a swift river flows to the ocean.[9] Indeed, 'there is no river like the river of desire'. The 'stream of death' which enlightened monks have 'cut, and crossed safely' is naturally explained by the commentary as the stream of desire. The image of 'cutting' this stream is very frequent: those who 'cut the stream which is hard to cross, reach final *nibbāna*'. A released monk is called 'one who has cut the stream'; it is elsewhere explained that: '"stream" is a term for desire . . . so a monk who has destroyed the corruptions is called "one who has cut the stream"'.[10]

In contrast with this, the man who still sees the constituents of personality as a self comes to misery and destruction like one carried away and drowned by the current of a fierce mountain stream. The process of Dependent Origination, which keeps one within the temporal world of *saṃsāra*, is compared to the flow of rainwater down hillsides, into streams, lakes, and rivers, and finally into the sea; while the 'swelling' of the sea, flooding the rivers, lakes, and streams in turn, and then their subsequent 'ebbing' back when the sea ebbs, illustrates the increase and decrease of the conditioning process as each of its twelve members 'swells' and 'ebbs' in turn.[11]

The image is indeed applied generally to life-in-*saṃsāra* in just this way. Those who are 'insatiate for sense-pleasure', and those who are under the sway of death because of their 'lust for existence', and those for whom thus 'far away is destruction of the fetters', are all said to 'float down the stream of existence' (or 'rebirth'). All such people are 'carried along by the stream of *saṃsāra*'.[12]

From this fundamental, negative, association between the idea of desire and that of a flowing stream, we can trace two further applications of the image: one general, and one particular. In general, life-in-*saṃsāra* is seen as drowning in a river, or ocean, while attaining *nibbāna* is 'crossing over' to the 'further shore',[13] by means of a ship or a raft. (Buddhist teaching is likewise an island by which one can escape drowning in the sea.) The image is so common that the epithets *pāraga*, *pāragato*, and *pāragū*, 'crossing' or 'crossed over' come to be used in these meanings without any explicitly marked simile.[14] In the same general pattern of imagery can be classed the opposition between those who 'go with the stream' and those who 'go against the stream'. The former succumb to sense-desire, and so on, while the latter – par excellence, of course, the Buddha and his teaching – go against that stream. The idea receives a neat symbolic expression in the legendary biography of the Buddha. After he had abandoned the 'fruitless' extreme of asceticism, and had decided to take food again, he accepted a bowl of milk-rice from the woman Sujātā. After eating, he placed the bowl in a nearby river, saying that if that day he were to be able to become a Buddha, the bowl should go upstream; if not, it should go downstream. It floated upstream, and then sank, coming to rest next to the bowls of the three previous Buddhas. In the same vein, those who make progress in the Buddhist Path are regularly said to go 'upstream'.[15]

The second, and particular, further way of applying the imaginative identification of the ideas of desire, pleasure, and so on with that of a flowing stream or river, is its use to illustrate more specific matters of individual psychology. An extended example of this is the following, which also serves to summarise much of what we have already seen of river imagery:

> Suppose a man is carried away by a flowing river, which has the appearance of being pleasant and enjoyable. Then a wise man standing on the bank sees him and says 'my good man, you are being carried away by a flowing river . . . further down there is a lake with waves and whirlpools, with demons and monsters. When you reach there you will find suffering and death!' Then the man, hearing the other's words, struggles against the stream with hands and feet.

I use this simile, monks, to explain my meaning – which is this: 'the flowing river' is a term for desire; 'which has the appearance of being pleasant and enjoyable' is a term for the six organs of sense; 'the lake further down' a term for the five lower fetters; 'with waves' a term for the turbulence of anger; 'with whirlpools' a term for the five strands of sense-pleasure; 'with demons and monsters' a term for womenfolk; 'against the stream' a term for renunciation; 'with hands and feet' a term for the application of energy; 'a wise man' is a term for the Buddha.[16]

We read elsewhere that 'the misguided man in whom the thirty-six streams* that flow toward sense-pleasures are strong, is carried away by the waves of lustful thought'. More briefly, it is said that 'the streams flow everywhere', and that 'mindfulness is their dam'. One is urged to 'cut the stream, discard sense-pleasure', whereas foolish ordinary men, who delight in the senses and their objects, 'are carried away by that stream'. In the ordinary processes of mind, mental consciousness is said to follow habitually after sense-consciousness, as drops of water follow each other down a slope.[17]

In the end, the flowing streams of sense-desire must be 'cut' or 'crossed' completely; nevertheless, for the duration of the Path, a monk must perforce work with motivational and perceptual processes as they ordinarily are, that is to say, based on desire. Accordingly, for this specific context, the imagery can be used without the extreme condemnation it carries in the passages I have cited so far.† Thus, during mental training, the stream is not to be 'cut' immediately, but guided, like water along viaducts. The meditative steadying of the mind by counting in- and out-breaths (in the mindfulness of breathing) is compared to the steadying of a boat in 'a fierce current' by its rudder. The disturbance of the flow of a mountain stream by irrigation channels cut into its sides is used to illustrate the weakening of insight by the five 'hindrances'.[18]

Apart from this secondary use of the image to illustrate the monk's psychology during training, the overwhelmingly important use of stream and river imagery, then, in its negative side, is to picture the continuance of life through the uncontrollable forward rush of desire. Given the place of the idea of *bhavaṅga* in the logic of continuity in Buddhist thought, it is perhaps now not surprising that it is seen as a 'flowing stream'. As long as there is a continuing mind caught in the temporally extended sphere of *saṃsāra*, rushing along as the 'stream of desire', for so long will

* That is, the six senses and their respective six objects, considered in relation to the three desires for sense-pleasure (*kāma*), further existence (*bhava*) and non-existence (*vibhava*).

† The relationship between this kind of use of stream imagery in descriptive psychology, and the more basic condemnation of 'the stream of desire', has the same form as the relationship between the idea of 'seeds of good *karma*' and the basic condemnation of 'planting seeds for the growth of consciousness' which I described in Chapter 7; and as that between the use of the idea of 'living in the body-house of individuality' during the course of training, and the ultimate goal of 'leaving home' which I described in Chapter 5.

mind – when not functioning in 'mental processes' – be in the *bhavaṅga* state. Hence *bhavaṅga* occurs 'unbrokenly like a flowing river'.

8.4.3. The Doctrine of Flux and the stream of consciousness

As an example of the assimilation of Buddhist thought in this connexion to that of a Heraclitean Doctrine of Flux, I will discuss Rāhula's treatment of another instance of this pattern of negative river imagery.[19] It occurs in a story of a former teacher called Araka, who lived in an era when a human lifetime lasted sixty thousand years, and girls were marriageable at five hundred; nonetheless, Araka taught that 'just as a mountain river, going here and there, flowing swiftly, taking all with it, does not pause even for a moment, an instant, a second, but goes along, moves along, flows on, so like a mountain river is the life of man, trifling, short'. The moral is drawn: 'for the born there is no immortality'. Nowadays, a man is said to live long if he lasts for a hundred years or a little more, and life is plagued with more afflictions. How much more true are Araka's words now?[20] Because of the presence of terms for very short amounts of time – especially the word *khaṇo*, 'moment' – this passage is often quoted as a forerunner of the theory of momentariness, and is taken to illustrate, as Rāhula says, that the *khandhā* 'are not the same for two consecutive moments . . . They are in a flux of momentary arising and disappearing.' In fact, as can be seen from the context of the simile, it is the brevity of life, not its changeability, which is being illustrated.[21] The passage is quoted by the *Visuddhimagga* in the sequence of reflections on death which I discussed earlier in this chapter (8.2.1 above). The simile is given, however, to illustrate life's 'limitedness of extent' – in that it lasts only for a hundred years or thereabouts – and *not* to illustrate 'momentary death'. In the same chapter of the *Visuddhimagga*, a similar image is used to illustrate the fact that death (taken as the death which is called in 'ultimate' terms 'the cutting off of the life-faculty') is inevitable for one who is born: 'A being, from the time of his birth goes toward death, not turning back even for a short while . . . just as a mountain stream, swiftly flowing, never turns back.' This simile is used of death in the usual sense, which is specifically differentiated from 'death' used in the sense of 'momentary death'.[22] The former passage, when it occurs in the Suttas, is one of a series given not to illustrate any philosophical point, but to dramatise the brevity of life and to reinforce the injunction 'live the holy life! Don't be indolent!'

I think it is clear that the image has nothing to do with the significance of change in systematic theory, or with paradoxes of identity and difference; and so Rāhula's collocation with the Buddhist passage of a version of the idea attributed to Heraclitus, 'you cannot step twice into the same river, for fresh waters are ever flowing in upon you', obscures rather than clarifies the wider imaginative world in which the river image in Buddhism is set. Indeed, the sentence quoted by Rāhula may well obscure the wider speculative thought of Heraclitus himself. The quote he gives is in fact a conflation of two of the extant fragments, the first clause being found by itself, and the second as the second half of a separate fragment, the whole of which runs 'on those who step into the same rivers, different and different waters flow'. According to a widely held view in modern Pre-Socratic scholarship, the real intention of Heraclitus' river-statement is to exemplify his fundamental doctrine of unity-in-difference; that is, the opposition is one between a genuine and real identity in the river with an equally real change in its waters. The same point is held to be made by another of the fragments, 'the barley-drink comes apart if it is not stirred': that is, the (real) being of a single thing depends on plurality and diversity in the things which make it up (in the latter case, the drink's ingredients, barley, honey, and wine). On this view, the version which speaks of the impossibility of stepping twice into the same river is held to be a later development, possibly made by the fifth-century sophist Cratylus, who would have used it – quite logically, indeed – to introduce his own idea, that it is impossible to step even *once* into the same river. In this doctrine change over time is held to deny *any* validity to the idea of identity: not, as in Heraclitus, to contrast the validity of identity with the complementary validity of change and difference.[23]

Whatever are the possible similarities or differences between the doctrines of Buddhism and Heraclitus, I think it is clear that we will not gain any insight from the apparent similarity in imagery: rather, our interpretation of the imagery will depend on a separate analysis of doctrinal theories and attitudes. The same is true of the other phrase, from modern western thought, which is used to describe the Buddhist idea of mental continuity; that of a 'stream of consciousness'. The term was first used by William James, but has perhaps become most widely known as a term of art in literary criticism, used first of the novels of Dorothy Richardson, and subsequently those of, amongst others, Virginia Woolf and James Joyce. Although one might mention here the claim that 'applied to the novel, it is, as Dorothy Richardson once said, a term characterised by its "perfect imbecility"',[24] it is doubtless too firmly entrenched in popular discourse ever to be rejected or clarified. It can be used on this level, perhaps, in the sense that it

> is reserved for indicating an approach to the presentation of *psychological* aspects of character in fiction, . . . Stream of consciousness fiction differs from all other psychological fiction precisely in that it is concerned with those levels that are

more inchoate than rational verbalisation – those levels on the margin of attention.[25]

If we turn from this vague but popular sense in literature to the precise function which the image has in the thought of the psychologist James, and of the philosopher Bergson, who is closely similar in this respect, a quite clear and fundamental contrast can be seen; this contrast is not only with the fact that the over-riding sense of the image in Buddhism is moral, but also with the technical picture of psychology and mental functioning which is illustrated by the use of the term in developed *Theravāda* philosophy. Some modern *Theravāda* writers have taken an opposite view: the western monk Ñāṇajīvako declares that

> in the oldest Buddhist texts of *Abhidhamma* ('about phenomena') the central conception of phenomenological analysis (*vibhajja-vādo*) was concentrated on the idea of a 'stream of existence' (*bhavaṅga-soto*): articulation (*aṅgaṃ*) of the existential (*bhavo*) flux (*soto*) or, in a free translation, emergence of a fluctuating articulation . . . Thus the core of the *abhidhamma* conception of the 'stream of existence' consists in its theory of momentariness. Its modern analogy (is) the philosophy of William James . . .[26]

Similarly, it is argued by the Sinhalese lay Buddhist Gunaratna that

> According to Buddhist psychology mind is nothing but a constant stream or flow of thoughts . . . Since innumerable thoughts arise and fall one after another during the day, as innumerable are these momentary interruptions to the flow of unconscious *Bhavaṅga* during the day . . . In this connection it is important to remember that not only is there a rapidity of succession of thoughts but that there is no boundary line between one thought and another. One thought merges into the other so that the expression 'Succession of thought' does not quite accurately describe the position. Hence the description by reference to a river where there is not so much a succession of waters as a flow of waters. That eminent psychologist William James . . . has a whole chapter entitled 'The stream of consciousness'.[27]

The writer here goes on to quote the passage in which James first used the image of the stream. It was indeed an image which impressed itself on him because of the inadequacy of the view of mind as a series of discrete momentary 'awarenesses' or 'impressions', in the manner of the philosopher Hume:

> The chain of distinct existences into which Hume thus chopped up our 'stream' was adopted by all of his successors as a complete inventory of the facts. The associationist philosophy was founded. Somehow, out of 'ideas', each separate, ignorant of its mates, but sticking together and calling each other up according to certain laws, all the higher forms of consciousness were to be explained, and among them the consciousness of our personal identity.[28]

The passage in which he introduced the stream image denies this view *on the grounds of its phenomenological inadequacy*:

Consciousness, then, does not appear to itself chopped up in bits. Such words as 'chain' or 'train' do not describe it fitly as it presents itself in the first instance. It is nothing jointed: it flows. A 'river' or a 'stream' are the metaphors by which it is most naturally described. In talking of it hereafter let us call it the stream of thought, of consciousness, or of subjective life.[29]

It is this fact of the *manner in which consciousness appears to itself* which is basic also to the use of the image by Bergson. He spoke, on the one hand, of the 'spatialised time' necessary and useful for 'positive science', where

what it [i.e. science] refers to is the movement of a certain mobile T on its trajectory. This movement has been chosen by it as its representative of time, and it is, by definition, uniform. Let us call T_1, T_2, T_3, . . . etc., points which divide the trajectory of the mobile into equal parts from its origin T_0.[30]

In contrast to this, however, he set 'real time' or 'real duration', in which there was no such series of discrete moments, T_1, T_2, T_3, . . . etc., but a 'flux of experience' (*flux de vécu*), in which different phases were essentially 'mutually interpenetrating', and in which the scientific series of quantitatively uniform moments was replaced by one of a qualitative variety of phases.

Which amounts to saying that real time, regarded as a flux, or, in other words, as the very mobility of being, escapes the hold of scientific knowledge . . . [Science] has no sign to express what strikes our consciousness in succession and duration. It no more applies to becoming, than the bridges thrown here and there across the stream follow the water that flows under their arches.[31]

There are certainly some strong resemblances between the thought of James and Bergson, and that of Buddhism. I myself used a quotation from James as a motto for Chapter 3; and modern *Theravāda* writers like those I have just mentioned naturally and rightly quote with approval, in support of the denial of a permanent self 'underneath' experience, the idea of Bergson that 'there are changes, but there are underneath the changes no things which change: change has no need of a support. There are movements, but there is no inert or invariable object which moves: movement does not imply a mobile.'[32] In the present context, however, which is the systematic picture of psychological continuity in one 'stream' of mental life, there are crucial differences. The strictures of James on the Humean supposition of a series of discrete 'ideas', and Bergson's strictures on the scientific view of time as a series of discrete moments, both apply to the Buddhist idea of momentariness: and so, from the point of view of historical scholarship, the assimilation of these different points of view is not justified.* That this conclusion is necessary can be seen from a number of considerations.

In the first place, the doctrine of momentariness, as we have seen, is not a *phenomenological* truth, since its 'moments' are subliminal – there are sixty-four, or even billions, to a 'finger-snap'. Its truth, then, must be argued and assessed on the level of the theoretical elaboration of a conceptual, *a priori* account of mind, and not on that of one which might be qualitatively true to experience. We saw that this conceptual representation of continuity in terms of momentariness developed out of the meditative project of reducing the scope of 'a lifetime' – birth, life, and death – until it reached the infinitesimal, subliminal (and hence intensely 'self-mortifying') moment, with its 'arising, presence, and cessation'. In the words of a modern *Theravāda* writer I quoted at the start of the chapter, 'each conscious moment in its arising and passing away is a little birth and a little death'. This presents a clear parallel to the mathematical time denied psychological validity by Bergson: 'In short, the world the mathematician deals with is a world that dies and is reborn at every instant . . . He is always talking of a given moment, a static moment that is – and not of flowing time.'[33] Similarly, I argued earlier – using the fact that the simile of the mind as a monkey jumping from one branch to another is used to illustrate both changes in the object of consciousness and changes in consciousness itself – that for *Theravāda*, change in content is equivalent to change in form; and change of form is equivalent to change in being. James specifically confronts such a position, and rejects it, arguing that 'the transition between the thought of one object and the thought of another is no more a break in the *thought* than a joint in the bamboo is a break in the wood . . . Our Thought is not composed of parts, however so composed its objects may be.'[34] As I have already mentioned,† the theory of momentariness as a conceptual, *a priori* account of mind was brought up against the logical problems it contains by other Buddhist schools – that is, they asked the question (which closely parallels the paradoxes of Zeno): what about the sub-moments of 'arising, presence, and cessation'? Did they too have sub-moments of 'arising, . . .' and so on in an infinite regress? In the versions of Buddhism held by those who made this criticism, there are perhaps more affinities with James' and Bergson's ideas of a partless and mutually interpenetrating flux, and with their criticism of the conception of mind as 'broken' or 'chopped up' into a succession of 'juxtaposed' particular

* As I mentioned in connexion with the assimilation of the *bhavaṅga*-mind and the 'unconscious', however, this does not preclude such a development of Buddhist philosophy by creative *Theravāda* thinkers.

† In n.22 of Chapter 8.2.2 above.

ideas or moments. But this version of Buddhism is precisely *not* the *Theravāda* one.

Secondarily, the point can be made by looking at the terminology in which the succession of moments, and therein the continuity of *bhavaṅga*-mind, are described. Words from the roots *bhañj*, 'to break', and *chid*, 'to cut' or 'chop' are fundamental. Each mind-moment comes to its 'cessation' (*bhaṅga*, from *bhañj*) before another can 'arise'. When a thought process occurs, after a series of moments of contentless *bhavaṅga*, the *bhavaṅga*-mind is said to be 'cut off' (*bhavaṅga-upaccheda*, from *chid*), in the third moment of the seventeen-moment series. In the case of the meditative attainment of 'cessation', personal identity is carried by the body, and not by the identity of a continuing level of mind or consciousness: in it, as we saw, 'mental continuity is suspended' (literally 'cut off', *vocchijjati* from *chid*). This same pattern of terminology can be seen in the commentarial elucidation of the one occasion on which the phrase 'the stream of consciousness' (*viññāṇa-sota*) appears in the Canon. (Naturally, this phrase is much quoted by *Theravāda* writers who wish to make the kind of assimilation I am arguing against.)[35]

The occurrence of the phrase is found in a strange and unusual passage.[36] There are, we read, four 'attainments of vision'. In the first and second, a monk meditates on the human body as a foul and decaying object. In the third he 'knows a person's stream of consciousness as unbroken on both sides, established in this world and the other'. In the fourth, he knows almost the same thing, with the difference that the consciousness he knows is 'not established' either in this world or the other. ('The other' here means the next world, after death.) We saw in Chapter 7 that the idea of consciousness being 'established' or 'stationed' in either the four or seven 'stations of consciousness' resulted from the combination of a number of different ethical, eschatological and cosmological ideas. The commentaries here repeat the idea, explaining that in the third attainment, the object of the knowledge is the consciousness of the 'ordinary man' and 'learner' on the Path, which is established in this world 'by means of lustful desire'. It is established in both this world and the next in that it 'drags on karmic existence' into the next world. As we saw also in Chapter 7, consciousness, seen in the light of karmic activity and its results, is called 'construction-consciousness'. Accordingly, the sub-commentary tells us that this is what is meant here. In the fourth attainment, the commentary tells us what is known is the consciousness of the *Arhat*, which is not 'established' because of the absence of all these things.

The image of the 'stream' is explained in the sub-commentary – the commentary merely glosses the term by the simple word *viññāṇa*, 'consciousness' – in this way: 'because of its similarity to a stream through its occurring unbrokenly, consciousness is a "stream of consciousness"'. Each moment of consciousness moreover, it says, is conditioned by the previous moment, and is itself a condition for the next moment, and it is in this way that it is similar to a stream. The words which I have translated as 'unbroken', in the *Sutta* text, and here as 'unbrokenly' in the sub-commentary, *are* both derived from the root *chid*, 'to cut'. (I choose 'unbroken(ly)' as it is more natural in English.) This terminology is not, however, to be taken as implying a systematic picture of mind as a partless flux à la James or Bergson. We have seen that the metaphor of 'cutting' the stream of desire and death is common: here, because in an 'ordinary man' or 'learner' who continues in the round of rebirth such a 'cutting' does not happen, their consciousness is said to proceed 'uncut'. The systematic picture of mind as a succession of parts, found in the theory of momentariness, is asserted by the sub-commentary here, in speaking of 'consciousness which is split up in each moment'. (The word translated as 'split up' is derived from *bhid*, 'to cut, cleave, split'.) Unusual though this idea of a 'stream of consciousness' is, we can see that the commentarial elucidation follows the pattern we have seen: for *Theravāda* a 'stream' of existence, life, or consciousness is so because it is an uncontrolled flow of desire, in which the hapless 'person' who appears in it is carried away to suffering and death, whether in this world or the next.

In this section, I have argued what might seem a wholly negative case, that river and stream imagery in *Theravāda* is *not* similar to that in Heraclitus, James, and Bergson. I think, however, that the argument finally makes a positive point, in that if one takes a step back from the complexities of this comparative argument, and tries to understand *Theravāda* thought and imagery in its own terms, and not in those of putative comparisons, the idea of *bhavaṅga*-mind 'flowing like a river' will stand out clearly as a detail in the overall canvas of river imagery used 'negatively' as an illustration of the Buddhist moral attitude to desire. It is as an aid in appreciating the specificity of Buddhist thought that it is worthwhile carefully to differentiate it from what might seem to be comparable ideas. The same is true of what I have called the 'positive' uses of river and water imagery in *Theravāda* – that is, those uses in which it is taken to illustrate ideas and attitudes which receive positive evaluation in Buddhism, unlike the 'stream of desire'. Here we can gain insight into the *Theravāda* idea of *bhavaṅga*-mind by differentiating it from other Indian styles of thinking (including some other schools of Buddhism), as well as in wider cross-cultural comparison.

8.4.4. Positive uses: calm, profundity, and the ocean

The 'positive' uses of river and water imagery in the *Theravāda* tradition cannot be brought into a single piece with the conceptual analysis of *bhavaṅga* and mind-in-*saṃsāra*. When images of water are applied to matters of individual psychology, the important idea is not that of a moving, flowing current, but of a still, cool, deep, and peaceful expanse, as in a lake or the ocean. In so far as the idea of *moving* water is used positively, it refers to the Buddhist religious life and community in its entirety, and not to matters of individual psychology.

When water imagery is used to picture psychology, the most frequent image is of the monk's mind – especially when in meditation – as a still, clear expanse of water. It is, for example, like the ocean, undisturbed by waves, or like a mountain lake, undisturbed by wind. In a frequent figure, the 'clear' mind of a meditator (in contrast to the 'muddy' mind of the ordinary man), in which all mental phenomena can be seen and classified 'as they really are' with ease, is said to be like a clear pond through which the stones, plants, and suchlike, on the bottom can be seen with ease. Equally, the man cooled from passions is like the cool waters of a lake, especially when he is in meditation. The monk plunged in meditation is like a tortoise plunged in water; speaking of a group of seven contemplations, the *Visuddhimagga* says

> just as a golden swan that loves the foothills of Citta Peak finds delight, not in a filthy puddle at the gate of a village of outcastes, but only in the Seven Great Lakes, so too this meditator-swan finds delight, not in the manifold formations seen clearly as a danger, but only in the Seven Contemplations, because he delights in development [or 'mental culture', *bhāvanā*].

The difference between fools and wise men is like the difference between noisy, gushing streams, and the smooth, silence of the great sea.[37]

The mind of a monk in meditation is 'like the Ganges, far-reaching, wide, immeasurable', as is the merit gained from the religious life of Buddhism. We saw earlier that the released man, the *Tathāgata*, is 'deep, immeasurable, unfathomable as is the great ocean'.[38] The use of ocean imagery, of what Freud called 'oceanic feeling', in the description of religious and 'mystical' states of mind has often been remarked.[39] I have mentioned more than once that there is some similarity between the *Vijñānavāda* Buddhist idea of *ālaya-vijñāna*, the 'home-consciousness', and the *Theravāda bhavaṅga*. The 'home-consciousness' is said to be like a stream, flowing onward throughout *saṃsāra*; and it is also like an ocean, on the surface of which, like waves, occur conscious processes of thought.[40] Such imagery, however, is *not* appropriate to the *bhavaṅga*, and so is not found in the *Theravāda* texts. As we have seen, when conscious processes occur, the *bhavaṅga* is interrupted, 'cut off', as it is also during the state of 'cessation'. The *Vijñānavāda* home-consciousness *does* continue to exist on both of these occasions, and so can be seen as an ocean continuing under the waves of conscious activity, and as existing quietly in the undisturbed calm of cessation. *Bhavaṅga* is not such an 'ocean'.

The last positive use of water imagery I will mention provides another example of what *bhavaṅga* is not. Just as the released man, the *Tathāgata*, is like an ocean, so the state of *nibbāna* itself is likened to an ocean, in various ways. It is said that just as an ocean is not over-filled or disturbed by the rivers that flow into it, so the *Tathāgata* is not disturbed by the minor inconveniences of life; just as the ocean rejects a corpse, bringing it up on the shore, without anger, so the *Tathāgata* dismisses those who act wrongly, but without anger. Similarly, *nibbāna* itself is not 'filled up' by the number of men who reach it, just as the ocean is not filled up by rivers. It is immeasurable, like the waters of the ocean, while the movement of the Buddhist religious life toward *nibbāna* is like that of rivers toward the ocean. So long as one does not cling to the two banks of the sense-organs and their objects, nor sink in mid-stream through 'lust for pleasure', nor become caught in the whirlpools of the five strands of sense-pleasure, one will reach *nibbāna*. The Eight-fold Path is described as a stream, and as we have seen, the first stage on this path is that of the 'stream-winner'. The monkhood as a whole flows toward *nibbāna* like a stream. Insofar as Buddhist teaching and its practice shares some of the calm peacefulness of its goal, *nibbāna*, it too is like a lake.[41]

Many of these ideas come together in a passage which compares the eight 'marvellous, wonderful things' of the ocean with those of Buddhist teaching and practice (the *Dhamma*).[42] These are:

(i) as the ocean deepens gradually, falls away from land without any sudden precipice, so the *Dhamma* is gradual, without any 'sudden attainment of insight';
(ii) as the ocean stays in one place, not overstepping its bounds, so Buddhist monks do not transgress their discipline;
(iii) as the ocean rejects a corpse, so the monkhood rejects evildoers;
(iv) as rivers lose their 'former names and lineages' and 'are reckoned simply as the ocean', so individuals of all four sections of caste society – brahmins, kṣatriyas, vaiśyas or śūdras – lose their former names and lineages when they go forth from home to homelessness, and 'are reckoned simply as "ascetics, sons of the Buddha"';
(v) as the ocean is neither depleted nor filled by the number of rivers which reach it, so *nibbāna* is not depleted or filled by the number of men who reach it;
(vi) as the ocean has one taste, that of salt, so the *Dhamma* has but the one 'taste of freedom';

(vii) as the ocean contains many treasures, so the *Dhamma* contains treasures like the Foundations of Mindfulness;
(viii) as the ocean contains many great beings, so the *Dhamma* contains the 'Eight Noble Persons'.

Clearly there are many connotations of these images, some of which might share the flavour of ocean imagery in other types of religious thought. There is one difference, however, which should be firmly remarked. The fourth comparison, concerning the loss of identity suffered by individual rivers when they reach the ocean, is the *only* place in the *Theravāda* texts where this precise simile occurs. The poetry of many other religions knows the image of the individual's relation to the Absolute reality, God, or whatever, as that of a drop of water, or a river, to the ocean. Edwin Arnold's poem on the life of the Buddha, *The Light of Asia*, which has been very influential in western understanding, ends with the line speaking of the Buddha's death, 'and so the dewdrop slips into the shining sea'. In the *Upaniṣads*, we read that the relation of all beings to Being is that of individual rivers arising from, and returning to, the sea; and that 'as flowing rivers disappear in the ocean, leaving behind [their individual] name-and-form, so the man who knows, liberated from name-and-form, goes to the divine person, higher than the high'.[43] Many other examples could be cited. When the simile appears in *Theravāda*, however, it does not concern any metaphysical questions of identity in the ultimate state, but a question of *social* identity, a losing of individual householder's identity in the 'ocean' of the monkhood. Metaphysically, neither monks nor householders have a real individuality. Accordingly, the 'stream' of *bhavaṅga*, however much it might be 'the true and innermost nature of man', as Nyanatiloka says,[44] could not be said to flow into the 'ocean' of *nibbāna*. To use river imagery in that way would be, in Buddhist eyes, simply a poetic variant of 'eternalism'.

Conclusion

True it is that man for the most part thinks in set phrases and fixed formulas; not such as he searches out for himself, but as he remembers the traditional.

Thomas Mann (1978) p. 455*

What a given religion is – its specific content – is embodied in the images and metaphors its adherents use to characterise reality . . . But such a religion's career – its historical course – rests in turn upon the institutions which render these images and metaphors available to those who thus employ them.

Clifford Geertz (1968) pp. 2–3

I hope in the main body of this work to have given some substance to the words of Thomas Mann and Clifford Geertz with which I conclude it. I suggested in the Introduction that Buddhist thought embodies certain specific conceptual hypotheses, which are addressed to quite specific and socially derived concerns. I hope now to have shown how the conceptual framework of Buddhist thinking is addressed to the particular concern of elaborating an account of selfhood, persons and their continuity, in the light of the overall *saṃsāra–nirvāṇa* dichotomy, itself predicated on the social dichotomy of layman–monk; and how this account has embodied the hypotheses of the creation of temporality by the 'constructive activity' of *karma*, the need for a coherent picture of the cessation of such creative activity if the religious goal of release is to appear intelligible, and the supposition that such a cessation takes place in the consciousness of the religious virtuoso. Let me summarise the crucial facts and ideas which I take the two quotations to point out and emphasise.

In the first, from Mann, I take it that the 'set phrases and fixed formulas' in which Buddhist thinking has been carried out refer to two things. In the first place, both the Buddha's teaching of a way to *nirvāṇa* – a religious 'absolute' independent of time and space – and the doctrines of Buddhism which describe in detail the cosmological and

* Original text: *Es ist einmal so, dass der Mensch ganz vorwiegend in Schablonen und Formeln fertigen Gespräches denkt, also nicht, wie er sichs aussucht sondern wie es gebräuchlich ist nach der Erinnerung.*

psychological reality in which it appears as a soteriological project, were articulated with the conceptual tools of Indian culture, in all its given historical and social specificity. In Chapter 1 I attempted to give some idea of the pre-Buddhist Brahmanical picture of society, religious cosmology, and eschatology, arguing that this picture was 'culturally hegemonous' for all Indian thinking. In the chapters on Buddhism, I have tried to show how – including, as a necessarily connected symbolic opposition, the negation of the fundamental Brahmanical doctrine of *ātman*, by means of the Buddhist 'denial of self' (*anattā*) – the conceptual universe elaborated in the *Theravāda* tradition has built, 'for the most part', on this traditional foundation. This is true not only in the case of the basic framework of *saṃsāra–nirvāṇa*, the particular view of temporality, and so on, but in many of the crucial connexions of ideas and particular details of its psychology and mythology. Equally, it has been the continuing social position and role of the intellectual tradition of the *Theravāda*, which has given meaning and legitimation to that conceptual 'formula' – the dichotomy between 'conventional' and 'ultimate' truth – by means of which alone the technical details of theoretical and personal analysis, used as strategies by specialist scholars and virtuoso meditators, have been inserted into a wider and more comprehensive ethical and psychological doctrine.

In the second place, this ultimate picture of psychological analysis, which, as we have seen, replaces the hotly denied conception of a transcendental self or soul, consists in fact of a traditional system of lists, or systematic categories rigidly adhered to by those monks, whether scholars or meditators or both, for whom there is nothing but 'remembering the traditional'. It is precisely the introjection of these categories and formulas – their 'point', if not all their 'details' – and the 'realising' of them personally through insight meditation, which forms in practice the most important part of the Buddhist Path to *nirvāṇa*.

In terms of apparently abstract conceptual analysis, as we have seen, the Buddhist attitude to selfhood, to personality and continuity, is that impersonal mental and material elements are arranged together in a temporarily unified configuration. What unifies and prolongs this configuration is desire; it is in desire for the enjoyment of these constituents of personality, and for their continuance, that there arises for the unenlightened man 'the conceit "I am"' (*asmimāna*), a 'conceit' which is not so much asserted propositionally as performed automatically by 'the utterance "I"' (*ahaṃkāra*). Desire here, indeed, brings about its own object – that is, the continuance of life-in-*saṃsāra*; a form of existence seen from the *nirvāṇa*-oriented virtuoso perspective as unsatisfactory, as 'suffering'. In the detailed ultimate accounts of continuity produced by Buddhist scholasticism, which we have seen in Chapters 7 and 8, the temporal extension of these 'momentary' impersonal elements is seen as their being held together and propelled by certain regularities of conditioning (loosely, 'causal laws'), in which certain types of element, such as consciousness, the 'life-faculty' and the *bhavaṅga*-mind, are held to be particularly important.

It is evident – and has been evident since the first discovery of Buddhism by the west – that such doctrines, supposedly negative and pessimistic, and certainly difficult, counter-intuitive and abstruse, are extremely unlikely religious vehicles for the worldly and other-worldly aspirations of the ordinary man. We have seen, however, both through modern anthropological research and through the ideas of Buddhism itself, that the ideas of the canonical tradition, and related practices derived from it, in fact co-exist in society with a differing but complementary religious system. In this complementary range of religious thought and practice, interaction with gods and spirits, and the use of alternative explanations of good or bad fortune – such as astrology and magic – are of more immediate concern than the conceptual subtleties of Buddhist intellectualism. I have tried to show how Buddhist doctrine can be integrated with the thinking and practice of the 'ordinary man': and it is this which is pointed to by the second quotation, that of Clifford Geertz on imagery. I take it that the patterns of imaginative perception disclosed by the images I have discussed are the basic and unifying structures of *Theravāda* Buddhist culture. Where Buddhist intellectuals, in the textual tradition, take these patterns of imagery to be merely illustrative of an abstract conceptual account, I take the theoretical constructions of intellectuals to be themselves also illustrations of the underlying, unconscious patterns of imagination to which the imagery found in the textual tradition gives *us* access. (The methodology here perhaps bears some resemblance to the Freudian use of jokes and slips of the tongue to discover unconscious phenomena.) It is in this way, I think, that the 'specific content' of *Theravāda* 'is embodied in the images and metaphors its adherents use to characterise reality'.

Equally, I have tried to make clear how the 'historical career' of Buddhism has rested on certain institutions which have been able to 'render these images and metaphors available to those who thus employ them'. It is, as I have stressed, following Dumont, the fundamental social dichotomy between layman and monk, between the man-in-the-world living in his house, and world-renouncer oriented towards 'homelessness' in every sense, which has been the institution on which the psychological and ontological dichotomy of *saṃsāra* and *nirvāṇa* has rested. Thus also, the peasant farmer's activity of agriculture, of planting seeds and reaping their fruit, has been converted into the eschatological picture of continuing life-in-*saṃsāra*, while the monk's inactive abstinence from agriculture has been the paradigmatic symbol of the transcendence of the karmic sphere, in *nirvāṇa*. Again, within the monkhood, in the metaphorical agriculture of *karma*, there have been the reform movements, attempting to regain the 'original' Buddhist way of life in the face of the ubiquitous domestication of the monkhood,[1] and recognised by the tradition in the dichotomy of 'village-dwelling' and 'forest-dwelling' monks; these have periodically re-vivified and re-embodied the old *saṃsāra–nirvāṇa* dichotomy, once the charisma of the *nirvāṇa*-seeking renouncer has been routinised into the figure of the monk as parish priest, officiant at funerals and sundry merit-making rituals.

At the beginning of this book, I said that my main interest in writing about Buddhism was philosophical, and that in my view philosophy in the west should proceed in constant contact with intellectual history and anthropology, with the investigation and comparison of cultures. I hope that I have here given some material toward that end. As one means of approach to the general task of comparison, I would suggest that we can profitably see systems of imagery and the institutions which embody them, as constituting those 'collective representations' and 'forms of life' which give to each culture its specificity and internal unity. These unconscious systems of imaginative perception, thought, and behaviour can be seen to permeate experience, discourse and practice, in an impersonal – or, perhaps, supra-personal – mode of automatic cultural self-transmission. Different individuals and texts, and particular individuals and texts at different moments of greater or lesser abstraction, can be seen as placing themselves at various points on a continuum; a continuum which stretches from the concrete, 'everyday' and unconscious obviousness with which such patterns of imagination are simply built into, and given with, experience and action, to the most abstract and self-conscious levels of theoretical reflection, in which the images are appropriated consciously, as explanatory metaphors illustrative of what are taken to be historically and logically prior structures of thought.

I have argued that the ideas of Buddhist theory, the conceptions within Buddhism which correspond to the English terms 'self', 'person', 'identity' and 'continuity', are of a single piece with quite ordinary, socially institutionalised and 'everyday' forms of perception and behaviour; and I have in this way tried to present Buddhism as indissolubly a single cultural world. I have tried to show that the most abstract forms of its imaginative representation – what we call its 'ideas' – are intimately connected with, and inextricable from, the presuppositions and institutional framework of Buddhist culture and society. The next task is to attempt, with the help of the mirror of Buddhist thought, to achieve a similar understanding of our own.

Notes

The following abbreviations are used in the notes and the bibliography. In the case of Pali texts, the addition of A to the name of a text indicates the commentary to it. For example, DA refers to the *Dīgha Nikāya Aṭṭhakathā*, otherwise known as the *Sumaṅgala Vilāsinī*.

A	*Anguttara Nikāya*
Abh.S.	*Abhidhammattha-saṃgaha*
Ait.Ār.	*Aitareya Araṇyaka*
Ait.B.	*Aitareya Brāhmaṇa*
Ait.U.	*Aitareya Upaniṣad*
AK	*Abhidharmakośa*
Asl.	*Atthasālinī*
AV	*Atharva Veda*
BAU	*Bṛhadāraṇyaka Upaniṣad*
BE	*Buddhist Encyclopaedia*
BHSD	*Buddhist Hybrid Sanskrit Dictionary*
BPS	Buddhist Publication Society
Ch.U.	*Chāndogya Upaniṣad*
CPD	*Critical Pali Dictionary*
D	*Dīgha Nikāya*
Dhp.	*Dhammapada*
Dhs.	*Dhammasanganī*
Dīp.	*Dīpavaṃsa*
DPPN	*Dictionary of Pali Proper Names*
ERE	*Hasting's Encyclopaedia of Religion and Ethics*
It.	*Itivuttaka*
J	*Jātaka*
Kaṭh.U.	*Kaṭha Upaniṣad*
Kauś.U.	*Kauśītaki Upaniṣad*
KSP	*Karma-siddhi-prakaraṇa*
Kvu.	*Kathāvatthu*
M	*Majjhima Nikāya*
Mait.U.	*Maitri Upaniṣad*
Māṇ.U.	*Māṇḍukya Upaniṣad*
Miln.	*Milinda-pañha*
MSA	*Mahāyāna-saṃgraha*
Muṇḍ.U.	*Muṇḍaka Upaniṣad*
Nd.1	*Mahā-niddesa*
Nd.2	*Culla niddesa*
Nett.	*Netti-pakaraṇa*
Peṭ.	*Peṭakopadesa*
Pj.1.	*Paramattha-joṭikā*, vol. 1
Praśn.U.	*Praśna Upaniṣad*
Ps.	*Paṭisambhidā-magga*
PTC	*Pali Tipitikaṃ Concordance*
PTS	Pali Text Society
PTSD	*Pali Text Society Dictionary*
Pugg.	*Puggala-paññatti*
Pv.	*Petavatthu*
RV	*Ṛg Veda*
S	*Saṃyutta Nikāya*
Sarvad.	*Sarvadarśana-saṃgraha*
ŚB	*Śatapatha Brāhmaṇa*
SBB	Sacred Books of the Buddhists
SK	*Sāṃkhya Kārikā*
Sn.	*Sutta Nipāta*
Śvet.U.	*Śvetāśvatara Upaniṣad*
Tait.U.	*Taittirīya Upaniṣad*
Thag.	*Theragāthā*
Thig.	*Therīgāthā*
TS	*Taittirīya Saṃhitā*
Ud.	*Udāna*
Utt.S.	*Uttarajjhāyana Sutta*
Vbh.	*Vibhaṅga*
Vin.	*Vinaya Piṭaka*
Vism.	*Visuddhimagga*
VS	*Vājasanehi Saṃhitā*
Vv.	*Vimāna-vatthu*
YS	*Yoga Sūtra*

Introduction

1. Dumont (1973) p. 104. He adds in a footnote 'If history is the movement by which a society reveals itself as what it is, there are, in a sense, as many qualitatively different histories as there are societies' (taken from Dumont and Pocock (1957) p. 21). The original text continues: 'and India, precisely because she is indifferent to history, has carefully laid it down in the form of her society, her culture, her religion'. The great Sanskritist Louis Renou writes, (1953) p. 51, 'In Indian studies [both] ancient and modern evidence must be taken into account.'
2. Dumont (1972) p. 19.
3. Geertz (1974) pp. 30–1.
4. On which see, *inter alia*, Lukes (1973), Dumont (1977).
5. Rāhula (1967) p. 51.
6. Malalasekera (1957) pp. 33–4.
7. In BPS (1973) pp. 2–3. For 'Eternalism' and 'Annihilationism' see Chapters 1.1.2, 3.2.5.
8. Durkheim (1915) pp. 29ff.
9. Spiro (1966) p. 96.
10. Rhys Davids, C. A. F. (1938) pp. 33–5, 53; (1934) p. 67. For the phrases quoted by Mrs Rhys Davids as '[this] is not of me . . .', see Chapter 3.2.1.
11. Rhys Davids, T. W., *Dialogues of the Buddha*, I, SBB II, p. 189.
12. Humphries (1962) pp. 85–6; (1976) pp. 32, 37.
13. R. F. Gombrich, private communication. Quotations in the text from Zaehner (1957) pp. 237, 22, 126.
14. Radhakrishnan (1929) p. 385.
15. Coomaraswamy (1916) pp. 198–9.
16. Bhattacharya (1973).
17. Grimm (1958).
18. Frauwallner (1953). E.g. pp. 217ff.
19. Bareau (1973) pp. 94–5.
20. Oldenburg (1882) pp. 319ff. His exact position has been the subject of some debate. See Welbon (1968) Chapter 6.
21. Stcherbatsky (1926) p. 357; (1927) *passim*.
22. Monier-Williams (1890) pp. 149, 151, 162.
23. Eliot (1921) pp. xciii–iv.
24. Dharmapāla (1965) pp. 27, 217, 495. The best account of Dharmapāla and Buddhist modernism in Ceylon is Bechert (1966) pp. 47ff. See also Gombrich (1971) pp. 52ff.
25. Zaehner (1966) p. 187.
26. Pocock (1973) p. xiv.
27. Poussin (1917) pp. 1–8.
28. Spiro (1970) p. 12. He acknowledges the previous discussions of Edgerton (1942) and King (1964).
29. Tambiah (1970) pp. 3–4. See also *ibid.* pp. 367ff; Obeyesekere (1963), Gombrich (1971) pp. 153f.
30. See, *inter alia*, Schayer (1934); Regamey (1935); Law (1936); Masson (1942).
31. Gombrich (1966); (1971). Quotation in text from (1971) pp. 4–5. See further Chapter 5.1.2 for examples of the distinction applied.

32. Short accounts are Zurcher (1962); and Robinson (1970). The authoritative scholarly work on Buddhism in India is Lamotte (1967).
33. There are, of course, for other purposes many differences to be drawn between the *Sutta* and *Vinaya Piṭaka*. The final form of the *Vinaya* contains a variety of material, not all of which is narrative. On the early history of Buddhist literature see Frauwallner (1956); Lévi (1915).
34. E.g. D.II.125; A.I.117; II.147; III.179, 360; Vin.I.119. See further Frauwallner (1964).
35. See Johnston (1937).
36. Ñāṇamoli (1975) p. xxix.
37. Gombrich (1971) p. 43. On the continuing contemporary importance of the *Visuddhimagga* see Carrithers (forthcoming) Chapter 3.
38. Coulson (1976) p. xxi. On the history and use of Pali see Geiger (1943), Norman (1978).
39. Dharmapāla (1965) p. 519.
40. M. B. Carrithers, private communication.
41. I cannot argue for these remarks on the *Mahāyāna* here. The crucial philosophical legitimation for the inclusion of 'popular' ideas and practices (though it was not conceived as such) was the rejection of any linguistic form, even cherished Buddhist ones, as finally appropriate to 'ultimate truth'. See further Chapters 4.1.3, 5.1.3 (footnote), 8.2.2 n.22.
42. A detailed account would have to deal far more thoroughly with differences between *Mahāyāna* Buddhism and Hinduism, and with paradoxes within the overall similarity which I have claimed for them – the most obvious point being the status of Sanskrit *per se*, which for the majority of Hindu schools of thought was a sacred language, uniquely appropriate to reality, indeed a part of reality itself. This contrasts strongly with the *Mahāyāna* rejection of any language as 'ultimately true'. See further Chapter 3.2.5.
43. See, for example, the works of Chogyam Trungpa and, especially, Tarthang Tulku.

1. The origins of rebirth

1.1. Buddhism and early Indian religion

1. The term was introduced by the anthropologist Srinivas (1952). In an excellent review of the idea and the literature it inspired, Staal (1963) stresses that its usefulness lies in historical, diachronic analysis, and not in synchronic, sociological study. Thus, although it has been 'established beyond doubt that Sanskritisation was . . . a historical process', still 'it should be clear that the concept of Sanskritisation describes a process and is a concept of change. It is not a concept at which synchronic analysis could ever arrive.' As an instrument of cultural history, 'we can accept the term Sanskritisation only if it is made clear that its relation to the term Sanskrit is extremely complex'; in both cultural history and linguistic analysis, 'the term can be used . . . as a conceptual tool only for a first approximation, and covers only part of the material . . . While [it] is undoubtedly a useful heuristic concept, other more specific processes are at work.'
2. E.g. TS.I.7.3.1; ŚB.II.2.2.6, IV.3.4.4.
3. Von Fürer-Haimendorf (1953) pp. 42, 43, 45. See also his (1964) especially

pp. 290–1; and Horsch (1968). It should be made clear that the term 'Aryan' is used here culturally and not racially.

4. 'By "hegemony" Gramsci seems to mean a socio-political situation, in his terminology a "moment", in which the philosophy and practice of a society fuse or are in equilibrium; an order in which a certain way of life and thought is dominant, in which one concept of reality is diffused throughout society in all its institutional and private manifestations, informing with its spirit all taste, morality, customs, religious and political principles, and all social relations, particularly in their intellectual and moral connotation. An element of direction and control, not necessarily conscious, is implied' (Williams G. (1960)). In the Indian case, Brahmanical hegemony would be overstated if this phraseology were all taken literally.
5. The classic treatment of caste society is now Dumont (1970a).
6. Good treatments of the issue are Warder (1956); Dutt (1960); Olivelle (1974); and Rhys Davids' Introduction to the *Samaññaphala* and *Kassapa-Sīhanāda Suttā* of the *Dīgha Nikaya* (*Dialogues*, pp. 56ff, 206ff). Ling (1973) is a popular summary.
7. 'Thus the *dvandva* (co-ordinative) compound *śramaṇa-brāhmaṇa* is used extensively in both Buddhist and orthodox writings to indicate the entire class of *religieux* and philosophers whether inside or outside the orthodox tradition. The two groups are put on a par for purposes of honour and reverence. [E.g. in the Edicts of King Aśoka.] The *Brāhmaṇas* were, however, bitterly opposed to the *śramaṇas*. Patañjali, the grammarian of the second century B.C., uses the compound, . . . to illustrate the case of *dvandva* (co-ordinative compounds) where the two members are in perpetual opposition: *yesañ ca virodhaḥ śāśvataḥ*. (*Mahābhāṣya*, 1475 on Pāṇini II.4.12). Kleitarches, quoted by Strabo, says: "The pramnai (*śramaṇas*) are philosophers opposed to Brachmanes . . . They ridicule the Brachmanes . . . as fools and imposters" (Strabo, *Geography*, XV.60). (Olivelle (1974) p. 4.)
8. Basham (1967) p. 246.
9. The classic account is Basham (1951).
10. Scepticism is given in both the lists of views in the *Brahmajāla Sutta*, as the view held by the 'Eel-wrigglers', and in the *Sāmaññaphala Sutta*, where Sañjaya Belaṭṭhiputta is represented (in the same words as the *Brahmajāla*) as saying 'If you ask me whether there is another world – well, if I thought there were, I would say so. But I don't say so. And I don't think it is thus or thus. And I don't think it is otherwise. And I don't deny it. And I don't say there neither is, nor is not, another world. And if you ask me about the beings produced by chance; or whether there is any fruit, any result, of good or bad actions; or whether a man who has won the truth continues, or not, after death – to each or any of these questions do I give the same reply' (D.I.58, translated by Rhys Davids).
11. A detailed treatment of the views of the various non-Brahmanical thinkers is found in Jayatilleke (1963).
12. D.I.53–4.
13. Basham (1951) p. 3.
14. D.I.52–3.
15. Basham (1951) pp. 17, 90f, 262f.
16. D.I.56.
17. Basham (1951) p. 269.

18. D.I.55.
19. This has been argued particularly by Thapar (1966), (1975); and Warder (1956), (1970).
20. All three quotes in this paragraph from Basham (1951) pp. 6, 132.
21. Basham (1951) pp. 5–6.
22. Sarvad. 2.
23. Basham (1967) p. 172.

1.2. Time: *saṃsāra*

1. In the remaining sections of Chapter 1, I shall only give references to primary source material where I have quoted from it directly, or where I think something of particular importance. For the main part of the argument, the general reader will have no use for such textual citation; and the specialist Indologist who might wish to take the matter further must needs look at the existing secondary material, which, along with the original version of my work (Collins (1979)), contains the appropriate references. In any case, much more work on the primary material needs to be done before we have anything like a complete picture.

   Among the many secondary sources quoted in these notes, I have profited most from Cone (1971); Silburn (1955); Boyer (1901); and Gonda (1966), for the evolution of Brahmanical ideas; and from Heesterman (1964); and Dumont (1970b) Chapter 3, for the sociological interpretation of these ideas.
2. The classic account is Lévi (1966) (2nd ed.); Biardeau and Malamoud (1976) follow a similar line, stressing the continuity and ubiquity of the classical pattern of sacrifice in India. Heesterman (1964) argues plausibly for a pre-classical form of agonistic ritual, in which competition and exchange predominated. The classical sacrifice, he argues, already contains an individualisation of this pattern into the single figure of the *yajamāna*; the subsequent internalisation of sacrifice in the renouncer is then only an extension of this same development. See further Chapter 1.4.2.
3. Gonda (1975) p. 67. Cf. Silburn (1955) pp. 21ff on 'Kavi: le poète mensurateur'.
4. Cf. Kane (1946) III, Chapter xxxiv, p. 890.
5. Silburn (1955) p. 9. Two late hymns of the *Atharva Veda* celebrate Time (*kāla*) as a force in itself. See Silburn (1955) pp. 136ff, and Chapter 8.1.3 below.
6. Heesterman (1964) p. 2.
7. Gonda (1975) p. 367.
8. Cf. Silburn (1955) pp. 44–5; Varenne (1976) pp. 20–2. *Saṃsāra* derived from *sar* – 'to run, hasten, flow, stream': Gonda, *Selected Studies* IV, p. 310. (Cf. Chapter 8.4.1 and n.8 below.)
9. Durkheim (1915) pp. 38, 346.
10. Lévi (1966) pp. 80–1.
11. ŚB.9.5.1.10, and 10.1.5.4. This point, as many others in this account, was first made by Boyer (1901). On *sarvam āyus* see Gonda (1965) p. 66 and m.157; and Gonda, *Selected Studies* IV, pp. 495ff.
12. RV.1.125.6, cf. 10.107.2.
13. This is slightly less true of the tenth *maṇḍala* of the *Ṛg Veda*, where we begin

to enter the speculative world of the *Brāhmaṇas*. See Gonda (1975) pp. 138–9.

14. Cf. O'Flaherty (1977) pp. 213–14.
15. See Oldenburg (1917) pp. 536f; Keith (1925) pp. 409–10.
16. Gombrich (1975) p. 130.
17. Gonda (1966) p. 110 and *passim*.
18. According to Gonda (1966) pp. 1–41, this was because, *inter alia*, of the general religious significance in early Indo-European culture of clearings, glades, and the like; and because of the need of the invading Indo-Aryans in India, in their life of war and migration, for secure tracts of land for agricultural and pastoral use.
19. As late as the *Upaniṣads*, *loka* is used, both in the singular and in the plural, as an unspecified good which man might attain or be deprived of. (Cf. Gonda (1966) pp. 51, 104, for examples.) The new concept of *brahman*, and man's aim for it, is often expressed there in terms of a *brahma-loka* to be attained by the successful.
20. On the term *svarga* see Gonda (1966) p. 73. On the relation between the *deva-* and *svarga-loka, ibid.* pp. 84–7 and notes.
21. Well described by Cone (1971) pp. 95–106.
22. Gonda (1966) p. 80.
23. ŚB.2.1.4.9.
24. ŚB.1.9.3.1.
25. Cf. Gonda, *Selected Studies* IV, pp. 317ff.
26. Gonda (1966) p. 130.
27. *mṛtvā punaḥ sambhavanti*, ŚB.10.4.3.10. This verse makes a distinction between those who are reborn after death for *amṛtam*, and those who are reborn to become 'again and again the food of that one [Death]' (*etasyaivan-naṃ punaḥ punar bhavanti*). This is not, I think (pace Keith (1925) p. 583), a difference between an endless 'immortality' and being subject to repeated (a second) death, but a difference between obtaining *amṛtam* in the sense of a 'full life' (*sarvam āyus*) after death, and obtaining a weak *āyus*, which is brought to an end before its time. We have seen how *amṛtam* for man means a 'full life' of a hundred years; and the earlier verses of this *Brāhmaṇa* (ŚB.10.4.3) speak of attaining a 'full life' by avoiding having the sequence of days and nights come to an end before old age (*purā jaraso*). 'Repeated death' (*punarmṛtyu*) can mean simply being subject to life in time, that is to death, during the first lifetime (*āyus*) on earth: 'he who knows this conquers repeated death and attains a full life' (*apa punar-mṛtyuṃ jayati sarvam āyur eti ya evaṃ veda*) (SB.10.2.6.19).
28. See, *inter alia*, Oldenburg (1915) pp. 27f; Lévi (1966) pp. 93–5; Horsch (1971) pp. 136f; Gonda (1975) p. 367 and n.56.
29. Examples will be found in Gonda (1966) *passim*, who is concerned particularly to stress this point.
30. See Gonda (1965) pp. 315f; Lévi (1966) pp. 102–8.
31. Durkheim (1915) p. 39; also stressed by Hubert and Mauss (1964) pp. 62ff.
32. On these analogies, or identifications, see Oldenburg (1919) pp. 110ff; Gonda, *Selected Studies* II, pp. 402ff.
33. Cf. Boyer (1901) pp. 465–6. Insofar as 'joining the gods' was frequently accomplished by the taking of *soma*, whether this was an hallucinogen as some have alleged, or simply a strong intoxicant, madness as a result of

prolonged use is perhaps not surprising. The later ascetic renouncers, who did want to remain permanently in a sacred sphere of reality, were, accordingly, excluded from human society (see Chapter 1.4.3 below).

34. On *dīkṣa* in sacrifice and society see Biardeau and Malamoud (1976) pp. 36–8, 161–2; the idea of a 'birth' into the sacrifice is elaborated in the ritual image of the *yajamāna* as an embryo; cf. Hubert and Mauss (1964) p. 21; Keith (1925) pp. 461–2.
35. *sa yat tataḥ sambhavati tat tṛtīyaṃ jāyate* (ŚB. 11.2.1.1; cf. Ait.Ār.II.5).
36. SB.10.3.3.8.
37. Frauwallner (1953) pp. 49ff: '*Die Atem-, Wasser-, und Feuerlehren*'. He is concerned to stress the supposed *kṣatriya* origin of some of these ideas.
38. Cf. Boyer (1901) p. 499.
39. 'Let him not live . . .' RV.10.5.25; cf. RV.3.53.21; AV.7.31. On *asu* see Oldenburg (1917) pp. 524f.
40. 'Everything which . . .' (*sarvam ātmanvad yat prāṇat*) (AV.10.8.2, 11.2.10).
41. Cf. Frauwallner (1953) p. 61.
42. ŚB.2.3.3.7. Cf. Lévi (1966) pp. 96–7.
43. Cf. Gonda (1965) Chapter 2: '*Soma*, *amṛta* and the Moon'.
44. Heesterman (1964) p. 24.
45. *Upāsate*: 'worship' (Hume (1931) p. 232; Zaehner (1966) p. 100); 'meditate on' (Radhakrishnan (1953) p. 431).
46. Both passages add a third fate: that of insects, 'repeatedly returning creatures', of whom it is simply said 'be born! Die!'. Neither of the two ways are open to these.
47. Spiro (1970) pp. 76ff; Gombrich (1971) p. 155.

1.3. Action and the person: *karma*

1. Gonda (1966) pp. 72–3.
2. ŚB.6.2.27. Eggeling's translation (1964) Part 3, pp. 180–1. Compare Gonda (1966) p. 29 on the same passage.
3. On *iṣṭāpūrta* see Biardeau and Malamoud (1976) p. 165; Gonda (1964) p. 236; Keith (1925) p. 250.
4. This idea of a 'store' of good deeds remained alive later in Buddhism: cf. Gonda (1964) pp. 186–93, (1966) p. 236.
5. ŚB.8.6.1.10.
6. AV.10.2, 11.8. On these two hymns see Renou (1956) pp. 69–79.
7. ŚB.11.2.6.13; Ait.B.2.40.1–7; Kauś.U.2.6; Tait.U.2.7.1; Ait.U.2.3.
8. E.g. RV.10.15.1. For other references and discussion, see Geldner (1951) III, p. 185. The medieval commentator's remarks, on certain of these passages, that the differences result from differences in sacrificial merit, is certainly true to the spirit of the tradition, but doubtless anachronistic.
9. Obeyesekere (1968) pp. 12f, following Weber.
10. *Mahāyajña*, incumbent daily on the Brahmin householder. See Biardeau and Malamoud (1976) pp. 41, 66ff.
11. Biardeau and Malamoud (1976) pp. 57ff; Heesterman (1964) p. 27. On the 'mental sacrifice' (*mānasa yajña*) of the renouncer, see Varenne (1960) II, p. 53. On the 'fire-sacrifice of the breath' (*prāṇāgnihotra*) see *ibid.* pp. 69ff.
12. D.I.127ff, the *Kūtadanta Sutta*. Cf. Heesterman (1964) pp. 27–8.
13. BAU.3.2.13.

14. Cf. Silburn (1955) pp. 1–2 on '*kratu: intention ardente*', and pp. 52–3 on '*désir procréateur*'.
15. E.g. Śvet.U.5.11–12; Mait.U.3.1–2.

1.4. Timelessness: *mokṣa* (*nirvāṇa*)

1. Edgerton, above all in his (1929) article. See also Edgerton (1925), and a summary of his ideas in (1965) pp. 21ff.
2. On this idea in India, see Gonda (1970) *passim*, especially pp. 21ff, 60ff.
3. For examples in the BAU and Ch.U. see Edgerton (1929) p. 104 n.12.
4. See Gonda (1950) *passim*.
5. On this idea in the *Ṛg Veda* see Edgerton (1929) p. 100 n.6.
6. Edgerton (1929) pp. 116f; Renou (1949).
7. This is Gonda's preferred sense: (1950) Chapters 2–4.
8. ŚB.2.3.2.13.
9. From the root *yam*, 'to tame' or 'restrain', as with horses. For the horse-metaphor, see Varenne (1976) pp. 100–1.
10. BAU.3.7; Māṇḍ.U.6.
11. Heesterman (1964) pp. 27, 22.
12. Edgerton (1929) pp. 98–9, quoting from Oldenburg (1919).
13. ŚB.12.9.3.12.
14. See Silburn (1955) pp. 56–7, 84, 90–4.
15. Heesterman (1964) p. 27.
16. Dumont (1970b) p. 46.
17. Dumont (1965), (1970a), (1970b) Chapters 3, 7, (1973), (1975), (1977).
18. Kauś.U.1.2; BAU.1.4.15; Ch.U.8.2.1–10; BAU.4.4.2–3, 1.4.10.
19. Malamoud (1976) p. 13.
20. Dumont (1970b) pp. 47–9.

2. Varieties of Buddhist discourse

2.1. Buddhist thought in context

1. Rāhula (1956) pp. 158–61, 196–7.
2. Perhaps the most famous example is Nālandā. See Dutt (1962) especially Parts IV–V; Darian (1971).
3. Gombrich (1971) pp. 63–4.
4. Tambiah (1968).
5. These stories are also recounted on festival occasions, for general cultural purposes which have little immediate connexion with the religious concerns of doctrinal Buddhism. See for example Tambiah (1970) Chapter 10, on such a use of the great *Vessantara Jātaka*. On this important and widely used *Jātaka* see Cone and Gombrich (1977).
6. Tambiah (1968) p. 118. His description of the meditative life as 'entering into mystical realms' is perhaps a little misleadingly flamboyant.
7. Obeyesekere (1968) pp. 21ff; Gombrich (1971) Chapter 5; Spiro (1970) Chapters 3–6.
8. Sharma (1973); Pocock (1973) pp. 37–8, 107.
9. Obeyesekere (1976) p. 206.
10. On the role of *upāsaka* see Obeyesekere (1968) pp. 31ff.

11. Hopkins (1906), (1907).
12. O'Flaherty (1977).
13. Diseases (*ābādhā*) S.IV.230; A.II.87, III.131, V.110. 'Things experienced' (*vedayitāni*) Miln.134–5.

2.2. Different ways of talking about 'self' and 'person'

1. *Suddhaṃ attānaṃ pariharati* (A.I.148–9, IV.109f; Asl.128). A closely similar phrase *khataṃ upahataṃ attānaṃ pariharati* is translated in the PTS editions as 'he carries about with him an uprooted, lifeless self' (A.II.2, 228, 252, V.308). 'Sees in himself complete purity, . . .' (*parisuddhakāyakammantataṃ attani samanupassamāno*) (M.I.17).
2. For examples see CPD and PTC entries for *attā* and its use in compounds.
3. 'Exalts himself . . .' (*attukkaṃsako . . . paravambhī*) (M.I.19, 200, 402f; *et freq.*). 'For one's own benefit' (*attahita*) (A.II.95 *et freq.*) (*atta-d-attham*) (Dhp.166). 'Self-born, -caused' 'no-one purifies another' (*attaja, -sambhava, nāñño aññaṃ visodhaye*) (Dhp.161, 165). 'Action of oneself, . . . by another' denoting 'initiative' (*ārabbha*) (A.III.337). The denial of these as a spiritually enervating heresy at D.I.53.
4. 'No one is dearer than oneself' (*natthi . . . koci añño attanā piyataro ti*). 'Surveying . . .' (*sabbā disānuparigamma cetasā, n'ev' ajjhagā piyataraṃ attanā kvaci; evaṃ piyo puthu attā paresaṃ, tasmā na hiṃse paraṃ attakāmo*) (S.I.75).
5. S.II.82.
6. *attānam gaveseyyātha* (Vin.I.22).
7. Nakamura (1976) p. 11; cf. his (1964) pp. 91–2. Professor R. F. Gombrich has kindly pointed out to me the occurrence in a Jain text (Utt.S.16.13) of the idea that sense-pleasures are like poison for the man who is 'seeking himself' (*attagavesissa*). Since the term *ātman* has no use – whether positively or negatively – as a technical term in Jainism, it is clear that in both Buddhism and Jainism such terms are used as simple and non-theoretical behavioural description and injunction.
8. 'Taking refuge . . . in oneself and the *Dhamma* as an island' (Dhp.236, 238; D.II.100; S.III.43; *et freq.*). *Attā hi attano nātho* (Dhp.160, 380). 'Watch oneself', *attānupekhin* (A.III.133); 'self-guarded', *attagutta* (S.V.169; A.III.6; Dhp.379; A.II.27f; *et freq.*). 'Self-developed', (A.IV.26; *et freq.*). CPD contains references to a great many other similar uses of *atta*-compounds.
9. D.III.252; A.IV.113.
10. The 'individuality' of each lifetime as *attā* (D.I.195–6; some mss. of S.II.283). Cf. also Chapters 4.2.3 and 5.2.1, 5.2.2 below. 'Great-' and 'small-souled' (*mahattā, appatumo*) (A.I.249).
11. M.II.341 *et freq.* On these phrases see Zaehner (1969) pp. 214–15, who uses the Upaniṣadic 'with his self become *Brahman*' as a translation.
12. 'One reproaches oneself' (A.I.57). 'Do you reproach yourself . . .?' (*kacci pana tvam attā sīlato upavadati*) (S.IV.47; cf. S.III.103). 'You know yourself, man, . . .' (*attā te purisa jānāti saccaṃ vā yadi vā musā. Kalyāṇaṃ vata bho sakkhi attānaṃ atimaññesi, yo santaṃ attani pāpaṃ attānaṃ parigūhasi*) (A.I.149).
13. *Attā* as 'friend' or 'enemy' (literally as 'dear' or 'not-dear' *piyo, appiyo*) (S.I.71 *et freq.*). 'Themselves as enemy' (*amitten' eva attanā*) (Dhp.66;

S.I.57). *Attanā* as 'by his own efforts' (A.III.81); as 'in themselves', 'inherently' (M.I.161).

14. A.I.53; M.I.8 respectively.
15. D.III.230; S.II.3; M.I.51; *et freq*. See also *Buddhist Dictionary* pp. 184–5.
16. *Attānudiṭṭhi* (D.II.22; S.III.185; A.III.447; *et freq*.). For references to such later terms as *attagaha, attadiṭṭhi(n-jaha), attupaladdhi*, etc., see CPD.
17. 'Views . . . of self and universe' (*atta- . . . loka-vādasampayuttā diṭṭhiyo*)(M.I.136–7). These as a 'net' of views (D.I.13). 'There is no grasping of a doctrine . . .' (M.I.137). 'A person is not to be found' (e.g. Kvu.1f; Miln.25). On this latter see Chapter 6.1 *passim*.

2.3. Elements of personality and (not-)self

1. In the *Brāhmaṇas*, ŚB.10.1.3.4, 10.1.4.1–3. On this topic generally see Deussen (1906) pp. 265f; and, especially, Johnston (1937) *passim*. 'Wisdom' translates *prajñā*.
2. Kaṭh.U.3.10–11.
3. For as long as one possessed mind . . . (RV.10.59.5). *Manas* going to Yama at death (AV.5.30.6; RV.10.5.8). Mind as the charioteer . . . (VS.34.1–6). The image of the chariot is frequent in all Hindu thought: see Varenne (1976) pp. 84–6, 100, 129. On the motif in Buddhism see Chapter 8.1.3 below.
4. ŚB.2.3.3.2.
5. Ch.U.7.15 and 26; BAU.3.4.1; 4.5.15.
6. *Ātmānas tu kāmāya sarvaṃ priyam* (BAU.4.5.6f).
7. Prajāpati as 'spirit having *ātman*' (*yad yakṣam ātmanvat*) (AV. 10.2.11.8). (On these hymns see Renou (1956) pp. 69–79.) Identified with *brahman* at SB.7.3.14.2. For further references see Eggeling (1964) v, pp. 556–8. As animating the universe (Mait.U.2.3). 'In the beginning . . .' (BAU.1.4.5; 2.5.1–15).
8. Hubert and Mauss (1964) Conclusion.
9. In the *Upaniṣads*, e.g. Kaṭh.U.1.26; Mait.U.1.3–4, 3.4. On *dukkha* in Buddhism, see Chapter 6.3.2 below.
10. Both these are found in the Brahmanical tradition, from its earliest times.
11. E.g. Dhp.277–9; M.I.230; S.III.132; A.I.286; Thag.677–8. On this point see Rāhula (1967) p. 81.
12. See Nyanaponika (1971), who provides many examples.
13. E.g. S.II.85, IV.19–20; Dhp.202–5.
14. Gombrich (1972) p. 492.
15. E.g. M.I.487; S.IV.399.
16. Welbon (1968) has devoted a book to the history of attempts to define *nirvāṇa*. A great deal of confusion has occurred precisely because of the failure to distinguish the two forms of it.
17. Gellner (1962).

3. The denial of self as 'right view'

3.1. Different kinds of 'right view'

1. E.g. M.I.287, 401, III.22, 52, 71; D.I.55.
2. M.I.400f.

3. On this form of 'Pascalian' wager, see Jayatilleke (1963) pp. 405–6.
4. For the meaning and history of this term, literally 'worthy ones', the regular *Theravāda* term for an enlightened saint, see Rhys Davids' introduction to the *Pāṭika Sutta*, *Dialogues* III, pp. 3–6.
5. D.II.329ff.
6. Nowell-Smith (1954) pp. 111ff.
7. For example, at M.I.493 it is said that the whole 'company of Gotama, householders and renouncers' (*Gotamassa parisā sagahaṭṭhapabbajitā*) flows towards *nibbāna*, like the river Ganges to the sea.
8. Right view as the Four Noble Truths: e.g. M.III.251; S.V.8 (this is perhaps the most common explanation given by commentaries); as Dependent Origination S.II.17.
9. M.I.46ff.
10. In the Canon at M.I.301. Of course, the three terms arranged in the order *sīla, samādhi, paññā* are very common: see Barua (1971) Chapter 3. The entire *Visuddhimagga* is arranged on this pattern. Sometimes, *samādhi* and *paññā* are replaced by *samatha* and *vipassanā*, 'tranquility' and 'insight' (e.g. MA.II.106; Vism.I.8). I shall deal with these in Chapter 3.3 below.
11. 'Learner' (*sekho*), 'adept' (*asekho*). D.II.217, III.271; M.I.42; A.II.89, V.221.
12. E.g. at D.II.122–3, and of course ubiquitously in the later literature. The 'right view' and 'right resolve' of the first and preliminary form of *paññā* are related to the 'right knowledge' and 'right release' of the second, 'liberating' form of *paññā* as intention to attainment, as goal set to goal achieved.
13. M.III.71ff. The right view which 'has corruptions . . .' (*sāsavā puññabhāgiyā upadhivepakkā diṭṭhi*). 'When one knows . . .' (*sammādiṭṭhiṃ sammādiṭṭhīti pajānāti, sā 'ssa sammādiṭṭhi*). 'That view which is noble . . .' (*ariyā anāsavā lokuttarā maggaṅgā diṭṭhi*).
14. There are seven such 'constituents' (*sambojjhaṅga*): mindfulness (*sati*); investigation of *dhammā*; energy (*viriyā*); rapture (*pīti*); tranquillity (*passaddhi*); concentration (*samādhi*); and equanimity (*upekkhā*). All these terms denote high, and specialist, virtues, and are terms of art in Buddhist meditation theory.
15. S.V.200, 202.
16. *Diṭṭhi ariyā niyyānikā, takkarassa sammādukkhakkhayāya niyyāti.* (E.g. M.I.322; A.III.132).
17. *Yathābhūtassa dassanaṃ* (M.III.289; S.II.16–17).
18. 'Endowed with view' (*diṭṭhisampanno*), 'achieved view' (*diṭṭhipatto*); 'highest view' (*paramā diṭṭhi*) (Sn.471).
19. D.III.118–19.
20. MA.I.196. 'The ordinary man outside' Buddhism (*puthujjano bahīrako*). 'Learner within the teaching' (*sekho sāsaniko*). 'Not in accordance with the truth' (*na saccānulomika*). See also DA.I.59 (cf. MA.I.20–1) for a distinction between the 'good ordinary man' (*kalyāṇo puthujjano*) who appreciates Buddhist teaching, and the 'blind' (*andho*) one who does not.
21. On the 'ordinary' monk, see Gombrich (1971) pp. 324–5.
22. On these two codes of ethics, see Gombrich (1971) pp. 73f.
23. DA.I.231. 'Right view based on faith' (*saddhāmūlikā sammādiṭṭhi*).
24. M.I.299; S.III.158; IV.159.
25. For the full list, see *Buddhist Dictionary* p. 161.
26. S.III.126; cf. S.II.115f. 'He does not consider . . .' (*attānam attanīyaṃ vā na*

samanupassati). 'I have a *sense* of "I am" . . .' (*asmīti adhigataṃ . . . ayaṃ ahaṃ asmīti ca na samanupassati*). 'The conceit of "I am"' (*asmīti māna*). 'Desire for "I am"' (*asmīti chando*). 'Underlying tendency to "I am"' (*asmīti anusayo*).

27. In a ritual enactment of the same metaphor, still surviving, a young monk taking his ordination is washed, to remove his 'lay smell' (M. B. Carrithers, private communication). Of course, ideas of 'smell' of this sort fall into the pan-Indian attitude to physical and moral 'purity'.

3.2. Arguments in support of *anattā*

1. That is, it is a substantive of the *-an* declension, nominative singular. In Sanskrit grammatical terminology it is a *karmadharaya* rather than *bahuvrīhi* compound. There is only one definite exception to this. At S.III.56, 114, we read *anattaṃ rūpaṃ anattā rūpan ti yathābhūtaṃ na pajānāti* – 'he does not understand the selfless body as it really is, (thus) "body is a not-self"'. Here *anattaṃ* is an adjective in the *-a* declension (a *bahuvrīhi*), agreeing with and qualifying the substantives *rūpaṃ*, *saññā*, *vedanā*, *saṃkhāre* (and hence here the form is *anatte*), and *viññāṇaṃ*. The apparent reading *anattaṃ* at Ud.80, which is suspect because unmetrical, seems to be an error for *anantaṃ* (quoted by the commentary as a variant reading). See CPD, s.v. *a-nata*.
2. See von Glasenapp (1960); Norman (forthcoming) pp. 6–7. Chowdhury (1955) insists on the interpretation of *anattā* as a *karmadharaya*, but by translating 'not-Self' reaches the conclusion that the Buddha taught by implication the (real, Vedāntic, cosmic) Self.
3. *Anattā* here could be nominative singular or plural (in place of *anattāno*) of the *-an* declension; or nominative plural of the *-a* declension. The CPD remarks that some commentaries here take *anattā* to be an adjective, and cite NettA. on Nett.6.31, which glosses as *natthi etesaṃ attā*. (Cf. KvuA.33.)

   The Sanskrit version of the phrase is *sarve dharmāḥ anātmānaḥ* (see Lamotte, *Traité*, p. 1368 n.1. for references), which shows a similar ambiguity. According to Pāṇinian grammar (Pāṇini 5.4.68 to 5.4.160) *anātman* can be used as a *bahuvrīhi*, although the alternative *anātmaka* (or *nirātman*) is preferred. The adjectival use is found at ŚB.2.2.8; and Bhagavad Gītā 6.6.
4. Vin.v.86. *Aniccā sabbe saṃkhārā dukkhānattā ca saṃkhatā nibbānañ c'eva paññatti anattā iti nicchayā*. (I. B. Horner's (PTS) translation save 'conditioned things' instead of 'constructs' for *saṃkhārā*, and 'unsatisfactory' instead of 'painful' for *dukkhā*.) On *paññatti*, 'concepts', see Ñāṇamoli (1975) p. 257 n.11.
5. *Puthujjano . . . kiñci dhammaṃ attato upagaccheya* (whereas) *diṭṭhisampanno . . . anattato . . .* (M.III.64; cf. M.I.300; S.IV.31; A.III.444 *et freq.*).
6. M.I.435, 500; A.IV.422–3; A.II.18; Thag.1160–1.
7. M.I.140; S.III.33–4, IV.81–2, 128.
8. Norman (forthcoming) p. 7.
9. S.III.66f. It is also, of course, found elsewhere.
10. M.I.230.
11. 'The ordinary man regards . . .' (S.III.3). 'Being prey to' the *khandhā* as 'murderers' (S.III.87, 114, 142).

12. 'No exercising of mastery' (*avasavattana*) (e.g. Vism.xx.18; MA.II.113; AA.II.38; Nd.2.279). No 'leader' (*pariṇāyaka*) (Asl.129).
13. (E.g. *rūpaṃ*) *aniccaṃ; yad aniccaṃ taṃ dukkhaṃ; yad dukkhaṃ tad anattā.* (S.IV.1; *et freq.*)
14. *saññā-*, *citta-*, *diṭṭhi- vipallāsa* (A.II.52; *et freq.*)
15. E.g. S.III.23–4.
16. In the text, I quote the *Mahānidāna Sutta*, which speaks of a relation between 'feeling' (*vedanā*) and a postulated self. A similar argument is found in the *Poṭṭhapāda Sutta*, (D.I.180) which speaks of a relation between 'perception' (or 'ideas': *saññā*) and a self. In the *Chachakka Sutta* (M.III.282–3) there is discussion of the relation between a self and all six senses, sense-objects, and the resultant six forms of 'sense-consciousness', and 'sense-contact' (*phasso* – that is the conjunction of sense and sense-object which produces sense-consciousness), and also the 'craving' (*taṇhā*) which is held to be consequent on these processes of perception (at least in the unenlightened). It is said that because all these phenomena arise and decay, it 'is not possible' (*na uppajjati*) to regard them as a self. For brevity, I will summarise all these particular forms of the argument under the general heading of 'experience' and a self.
17. D.II.66f. 'Feeling is my self' (*vedanā me attā*); 'My self is insentient' (*appaṭisaṃvedano me attā*); 'My self feels, my self has the attribute of feeling' (*vedīyati me attā, vedanādhammo me attā*). 'Where there is no feeling at all . . .' (*yattha . . . sabbaso vedayitaṃ n'atthi, api nu kho tattha asmīti siyāti*). 'Where feeling is completely absent . . .' (*sabbaso vedanāya asati . . . api nu kho tattha ayem ahaṃ asmīti siyāti*).
18. Ud.70. (*Ahaṃkārapasutā pajā . . . etaṃ paṭigacca pasato ahaṃ karomi ti na tassa hoti.*)
19. BAU.1.4.1. On this point see van Buitenen (1957) pp. 17f; Norman (forthcoming) discusses verbal reminiscences of the *Upaniṣads* in the *Alagaddūpama Sutta* (M.I.130ff), arguing that the *Sutta* must be interpreted as explicitly denying an Upaniṣadic universal self.

    Biardeau (1965) is a valuable supplement to van Buitenen on *ahaṃkāra*, and offers some fascinating speculation on the possible sociological variety behind the use of the term as a category of cosmogonic and spiritual thought.
20. S.IV.196–8. '. . . but for him there is no "I", "mine", or "I am"' (*ahaṃ ti maman ti vā asmīti vā taṃ pi tassa na hoti*).

    There is another lute image of this sort at Miln.53, and a similar use of an analogy with the sound of a conch-shell at D.II.337–8. The need for a monk to maintain a correct level of practice – neither too eager nor too lazy – is compared to the need for a lute-string to be neither too taut nor too loose to produce the right note at A.III.374; Vin.I.181–2.
21. E.g. AK Chapter 3. See Jaini (1959); BE.I, pp. 775ff.
22. Having a mental object: Kvu.9.4. 'Young baby': M.I.432–3.
23. As 'obsessions' (*pariyuṭṭhāna*) at Vbh.383. Getting rid of *anusayā* by meditation at M.II.32; S.III.236.
24. Vism.I.13, XXII.60, XV.164.
25. *Abhimāna* SK.24; *asmitā* YS.III.47 and commentary. On *ahaṃkāra* and (the true) *ātman* in the *Mahābhārata*, see Biardeau (1965) pp. 83–4.
26. D.I.180ff.
27. M.I.256ff. 'One and the same consciousness . . .' (*tad ev 'idaṃ viññāṇaṃ*

sandhavati samsarati, anaññam). 'That which speaks and feels . . .' (*vado vedeyyo tatra tatra kalyāṇapāpakānaṃ kammānaṃ vipākaṃ paṭisamvedeti*). Consciousness, 'generated by causal conditions . . . is defined . . .' (*viññāṇaṃ paṭiccasamuppanaṃ . . . saṅkhaṃ gacchati*).

28. S.IV.67–8.
29. 'Who is conscious?' (S.II.13–14). 'Whose is this consciousness?' (S.II.62). 'Going beyond the teaching' (*sāsanam atidhavati*), 'what self do deeds . . .' (*anattakatāni kammāni kaṃ attānaṃ phusissanti*) (M.III.19).
30. M.I.8. On the terms 'eternalism' and 'annihilationism', see *inter alia* Silburn (1955) pp. 128–32.
31. M.I.137.
32. 'The same man acts . . .' (S.II.20; cf. 23). 'Existence' and 'non-existence' (S.II.17). 'Destruction . . . of a really existing being' (*sato sattassa . . . vināsam*) (M.I.140; cf. D.I.34). 'Annihilation of greed . . .' (Vin.I.234; A.IV.174–5, 182).
33. *Kārako na, kiriya vā vijjati* (Vism.XVI.90). Cf. *kammassa kārako natthi* (*ibid.* XIX.20).
34. See Vin.I.139; M.III.234; Lamotte (1967) pp. 607f; Warder (1974) p. 250.
35. Sāriputta as 'foremost in learning' (A.I.14; cf. DPPN pp. 1108ff). 'All that which has the nature . . .' (*yam kiñci samudaya-dhammaṃ taṃ sabbaṃ nirodhadhammaṃ)* (Vin.I.39–40; *et freq.*).
36. Rāhula (1967) p. 53. *Imasmiṃ sati, idaṃ hoti; imassuppādā idaṃ uppajjati* . . . (and in the negative) (M.III.63; S.V.387; *et freq.*).
37. *Nidāna Saṃyutta* (S.II.1–132). Rhys Davids in *Dialogues* II, p. 47.
38. S.II.25. In the same way, the fact that 'all *dhammā* are not-self' is true whether or not there is a Buddha (A.I.286), although it requires a Buddha to recognise it and teach it (unlike the truths of impermanence and suffering) (VbhA.49–50).
39. First two elements missing (S.II.66; A.I.176). Consciousness and name-and-form mutually conditioning (S.II.104). Elements in different order (S.II.101).
40. Frauwallner (1953) pp. 197ff.
41. Poussin (1913) pp. 1–5, on Sn.724–65. See also Silburn (1955) pp. 197–9.
42. 'Different ways of teaching' (*desanābheda*) (Vism.XXVII.28–34). 'Profound in teaching' (*desanāgambhīra*) (*ibid.* 307).

    These different sections are: (a) the four of nos. 1–2, 8–10 as karmic cause, with nos. 3–7, 11–12 as karmic result; (b) the three of nos. 1–2 (past life) 3–10 (present life) and 11–12 (future life); (c) the two of nos. 1–6 (from the past to the present moment) and 7–12 (from the present into the future). See further Chapter 7.1.2; and Poussin (1917) pp. 37–8, 38 n.2.
43. Vism.VII.8; cf. Vism.XVII.57, 273, 285; VbhA.138–94; Poussin (1913) p. 38 and n.2.
44. For these ideas, with particular reference to Thai social and political history, see Tambiah (1977); Bechert (1966) I, Sects. 1–2. On wheel-imagery in the *Theravāda* see Karunaratne (1969). A good modern example of the point here is provided by the Buddhist Publication Society of Ceylon, who call their series of pamphlets *The Wheel.*

3.3. The denial of self as a strategy in 'mental culture'

1. 'Mental culture' is a better, because more general and positive, translation of *bhāvanā* than is 'meditation', which implies too specialised and passive a

form of behaviour. See *Buddhist Dictionary*, pp. 31–2; and Carrithers (forthcoming) Chapter 3.
2. See *Buddhist Dictionary*, pp. 157–8, 197–8.
3. For 'dry-visioned' saints see *Buddhist Dictionary*, p. 175.
4. E.g. Vism.I.1f.
5. Carrithers (forthcoming) Chapter 1: following Douglas (1966); and James (1960).
6. *Sīla-* and *diṭṭhi-visuddhi* (D.III.234; A.I.95; Dhs.1365–6). The seven-fold list of purities (M.I.147ff). At D.III.228, the seven-fold sequence is found, with the addition of 'purity of wisdom' and of 'release', in much the same way as we saw (in Chapter 3.1.3) that the eight-fold Path was increased to the ten-fold Path of the 'adept'. At A.II.195 'purity of behaviour', of 'mind', and of 'release' are found together.
7. Ñāṇamoli (1975).
8. Ñāṇamoli (1975) p. xxix. On *mātikā*, see my own Introduction, and Frauwallner (1964); Lamotte (1967) pp. 197f.
9. See, for example, Tables 1–3 in Ñāṇamoli (1975).
10. Something of the same function might be seen in the twenty-five categories (*tattva*) of the *Sāṃkhya* system. Although the person (*puruṣa*) is the object of the highest spiritual value, and is thus placed in a dichotomy with *prakṛti*, which is non-valued, in terms of content it is empty, and so is merely tacked on to the end of the twenty-four categories of *prakṛti* which do have recognisable and nameable content.
11. A.V.109.
12. S.III.184.
13. A.III.444.
14. A.IV.51. For the translation of *paricita* as 'familiar with' in *aniccasaññā-paricitena cetasā*, see PTC.III.170–1.
15. S.III.155–6.
16. M.III.227–8, reading *na ca apekkhavā upādāya ca na paritassati*, with PTC.I.411; and CPD p. 295.
17. Vism.XXI.49–50.
18. Eighteen elements 'for the purpose of abolishing . . .' (Vism.XV.22, 32). Investigating *nāma-rūpa* 'in order to abandon . . .' (*ibid.* XVII.25–8).

4. Views, attachment, and 'emptiness'

1. Mackie (1967) pp. 177–8.
2. For an extended use of the image of the 'tumour' or 'boil' of conditioned *saṃsāric* life see Vism.XVII.303. In general, the analogy between Buddhist teaching and the remedies of medicine is close: see Kern (1896) pp. 46–7; and (e.g.) Miln.334f.

4.1. Views and attachment

3. M.I.300, III.17; A.II.214–15; *et freq.*
4. S.II.96.
5. S.III.44.
6. M.II.228ff. (Self as 'conscious', *saññī*: literally, 'having ideas', or 'perceptions'.)
7. M.I.6ff.

8. *Diṭṭhivagga* S.III.180ff; *Diṭṭhisaṃyutta* S.III.202ff.
9. S.III.46–7; S.III.105.
10. D.I.82; M.I.348; *et freq.*
11. M.III.297ff.
12. 'Nothing so apt . . .' (A.I.31). 'Lower, middling, and excellent ideas . . .' (S.II.153–4).
13. M.I.147ff.
14. *Alagaddūpama Sutta*, M.I.134f. See Norman (forthcoming).
15. Sn.21.
16. M.I.260.
17. M.I.497ff. 'All is not pleasing to me' (*sabbaṃ na me khamati*). 'This would just be such . . .' (*taṃ p'assa tādisaṃ eva, taṃ p'assa tādisaṃ evāti*). This could mean that, in that case, everything would be equally valueless, and thus no motivation for religious action.
18. 'At peace am I . . .' (*nibbuto 'haṃ asmi, santo 'haṃ asmi, anupādāno 'haṃ asmi*). 'Declares that what is only . . .' (*nibbānaṃ sappāyaṃ eva paṭipadaṃ abhivadeti*). 'Is shown to be an act . . .' (*tad ap' . . . upādānaṃ akkhayati*).
   In a similar vein, the *Laṭukikopama Sutta* (M.I.447ff) speaks in turn of the 'transcending' (*samatikkamo*) of household life and its pleasures, then the sequence of states attained in meditation by the monk, up to 'cessation of perception and feeling'.
19. For a full list and discussion of the *jhānā*, see *Buddhist Dictionary*, p. 70. The *jhānā* as 'constructed' (M.III.244).
20. M.III.104ff. 'He knows it is existent, saying "it is"' (*taṃ santaṃ idaṃ atthīti pajānāti*).
21. 'Concentration of mind that is signless' (*animitta cetosamādhi*). In the 'Greater Discourse on Emptiness' (M.III.109ff), it is said that a monk who 'dwells alone, apart from society, . . . (and) enters into and abides in emptiness' does so by 'not paying attention to any sign' (*sabbanimittānam amanasikāra*), both internally and externally. 'Paying attention to a sign' here means to be aware of the specific, linguistically describable content of any object of perception or cognition – that is, to see by 'insight' what *dhamma* it is.
22. S.IV.54, *suññam attena vā attanīyena vā*.
23. For references see Lamotte, *Traité*, pp. 357f, 370. Although sometimes it is said that the earlier schools do not know 'the selflessness of things', frequently Suttas are quoted – including many of those I have discussed – to show that they do; see Lamotte, *Traité*, pp. 1079f, 2005–6, 2141f. Rāhula (1978) Chapters 7 and 9, argues strongly for the position that in this, as in other ways, all Buddhist schools teach the same thing.
24. On this, as on all matters of the *Madhyamaka* school discussed here, see P. M. Williams (1978), (1980); (forthcoming).
25. Dhs.1306–8. *Sabbe dhammā adhivacana-, nirutti-, paññatti-pathā.*
26. 'Body is like a heap of foam . . .' (S.III.142). 'Not seen by the King of Death' (Dhp.46, 170). *Khandhā* like sandcastles (S.III.189f). 'Having the nature of falsehood' (*mosadhamma*) said of feeling (M.III.245), name-and-form (Sn.756–8), in contrast to *nibbāna*, which has 'the nature of genuine truth' (*saccam amosadhammaṃ*). *Khandhā* as 'impermanent, unsatisfactory, a disease, . . .' (M.I.435; *et freq.*).
27. Reflecting on emptiness 'in the forest . . .' (M.I.297; S.IV.296–7; cf.

M.II.263). Reflecting on 'emptiness . . . in an empty place' is part of the same attitude which related external and internal 'emptiness' in the *Cūlasuññatā Sutta* quoted earlier in the text; and which we shall see again in Chapter 4.3 below. 'See the world is empty . . .' (Sn.1119).

28. 'With tender insight' (*taruṇavipassana*) (Vism.XX.105–27). 'Surely I have reached . . .' (*addhā maggapatto . . . phalapatto 'smi*) (*ibid.* 122–3).
29. Vism.XIV.224. Compare, with regard to body's not enduring 'being pounded', the phrase 'body is . . . of a nature to be constantly rubbed away, pounded away, broken up, and scattered' (M.I.144, 500 *et freq.*; Horner's (PTS) translation). The image of things 'having no core' is frequently used to express the idea of the lack of any 'central self' (e.g. Vism.XXI.56, quoting Nd.2.279).
30. Vism.XX.19.
31. 'The contemplation of emptiness is the contemplation of not-self' (Vism.XXII.117). 'One in meaning . . .' (*ekatthā byañjanam eva nānaṃ*) (Vism.XX.91). 'Paying attention to not-self . . .' (Vism.XXI.69, quoting Ps.II.48). Different 'gateways' for different temperaments (Nett.90). 'When a *learned man* . . .' (Vism.XXI.70, quoting Ps.II.58).
32. A.I.66–7.
33. A.II.10. The four are also called 'floods' (*ogha*) (D.III.230, 276).
34. Coulson (1976) p. 111.
35. D.I.1ff.
36. These parts of the *Sutta Nipāta* have been called 'Proto-*Mādhyamika*' (by Gomez (1976)), because of the radical devaluation of views, of whatever sort. While there is certainly some sense in this description, we must remember that the later *Madhyamaka* school knew of the strong distinction between right and wrong views in other parts of the Buddhist tradition, and so its radical stance could have a clear relation to that tradition; in the *Sutta Nipāta*, we cannot presume that the sentiments expressed have taken cognisance of that distinction, and are speaking to it.

    The verses from the *Sutta Nipāta* which I quote are (in order) Sn.898–900,796, 894.
37. S.III.138f; cf. M.I.108.
38. 'Makes use of conventional terms' (*loke vuttaṃ tena voharati*). It is interesting to note that the monk Sāriputta, 'foremost in wisdom', who was later taken to be the ideal type of *Abhidhamma* dogmatism by the schools emphasising 'emptiness', is said to reach Arhatship after listening to this discourse while standing behind the Buddha, fanning him. (M.I.501). This is surely a significant representation – on the level of legend – of the ideal *Theravāda* attitude to wisdom as an end in itself.
39. 'Worldly forms of speech, and expression . . .' (*loka-samañña, -nirutti, -vohāra, -paññatti*) (D.I.202). 'I speak' (*ahaṃ vadāmīti*) and '(others) speak to me' (*mamaṃ vadantīti*) as 'conventional usages' (*vohāramatta*) (S.I.14).
40. Verses quoted, in order, Sn.911. 787, 1074, 1076; A.II.9 (reading here *vādapathātivattaṃ*, with Gomez (1976) p. 158 n.5, in place of PTS's *vādapathāti vuttaṃ*, which seems corrupt).

4.2. The Unanswered Questions

1. These ten questions are expanded to fourteen in other parts of the Buddhist tradition by the addition of the 'both . . . and' and 'neither . . . nor'

alternatives of nos. 9, 10 to the two sets of questions, nos. 1–2, 3–4. In *Theravāda* the first four usually refer only to 'the world'; I have used a version mentioning 'self' (cf. M.II.233; D.I.16, III.137, where nos. 3 and 4 are *sayaṃkato attā ca* . . . ('self and world are self-made') and *paraṃkato* . . . ('. . . are other-made'))'. The later tradition knows this version (see Lamotte, *Traité*, p. 154 n.1) which gives the overall sense of the questions, and what has always been taken as their most important meaning. Often, the commentaries explain 'world' as *attā* (e.g. UdA 339).

2. S.II.60–2. Cf. Chapter 3.2.5 on the notion of 'unfit' questions.
3. As 'being' at SA.II.311, SA.II.201; DA.I.118; MA.II.117; as 'self' UdA.340.
4. Vajirā at S.I.135; Selā at S.I.134; 'See the painted puppet . . . a composite thing' (*samussitaṃ*) Thag.769; Dhp.147; M.II.64. The commentaries to all of these passages gloss 'puppet' as *attabhāva.*
5. Vism.XVIII.32 (Ñāṇamoli's translation, slightly adapted). The verse quoted as from 'the Ancients' is not among those recorded in the Canon.
6. E.g. M.I.300, III.17.
7. Sāriputta S.IV.287; the Buddha S.IV.394.
8. Smart (1964) pp. 33–4. Cf. Gombrich (1971) p. 7 n.9.
9. D.II.68 (*adhivacanaṃ, adhivacana-patho* . . . *nirutti* . . . *paññatti* . . . *paññā* . . . *paññāvacaraṃ* . . . *vaṭṭaṃ, yāvatā vaṭṭam vaṭṭati* . . .).
10. A.V.196–8.
11. Knowing what can be named (*akkheyyāni*), 'has no conceits' (*na maññati*) (S.I.11). 'Freed from denotation by the *khandhā*' (*rupādi – saṅkhāvimutto*) (M.I.487–8). 'No mind' to describe the *Tathāgata* (S.IV.52). 'Any reason or grounds . . .' (*hetu paccayo paññāpanāya* . . . *aparisesam nirujjhati*) (S.IV.400). The *Tathāgata* not found in this life (S.III.109f).
12. Sāriputta (S.IV.383–90). Moggallāna to Vacchagotta (S.IV.394). Being under the sway of Māra (M.I.157). Anāthapiṇḍika, such a view as 'constructed . . .' (*saṃkhata cetayitā paṭiccasamuppannā*) (A.V.185). Such a view as 'a prejudice . . .' (*diṭṭhigataṃ, taṇhā-, saññā-, upādānagataṃ, maññitaṃ, papañcitaṃ, vippaṭisāro*) (A.IV.67–8).
13. 'Untraceable' (*ananuvejja*) mind of the *Tathāgata* (M.I.140). 'With consciousness unestablished' (*appatiṭṭhena viññāṇena parinibbuto*) (S.I.122). On this idea of 'establishing' or 'stationing of consciousness' (*viññāna-ṭṭhitiyo*) see Chapter 7.2.2 below.
14. The *Tathagata* like an ocean at S.IV.374ff. Cf. M.I.487–8; It.80. The mind of a meditating monk like the Ganges at M.I.128.
15. By Frauwallner (1953) pp. 218–19, amongst many others.
16. This is what Lamotte (*Traité*, p. 2003) calls '*la raison d'ordre pratique*' as opposed to '*la raison d'ordre logique*', which I discussed in Chapter 4.2.1.
17. Rāhula (1967) pp. 62–3, on S.IV.400–1.
18. M.I.429ff.
19. D.I.178ff. 'Rely on' (*pacceti*). 'Made of awareness' (*saññā-mayaṃ*), 'without any good ground' (*appaṭihīrakaṃ*).
20. Rhys Davids' (PTS) translation of *attabhāva-paṭilābha*. See Chapter 5.2 below.
21. 'Unprofitable reasonings' (S.V.418). Advice to Cunda (D.III.135–40). Sāriputta to Kassapa (S.II.222).

4.3. Quietism and careful attention

1. E.g. *Kosambi Sutta* (M.I.320ff); *Kinti Sutta* (M.III.156ff).
2. 'Unpleasant even to think about . . .' (A.I.275). 'When, in a dispute, . . .' (A.I.79, adapted from Khantipalo's ((1964) p. 163) translation).
3. Sn.895–6, 831–3.
4. Sn.793, 914; S.I.141; and Sn.1078 respectively. K. R. Norman (private communication) suggests that *visenikatvā* may well mean 'something like "free from human society, alone"' (following the Buddhist Hybrid Sanskrit tradition, deriving the term from *viśreṇayati*, 'dissociates (from) himself', from *śreṇi*, 'association' 'company', and not from *senā*, 'army'). Nyanaponika (1955) takes the terms from *senā*, perhaps deriving from *sī*, 'to bind' (he gives *liegen, lehnen, neigen*), and translates *visenikatvā* as '*keiner Seite sich verbindend*', or '*nirgend sich verbunden*' ((1955) pp. 320, 325, 356).
5. 'Waging warfare in talk' (Sn.390), as 'mutual quarrelling' (etc.) (A.II.215).
6. 'Weapons of the tongue' (*mukha-sattīhi*) (M.I.320; Ud.67; A.I.70; Vin.I.341; *et freq.*).
7. M.I.108ff. 'Imaginings, ideas, and estimations' (*papañca-saññā-saṅkhā*). 'Has ideas about' (*sañjānāti*), 'reasons about' (*vitakketi*), 'has (vain) imaginings about' (*papañceti*).
8. Ñāṇānanda (1971), quotation from p. 4.
9. Ideas as their cause (*saññā-nidāna*) (Sn.874). 'Root of imaginings and estimations' (*papañca-saṅkhā-mūla*) as 'I am the thinker', an 'internal craving (*taṇhā ajjhattaṃ*) (Sn.916).
10. S.IV.202–3. 'Something conceived' (*maññitaṃ*), 'shaken' (*iñjitaṃ*), 'caused to quiver' (*phanditaṃ*), '(vainly) imagined' (*papañcitaṃ*).
11. M.I.1ff.
12. See Johnston (1937) pp. 22–3.
13. A.II.24. 'Has no conceits' (*na maññati*) about 'the seer' (*daṭṭhā*).
14. The way to destroy all conceits (S.IV.24). 'In the seen there will be only the seen . . .' (*diṭṭhe . . . diṭṭhamattaṃ bhavissati*) (Ud.8; S.IV.72). The sage living '[with] clear [mind]' (Sn.793).
15. The cessation of perception and feeling (*saññā-vedayita-nirodha*) (M.I.392; S.IV.293–4).
16. *Khīṇā jāti, vusitaṃ brahmacariyaṃ, kataṃ karaṇīyaṃ, nāparaṃ itthattāya* (D.I.84; M.I.139; S.I.140; *et freq.*).

    As the Buddha remarks, punning on *attha*, 'goal', and *attā*, 'self', a truly enlightened monk 'speaks of the goal, without bringing himself into it' (*attho ca vutto, attā ca anupanīto*) (A.I.218. III.359; Vin.I.185). The commentary to the last passage (Vin.A.1083) explains that this is because he does not say 'I am an *Arhat*' (*aham arahā ti*).

5. The individual of 'conventional truth'

5.1. 'Conventional' and 'ultimate truth'

1. In speaking of a 'taboo' here, I should make it clear that the term is being used in its most general acceptation. Steiner ((1956) pp. 20–1) argues that 'Taboo is concerned (1) with all the social mechanisms of obedience which have ritual significance; (2) with specific and restrictive behaviour in

dangerous situations. One might say that taboo deals with the sociology of danger itself, for it is also concerned (3) with the protection of individuals who are in danger, and (4) with the protection of society from those endangered – and therefore dangerous – persons.' No doubt in particular cases of individual psychology or institutional dogmatism one might want to apply any or all of these definitions to the way in which the *anattā* doctrine is held and promulgated. In a generally valid sociological account, however, only the first definition can apply.

2. Gombrich (1971) pp. 73, 243.
3. Gombrich (1971) pp. 325–6.
4. DhpA.I.118ff.
5. *Paṇḍitasattavāhaputto aham eva ahosiṃ ti* (J.I.106, Cowell's (PTS) translation).
6. Sāti, *appasuto jātakabhāṇako*, misinterpreted *ahaṃ, bhikkhave tena samayena Vessantaro ahosiṃ ti* (MA.II.305).
7. It was not, however, admitted to printed editions of the Canon in Thailand: see Gehman's introduction to his translation of Pv. (Gehman (1974) p. xii.)
8. For examples, see the works cited in n.30 of the Introduction.
9. See Gombrich (1971) pp. 226ff.
10. Spiro (1970), discussed in the Introduction.
11. For references see Jayatilleke (1963) pp. 361ff. His whole discussion of the two truths is excellent.
12. A.II.60. Cf. Kvu.3; Dīp.36; Nett.21. These terms are translated as 'of direct (and) indirect meaning' (Jayatilleke, (1963)), as 'of explicit (and) implicit meaning' (Ñāṇamoli (1962) p. 36), and as 'of literal (and) symbolic meaning' (Schayer (1935) p. 121); and as '*de sens explicite*' and '*de sens indéterminé, de sens à déterminer*' (Poussin, AK.IX.p. 247).
13. AA.II.118, translated in full by Jayatilleke (1963).
14. SA.II.77, on S.II.82. (*Ubhayena pi sammuti-kathaṃ katheti. Buddhānaṃ hi sammuti-kathā paramattha-kathā dve kathā honti. Tattha satto, naro, puriso, puggalo, Tisso, Nago ti evaṃ pavattā sammuti-kathā nāma. Khandhā, dhātuyo, āyatanānī ti evam pavattā paramatthakathā nama . . .*
    Duve saccāni akkhāsi sambuddho vadatam varo,
    Sammutiṃ paramatthañca tatiyaṃ nūpalabbhati.
    Saṃketavacanaṃ saccaṃ lokasammutikāranā,
    Paramattha-vacanaṃ saccaṃ dhammānaṃ bhūtakāraṇā.)
15. AA.I.95, on AI.22. (*Buddhassa bhagavato duvidhā desanā: sammuti-desanā paramatthadesanā cā ti. Tattha puggalo, satto, itthi, puriso, khattiyo, brāhmaṇo, devo, Māro, ti evaṃrī pā sammutidesanā. Aniccaṃ dukkham, anattā, khandhā, dhātuyo, āyatanāni satipaṭṭhānā ti evaṃrūpā paramatthadesanā.*)
16. *Puggalo na upalabbhati saccikaṭṭhaparamatthena ti* (Kvu.I.1ff). At Pj.1.76f, the phrase 'all beings subsist by food' (*sabbe sattā āhāraṭṭhitikā*), which we shall meet in Chapter 7.1.4, is explained as being 'teaching in terms of a person' (*puggala-diṭṭhanāya desanāya*); this is said to use 'person' as a metaphor (*upacara*) for the five *khandhā*, just as a village is a metaphor for the houses in it. In terms of the theory of momentariness (which we shall meet in Chapter 8.2) 'ultimately, as the *khandhā* are born and grow old moment by moment, so you, monk, are born, grow old and die' (*paramatthato ca khandhesu jāyamānesu jīyamānesu ca khaṇe khaṇe*

tvam bhikkhu jāyase ca jiyase ca mīyase cā ti) (*ibid.* 78; cf. Ñaṇamoli's (PTS) translation and notes).

17. *Rūpasmiṃ* (etc.) *pana sati evaṃnāmo evaṃgotto ti vohāro hoti* (KvuA.33).
18. Vism.XVII.113–15. He is confused (*vimuyhati*), thinking about the breaking up of the *khandhā, satto marati, sattassa dehantarasaṃkamanan ti*, and of *saṃsāra* as a whole *satto asmā lokā paraṃ lokaṃ gacchati, parasmā lokā imaṃ lokaṃ agacchati*, instead of *khandhānañ ca paṭipati dhātu-āyatanānañ ca abbocchinnaṃ vattamānā saṃsaro ti pavuccati*. Similarly, in a pun on the word *avijjā*, 'ignorance', it is said 'amongst women, men, etc., which are in the ultimate sense non-existent, it hurries on (*paramatthato AVIJjamānesu itthipurisādisu JAvati*) and amongst the constituents (of personality) etc., which are existent, it does not hurry on' (*VIJjamānesu pi khandhādisu JAvati na*) (Vism.XVII.43).
19. *Phalass'uppattiyā eva siddhā bhuñjakasammuti, phaluppādena rukkhassa yathā phalati-sammuti. Yathā hi rukkhasaṃkhātānaṃ dhammānaṃ ekadesabhūtassa rukkhaphalassa uppattiyā eva, rukkho phalati vā, phalito ti vā vuccati, tathā devamanussasaṃkhātānaṃ khandhānaṃ ekadesabhūtassa upabhogasaṃkhātassa sukhadukkha-phalassa uppāden'eva, devo manusso vā upabhuñjati ti vā, sukhito dukkhito ti vā vuccati. Tasmā na ettha aññena upabhuñjakena nāma koci attho atthīti* (Vism.XVII.171–2).

Other examples of the discussion of the two truths can be found at SA.II.13; DA.II.382, III.889; MA.I.137.

5.2. *Attabhāva* 'individuality', *puggala* 'person'.

1. D.I.176; Sn.102.
2. 'Through either the body's . . .' (*ayaṃ me attā ti balajanena pariggahitattā attabhāvo vuccati sarīraṃ pi khandhapañcakaṃ pi*) (Asl.308). Four 'grounds for individuality' (*attabhāva-vatthu*) (Nett.85). '*Attabhāva* is what the body is called . . .' (*attabhāvo vuccati sarīraṃ, khandhapañcakaṃ eva vā, taṃ upādāya paññattimatta-sabbhavato*) (Vism.IX.54).
3. M.II.181. 'Wherever there is the production of individuality, it is reckoned accordingly' (*yattha yatth' eva attabhāvassa abhinibbatti hoti, tena ten' eva saṅkhaṃ gacchati*).
4. 'In whatever individuality . . .' (*yasmiṃ yasmin attabhāve abhinivuttha-pubbaṃ hoti*) (D.I.111). Individuality 'reckoned as a man or woman' (*attabhāvo . . . itthī ti vā puriso ti vā saṅkhaṃ gacchati*) (Vism.XV.18).
5. As gods (Vin.II.185; A.III.122; DhpA.I.131, III.7); as spirits (A.IV.66; S.II.255f; Vin.III.104f); as men (Vism.XVII.168; VinA.II.437); as animals (a jackal, S.II.272). As all four (Nd.2.231–2) (cf. J.I.14).
6. In his Buddhist Hybrid Sanskrit Dictionary, Edgerton emphasises the frequency of this meaning of *ātmabhāva* in the texts he deals with there (BHSD p. 92).
7. The ocean containing *attabhāva* of various lengths (A.IV.200; Ud.54; Vin.II.237). Simile of animals floating or sinking (A.V.202). 'Stooping' and 'bent decades' (Vism.XX.51). Gods and monks creating *attabhāva* (Pj.I.124; Thag.1183; D.II.210–11, 266; A.I.279). *Attabhāva* means bodily size also at A.II.17; S.V.447; Pj.I.245f.
8. D.I.195f; discussed in Chapters 2.2.2 and 4.2.3.
9. 'Mind-made' (A.III.122; Vin.II.185). 'As material, immaterial . . .' (D.III.111); without body in the formless worlds (Kvu.263). In one passage

the 'acquisition of individuality' is said to be four-fold, according to whether it results from one's own or another's volition (or both, or neither). In the case of the first three, in the lower celestial regions, dying from such a state is phrased as 'falling (dying) from *that body*' (*tamhā kāyā cuti*); in the case of the last, however, which is the realm of neither perception nor non-perception, and thus a 'formless' world, the phrase becomes simply 'dying from *there*' (*tato cuti*) (A.II.159; cf. D.III.231).

10. E.g. Kvu.326f.
11. 'A hundred, a thousand . . . individualities' (DhpA.I.78). 'From birth to (re)birth' (*bhavābhāvāya*) as 'the repeated production of . . .' (*punapunnaṃ attabhāvabhinibbatti*) (Nd.I.109, 289). A man 'produces an individuality . . .' (*tajjaṃ tajjaṃ attabhāvaṃ abhinibbatteti*) (A.III.411–14). 'Wherever the individuality is produced' (*yatth' assa attabhāvo nibbattati*) (A.I.134). 'In the present (and) . . . the next individuality' (*imasmiṃ . . . anantare attabhāve*) (Vism.XIX.114). One-seeder 'produces only one (more) . . .' (*ekaṃ eva attabhāvaṃ jānetvā*) (SA.III.238, on S.V.204; cf. Pugg.38). The sage 'not producing individuality . . .' (*āyatiṃ attabhāvaṃ anabhinibbattento*) (SnA.II.547, on Sn.844). *Diṭṭhe va dhamme* as *imasmiṃ attabhāve* (DA.I.313; MA.III.453; AA.III.404; *et freq.*). Not understanding the Four Truths 'in the present . . .' (Miln.171). In the same way, the series of lives culminating in that of the Buddha, and beginning from the time of 'his' decision, as Sumedha, to attain enlightenment, is referred to as a series of *attabhāvā* (e.g. J.I.2, 14).
12. Pun on *viharati* (Pj.I.111). 'Dedicates his individuality' (*attabhāvaṃ pariccajāmi*) (Vism.III.124, 126).
13. There is an interesting, though rather complex series of phrases found in the Canon which help to make clear the attitude toward this sense of self which the most orthodox level of doctrinal thought recommends: 'Had it not been, it would not be mine; (if) it will not be, it will not be mine' (*no c'assa, no ca me siyā; na bhavissati, na me bhavissati*) (A.IV.70; M.II.264–5; S.III.55). The commentaries here explain that 'had it not been' refers to *kamma* incurred in previous individualities; 'it would not be mine' refers to the present individuality, the present five *khandhā*; '(if) it will not be' refers to *kamma* produced in the present or future individualities; and 'it will not be mine' refers to the production of further groups of *khandhā*, further individualities. What we are dealing with here is plainly a rather elaborated version of the simple doctrinal idea that *karma* produces rebirth in *saṃsāra*. What gives this elaborate version point, however, what makes the introduction of the technical terms *attabhāva* and *khandhā* significant, can be seen by the existence of a very closely similar series of phrases – the only difference being that they are couched in the *first* rather than the *third* person singular. I have argued that the point of the various lists of impersonal elements which constitutes the pattern of the ultimate truth about personality and continuity is the project of de-personalisation as a particular soteriological strategy. Here also, although we are in the realm of conventional truth, something of the same project may be seen. Whereas the third person version was acceptable as a statement of the Buddhist attitude (it was spoken by the Buddha at A.IV.70; S.III.55; by Ānanda at M.II.264–5), the first person version, which runs 'Were I not (then), it would not be for me; (if) I will not

be, it will not be for me' (*no c'assaṃ, no ca me siyā; na bhavissāmi, na me bhavissati*) is given as an example of a 'conditioned . . . annihilationist view' (*yā sā . . . ucchedadiṭṭhi, saṅkhāro so*) (S.III.99); it is said to be a view which is caused by grasping the *khandhā* (S.III.183), and is quoted by a commentary as an example of the view 'I will be annihilated, destroyed, I will surely not exist' (MA.II.112 on M.I.137). One of the commentaries to the third person version says that a foolish 'ordinary man' is frightened by these phrases because he thinks 'I will now be annihilated, I will now cease to exist!' (*idān 'aham ucchijjissāmi, na dāni kiñci bhavissāmi*) – an idea which shows he cannot 'exhaust his self-attachment' (*attasinehaṃ pariyādātuṃ*) (SA.II.276, on S.III.55). (To be sure, even in the 'approved' version, the genitive pronoun *me*, 'of' or 'for me', shows that first person reference cannot be entirely expunged from linguistic usage. For Buddhist doctrine, however, this use of the pronoun might reasonably be seen as a weak, ostensive one, having the function almost of a particle in simply pointing to the focus of linguistic and spiritual attention. We are certainly here in the midst of the paradoxes which I have suggested arose from the attempt to teach ordinary men, in ordinary language, the doctrine that ordinary psychology and language are based on an illusion – the illusion of enduring self-hood.)

14. Some reply to the point . . . (A.II.135); like a carving on a rock . . . (A.I.283); 'self-tormentors' (etc.) (A.II.205).
15. D.I.176; S.II.21; Sn.102.
16. Differences in temperament and different meditation practices (Vism.III.74ff; Nett.140). Six 'roots of the person' (Pet.575). Source (*nidāna*) of temperaments as karmic habit (*pubbaciṇṇa*), elements (*dhātu*), and humours (*dosa*) (Vism.III.80).
17. 'Four persons found in the world' (M.III.209). 'Ten persons . . .' (A.V.139f). The four-fold pattern of 'light' and 'darkness' (D.III.233; S.II.85; S.I.93; *et freq.*). The 'four pairs' and 'eight persons' (D.III.255; A.IV.292; S.I.220; *et freq.*). 'Nine persons' (e.g. A.IV.372).
18. Of D.I.81.
19. M.II.32. 'I, lord, even in so far . . .' (*ahaṃ, bhante, yāvatakaṃ pi me iminā attabhāvena paccanubhutaṃ, taṃ pi nappahomi iti sakāraṃ sa-uddesaṃ anussarituṃ*).
20. Expressed most elegantly perhaps by Mauss (1938); and Geertz (1974), (1975) Chapter 14.
21. Dumont (1970b) p. 47.
22. D.I.13–15.
23. Dumont (1970b) p. 49.
24. S.III.25f; and SA.II.163–4. '"The person" is what should be said . . .' (*puggalo ti 'ssa vacanīyaṃ; yoyaṃ āyasmā evaṃnāmo evaṃgotto*). 'In this way, in using . . .' (*iti vohāra-matta-siddhaṃ puggalaṃ bhārahāro ti katvā dasseti*).
25. For example, Warren (1909) p. 159; and Keith (1923) p. 82.
26. It is conceivable that taken by themselves, *bhārādāraṃ* and *bhāranikkhepanaṃ* could be adjectives agreeing with an understood *purisaṃ*; but later in the *sutta* the Buddha asks *katamaṃ . . . bhārādānaṃ, . . . -nikkhepanaṃ*, and here they are definitely neuter nouns.

5.3. House imagery

1. Freud (1973.1) p. 186, (1976) pp. 156–7, 320–1. (Cf. also the discussion in Rycroft (1979) pp. 91–3.)
2. Buber (1970) p. 150.
3. Eliade (1959) pp. 175, 177–8.
4. Bachelard (1957) p. 34, (1964a) p. 17.
5. Vism.XVIII.28, quoting original found at M.I.190. The *Visuddhimagga* quotes this image, along with that of the chariot and its parts (as in Chapter 4.2.1), and explains that as 'mere conventional speech' 'house' and 'chariot' may be said to exist, but that 'ultimately', they do not.
6. The guest-house (*āgantukāgāra*) (S.IV.219); alms-food and the body (Vism.I.91).
7. A.I.261–2; Dhp.13–14.
8. DhpA.I.121, on Dhp.13.
9. See SnA.I.31f; and ThagA.I.28–9, and the references cited there.
10. *Khandhā* as sandcastles (S.III.189–90); old house thatched with dry grass (S.IV.174); sleeping house-owner (Vism.XXI.94); foolish man prey to fears and misfortunes (A.I.101).
11. Six sense-bases as an empty village (S.IV.174; Vism.XV.16, XXI.35). Birth, old age, and death like village-robbers (Vism.XVI.58). Body as a village with thirty-two families (Vism.VIII.70–1).
12. Memory of former lives like sequences of villages, and seeing the death and rebirth of others like watching them go from house to house (D.I.83; M.I.279, II.21, III.178); entering heaven like entering a palace (M.I.76); desire as the house-builder (Dhp.153–4; Thag.183). *niketa* as 'former dwelling-place' (D.III.145).
13. Subduing 'householders' ways' (M.II.136); the Buddha and Vipassi (M.I.504; D.II.16); 'giving up the five strands . . .' (Sn.337); 'living homeless' (*aniketa-vihāro*) (Thag.36 and ThagA.I.106); the monk who has forsaken the sense-pleasures (A.I.147–8); 'leaving father and mother, . . .' (Thag.892, Norman's PTS) translation). *Aggañña Sutta* (D.III.88–9).
14. Sn.844; and SnA.547.
15. S.III.9ff; also at Nd.1.197ff.
16. Thus Nyanaponika's German translation, (1955) p. 183, reads '*nicht ersehnend*', and he comments on this as '*nicht vorwegnehmend, antizipierend*' (p. 327).
17. SnA.II.547. 'Rejecting . . .' (*rūpavatthādiviññānass' okāsaṃ tatra chandarāgapahanema chaḍḍetvā*); 'not frequenting . . .' (*rūpanimmitaniketādini taṇhāvasena asaranto*); 'producing no future . . .' (*āyatiṃ attabhāvaṃ anabhinibbattento*).
18. See PTSD pp. 46, 162. In the same way, the word *nekkhamma*, 'renunciation', can mean the act of leaving home for the monkhood, the attitude of renunciation which the monk practises, and the final abandonment of rebirth in *nirvāṇa*. See PTSD p. 377, Norman's notes to Thig.226, 339, 403 (PTS translation), and the remarks on *nikkhamati* in the text and note 20 below.
19. *Ālayarāma, ālayarata, ālayasammudita* (Vin.I.4; D.II.36; M.I.167; S.I.136; A.II.131).
20. DA.II.464; MA.II.174–5; SA.I.195–6. 'Take pleasure in . . .' (*kāmālayehi*

tanhālayehi sattā ramanti); 'dwell in the round of *saṃsāra*' (*saṃsāra-vaṭṭe vasanti*).
21. Miln.211f.
22. E.g. D.II.31; S.III.26, 158, IV.172; *et freq.*
23. Vin.III.20, 111; It.88; A.II.34.
24. Dhp.411; Sn.535. I think a great deal of light could be thrown on the *Vijñānavāda* school of Buddhism's idea of an *ālaya-vijñāna*, 'home-consciousness', if it were examined in relation to this pattern of imagery.
25. *Kāya*, *citta-*, and *upadhi-viveka* (e.g. Nd.I.26–7; MA.II.143; DA.I.169; AA.III.313).
26. An occasional variant is *okā anokaṃ āgamma* (S.V.24; A.V.232; Dhp.87).
27. D.I.62; M.I.179, II.211; *et freq.*
28. E.g. Nd.I.26.
29. 'Living alone . . .' (*ekavihārī ekavihārassa vaṇṇavādi*) (S.II.282–3). On this *Sutta* and others of the same pattern, see Ñāṇānanda (1973). Living with (desire as) a companion (S.V.35–7, cf. V.60–1). The two monks (Vism.III.31–4).
30. James (1960) pp. 290, 348–9.
31. Nyanaponika (1971a), quoting SnA.I.339, on Sn.334.
32. D.I.70; S.II.218; Vism.XIV.141. The process of perception and cognition, described in terms of the arising of mental contents interrupting the contentless *bhavaṅga*-mind (which I will discuss in Chapter 8) is compared to the arrival of a guest in one's house (VbhA.357; DA.I.195).
33. S.IV.194–5. The image of the body and mind as a town or city is widespread, and fits often into the pattern of house- and village-imagery I have outlined (e.g. A.IV.106f; Dhp.40, 150, 315; Thag.653, 1005). For a modern *Theravāda* treatment, see Nyanaponika (1974).
34. Miln.54–7; quotation in the text from p. 57.
35. The use of this phrase is given added significance if we remember that the *Milinda Pañha* is thought to show traces of *Sarvāstivāda* influence (cf. Horner (1964) pp. xvii–xviii). It was a tenet of this school that space and *nirvāṇa* both share the characteristic of being unconditioned *dharmāḥ*, whereas *Theravāda* scholasticism held that to be true of *nibbāna* alone: the *Milinda* (pp. 268, 271) holds the *Sarvāstivāda* tenet. Accordingly, the comparison between the 'great space' which remains after the destruction of the 'body-house' with its 'sense-doors' and the state of *nirvāṇa* which remains after the destruction of individuality is made more pointed.
36. A little later in the conversation he repeats his rejection of the picture of experience as a soul (*jīva*) apprehending the objects of its sensory and mental experience by means of the senses (and mind) in the same words: if (e.g.) the 'eye-doors' were removed, could such a soul see anything in the 'great space' which would remain? (Miln.86).
37. *Yathā gāmato/gehato nikhamma aññaṃ gāmaṃ/gehaṃ pavisati, evaṃ evaṃ pi so jīvo aññaṃ kāyaṃ (bondiṃ) pavisati* (Pv.IV.31–2).
38. On two occasions (Asl.164; Vism.IV.82) *kāya-* and *citta-viveka* are completed by *vikkhambana-viveka*, 'seclusion by suppression'. This is a term used for the suppression of defilements (*kilesa*) or 'hindrances' (*nīvaraṇa*) during meditative absorption (cf. Vism.IV.31; and Ñāṇamoli (1960) p. 273 n.1).
39. See PTSD p. 142 for details and references.

40. Nd.I.26–7. This type of seclusion is said elsewhere to be synonymous with *nibbāna* (DA.III.1019; MA.II.143).
41. 'Condition of seclusion' (*viveka-dhamma*) (Sn.1065); 'the state of *nibbāna*, . . .' (*sabba-saṃkhāra-viveka-nibbāna-dhamma*) (SnA.593).
42. Dhp.153–4. The commentary, as so often, explains the house here as the *attabhāva*; similarly, when a monk, who acquired the name 'Reed-breaker' (*sara-bhaṅga*) through breaking off reeds with his hands to make a hut, claims that as he is enlightened it is not fitting for him to break off reeds, the commentary again says it is because he has no more use for an *attabhāva*-hut. (Thag.487–93).

6. 'Neither the same nor different'

6.1. 'A person is not found'

1. On the councils, see Thomas (1951) Chapter 3; Bareau (1955a).
2. Ñāṇamoli (1975) p. xxx.
3. The main sources are AK Chapter 9, and the *Tattvasaṃgraha*. A translation of a Chinese version of a text of the school, the *Āśrayaprajñaptiśāstra*, was published in the *Visva-Bharati Annals*, V, 1953.
4. 'Known in real and ultimate fact' (*saccikaṭṭhaparamatthena upalabbhati*). The commentary (KvuA.8) glosses *upalabbhati* as *paññāya upagantvā labbhati*, 'is found, arrived at by the understanding'.
5. Kvu.I.1–16, and 16–157.
6. Kvu.I.158–9. 'A person transmigrates' (*puggalo sandhavati*).
7. 'One person acts . . .' (*so/añño karoti . . . so/añño patisaṃvedayati*) (S.II.76f). 'Caused by self/other' (*sayaṃ-, paraṃkataṃ*) (S.II.112f).
8. Kvu.I.160–3.
9. Kvu.I.170. (*Khandhesu bhijjamānesu so ce bhijjati puggalo, ucchedā bhavāti diṭṭhi yā Buddhena vivajjitā. Khandhesu bhijjamānesu no ce bhijjati puggalo, puggalo sassato hoti nibbānena samasamo ti.*)
10. (*Rūpādiyo*) *upādāya puggalassa paññatti* (Kvu.I.171–82).
11. Kvu.I.183–8.
12. Kvu.I.229–35. 'He who feels' (*yo vedanaṃ vedīyamāno*) (*ibid.* 229); 'the contemplator' (*anupassī*) (*ibid.* 231–3); 'he who looks on' (*avekkhati*) (*ibid.* 235).
13. Kvu.I.200–16. 'Doer' (*kattā*); 'instigator' (*kāretā*); 'experiencer of the person' (*puggalassa paṭisaṃvedi*); 'series of persons' (*puggalassa paramparā*).
14. 'There is the person . . .' (*atthi puggalo attahitāya paṭipanno*) (cited at Kvu.I.74; *et freq.*); 'that person . . .' (*so sattakhattuparamaṃ sandhavitvāna puggalo*) (Kvu.I.159); the 'Four Pairs' and 'Eight Persons' (Kvu.I.223).
15. Kvu.I.238, 240, 241, respectively.
16. Kvu.I.243. 'In real and established fact' (*saccato thetato*). This is the ancient pattern which the modern monk Nyanatiloka adapts in the quotation I gave in the Introduction.
17. Kvu.I.244 and KvuA.33. 'The meaning of teachings . . .' (*sabbā va desanā yathārutavasen' eva atthato na gahetabbā*).
18. Vism.XIX.19–20. 'No doer . . . experiencer' (*na karaṇato uddhaṃ kārako . . . na vipākapavattito uddhaṃ vipākasaṃvedaka*).
19. Miln.25. (*Nāgaseno ti ahaṃ mahārāja ñāyāmi, Nāgaseno ti maṃ mahārāja*

sabrahmacārī samudācaranti, api ca mātāpitaro nāmaṃ karonti Nāgaseno ti . . . api ca kho maharāja saṅkhā samaññā paññatti vohāro nāmamattaṃ yad idaṃ Nāgeseno ti, na h' ettha puggalo upalabbhati.)

20. Miln.25; cf. Miln.268, where one of the things which 'do not exist in the world' (*loke natthi*) is 'the occurrence of a being in ultimate truth' (*paramatthena sattupaladdhi*).
21. Steiner F. (1956) p. 20; cf. Chapter 5.1 and n.1.
22. Steiner F. *ibid.*, p. 147.
23. Miln.30f. 'Soul, inner wind' (*abbhantare-vāyo jīvo*); 'activities set in motion by the body' (*kāyo-saṃkhārā*).

6.2. Images of identity and difference

1. Miln.46. 'Who is reborn?' (lit. 'reconnects') (*ko paṭisandahati*). 'One does a good or evil deed . . .' (*iminā pana mahārāja nāma-rūpena kammaṃ karoti, sobhanaṃ vā pāpakaṃ vā, tena kammena aññaṃ nāma-rūpaṃ paṭisandahatīti*).
2. Miln.48. (*Kiñcāpi aññaṃ maraṇantikaṃ nāmarūpaṃ aññaṃ patisandhismim nāma-rūpaṃ, api ca tato yeva taṃ nibbattaṃ.)*
3. Miln.40. (*Yo so uppajjati so eva so udāhu añño ti.*) 'The young boy, tender, . . .' (*añño so daharo . . . ahosi, añño ahaṃ etarahi mahanto*). 'I was a young boy . . .' (*ahañ ñeva . . . daharo ahosiṃ . . . ahañ ñeva etarahi mahanto; imañ ñeva kāyaṃ nissāya sabbe te ekasaṅgahitā ti*).

   'Even so, a continuity of elements . . .' (*evaṃ eva dhammasantati sandahati, añño uppajjati, añño nirujjhati*).
4. Miln.71. (Literally 'pass over' (*saṅkamati*) and 'reconnect' (*paṭisandahati*).)
5. Vism.XIX.22 (Ñāṇamoli's translation, slightly adapted).
6. Miln.72–3. 'As long as a continuity is not broken off' (*abbocchinnāya santatiyā*).
7. Miln.77 (Horner's (PTS) translation).
8. Miln.31.
9. Vism.XVII.172, cited in Chapter 5.1.3 n.19.
10. Vism.XIX.20 (Ñāṇamoli's translation).
11. Vism.XIX.22; Miln.71; and Vism.XIX.22; Miln.54, respectively.
12. Vism.XVII.16–17. 'There is neither identity nor difference in a sequence of continuity' (*santānabandhato n'atthi ekatā nāpi nānatā*).

6.3. Self and other: compassion

1. E.g. M.I.8, 265, III.187f; S.II.26.
2. This was first pointed out by Demieville (1927).
3. James (1950) e.g. pp. 330f, 459, 650.
4. E.g. M.I.437; S.I.191; Pugg.31.
5. Quoted by Demieville (1927) pp. 293–4.
6. When this memory is attained or practised by an enlightened man, rather than someone on the Path to it, we can say that phrases such as 'the remembering self', and 'the present "I"', denote two related things as parts of the final 'lifetime': first, from birth until the attainment of *nibbāna*-in-life, there is the usual sense of 'individuality' (*attabhāva*) created by the operation of 'the conceit "I am"' on the fact of psycho-physical individuality. Second, from the attainment of this *nibbāna* until death (and final *nibbāna*), there is

the individuality which consists in the simple fact or event of a continuing body and mind, and also those particularities of character and personality-type which remain through the force of *karma*. On these particularities, said to be caused by *vāsanā*, 'impregnations', see Lamotte (1974).

7. Demieville (1927) p. 290.
8. Vism.XIV.73, XVIII.14, XXII.39.
9. S.I.12, III.48; D.III.216; Thag.1074–6; Dhs.1116. There are seven forms (*vidha*) at Vbh. 950, nine at Vbh.962, ten at Nd.I.80.
10. *Pānānaṃ yeva anuddayāya anukampāya paṭipanno hoti* (A.II.176–7).
11. Vism.III.28, 57–133.
12. 'Beings, persons, those endowed with individuality' (*sattā, puggalā, attabhāva-pariyāpannā*) (Vism.IX.52–4). 'Breaking down the barriers' (*sīma-sambheda*) (Vism.IX.40). 'Equality . . . to himself' (*atta-samatā*); 'not making the distinction . . .' (*ayaṃ parasatto ti vibhāgaṃ akatvā*) (Vism.IX.47). 'Sees the equality of all beings' (*sattesu samabhāvadassana*) (Vism.IX.96). 'Mental objects consisting in concepts' (*paññattidhamma-vasena . . . ārammaṇaṃ*) (Vism.IX.102; cf. *ibid.* IX.54, quoted in Chapter 5.2.1).
13. S.IV.259, V.56; D.III.216; Vism.XVI.34. 'Ordinary suffering' (*dukkha-dukkha*), 'suffering through change' (*pariṇāma-dukkha*), suffering through (the fact of) conditioned existence (*saṃkhāra-dukkha*).
14. S.II.53.
15. D.II.30–1.
16. S.IV.216.
17. Robinson (1970) p. 29; cf. Rāhula (1967) pp. 16–19.
18. E.g. SA.III.170.
19. *Mahāsatipaṭṭhāna Sutta* D.II.290f.
20. Poussin (1917) pp. 49–50.
21. Dumont (1970b) p. 48 n.24.
22. See, above all, Parfit (1971); and Nagel (1970). The homology between contemporary 'others' and past and future 'selves', in relation to a given 'person', is explicitly broached by Parfit (1973).
23. *Parātma-samatā*. On the *Bodhisattva* see Dayal (1932). Rāhula (1978) Chapter 6, discusses the ideal of the *Bodhisattva* in *Theravāda* tradition, arguing strongly for its being recognised there.
24. Sumedha J.I.13–14; 'the one person . . .' (A.I.22). The decision to preach (e.g. Vin.I.4). 'Whatever is to be done . . .' (M.I.46, II.266; S.IV.367 *et freq.*). Begged to stay alive (D.II.104; S.II.274, V.259). Preaching 'for the good of the many . . .' (Vin.I.21; D.II.45; S.I.105; *et freq.*). The released man teaching 'out of mercy and compassion' (S.I.206), as monks generally (e.g. M.I.161, II.113). Mahākassapa (S.II.202–3); on some ambiguities in the idea of the ascetic monkhood preaching to the laity, see Carrithers (1978).
25. E.g. Gombrich (1971), especially the Conclusion; and Ortner (1978) respectively.

7. Conditioning and consciousness

1. Nārada Thera (1948) is an admirable example.

7.1. The construction(s) of temporal existence

1. Silburn (1955) p. 213, quoting ŚB.4.5.6.5.
2. Poussin (1913) p. 9.
3. Frauwallner (1953) pp. 200–2: 'It means . . .' (*es besagt, dass etwas in einen Zustand der Bereitschaft gesetzt wird, der sich weiterhin auswirkt*).
4. Gombrich (1971) p. 346.
5. 'People form a construction . . .' (S.III.87; Vism.XVII.44). Those who 'delight in formations . . . construct . . .' (*saṃkhāresu abhiramanti . . . jāti-saṃvattanike saṃkhāre abhisaṃkharonti*)(S.V.449). 'Meritorious, demeritorious, neutral' (literally 'imperturbable') (*puññaṃ, apuññaṃ aneñjañ ce saṃkhāraṃ abhisaṃkharoti . . . puññ-, apuññ-, aneñjūpagaṃ viññāṇaṃ*) (S.II.82). According to *Buddhist Dictionary*, p. 162, here 'meritorious action leads consciousness to rebirth in the *kāma-* and *rūpa-lokas*' (sense- and fine-materal spheres) 'demeritorious action to the sense-sphere alone', while what is 'neither' (lit. 'imperturbable', 'immovable') leads to the immaterial-sphere (*arūpa-loka*). See further Table 2 in the text.
6. The body as 'something constructed . . .' (*nāyaṃ kāyo . . . tumhākaṃ pi na pi aññesaṃ . . . purāṇaṃ idaṃ . . . kammaṃ abisaṃkhātaṃ abhisañcetayitaṃ*) (S.II.64). 'Whatever a man wills, . . .' (*ceteti pakappeti anuseti . . . ārammaṇaṃ viññāṇassa ṭhitiyā . . .; patiṭṭhite viññāṇe virūḷhe āyatiṃ punabbhavābhinibbatti hoti*) (S.II.65f). 'Consciousness not persisting . . .' (*apatiṭṭhitam viññāṇaṃ avirūḷhaṃ anabhisaṃkhārañ ca*) (S.III.53–4).
7. Vism.XVII.307. On these different interpretations as aids to teaching cf. Chapter 3.2.5 n.42.
8. See Nārada Thera's (1975) translation of the medieval *Abhidhammatthasaṃgaha* (VII.3) pp. 354ff, and esp. Diagrams XVI and XVII.
9. M.I.297; Vism.XXIII.12.
10. A.I.112.
11. S.II.82, quoted in Chapter 7.1.1 above; D.III.217; Vbh.135, 340; Nd.1.334, 442; SnA. 505, 569; Nett. 99.
12. 'Basis of constructions' (*abhisaṃkhārupadhi*) (SnA.44–5; Nd.1.27, 141, 342).
13. Sn.18–34; and SnA.I.39.
14. 'Living homeless' (*anoko*). 'He makes no occasion . . .' (*abhisaṃkhāra-sahagata-viññāṇassa okāsaṃ na karoti*) (Nd.1.487); 'there is for him . . . (*abhisaṃkhāra-viññāṇādinaṃ anokāsabhūto*) (SnA.573).
15. Asl.236, 357, Nd.2.569. (*Sotāpattimaggañāṇena abhisaṃkhāra-viññāṇassa nirodhena satta bhāve thāpetvā anamatagge saṃsāre ye uppajjeyyuṃ nāmañ ca rūpañ ca etth' ete nirujjhanti, vūpasammanti, atthaṃ gacchanti, paṭipassambhanti.*)
16. Sn.832–4; and SnA.505–6. (*Kammasahajātābhisaṃkhāraviññāṇa.*)
17. *Viññāṇaṃ bhave na tiṭṭhe* (Sn.1055); . . . *uparujjhati* (Sn.1110); and SnA.591, 600 respectively.
18. See Lamotte (1974); cf. Chapter 6.3.1, n.6 above.
19. *Anidassanaṃ anantaṃ sabbato-pabhaṃ* (D.I.223).
20. 'Widespread, immeasurable . . .' (*vipulena mahaggatena appamāṇena*) (M.II.195, 207). 'Immeasurable mind' of the fourth *jhāna* (*appamāṇacetaso*) (M.I.270).

21. Asl.236, Nd.2. 569. (*arahato anupādisesāya nibbānadhātuyā parinibbāyantassa carimaviññāṇassa nirodhena paññā ca sati ca nāmañ ca rūpañ ca etth'ete nirujjhanti.*)
22. *Carimaka-viññāṇaṃ pi abhisaṃkhāra-viññāṇaṃ pi* (DA.II.393, commenting on the 'indescribable, infinite, radiant consciousness' of D.I.223, mentioned in the text and n.20 above).
23. 'From food arise all beings . . .' (Tait.U.2.2). 'The sun takes food to itself . . .' (Mait.U.6.12). 'Food is the source . . .' (*ibid.* 14). 'The oblation which is offered . . .' (*ibid.* 37). 'There is something else . . .' (*ibid.* 10).
24. Bachelard (1938) pp. 131, 136, (1964) pp. 64, 67.
25. Many references could be cited: see, for example, the articles 'Food'; 'Food (Hindu)'; 'Food for the Dead', ERE VI, 59–68. 'Not only from the physiological, but also from the sociological point of view, food, the food-quest and the food-supply, constitute the permanent basis of human action' (*ibid.* 59).
26. For the continuing role played by offerings of food in contemporary Buddhism, see Ames' article (1964) pp. 33ff.
27. *Āhāraṭṭhitikā* (D.III.211, 273; A.V.50–1; Thag.123; *et freq.*).
28. *Kabaḷiṅkāra, phasso, manosañcetana, viññāṇa* (D.III.228, 276; S.II.11, 12f; M.I.47–8, 261; *et freq.*).
29. The two terms *upādāna* and *āhāra* are closely parallel. Both come from verbal roots meaning to 'take up' (*upa-ā-dā, ā-hṛ*), both can be used for the fuel of the 'lamp of life' in the standard image; *āhāra* (like *upādāya*) can refer colourlessly to the idea of a cause (e.g. DA.III.1056); it is one of the twenty-four 'modes of conditionality' (*Buddhist Dictionary*, pp. 115ff).
30. 'For the maintenance of beings . . .' (*bhūtānaṃ vā sattānaṃ ṭhitiyā sambhavesinaṃ vā*) (M.I.261); lamp 'goes out without nourishment' (*anāhāro nibbāyeyya*) (S.II.86, III.126, IV.213); the Four Foods 'have desire as their cause' (*ime cattaro āhārā taṇhā-nidānā, taṇhāsamudayā, taṇhā-jātikā, taṇhā-pabhavā*) (S.II.11–12). 'What is born, become . . .' (*jātaṃ bhūtaṃ samuppannaṃ, kataṃ saṃkhatam addhuvaṃ jarāmaraṇa-saṃkhatam, roganīḷaṃ pabhaṅgunaṃ, āhāranetti pabhavaṃ, . . . tassa nissaraṇaṃ santaṃ, . . . saṃkhārūpasamo sukho ti*) (It.37). The commentary here (It.A.II.164) explains *āhāra* as either the Four Foods or 'all (kinds of) cause' (*sabbo pi paccayo*).
31. Sub-commentary to S.II.12, *apud* Nyanaponika (1967) pp. 48–9, n.8, p. 50 n.1.
32. 'Of what is consciousness the food?' (*kissa . . . viññāṇāhāro ti*) (S.II.13). 'Consciousness is established and grows . . .' (*patiṭṭhitam viññāṇaṃ virūḷhaṃ, . . . atthi tattha nāmarūpassa avakkanti, . . . saṃkhārānaṃ vuddhi, . . . āyatim punabbhavābhinibbatti*) (S.II.101).
33. Poussin (1917) p. 11.
34. For the *gandharva* in early mythology, see Wijesekera (1945), who also deals with the Buddhist idea of *gandhabba*.
35. Conjunction of three things (M.I.265–6, Horner's (PTS) translation; cf. M.II.157). Mythological birth (Miln.123). In some versions of the Buddha's birth, he descends in the form of a white elephant (D.II.12f; M.III.119f; Thomas (1949) Chapter 3).
36. It is usually used of consciousness and name-and-form, as we shall see, but

also on one occasion of 'the descent of the five sense-faculties' (*pañcannaṃ indriyānaṃ avakkanti*) (S.III.46).

37. 'Birth, origin . . .' (*jāti, sañjāti, okkanti, nibbatti*) (M.I.50, III.249; S.II.3, II.225; *et freq.*). 'Descent of consciousness' (S.II.91); 'when there is descent . . .' (*okkantiyā sati, nāma-rūpaṃ*) (A.I.176); 'were consciousness not to descend . . .' (D.II.63).
38. Consciousness and name-and-form mutually conditioning (S.II.104; D.II.63), like two bundles of reeds (S.II.114); 'descent of name-and-form' (S.II.90); 'whatever a man wills . . .' (S.II.66); 'consciousness thus persisting and having grown . . .' (S.II.101); consciousness as 're-linking', and name-and-form as 'descent' (Vism.XVII.294, quoting Ps.I.52).
39. *Tatrūpākasatta*, as at MA.II.310, in exegesis of the word *gandhabba* in the 'conjunction of three things' passage cited earlier in the text.
40. Nyanatiloka (1964) pp. 2–3.

7.2. The stations of evolving consciousness

1. In the dialogue with Sāti (M.I.256ff), discussed in Chapter 3.2.5.
2. 'With consciousness gone' (*apeta-viññāṇo*) (Dhp.41, 468). 'Vitality, heat and consciousness' (*āyu, usmā, viññāṇa*) (M.I.296; S.III.143). (On these terms see further Chapter 8.1.1 below.) 'Senseless' (*acetana*) lump of wood (*ibid.*). 'Mind . . . reaches the heights' (*uddhaṃgami, visesagami*) (S.V.370). 'What part of a man transmigrates?' (*kiṃsu tassa* [*purisassa*] *vidhāvati*) (S.I.38).
3. *Yañ ca kho . . . vuccati cittaṃ iti pi mano iti pi viññāṇam iti pi* (S.II.94). Elsewhere, 'consciousness-food' is glossed as 'whatever is mind' (*yaṃ kiñci cittaṃ*) (A.I.209).
4. PTSD p. 619 (italics in original).
5. Gonda (1966) pp. 143–4, quoting ŚB.6.2.2.2 (*kṛtaṃ lokaṃ puruṣo 'bhijāyate*).
6. Gonda (1966) p. 144.
7. Ch.U.7.5.3. 'Mind-worlds' (*cittān lokān*). Gonda (1966) has 'the *lokas* which he has made the object of his *cittam*'; Hume ((1931) p. 254) 'mind-worlds'; Zaehner ((1966) p. 115) 'states of being which have been properly thought out'.
8. 'Constructions which lead to rebirth' (*jāti-saṃvattanike saṃkhāre*) (S.V.49, cited in Chapter 7.1.1 above). 'Beings coming to (rebirth)' (*ābhassara-saṃvattanikā sattā*) (D.I.17). Meritorious acts which 'lead to heaven' (*sagga-saṃvattanika*) (A.II.54, III.46; D.I.51, III.66; *et freq.*), and bad deeds which 'lead to hell, . . .' (*niraya-tiracchāna-yoni-, pittivisaya-saṃvattanika*) (A.IV.247; Kvu.XXII.7). 'Ways of thinking which do (do not) lead to *nibbāna*' ((*a-*)*nibbānasaṃvattanikā vitakkā*) (It.82).
9. M.II.262f; and MA.IV.61f. 'Evolving consciousness might reach imperturbability' (*saṃvattanikaṃ viññāṇaṃ assa ānañjūpagaṃ*).
10. S.II.65. (. . . *viññāṇassa ṭhitiyā . . . patiṭṭhite viññāṇe*.)
11. Sn.1113; and Sn.A.601 (cf. Nd.2.570). Four 'by virtue of constructions' (*abhisaṃkhāra-vasena*), seven 'by virtue of rebirth' (*paṭisandhi-vasena*).
12. S.III.53; D.III.228. (*Tiṭṭhamānaṃ tiṭṭheyya.*) Commentaries: SA.II.271; DA.III.1021 respectively.
13. S.III.9f, discussed in Chapter 5.3.1. 'The stationing of construction-consciousness' (*abhisaṃkhāra-viññāṇa-ṭṭhiti*) (SA.II.259).

14. *Paṭisandhi-viññāṇa-ṭṭhānāni* (D.II.68, III.253, 282; A.IV.39, V.53, and commentaries).
15. *Sattāvāsa* (A.IV.401, V.54; D.III.263, 288; Pj.I.86–7).
16. The seven stations and nine abodes together (Vism.VII.69, XVII.148, XXI.35). Death explained as 'having passed away from one becoming, . . .' (Vism.XIII.69; cf. Kvu.362f).
17. Consciousness 'not stationed' in release (S.II.65, III.53). Not found by Māra (S.I.122, III.124) or the gods (MA.II.117).
18. For more details of these 'Planes of Existence' see Nārada Thera (1948); *Buddhist Dictionary*, p. 76; PTSD p. 187. On Indian cosmology generally, Gombrich (1975). Four 'incalculable aeons' (*asaṅkheyyakappa*) equal one 'great aeon' (*mahākappa*).

7.3. Vegetation imagery

1. Cited in Gonda (1965) p. 225 (his translation).
2. 'Like fields are the *Arhats* . . .' (Pv.I.1). 'Men offering sacrifice . . .' (*yajamānānaṃ manussānaṃ . . . karotaṃ opadhikaṃ saṅghe dinnaṃ mahāphalanti*) (S.I.233; A.IV.292). To a similar use of the phrase *opadhikam puññaṃ*, 'meritorious deeds which bring rebirth', (It.20, 78; Vv.34.21), the commentaries give the explanation 'producing (an) individuality, (and) providing for the ripening of phenomena in rebirth' (*attabhāva-janaka paṭisandhipavattivipāka-dāyaka*).
3. 'Gifts to those who . . .' (S.I.233; cf. an extended treatment at A.IV.237). 'Unsurpassable field of merit' (*anuttara puññakkhetta*): the Buddha (S.I.167; Sn.486; It.98); individual accomplished monks (M.I.446; A.I.244, II.113, III.158, 248, 279, 387, IV.10, 292; Miln.416; Pv.IV.1); the monkhood as a whole (D.III.5, 227; M.III.80; S.I.220, V.343, 363, 382; A.II.34, 56; It.88).
4. Seed of the *dhamma* (S.IV.314); young monks like seedlings (M.I.457; S.III.91–2); women like mildew (A.IV.278).
5. Vin.II.180–1. 'What belongs to the houshold life' (*gharāvāsatthaṃ*).
6. 'Like the seed that is sown . . .' (S.I.227); actions performed with greed, hatred, and delusion (A.I.134–5); 'roots' (*mūla*) of good and evil (Dhp.356–9; for further references and a modern elucidation of the image see Nyanaponika (1978)); these 'roots' not cut off (A.III.404); bitter and sweet seeds (A.I.32, V.212–13); Brahmanical sacrifices as bad seed in unfavourable soil (D.II.353).
7. 'With such nourishment. . .' (*tadāhāro tadupādāno ciraṃ dīghaṃ addhānaṃ tiṭṭeyya*); 'like a palm-tree stump . . .' (*ucchinnamūlo tālavatthukato anabhāvakato āyatiṃ anuppādadhammo*) (S.II.87–9). The phrase used without explicit vegetation imagery (e.g. M.I.370, 488; S.I.69, II.62). 'Just as a tree, whose roots . . .' (Dhp.356). 'Just as when someone cuts a living tree . . .' (S.IV.60).
8. S.I.172f; Sn.12f. The commentaries (SA.I.250; Sn.A.144) explain that the 'seed of faith' grows by putting out the 'root of morality' (*sīla-mūla*) and the 'shoot of meditation and insight' (*samatha-vipassanaṅkuro*).
9. Miln.75–6.
10. Growth in the religious life depends on *sīla* (S.V.46); right or wrong attitude in hearing or practising the *dhamma* (Thag.363, 388, 391); good and bad preaching (S.V.379; cf. Miln.353); *sīla/samādhi/paññā* like seeds to fruit (A.III.20, IV.336; *et freq.*).

11. A.I.239–40; cf. A.I.229–33. 'Urgent duties' (*accayikāni karaṇīyāni*); 'magic powers or influence' (*iddhi vā anubhāvo vā*); 'natural process of seasonal change' (*utu-pariṇāma*).
12. 'Non-interruptedness of continuity' (*santānanupacchedo*) (Vism.XVII.301); 'six-fold sense-base planted in name-and-form . . .' (*ibid.* 303); formations 'like the seeds of a poison tree . . .', 'cause of the continuity of the *khandhā*' (*khandha-santānassa hetu*) (Vism.XV.42); birth, old age and death like weeds and creepers (Vism.XVI.58); 'continuing the tree's lineage . . .' (*mahārukkhe yāva kappavāsanā bījaparamparāya rukkha-paveniṃ sandhayamāne*) (Vism.XXII.87–8).
13. 'Human puppet' 'by reason of a cause' (*hetuṃ paṭicca*) (S.I.134). Different *puggalā* from different 'seeds' (Miln.65). The 'one-seeder' (*ekabījin*) (S.V.204; A.I.233, IV.380; Kvu.XII.16; Pugg.16; Nett. 189). 'Rendered consciousness seedless' (*abījaṃ viññāṇaṃ kataṃ*) (Miln.146).
14. 'A mind with no desire . . .' (*virattacittā āyatike bhāvasmiṃ*), 'no desire for growth' (*avirūḷhacchanda*), 'seeds are destroyed' (*khīṇabīja*) (Sn.235); 'destroyed rebirth' (*khīṇapunabbhavā*) (Sn.514, 656); the sage 'examines the ground . . .' (*saṃkhāya vatthuni pamāya bījaṃ . . . jātikhayantadassī*) (Sn. 209; SnA.257). 'Consciousness stationed in the field of *kamma* . . .' (A.I.223–4; AA.II.334). The four stations of consciousness as the earth . . . (S.III.54).

8. Momentariness and the *bhavaṅga*-mind

1. Nyanatiloka (1964) pp. 6–7, and (1972); *Buddhist Dictionary*, p. 33.
2. Aung (1910), p. 11.
3. Saratchandra (1958) p. 81.
4. Nyanatiloka (1964) p. 5.
5. Storey (1975) p. 65.
6. Storey (1975) p. 32.

8.1. 'Impermanent are conditioned things'

1. *Yaṃ kiñci samudaya-dhammaṃ sabbaṃ taṃ nirodhadhammaṃ ti* (Vin.I.11, the phrase is regularly used in descriptions of conversion or enlightenment: Vin.I.16; M.I.380; A.IV.186; *et freq.*).
2. *Vayadhammā saṃkhārā* (D.II.156).
3. S.III.155–7. (This passage, of course, fits nicely into the pattern of vegetation imagery in Chapter 7.)
4. *Buddhist Dictionary*, p. 14. Many other passages from the Suttas are cited and discussed in BPS (1973) Wheel 186–7.
5. *Āyu, usmā, viññāṇa*; as discussed in Chapter 7.2.1.
6. Human being lighter when alive . . . like a conch-shell . . . (D.I.334f). Sense-organs 'continue to exist dependent on life' (*āyuṃ paṭicca tiṭṭhanti*) 'phenomena to be experienced' (*vedanīyā dhammā*), 'life not spent . . .' (*āyu aparikkhīṇo, usmā avūpasantā indriyāni vippasannāni*) (M.I.295–6; cf. S.IV.293–4).
7. 'Life-formations pass away . . .' (*āyu-saṃkhārā khīyanti*) (S.II.266). The Buddha 'took control . . .' (*jīvita-saṃkhārā adhiṭṭhāya vihāsi*) (D.II.106; A.IV.311, Ud.62), and could have lived till the end of the aeon (S.V.259).

possible to know one's 'life-term' (*āyu-antaraṃ*) (Vism.VII.243). Of course, this is only possible in life in the human sphere, and those below it; in the heavens above, 'duration of life' (*āyu-pamāṇa*) is fixed in advance (D.I.3; A.I.213, 267; *et freq.* (cf. Table 2, Chapter 7)). It is in either case good or bad karmic behaviour which 'conduces to long (or short) life' (*dīgh-(app-)āyu-saṃvattanika*) (M.II.203–4).

8. Molière, *Le Malade Imaginaire, Troisième Intermède.*
9. SA.II.323, MA.II.350.
10. *Dhammānaṃ āyu, ṭṭhiti, yapanā, yāpanā, iriyanā, vattanā, pālanā jīvitaṃ* (Dhs.19, 82, 295, 380; Vbh.122–3; *et freq.*).
11. 'Most important factor of continuity' (*pavatta-sīsam*) (Ps.II.231). Known as 'a real and ultimate fact' (Kvu.I.1, 60). Life and death as the existence and 'breaking off' (*upaccheda*) of the life-faculty (Asl.97; Vin.III.73, IV.124; Vbh.236; Nett. 29; *et freq.*).
12. *Rūpa-, arūpajīvitindriya* (Vbh.123; Vism.X.19); as part of *rūpakhandha* (Vism.XIV.59) and *saṃkhāra-khandha* (*ibid.* 138) respectively. Mental life-faculty as one of the 'concomitants of consciousness . . .' (*sabbacitta-sādhāraṇā cetasikā*) (Abh.S.II.2; cf. Table II in *Buddhist Dictionary*).
13. 'The function of the life-faculty . . .' (*kicca . . . jīivitindriyassa saha-jātadhammānupālanam*) (Vism.XVI.10); the 'controlling factor . . .' (*pavat-tasantatādhipateyyaṃ*) (Asl.123). 'Watches over' elements but not independent of them (Asl.123; Vism.XIV.59).
14. The 'worlds without matter' are the *arūpa-lokā*, as in Table 2 of Chapter 7. 'Unconscious beings' (*asañña-sattā*) and states (Vism.XVI.11, XVII.192; Kvu.VII.10). On the need for a *material* basis for the attainment of 'cessation', see further 8.3.2.(iv) and n.34 below.
15. See KSP.22f; Hakamaya (1975). As we shall see, the *Theravāda* idea of '*bhavaṅga*-mind' was held to exist during deep sleep, but not during 'cessation'.
16. MA.II.350f, on M.I.296. 'The occurrence of a fire' (*jālapavatta*).
17. 'This life is weak . . . the life-formations are stopped' (*āyusaṃkhārā upacchijjanti*) (Vism.VIII.27–8). 'Breaking the sequence of the postures' (*iriyāpathabhañjaka*) avoided by the 'livelihood known as . . .' (*cirakālaga-manasaṃkhātā yātrā*) (Vism.I.84).
18. *Iriyati, vattati, pāleti, yapeti, yāpeti, carati, viharati.* (Vbh.194, 292). The PTS translation renders *iriyati* here as 'assumes the four postures', because of the verbal connexion with *iriyā*.
19. 'The carrying on of life . . .' (*iriyāpathena iriyāpathaṃ vicchinditvā jīvita-haraṇato*) (Vbh.A.262). Pun on *viharati* (Pj.I.111 cited in Chapter 5.2.2 and n.12). 'By abiding in a posture, he produces . . .' (*iriyāpathavihārena . . . attabhāvassa iriyanaṃ vuttiṃ pālanaṃ yāpanaṃ cāraṃ vihāraṃ abhinip-pādeti*) (Asl.167; Vism.IV.103, VinA.I.147).
20. 'The continuance of the chariot of the body . . .' (*iriyāpathacatukkehi kāyasakaṭavattanato*) (VbhA.262). The body as 'four-wheeled' (*catucakkaṃ*) (S.I.1.6), with the four postures (SA.I.53, quoted at MA.I.27; Ps.A.626). The 'wheel-turning king' (DA.I.259; MA.III.365; cf. PTSD p. 259), and 'mounting a chariot' (*cakkasamārūḷha*) (AA.II.284, on A.III.66, quoted at AA.I.120).
21. *Imassa kāyassa ṭhitiyā yāpanāya* (M.I.10, 355; A.II.40; *et freq.*).
22. 'Maintenance is a synonym . . .' (*ṭhitī ti jīvitindriyass' etaṃ adhivacanaṃ*;

tasmā imassa kāyassa ṭhitiyā yāpanāya ti ettavatā etassa kāyassa jīvitin-driya-pavattāpanatthaṃ) (Vism.I.91).

23. Chest-bones (Vism.VII.105), heart (*ibid.* XI.60), joints (*ibid.* XI.79).
24. The body decays like royal chariots (S.I.71; Dhp.151); the Buddha's body like a worn-out chariot (*jara-sakaṭaṃ*) (D.II.100; S.V.153); the world as a painted chariot (Dhp.171); 'the world turns by *karma* . . .' (*kammanā vattati loko, kammanā vattanti pajā, kammanibandhanā sattā rathassānīva yāyato*) (Sn.654).
25. One-wheeled chariot (S.IV.291; cf. Ud.76); regarding mind and mental factors like a charioteer his horses (Vism.XIV.153–4); monk practising mindfulness over the senses (S.IV.76), or trying for 'higher powers' (*iddhi*) (A.III.28; M.III.97) like a charioteer.
26. AV.19, 53; RV.1.164, verses 2, 11–14.
27. See Geldner (1951) 1 pp. 288–9; Silburn (1955) pp, 14ff, 138ff.
28. Kath.U.1.3.3–1.3.9. The self as chariot-owner (*ātman rathin*); 'reaches the end of the road' (*adhvanaḥ pāram āpnoti*). For other examples of the image see Hume (1931) p. 540; and cf. the illuminating discussion of Varenne (1976) pp. 78, 84–6, 129.
29. Enlightened man 'has reached the end . . .' (*gataddhin*) (Dhp.90); the unenlightened man 'a traveller' (*addhagū*) (Dhp.302) on 'the long road called . . .' (*vaṭṭa-saṃkhātaṃ addhānam*) (Dhp.A.III.463).
30. *Sāmī* (e.g. Vism.XX.19, cited in Chapter 4.1.3 above).
31. When used in compounds, they can also refer literally to a road. See PTSD p. 26; Gonda, *Selected Studies* IV, pp. 320–2.
32. *Tayo addhā* (D.III.216; It.53, 70); *addhāyu* (A.II.66); 'one who has reached the end of his road' (D.I.48; M.I.82; *et freq.*); *dīghaṃ addhānaṃ saṃsāraṃ* (Sn.740; A.II.10; It.9, 109; *et freq.*).
33. S.I.135; Kvu.I.240; Miln.25–6, cited in Chapters 4.2.1, 6.1.1, and 6.1.2 respectively.
34. Vism.VIII.39, translated and glossed by Ñāṇamoli. 'In the ultimate sense . . . single conscious moment' (*paramatthato hi atiparitto sattānaṃ jīvi-takhaṇo ekacittapavattimatto yeva*).
35. Asl.123–4; Vism.XIV.59, in 8.1.2 and n.13. 'It does not prolong . . .' (*na bhaṅgato uddhaṃ pavattayati attano ca pavattayitabbānañ ca abhāvā, na bhaṅga-kkhaṇe ṭhāpeti sayaṃ bhijjamānattā khīyamāno viya vaṭṭi-sineho padīpa-sikhaṃ*).

8.2. The 'ultimate' extent of a lifetime: momentariness

1. See Poussin (1931); Lamotte (1967) p. 665ff; Stcherbatsky (1962) pp. 79–118; Silburn (1955) pp. 255f, 277f, 298f, 332f.
2. Ñāṇamoli (1975) p. xxix; Stcherbatsky (1962) pp. 82, 117.
3. Stcherbatsky (1962) p. 83.
4. See Conze (1962) p. 282. Some of the estimates given by the tradition *are* closer to what might be perceptually distinguishable moments (cf. *ibid.*).
5. 'Finger-snap' (*acchāra*) (A.I.10, 34, 38, IV.396; Miln.102; Thag.405, Thig.67; *et freq.*).
6. Sixty-four at Lamotte (1967) pp. 667–8; billions at Aung (1910) p. 125 n.5.
7. A.I.10; Asl.60–1.
8. In the social history of Buddhism, the 'magical' physicalistic attitude to purity of Indian culture generally lives in unstable tension with the ethical,

psychological purity of virtuoso Buddhism, and often infiltrates anew into Buddhist practice. See Carrithers (forthcoming) Chapters 3, 5–7.

9. S.II.94–5. 'By night and by day . . .' (*rattiyā ca divasā ca aññad eva uppajjati aññad eva nirujjhati*). The image of the 'monkey-mind' jumping restlessly from one branch (object of thought) to another is frequent: e.g. S.II.95; It.23–4; Thag.1111; cf. S.V.48; Thag.125–6. (See further, on the implications of the monkey-image's being used both for changes in the *object* of the mind and (as here at S.II.94–5) in mind itself, Chapter 8.4.3 below.)
10. *Lahuparivattaṃ* (A.I.10).
11. Vism.XX.48f.
12. *Rattiṃ pavattarūpaṃ divasaṃ appatvā tatth' eva niruddhaṃ* (Vism.XX.59).
13. 'Thus formations keep breaking up . . .' (Vism.XX.65, Ñāṇamoli's (PTS) translation). 'A further act of mind' (*aparena cittena*) (Vism.XX.79).
14. 'Cutting off of the life-faculty . . .' (*ekabhāvapariyāpannassa jīvitindriyassa upacchedo*); 'momentary death, reckoned . . .' (*saṃkhārānaṃ khaṇabhaṅgasaṃkhātaṃ khaṇa-maraṇaṃ*) (Vism.VIII.1).
15. 'Limitedness of extent' (*addhāna-pariccheda*); 'in terms of the shortness of the moment' (*khaṇa-parittato*) (Vism.VIII.39).
16. 'Life is short' (*appaṃ jīvitaṃ*) (Sn.775); 'through the limitation of its duration' (*ṭhiti-parittatāya*) (Nd.I.42).
17. *Jīvitaṃ attabhāvo ca sukhadukkhā ca kevalā/ekacittasamāyuttā, lahuso vattati khaṇo . . . cullāsīti sahassāni kappaṃ tiṭṭhanti ye marū/na tveva te pi tiṭṭhanti dvīhi cittehi samohitā*. The second stanza is, in fact, omitted at Vism.VIII.39; but is included when the same sequence of verses is quoted at Vism.XX.72 (cf. SA.I.22).
18. 'Past, future, and present are two-fold, . . .' (*idam pana atītānāgatapaccuppannaṃ nāma Suttāntapariyāyato Abhidhammaniddesato ti duvidhaṃ. Taṃ Suttāntapariyāye bhavena paricchinnaṃ . . . Abhidhammaniddese pana khaṇena paricchinnaṃ*). 'The matter occurring between rebirth . . .' (*cuti-paṭisandhi-antare pavatta-rūpam paccuppannam*); 'matter passing through these three (sub-)moments . . .' (*ime tayo khaṇe sampattaṃ rūpaṃ paccuppannaṃ*) (Vbh.A.7; cf. Vism.XIV.187, 190–1, XVI.33).
19. *Uppāda, ṭhitassa aññathattam, vaya* (A.I.152; said of the *khandhā* at S.III.38).
20. 'Occurring moment' (*khaṇupapannaṃ*) has 'arising, . . .' (*uppāda, jarā, bhaṅga*) (Vin.A.II.438). The Indian *Sarvāstivāda* school divided the moment into *four* sub-moments, 'arising, presence, decay [*jarā*], and cessation'.
21. 'Continuity is destroyed' (*santati vikopitā*); 'arising, growing old, becoming otherwise' (*uppādavayaññathattabhāva*) (Vism.XX.14–16).
22. There is one parallel between the existence of a moment and that of a lifetime which might have produced unexpected and unwanted conclusions for *Theravāda* thought. The 'acquisition of individuality' (*attabhāva-paṭilābha* (Vism.A.280, *apud* Ñāṇamoli, (1973) p. 64; cf. AK.IV.2–3; and Conze (1962) p. 134)). In a lifetime, as we saw, was an event of conventional truth: 'individuality' is a concept derived from the unenlightened man's perception of himself as a self. In the case of the moment, however, we are dealing with ultimate truth; and so to find the phrase used for the 'arising' of such a 'real' element is surprising. Indeed, *Theravāda* ascribes to the momentary existent exactly the kind of existence it denies to the individual of a lifetime. For example, the *Visuddhimagga* speaking of the 'sense-bases', says that 'before

their rise, they have no own-being; after the decay, their own-being is destroyed' (*pubbe udayā appaṭiladdhasabhāvāni uddhaṃ vayā paribbhinna-sabhāvāni* (Vism.xv.15)). In a similar vein, Nārada Thera's commentary on the *Abhidammattha Saṃgaha* says 'past is defined as that which has gone beyond its *own state* [what I have translated as "own-being"] or the moments of genesis, development and cessation' (*attano sabhāvaṃ uppādā-dikkhaṇaṃ vā atīta vā atikkantā atīta*) (Nārada Thera (1975 p. 188 (my italics)). We saw that 'own-being' was the term used (in its Sanskrit form *svabhāva*) by the *Madhyamaka* school in relation to elements (*dhamma*) (which corresponded to 'person' or 'self' in relation to a lifetime) as part of its assertion of the 'selflessness of things' (Chapter 4.1.3). Accordingly, the *Madhyamaka* argued against the existence of 'real' momentary elements. Apart from subjecting the idea to logical ridicule – is there an arising, presence, and dissolution of the arising-moment (and so on, in infinite regress)? – they argued, with perfect Buddhist logic, that just as there was no real being between the limits of birth and death, so there was no real being between the limits of 'arising' and 'cessation', and thus the only ultimate truth was that of 'emptiness'.

8.3. The *bhavaṅga*-mind

1. *Tika-Paṭṭhāna* 159, 160, 169, 324f. See Cousins (1981).
2. A.II.79. There is an alternative reading *-agga*, in both sets of four. The commentary (AA.III.107) explains *bhavagga*, 'height of existence', as the final individuality (*attabhāva*), in the last lifetime, of an *Arhat*.
3. E.g. Nett. 29, 64, 65, 68.
4. Poussin (1913) p. 40.
5. Thus, for instance, Aung (1910) p. 9 n.2.
6. Nyanaponika (1965) p. 108 footnote. Aung (1910) pp. 265–6; and Sarat-chandra (1958) pp. 80–1, (1943) pp. 97–8, quote examples from the Ceylonese commentaries explaining *-aṅga* as *-kāraṇā*.
7. 'Occasions for the occurrence' (*vipaccanaṭṭhānaṃ*); '*bhavaṅga* for the length . . .' (*āyukālaṃ bhavaṅgaṃ*) (Asl.266).
8. *Kammādiko vipākassa, bhavaṅgādiko kiriyassa* [*nāmassa paccayo*] *ti* (Vism.XIX.8).
9. Miln.299–300. 'One who dreams . . .' (*yo so supinaṃ passati na so niddāyanto passati nāpi jagganto passati, api ca okkante middhe asampatte bhavaṅg' etth'antare supinaṃ passati*). 'When someone is deeply asleep . . .' (*middhasamārūḷhassa cittaṃ bhavaṅgagataṃ hoti bhavaṅgagataṃ cittaṃ na ppavattati . . . pavattamāne citte supinaṃ passati*). 'Monkey-sleep . . . the middle stage . . .' (*kapiniddāpareto . . . idam middhassa majjhaṃ*); 'the final stage . . .' (*bhavaṅgagati pariyosanaṃ*).
10. Vbh.A.408; cf. AA.III.317. 'One steeps (deeply) . . .' (*bhavaṅgacittena hi supati. Tañ ca rūpanimittādi-ārammaṇaṃ, rāgādisampayuttaṃ vā na hoti. Supinaṃ passantassa ca idisāni cittāni uppajjanti*). 'Conflict with *Abhidhamma* (and) the Code of Discipline' (*Abhidhamma-, Vinaya-virodho*). 'For just as the sleep of a monkey . . .' (*yathā hi makkaṭassa niddā lahuparivattā hoti, evaṃ yā niddā . . ., yassa pavattiyaṃ punappunaṃ bhavaṅgato uttaraṇaṃ hoti*).
11. Vism.XIV.114. (*Bhavaṅga-viññāṇaṃ nāma pavattati . . . asati santānavini-vattake aññasmiṃ cittuppāde . . . supinaṃ apassato niddokkamānakālād-*

isu aparimāṇasaṇkham.) The commentary here (Vism.A.478, *apud* Ñāṇamoli (1975) p. 515 n.45) remarks that 'the seeing of dreams is done only with the consciousness that is functional'.

12. The similarity was stressed by the *Vijñānavāda* itself: cf. MSA.I.11–12, *apud* Lamotte (1938) II, pp. 26–9; and KSP.35, *apud* Lamotte (1936) p. 250.
13. The *locus classicus* for the argument is *Viṃśatikā* 3–4.
14. *Manañ ca paṭicca dhamme ca uppajjati manoviññāṇaṃ* (e.g. M.I.112, 259; Vbh.88f).
15. Thus the commentaries to the three passages cited in n.14 gloss *manas* as *bhavaṅga-citta* (MA.II.77) and *bhavaṅga-manas* (MA.II.306; Vbh.A.81).
16. *Bhavaṅgamana-dhamma-manasikāre paṭicca uppajjati manoviññāṇaṃ* (Vism.XV.39).
17. *Sattarasa cittakkhaṇāni rūpadhammānaṃ āyu* (Abh.S.IV.3).
18. 'Short duration of the material life-faculty' (*rūpajīvitindriyassa parittako kālo*); 'while (one moment of) matter . . .' (*yāva pan' uppannaṃ rūpaṃ tiṭṭhati tava soḷasa cittāni uppajjitvā bhijjanti*) (Asl.60). 'While (one moment of) matter endures, *bhavaṅga*-mind arises and ceases sixteen times' (*rūpe dharante yeva hi soḷasavare bhavaṅgacittaṃ uppajjitvā nirujjhati*) (Vism.XX.24).
19. Vbh.A.26.
20. Details will be found in the ancient texts: Vism.XIV; Asl.269f; Abh.S. Chapter 4. In modern works: Aung's (1910); and Nārada's (1975) editions of Abh.S., *Buddhist Dictionary*, pp. 194–5; Saratchandra (1958) Part 2; Gunaratna (1971); Jayasuriya (1963) pp. 100ff; and Cousins (1981). There are, for instance, differences in the process when the object is weak (e.g. Aung (1910) pp. 31f), and when the process is not completed (Asl.269).
21. There are slight but unimportant differences in the details of the different versions. See Asl.271; Aung (1910) p. 28; the Ceylon commentaries, *apud* Saratchandra (1958) p. 46; Govinda (1969) pp. 134–5; Mrs Rhys Davids (1914) pp. 180–1.
22. See those authors and works cited in nn.1–6 at the start of this chapter; and Da Silva (1973); Gunaratna (1971).
23. Freud (1915) Section 2, pp. 172ff.
24. Freud (1973.2.) pp. 102, 104.
25. This has been studied by Da Silva (1973), who acknowledges that 'a concept of the Unconscious is basically related to motivation' (p. 49).
26. For further details here see the references cited in n.20, and Nārada (1948) pp. 33ff.
27. *Ekasmiṃ hi bhāve yaṃ sabbapacchimaṃ taṃ tato (bhavato) cavanattā cutī ti* (Vism.XIV.123; *bhavato* not in all mss.).
28. The three kinds are *āsanna/āciṇṇa kamma, kamma nimitta*, and *gati nimitta*. (See Vism.XVII.135f; Gunaratna (1971) pp. 44ff; Nārada (1975) pp. 179ff).
29. See, for instance, Edgerton (1926); ERE IV, p. 448.
30. Monks visiting laymen (M.II.91, III.258); the Buddha recommends the practice to lay followers (S.V.408).
31. E.g. KSP.30–2, in Lamotte (1936) pp. 244f; cf. Hakamaya (1975).
32. *Cittaṃ appavattaṃ* (Miln.300).
33. 'Without mind' (*acittako*) (Vism.XXIII.43, 47); 'mental continuity is suspended' (*cittasantati vocchijjati*) (Abh.S.IX.9).

34. 'Because of the absence of physical basis' (*vatthussa abhāvā* (Vism.xxiii.29). The commentary (Vism.A.902 *apud* Ñāṇamoli (1975) p. 828 n.12) explains that if anyone in an immaterial world were to attain 'cessation', he would become 'indefinable' (*appaññi(a)ttika*), 'owing to the non-existence of any consciousness or consciousness-concomitant' (*citta-cetasika*). He would thus be like a released *Arhat*, who has attained final *nibbāna* without substrate (*anupādisesa*).
35. MA.ii.350, cited in 8.1.2 above. Cf. Kvu.viii.10.
36. Cessation 'cannot ward off death' (*na . . . maraṇaṃ paṭibāhituṃ sakkoti*) (Vism.xxiii.42). The commentary here (Vism.A.904) *apud*, and translated by Ñāṇamoli (1975) p. 831 n.17.
37. *Bhavaṅgapāto* (Abh.S.iv.11; cf. Vism.xxiii.49; MA.ii.351).
38. For the theme in Indian Buddhism, see Bareau (1955) pp. 67–8; Ruegg (1969) Part 4: 'La Luminosité Naturelle de la Pensée', *passim*. In Chinese and Japanese Buddhism, the idea became almost a cliché – see for instance the famous dialogue in which the idea of mind as a 'bright mirror' receives paradoxical treatment from Shen-Hsiu and Hui-Neng, Robinson (1970) pp. 90–1.
39. 'Adventitious defilements' (*āgantukehi kilesehi*); 'naturally, when mind . . .' (*pakatiyā pana sakale pi paṭisandhi-bhavaṅgavāre paṇḍaraṃ*) (MA.i.167, on M.i.36f). 'Natural mind' (*pakati-citta*) (Kvu.A.193, on Kvu.xxii.3).
40. 'Purified and cleansed' (*parisuddha pariyodāta*) (D.i.76; A.i.164; *et freq.*); glossed as 'bright' and 'luminous' (*pabhassara*). (Vism.xii.14). 'Purified mind' as 'bright, like gold' (e.g. S.v.92; A.i.253, iii.16).
41. 'Mind, when freed from adventitious defilements . . .' (*pabhassaraṃ idaṃ cittaṃ . . . āgantukehi upakkilesehi vippamuttaṃ*) (A.i.10); and commentaries (AA.i.160; Asl.140).
42. As, for instance, in the famous first verse of the *Dhammapada*, 'things have mind as their fore-runner, mind as their chief, and are mind-made' (*manopubbaṅgamā dhammā manoseṭṭhā manomayā*); cf. 'the world is led by mind' (*cittena . . . nīyyati loko*) (S.i.39; A.ii.177), discussed by Rāhula (1978) Chapter 7.

8.4. River imagery

1. Storey (1975) p. 32, quoted at the beginning of this chapter.
2. One of the first works to deal with the *bhavaṅga*, and one which is still the most widely known secondary source for the concept, Aung's (1910) translation and commentary of the *Abhidhammattha-saṃgaha*, points out clearly, using the image of the 'stream of thought', that *bhavaṅga ceases to occur* when thought-processes begin: 'But it must not be supposed that the stream of being is a sub-plane from which thoughts rise to the surface. There is juxtaposition of momentary states of consciousness, subliminal and supraliminal, throughout a lifetime and from existence to existence. But there is no superposition of such states' (Aung (1910) pp. 11–12; cf. Chapter 8.4.4 and n.40 below).
3. *Asati vīthicittuppāde bhavassaṅgabhavena bhavaṅgasantatisaṃkhātaṃ mānasam abbhocchinnam nadī soto viya pavattati* (Abh.S.v.15).
4. 'Like a flowing river' (Vism.xiv.114); 'stream of *bhavaṅga*' (*bhavaṅga-sota*) (Abh.S.iv.11).

5. 'Registering' as water following 'a boat going upstream' (*paṭisotagatam nāvaṃ*) (Vism.XIV.122); 'across a fierce current' (*caṇḍasote tiriyaṃ*), 'with the stream' (*yathāsotam*) (Asl.265); 'the time when the water flows . . .' (*ettha hi nadiyaṃ udakappavattanakālo viya bhavaṅgavīthippavattanakālo*) (Asl.269–70).
6. This was first argued by the German scholar Reinhardt (for references see Barnes (1979) I, p. 319 n.19); and has been popularised in English by Kirk and Raven (1957) pp. 196ff; Kirk (1962) pp. 366ff; and Hussey (1972) pp. 54–5. (See further Chapter 8.4.3 and n.23 below.) The matter is, of course, still in dispute: see Barnes (1979) I, pp. 65ff; Kahn (1979) pp. 147ff, 166ff, 200ff.
7. See, for example, Rāhula (1967) pp. 25–6 (discussed in Chapter 8.4.3 below); Mrs Rhys Davids, in Aung (1910) p. xxi and p. 9 n.1; Keith (1923) p. 77; Nakamura (1976) p. 50. Saratchandra (1958) p. 75 speaks of 'the Buddhist philosophy of flux'; while Mookherjee's very influential work on the notion of momentariness in Buddhist thought generally was called *The Buddhist Philosophy of Universal Flux* (1935).
8. The word *saṃsāra*, as we saw earlier, is derived from the root *sar-*, 'run, hasten, flow, stream' (Gonda, *Selected Studies* IV, p. 310, cited at Chapter 1.2.3 and n.8).
9. 'Desire that flows along' (*taṇhā saritā*) (A.II.211); 'attachment and sense-pleasures that flow along' (*saritāni sinehitāni ca somanassāni*) (Dhp.341); 'the swift-flowing stream of desire' (*taṇhaṃ saritaṃ sīghasaraṃ*) (Sn.3); desire as *saritā, nadī* (Vism.XVII.308); 'greed, swollen with the river of craving' (*lobho taṇhānadībhāvena vaḍḍhamāno*) (Vism.XIV.162).
10. 'There is no river . . .' (*natthi taṇhāsamā nadī*) (Dhp.251); the 'stream of death' (*māra-sota*) (M.I.225–6; and MA.II.267); 'cut the stream which is hard to cross . . .' (*chetvā sotaṃ duracayaṃ asesaṃ parinibbāyanti*) (It.95); 'one who has cut the stream' (*chinnasoto*) (Sn.715, 948); '"stream" is a term . . .' (*soto ti taṇhāyetaṃ adhivacanaṃ . . . tasmā khīṇāsavo bhikkhu chinnasoto ti vuccati*) (S.IV.291–2).
11. Man who sees the *khandhā* as a self . . . (S.III.137–8); Dependent Origination like rainwater down a hillside (S.II.32); swelling and ebbing (*upayanto, apayanto*) of Dependent Origination (S.II.118–19).
12. Those who are 'insatiate for sense-pleasure' (*kāmesu analaṃkatā*) (S.I.15), who have 'lust for existence' (*bhavarāga*) (S.IV.128), and for whom thus 'far away is destruction of the fetters' (*tesaṃ . . . ārā saṃyojanakkhayo*) (Sn.736), all 'float down the stream of existence' (*bhavasotanusārino*). 'Carried along by the stream of *saṃsāra*' (*saṃsārasotena vuyhantā*) (Miln.204).
13. The idea is very frequent: e.g. S.I.1, 2, 32, 53, 142, 169, 182, II.158 (a man falling off a plank of wood in mid-ocean), IV.71, 210, V.24, 81, 168, 180; M.II.105; A.IV.411; Sn.173, 210, 471, etc.
14. Crossing over by a ship (Sn.316, 770–1; Thag.776; Miln.80, 195, 229, 377); by a raft (M.I.134, 260; S.IV.174–5). Buddhist teaching as an island (*dīpa*) (Thag.412; D.II.100, III.58, 77; S.V.154). For *pāraga* etc. see PTSD p. 454.
15. 'Going with, against the stream' (*anu-, paṭisotagami*) (e.g. M.I.168; S.I.136; A.II.5; Sn.319). The Buddha's bowl (J.I.70; cf. Thomas (1949) pp. 70–1). Making progress in Buddhism as 'going upstream' (*uddhaṃsoto*) (A.I.223; D.II.237; *et freq.*).

16. It.114; cf. S.IV.174–5.
17. The thirty-six streams (Dhp.339); 'the streams flow everywhere' (*savanti sabbadhi sotā*) (Dhp.340; Sn.1034; Thag.761); 'mindfulness is their dam' (*tesaṃ sati nīvaraṇam*) (Sn.1035; cf. Thag.762); 'cut the stream, discard sense-pleasure' (*chinda sotaṃ, parakkamma kāme*) (Dhp.383; S.I.49); 'are carried away by that stream' (*tena sotena vuyhanti*) (Miln.69); mental consciousness following after sense-consciousness (Miln.57–8).
18. Mind to be guided like water along viaducts (M.II.105; Dhp.80, 145; Thag.19, 877); steadying the mind in a 'fierce current' (*caṇḍasote*) (Vism.VIII.193); disturbance of a mountain stream by . . . 'hindrances' (*nīvaraṇa*) (A.III.64; on the hindrances, see *Buddhist Dictionary*, pp. 110–11).
19. Rāhula (1967) pp. 25–6.
20. A.IV.137–8. (*Seyyathā pi . . . nadī pabbateyyā dūraṅgamā sīghasotā hara-hariṇī, natthi so khaṇo vā layo vā muhutto vā, yaṃ sā āramati, atha kho sa gacchat'eva vattat'eva sandat'eva, evam eva kho . . . nadīpabbateyyūpamaṃ jīvitaṃ manussānaṃ, parittaṃ lahukaṃ . . . natthi jātassa amaraṇaṃ.*)
21. This is true also of the other phrase quoted by Rāhula, *upanīyati loko addhuvo*. He translates 'the world is in continuous flux and is impermanent'. *Addhuvo* is literally 'uncertain', 'unstable' or 'impermanent'; *upanīyati* is a passive form from *upa-nī*, 'to lead', and means 'is led away', or, as both PTSD and CPD gloss, 'to be brought to an end', 'to pass away'. It is a word found often in connexion with the idea that 'life is short' (M.II.68; S.I.2; A.I.155); some translators give 'is swept onward' or 'swept away' – but in this interpretation, the implicit comparison with a river concerns, as usually, its power to carry one away helplessly to old age and death, and not any postulated paradoxes of change and identity. (The commentaries to the texts in which the phrase appears gloss simply and colourlessly as 'is destroyed', *nirujjati*, 'wastes away', *parikkhīyati*, and so on.)
22. A.IV.137–8 quoted at Vism.VIII.35. 'A being, from the time of his birth . . .' (Vism.VIII.11).
23. See the references to Kirk and Raven, Kirk, and Hussey in n.6 above. Kirk and Raven (1957) and Kirk (1951) argue that it is not a linear change in the waters of the river which is at issue, but an oscillatory interchange between mutually balancing opposites, as an instance of the general cosmic fact or principle of 'measure' or 'balance' (*metron*).
24. Humphrey (1958) p. v.
25. Humphrey (1958) pp. 1, 2–3 (italics in original).
26. Ñāṇajīvako (1975) p. 28. Cf. his (1973) pp. 25–6.
27. Gunaratna (1971) pp. 16, 23, 17–18.
28. James (1950) p. 353.
29. James (1950) p. 239.
30. Bergson (1909) p. 364, English translation (1911) p. 356.
31. Bergson (1909) pp. 364, 366, English translation (1911) pp. 355, 357.
32. Bergson (1934) p. 163, English translation (1946) p. 173, quoted by Ñāṇajīvako (1975) p. 29; cf. *ibid*. pp. 29–40, and his (1973) p. 26. Such a synthetic approach might also quote Bergson's remark 'we perceive duration as a stream against which we cannot go' ((1909) p. 42, (1911) p. 41).
33. Bergson (1909) p. 24, (1911) p. 23. Cf. Stcherbatsky (1962) pp. 117–18.
34. James (1950) pp. 240, 363. Gunaratna ((1971) p. 18), in support of the

claim that 'this view of mind as being not a unity but a series of thoughts is held by almost all psychologists of note', cites Bertrand Russell's remark that 'psychologists find that mind has not the identity of a single continuing thing but is a series of occurrences bound together by certain intimate relations'; such a series, however, was in Russell's view a series of atomistic 'perceptions' in the Humean, associationistic sense, and so precisely what James (quoted by the author on the same page) was concerned to deny by the idea of a *stream* of consciousness. (On the ambiguous but largely hostile relationship between Russell and Bergson see Capek (1971) pp. 335ff.)

35. As for instance by Kalupahana (1976) pp. 52, 86, who tries to make Buddhism look like a (post-Humean) positivist empiricism.

36. D.III.104–5. 'Attainments of vision' (*dassana-samāpatti*). 'Knows a person's stream of consciousness . . .' (*purisassa ca viññāṇa-sotaṃ pajānāti ubhayato abbocchinnaṃ idha-loke patiṭṭhitañ ca paraloke patiṭṭhitañ ca*).

The commentaries: DA.III.888ff; DAA.III.88ff. 'Drags on karmic existence' (*kammabhavaṃ ākaḍḍhantaṃ*). 'Because of its similarity to a stream . . .' (*avicchedena pavattiyā sota-sādisatāya viññāṇaṃ eva viññāṇasotaṃ*). '(Of) consciousness which is split up in each moment' (*viññāṇassa khaṇe khaṇe bhijjantassa*).

The word *abbocchinnaṃ*, which I translate here as 'unbroken', is also used of the *bhavaṅga*, (Abh.S.V.5, cited in Chapter 8.4.1 n.3 above); since in systematic theory the *bhavaṅga* is a momentary existent, it is clear that *abbocchinnaṃ* used of the 'stream of consciousness' does not imply a systematic picture of mind as a partless flux, but simply describes it as continuing because not 'cut' by the attainment of final *nibbāna*.

37. Mind like the ocean (Sn.920; Thag.372); like a mountain lake (A.III.396; cf. Vism.XIV.165); 'clear' mind of the meditator like a pond . . . (M.I.279–80, II.22; D.I.84; A.I.9; cf. Dhp.82, 95; It.92); man cooled from the passions like the waters of a lake (Sn.467), especially when in meditation (Miln.385, 397); monk in meditation like a tortoise (Miln.370); the 'meditator-swan' (*yogi-rājahaṃso*) (Vism.XXI.43, Ñāṇamoli's (PTS) translation). Fools and wise men like streams and the silent sea (Sn.720).

38. Meditator's mind 'like the Ganges . . .' (M.I.128), as is the merit gained from Buddhism (A.II.54f, III.52, 336; S.V.400). The *Tathāgata* 'deep, immeasurable . . .' (as in Chapter 4.2.3 and n.14 above) (M.I.487–8; S.IV.274f; It.80; Miln.70, 105, 187, 224).

39. For some modern examples see Zaehner (1957) pp. 37ff.

40. The 'home-consciousness' *vartate śrotasaughavat* (*Triṃśika* 4). For other examples of water and ocean imagery here, see Saratchandra (1958) pp. 89ff, (1946) pp. 52ff, who is concerned to emphasise the similarities between the *ālaya-vijñāna* and the *bhavaṅga*. (Cf., however, n.2 above.)

41. The *Tathāgata* not disturbed by minor inconveniences (Miln.224); dismisses those who act wrongly (Miln.187; cf.250); *nibbāna* not 'filled up' (Miln.319; cf. the passages cited in n.42 and discussed in the text below); but immeasurable . . . (Miln.317); movement of the Buddhist life to *nibbāna* like rivers to the ocean (S.IV.191, V.40f, 53, 300, 306); so long as one does not cling to the two banks . . . (S.IV.179–80); the Eight-fold Path as a stream (S.V.348; Thag.349); the monkhood as a whole flows toward *nibbāna* (S.V.396; cf. M.I.459; A.I.243, II.123. At M.I.493 the laity are

included also as 'the company of Gotama' (*Gotama-parisā*) who flow to *nibbāna*); the *dhamma* like a lake (S.I.169, 183; Miln.132, 246).

42. *Acchariyā abbhutā dhammā* (A.IV.197ff; Vin.II.236ff; Ud.53ff).
43. Relationship of beings to Being like rivers to the ocean (Ch.U.6.10); 'as flowing rivers disappear . . .' (Muṇḍ.U.3.2.8; cf. Praśn.U.6.5).
44. Nyanatiloka (1964) p. 7, cited in Chapter 8 n.1.

Conclusion

1. The term 'domestication' of the monkhood is taken from Carrithers (1979), who argues that 'it is the play between ascetic reform and domestication which creates the pattern of Sangha [i.e. the monkhood's] history'; he traces this pattern to the conditions of its agrarian environment. I take it that my presentation of imagery and its institutional embodiment both supports and is supported by this view.

Bibliography

Ames, M. (1964) Magical-Animism and Buddhism: A Structural Analysis. In E. B. Harper (ed.) *Religion in South Asia* (Seattle).
Aung, S. Z. (1910) *Compendium of Philosophy* (Pali Text Society).
Bachelard, G. (1938) *La Psychanalyse du Feu* (Paris). English translation (1964) *The Psychoanalysis of Fire* (Boston).
(1957) *La Poétique de l'Espace* (Paris). English translation (1964a) *The Poetics of Space* (Boston).
Bareau, A. (1955) *Les Sectes Bouddhiques du Petit Véhicule* (Paris).
(1955a) *Les Premiers Conciles Bouddhiques* (Paris).
(1973) La Personne dans le Bouddhisme. In I. Meyerson (ed.) *Problèmes de la Personne* (Paris/The Hague).
Barnes, J. (1979) *The PreSocratic Philosophers*. The Arguments of the Philosophers' Series (London).
Barua, D. K. (1971) *An Analytical Study of the Four Nikāyas* (Calcutta).
Basham, A. L. (1951) *The History and Doctrine of the Ājīvikas* (London).
(1967) *The Wonder that was India* (London).
Bechert, H. (1966) *Buddhismus, Staat und Gesellschaft* (Wiesbaden).
Bergson, H. (1909) *L'Évolution Créatrice* (Paris). English translation (1911) *Creative Evolution* (London).
(1934) *La Pensée et le Mouvant* (Paris). English translation (1946) *The Creative Mind* (London).
Bhattacharya, K. (1973) *L'Ātman-Brahman dans le Bouddhisme Ancien* (Paris).
Biardeau, M. (1965) Ahaṃkāra in the Upaniṣads. *Contributions to Indian Sociology*, VIII.
Biardeau, M. and Malamoud, C. (1976) *Le Sacrifice dans l'Inde Ancienne* (Paris).
Boyer, J. (1901) Étude sur l'Origine de la Doctrine du Saṃsāra. *Journal Asiatique*, II.
Brohm, J. (1963) Buddhism and Animism in a Burmese Village. *Journal of Asian Studies*, XXII.
Buber, M. (1970) *I and Thou*. English translation by W. Kaufmann (Edinburgh).
Buddhist Dictionary – see Nyanatiloka (1972).
Buddhist Publication Society (1973) *Impermanence*. Wheel no. 186–7 (Ceylon).
(1974) *Egolessness*. Wheel no. 202–4 (Ceylon).
Buitenen, J. A. B. van (1957) Studies in Sāṃkhya II. *Journal of the American Oriental Society*, LXXVII.
Burnyeat, M. and Honderich, T. (1979) *Philosophy As It Is* (London).
Capek, M. (1971) *Bergson and Modern Physics*. Boston Studies in the Philosophy of Science, VII (Holland).
Carrithers, M. B. (1978) The Social Organisation of the Sinhalese Sangha in an Historical Perspective. *Contributions to South Asian Studies*, I.
(1979) The Modern Ascetics of Lanka and the Pattern of Change in Buddhism. *Man* n.s. XIV.
(forthcoming) *The Forest Monks of Lanka* (Delhi).

Chowdhury, R. P. (1955) Interpretation of the Anattā Doctrine of Buddhism; a New Approach. *Indian Historical Quarterly*, XXXI.
Collins, S. (1979) Personal Continuity in Theravāda Buddhism (unpublished D.Phil. thesis, Oxford).
Cone, M. (1971) Vedic and Upaniṣadic Ideas of Death, Deathlessness and Forms of Existence (unpublished M.Phil. thesis, London).
Cone, M. and Gombrich, R. F. (1977) *The Perfect Generosity of Prince Vessantara* (Oxford).
Conze, E. (1962) *Buddhist Thought in India* (London).
Coomaraswamy, A. K. (1916) *Buddha and the Gospel of Buddhism* (London).
Coulson, M. (1976) *Teach Yourself Sanskrit* (London).
Cousins, L. (1981) The Paṭṭhāna and the Development of the Theravādin Abhidhamma. *Journal of the Pali Text Society*, IX.
Darian, S. (1971) Buddhism in Bihar from the Eighth to the Twelfth Century with Special Reference to Nālandā. *Asiatische Studien*, XXV.
Da Silva, P. (1973) *Buddhist and Freudian Psychology* (Colombo).
Dayal, H. (1932) *The Bodhisattva Doctrine* (London).
Demieville, P. (1927) Sur la Mémoire des Existences Antérieures. *Bulletin de l'École Française de l'Extrême Orient*, XXVII.
Deussen, P. (1906) *The Philosophy of the Upaniṣads*. English translation (New York).
Dharmapāla, A. (1965) *Returns to Righteousness*. A collection of speeches essays and letters, edited by A. Guruge (Colombo).
Douglas, M. (1966) *Purity and Danger* (London).
Dumont, L. (1965) The Modern Conception of the Individual: Notes on its Genesis and that of Concomitant Institutions. *Contributions to Indian Sociology*, VIII.
(1970a) *Homo Hierarchicus*. English translation (London).
(1970b) World Renunciation in Indian Religions. In his *Religion Politics and History in India* (Paris).
(1972) Une Science en Devenir. *L'Arc*, XLVII, on Marcel Mauss (Paris).
(1973) L'Absence de l'Individu dans les Institutions de l'Inde. In I. Meyerson (ed.) *Problèmes de la Personne* (Paris).
(1975) On the Comparative Understanding of Non-Modern Civilisations. *Dedalus*, Spring 1975.
(1977) *From Mandeville to Marx* (University of Chicago).
Dumont, L. and Pocock, D. F. (1957) For a Sociology of India. *Contributions to Indian Sociology*, I.
Durkheim, E. (1915) *Elementary Forms of the Religious Life*. English translation (London).
Dutt, S. (1960) *Early Buddhist Monachism* (1st Indian edition, Bombay).
(1962) *Buddhist Monks and Monasteries in India* (London).
Edgerton, F. (1925) Atharvan Philosophy. In *Studies in Honour of M. Bloomfield* (New Haven).
(1926) The Hour of Death. *Annals of the Bhandarkar Oriental Institute*, VIII.
(1929) The Upaniṣads: What do they Seek and Why? *Journal of the American Oriental Society*, XLIX.
(1942) Dominant Ideas in the Formation of Indian Culture. *Journal of the American Oriental Society*, LXII.
(1965) *The Beginnings of Indian Philosophy* (London).

Eggeling, J. (1964) *Śatapatha Brāhmaṇa*. English translation. Sacred Books of the East (2nd impression, Motilal Banarsidas).

Eliade, M. (1959) *The Sacred and the Profane*. English translation (New York).

Eliot, C. (1921) *Hinduism and Buddhism* (London).

Frauwallner, E. (1953) *Geschichte der Indischen Philosophie* (Salzburg).

(1956) *The Earliest Vinaya and the Beginnings of Buddhist Literature* (Rome).

(1964) Abhidharma Studien II. *Wiener Zeitschrift für die Kunde Süd-Asiens*, VIII.

Freud, S. (1915) The Unconscious. *Collected Works*, XIV (London).

(1973.1) *Introductory Lectures on Psychoanalysis*. English translation. Penguin Freud Library, I (Harmondsworth).

(1973.2) *New Introductory Lectures on Psychoanalysis*. English translation. Penguin Freud Library, II (Harmondsworth).

(1976) *The Interpretation of Dreams*. English translation. Penguin Freud Library, IV (Harmondsworth).

Fürer-Haimendorf, C. von (1953) The After-life in Indian Tribal Belief. *Journal of the Royal Anthropological Society*, LXXXIII.

(1964) Die Religion der Primitivvolker. In J. Gonda (ed.) *Die Religionen Indiens*, III (Stuttgart).

Geertz, C. (1968) *Islam Observed* (New Haven).

(1974) 'From the Native's Point of View': On the Nature of Anthropological Understanding. *Bulletin of the American Academy of Arts and Sciences*, XXVII, no. 1.

(1975) *The Interpretation of Cultures* (London).

Gehman, H. S. (1974) Petavatthu: Stories of the Departed. In *Minor Anthologies*, IV. Sacred Books of the Buddhists, XXX (London).

Geiger, W. (1943) *Pali Literature and Language*. English translation (Calcutta).

Geldner, K. (1951) *Der Rg-Veda Übersetzt*. Harvard Oriental Series, XXXIII–XXXVI (London).

Gellner, E. A. (1962) Concepts and Society. In B. Wilson (ed.) (1970) *Rationality* (Oxford).

Glasenapp, H. von (1960) *Vedānta and Buddhism*. English translation (reprinted as BPS Wheel no. 2, Ceylon).

Gombrich, R. F. (1966) The Consecration of a Buddhist Image. *Journal of Asian Studies*, XVI.

(1971) *Precept and Practice* (Oxford).

(1972) Review of Spiro (1967), (1970). *Modern Asian Studies*, VI.

(1975) Ancient Indian Cosmology. In C. Blacker and M. Loewe (eds.) *Ancient Cosmologies* (London).

(1978) Review of Bhattacharya (1973). *Archives Internationales pour l'Histoire des Sciences*.

Gomez, L. O. (1976) Proto-Mādhyamika in the Pali Canon. *Philosophy East and West*, XIX.

Gonda, J. *Selected Studies*, 5 vols (Leiden 1975).

(1950) *Notes on Brahman* (Utrecht).

(1964) *The Savayajñas* (Amsterdam).

(1965) *Change and Continuity in Indian Religion* (The Hague).

(1966) *Loka: World and Heaven in the Veda* (Amsterdam).

(1970) *Notes on Names and Names of God in Ancient India* (Amsterdam).

(1975) *Vedic Literature* (Wiesbaden).

Govinda, L. A. (1969) *The Psychological Attitude of Early Buddhist Philosophy* (London).
Grimm, G. (1958) *The Doctrine of the Buddha*. English translation (2nd revised edition, Berlin).
Gunaratna, V. F. (1971) *Rebirth Explained*. BPS Wheel no. 167–9 (Ceylon).
Hakamaya, N. (1975) Nirodha Samāpatti. *Journal of Indian and Buddhist Studies*, XXIII.
Heesterman, J. C. (1964) Brahmin, Ritual and Renouncer. *Wiener Zeitschrift für die Kunde Süd-Asiens*, VIII.
Heidegger, M. (1971) *Poetry, Language and Thought*. English translation (New York).
Hopkins, E. W. (1906) Modifications of the Doctrine of Karma. *Journal of the Royal Asiatic Society*.
(1907) Further on the Doctrine of Karma. *Journal of the Royal Asiatic Society*.
Horner, I. B. (1954–9) *Middle Length Sayings* (Pali Text Society).
(1964) *Milinda's Questions* (Pali Text Society).
Horsch, P. (1968) Der Hinduismus und die Religionen der Primitivstämme Indiens. *Asiatische Studien*, XXII.
(1971) Vorstufen der Indischen Seelenwanderungslehre. *Asiatische Studien*, XXV.
Hubert, H. and Mauss, M. (1964) *Essay on the Nature and Function of Sacrifice*. English translation (London).
Hume, E. (1931) *The Thirteen Principal Upaniṣads* (Oxford).
Humphrey, R. (1958) *Stream of Consciousness in the Modern Novel* (3rd pr., University of California).
Humphries, C. (1962) *Buddhism* (London).
(1976) *Popular Dictionary of Buddhism* (London).
Hussey, E. (1972) *The PreSocratics* (London).
Jaini, P. S. (1959) The Sautrāntika Theory of Bīja. *Bulletin of the School of Oriental and African Studies*, XXII.
James, W. (1950) *The Principles of Psychology* (New York).
(1960) *The Varieties of Religious Experience* (London).
Jayasuriya, W. F. (1963) *The Psychology and Philosophy of Buddhism* (Colombo).
Jayatilleke, K. N. (1963) *Early Buddhist Theory of Knowledge* (London).
Johnston, E. H. (1937) *Early Sāṃkhya* (Royal Asiatic Society, London).
Kahn, C. H. (1979) *The Art and Thought of Heraclitus* (Cambridge).
Kalupahana, D. (1976) *Buddhist Philosophy: A Historical Analysis* (University of Hawaii).
Kane, P. V. (1946) *History of Dharmaśāstra*, III (Poona, 1930–62).
Karunaratne, T. B. (1969) *The Buddhist Wheel Symbol*. BPS Wheel no. 137–8 (Ceylon).
Keith, A. B. (1923) *Buddhist Philosophy in India and Ceylon* (Oxford).
(1925) *The Religion and Philosophy of the Veda*. Harvard Oriental Series, XXXI–XXXII (London).
Kern, J. C. (1896) *A Manual of Indian Buddhism* (Strassburg).
Khantipalo Bhikkhu (1964) *Tolerance: A Study from Buddhist Sources* (London).
King, W. L. (1964) *In the Hope of Nibbāna* (La Salle, Illinois).

Kirk, G. S. (1951) Natural Change in Heraclitus. *Mind*, LX, n.s. 237.
(1962) *Heraclitus: The Cosmic Fragments* (Cambridge).
Kirk, G. S. and Raven, J. E. (1957) *The PreSocratic Philosophers* (Cambridge).
Lamotte, E. *Traité de la Grande Vertu de Sagesse*. Translation of the *Mahāprajñāpāramitaśāstra*, 5 vols. (Louvain 1944–80).
(1936) Traité de la Démonstration de l'Acte (translation of KSP). *Mélanges Chinois et Bouddhiques*, V.
(1938) *La Somme du Grand Véhicule*. Translation of MSA. (Louvain).
(1967) *Histoire du Bouddhisme Indien* (2nd ed., Louvain).
(1974) Passions and Impregnations of the Passions in Buddhism. In Cousins, L., *et al.* (eds.) *Buddhist Studies in Honour of I. B. Horner* (Dordrecht).
Law, B. C. (1936) *The Buddhist Conception of Spirits* (2nd ed., Varanasi).
Lévi, S. (1915) Sur la Récitation Primitive des Textes Bouddhiques. *Journal Asiatique*, 11th Series, V.
(1966) *La Doctrine du Sacrifice dans les Brāhmaṇas* (2nd ed., Bibliothèque de l'École des Hautes Études, LXXIII, Paris).
Ling, T. (1973) *The Buddha* (London).
Lukes, S. (1973) *Individualism* (Oxford).
Mackie, J. L. (1967) Fallacies. In *Encyclopaedia of Philosophy* (New York).
Malalasekera, G. P. (1957) *The Buddha and his Teachings* (The Buddhist Council of Ceylon).
et al. (1961–) *Encyclopaedia of Buddhism* (Ceylon, in progress).
Malamoud, C. (1976) Village et Forêt. *European Journal of Sociology*, XVII, no. 1.
Mann, T. (1978) *Joseph and his Brothers*. English translation (London).
Masson, J. (1942) *La Religion Populaire dans le Canon Bouddhique Pali* (Louvain).
Mauss, M. (1938) Une Catégorie de l'Esprit Humain: La Notion de Personne, celle de Moi. *Journal of the Royal Anthropological Institute*, LXVIII.
Monier-Williams, M. (1890) *Buddhism* (London).
Mookherjee, S. (1935) *The Buddhist Philosophy of Universal Flux* (Calcutta).
Nagel, T. (1970) *The Possibility of Altruism* (Princeton).
Nakamura, H. (1964) *Ways of Thinking of Eastern Peoples* (ed. P. Wiener) (Hawaii).
(1976) The Basic Teachings of Buddhism. In Dumoulin, H. and Maraldo, J. (eds.) *Buddhism in the Modern World* (New York).
(1976a) *Buddhism in Comparative Light* (Delhi).
Ñāṇajīvako Bhikkhu (1973) Aniccam – the Buddhist Theory of Impermanence. Buddhist Publication Society (1973).
(1975) Karma – the Ripening Fruit. In BPS Wheel no. 221–4 (Ceylon).
Ñāṇamoli Bhikkhu (1960) *The Minor Readings and Illustrator* (Pali Text Society).
(1962) *The Guide* (Pali Text Society).
(1973) Impermanence according to Theravāda. In Buddhist Publication Society (1973).
(1974) Anattā according to Theravāda. In Buddhist Publication Society (1974).
(1975) *The Path of Purification*. Translation of the *Visuddhimagga* (3rd ed., BPS Ceylon).
Ñāṇānanda Bhikkhu (1971) *Concept and Reality* (BPS Ceylon).

(1973) *Ideal Solitude*. BPS Wheel no. 188 (Ceylon).
Nārada Thera (1948) *The Buddhist Doctrine of Rebirth* (Colombo).
(1975) *A Manual of Abhidharma* (3rd ed., BPS Ceylon).
Norman, K. R. (1969–71) *Elder's Verses I and II* (Pali Text Society).
(1978) The Role of Pali in Early Sinhalese Buddhism. In Bechert, H. (ed.) *Buddhism in Ceylon and Studies in Religious Syncretism in Buddhist Countries* (Göttingen).
(forthcoming) A Note on Attā in the Alagaddūpama Sutta. In *Studies in Indian Philosophy* (L.D. Institute of Indology, Ahmedabad).
Nowell-Smith, P. (1954) *Ethics* (London).
Nyanaponika Thera (1955) *Sutta Nipāta*. German translation and notes (Konstanz).
(1962) *The Heart of Buddhist Meditation* (London).
(1965) *Abhidhamma Studies* (BPS Ceylon).
(1967) *The Four Foods*. BPS Wheel no. 105–6 (Ceylon).
(1971) *Anattā and Nibbāna*. BPS Wheel no. 11 (Ceylon).
(1971a) *The Power of Mindfulness*. BPS Wheel no. 121–2 (Ceylon).
(1974) *The City of the Mind*. BPS Wheel no. 205 (Ceylon).
(1978) *The Roots of Good and Evil*. BPS Wheel no. 251–3 (Ceylon).
Nyanatiloka Mahāthera (1964) *Karma and Rebirth*. BPS Wheel no. 9 (Ceylon).
(1972) *Buddhist Dictionary* (3rd ed., revised and enlarged by Nyanaponika Thera, BPS Ceylon).
Obeyesekere, G. (1963) The Great Tradition and the Little in the Perspective of Sinhalese Buddhism. *Journal of Asian Studies*, XXII.
(1968) Theodicy, Sin and Salvation in a Sociology of Buddhism. In Leach, E. (ed.) *Dialectic in Practical Religion* (Cambridge).
(1976) The Ayur-Vedic Tradition in Sri Lanka. In Leslie, C. (ed.) *Asian Medical Systems* (University of California).
O'Flaherty, W. D. (1977) *The Origins of Evil in Hindu Mythology* (University of California).
Oldenburg, H. (1882) *Buddha: his Life, his Teaching, his Order*. English translation (London).
(1915) *Die Lehre der Upanishaden und die Anfänge des Buddhismus* (Göttingen).
(1917) *Die Religion des Veda* (Stuttgart).
(1919) *Die Weltanschauung der Brāhmaṇa-Texte* (Göttingen).
Olivelle, P. (1974) *The Origins and Early Development of Buddhist Monachism* (Colombo).
Ortner, S. (1978) *Sherpas through their Rituals* (Cambridge).
Parfit, D. (1971) Personal Identity. *Philosophical Review*, LXXX.
(1973) Later Selves and Moral Principles. In Montefiore, A. (ed.) *Philosophy and Personal Relations* (London).
Pocock, D. F. (1973) *Mind, Body and Wealth* (Oxford).
Poussin, L. de la Vallée (1913) *Théorie des Douze Causes* (Paris).
(1917) *The Way to Nirvāṇa* (Cambridge).
(1923–31) *L'Abidharmakośa de Vasubandhu*, 6 vols. (Paris).
(1931) Notes sur le Moment ou Kṣana des Bouddhistes. *Roznik Orjentalistyczny*, VIII (Krakow-Luow).
Radhakrishnan, S. (1929) *Indian Philosophy* (2nd ed., London).
(1953) *The Principal Upaniṣads* (London).

Rāhula, W. (1956) *History of Buddhism in Ceylon* (Colombo).
(1967) *What the Buddha Taught* (2nd ed., Bedford).
(1978) *Zen and the Taming of the Bull* (Bedford).
Regamey, C. (1935) *Bibliographie Analytique des Travaux Relatifs aux Éléments Anaryens dans la Civilisation et les Langues de l'Inde* (Paris).
Renou, L. (1949) La Notion de Brahman. *Journal Asiatique*, CCXXXVII.
(1953) *Religions of Ancient India* (London).
(1956) *Études Védiques et Paninéennes*, II (Paris).
Rhys Davids, C. A. F. (1914) *Buddhist Psychology* (London).
(1934) *Outlines of Buddhism* (London).
(1938) *What was the Original Gospel in 'Buddhism'* (London).
Rhys Davids, T. W. (1899–1921) *Dialogues of the Buddha*, 3 vols. Sacred Books of the Buddhists, II–IV (London).
Robertson, R. (1969) (ed.) *The Sociology of Religion* (London).
Robinson, R. (1970) *The Buddhist Religion* (California).
Ruegg, D. S. (1969) *La Théorie du Tathāgatagarbha et du Gotra* (Paris).
Rycroft, C. (1979) *The Innocence of Dreams* (London).
Saratchandra, E. (1943) Bhavaṅga and the Buddhist Psychology of Perception. *University of Ceylon Review*.
(1946) Abhidhamma Psychology of Perception and the Yogācāra Theory of Mind. *University of Ceylon Review*, IV.
(1958) *The Buddhist Psychology of Perception* (Colombo).
Schayer, S. (1934) Pre-Aryan Elements in Indian Buddhism. *Bulletin de l'Académie Polonaise des Sciences et des Lettres*.
(1935) Pre-Canonical Buddhism. *Archiv Orientalni*, VII.
Sharma, U. (1973) Theodicy and the Doctrine of Karma. *Man*, n.s. VIII.
Silburn, L. (1955) *Instant et Cause* (Paris).
Smart, N. (1964) *Doctrine and Argument in Indian Philosophy* (London).
Spiro, M. E. (1966) Religion: Problems of Definition and Explanation. In Banton, M. (ed.) *Anthropological Approaches to the Study of Religion*. ASA Monographs III (London).
(1967) *Burmese Supernaturalism* (Englewood Cliffs, New Jersey).
(1970) *Buddhism and Society* (London).
Srinivas, M. N. (1952) *Religion and Society among the Coorgs of South India* (Oxford).
Staal, F. J. (1963) Sanskrit and Sanskritisation. *Journal of the Royal Asiatic Society*.
Stcherbatsky, T. (1926) Review of Poussin's Nirvāṇa. *Bulletin of the School of Oriental and African Studies*, IV.
(1927) *The Conception of Buddhist Nirvāṇa* (Leningrad).
(1962) *Buddhist Logic* (New York).
Steiner, F. (1956) *Taboo* (London).
Steiner, G. (1979) *Language and Silence* (London).
Storey, F. (1975) *Rebirth as Doctrine and Experience* (BPS Ceylon).
Tambiah, S. J. (1968) Literacy in a Buddhist village in N.E. Thailand. In Goody, J. (ed.) *Literacy in Traditional Societies* (Cambridge).
(1970) *Buddhism and the Spirit Cults of N.E. Thailand* (Cambridge).
(1977) *World Conqueror and World Renouncer* (Cambridge).
Thapar, R. (1966) *A History of India* (London).
(1975) Ethics, Religion and Social Protest in the first Millennium B.C. in

Northern India. *Dedalus*, Spring 1975.
Thomas, E. J. (1949) *The Life of the Buddha* (3rd ed., London).
(1951) *The History of Buddhist Thought* (London).
Varenne, J. (1960) *The Mahānārāyaṇa Upaniṣad* (Paris).
(1976) *Yoga and the Hindu Tradition*. English translation (University of Chicago).
Warder, A. K. (1956) On the relationships between early Buddhism and other contemporary systems. *Bulletin of the School of Oriental and African Studies*, XVIII.
(1970) *Indian Buddhism* (Motilal Banarsidas).
(1974) *Introduction to Pali* (Pali Text Society, 2nd ed.).
Warren, H. (1909) *Buddhism in Translations*. Harvard Oriental Series, III (London).
Weber, M. (1948) The Social Psychology of the World Religions (English translation). In Gerth, H. H. and Mills, C. W. (eds.) *From Max Weber* (London).
Welbon, G. (1968) *The Buddhist Nirvāṇa and its Western Interpreters* (Chicago).
Wijesekera, O. H. de A. (1945) Vedic Gandharva and Buddhist Gandhabba. *University of Ceylon Review*, III.
Williams, G. (1960) The Concept of 'Egemonia' in the Thought of Antonio Gramsci: some Notes on Interpretation. *Journal of the History of Ideas*, XXI.
Williams, P. M. (1978) Language and Existence in Mādhyamika Buddhist Philosophy (unpublished D.Phil. thesis, Oxford).
(1980) Some Aspects of Language and Construction in the Madhyamaka. *Journal of Indian Philosophy*, VIII.
(forthcoming) Silence and Truth – some aspects of Madhyamaka Philosophy in Tibet. *Tibet Journal*.
Worsley, P. (1968) The Trumpet Shall Sound (as reprinted in Robertson (1969)).
Zaehner, R. (1957) *Mysticism Sacred and Profane* (Oxford).
(1966) *Hindu Scriptures* (London).
(1969) *The Bhagavad Gītā* (Oxford).
Zurcher, E. (1962) *Buddhism: its Origin and Spread in Words, Maps and Pictures* (London).

Glossary and index of Pali and Sanskrit terms

abhisaṃkhāra – construction, formation, act, 175 and n, 200–8
abhisaṃkahāra-viññāṇa – constructed/constructive consciousness, 205–8
acetana – senseless, inanimate, 81, 214
addhā/addhāna – life, lifetime, road, 233
ahaṃkāra – 'I-maker', the utterance 'I', 100–3, 263
āhāra – food, 208–10
ahiṃsā – non-violence, 139–42
ajjhattam/bahiddhā – inside/outside, in oneself/in others, 72, 192–3
ālaya – home, attachment, 170–1
ālaya-vijñāna – home-consciousness, 224, 259–60
amṛtam (amṛtatvam) – immortality, non-dying, 42–4, 46
anattā (Skt *anātman*) – not-self, 4–5, 7–12, 70–8, 95–6, 87–143, 178–82, 188–95
anicca – impermanent, 9, 97–8, 226–7, 235–7
antaryāmin – inner controller, self, 60, 97
anusaya – underlying tendency, 101
arhat – 'worthy one', enlightened man, saint, 88, 91, 92, 142, 206–8, 219, 223, 257
artha – wealth, power, 39
āsava – corruption, 91, 106, 116, 120, 127
asekho – 'non-learner', adept, 92
asmimāna – the conceit 'I am', 94–5, 96, 100–3, 119, 141–2, 153, 189, 263
āśrama – stage of life, 39
asu – breath, 50
asunīti – leading away of the breath, death, 50
ātmayajñā – self-sacrifice, 60, 209
attā (Skt *ātman*) – self (q.v. *anattā*); origin of *ātman*-concept in pre-Buddhist thought, 79–81; use of *attā* and *atta*-compounds in Pali, 71–4, 76
attabhāva (Skt *ātmabhāva*) – individuality, 74, 132 and n, 148, 156–60, 167, 190, 223, 239
attabhāva-paṭilābha – acquisition of individuality, 138, 158
avyākata – unanswered (questions), 131–8
āyatana – sense-base, 82, 112, 154
āyu(saṃkhārā) – life(-formations), 227–8
(sarvam) āyus – (a full) life, 44–7

bhārahāra – bearing the burden, 162, 164–5
bhāvanā – mental culture, 111–15, 139–42, 172–3
bhavaṅga – constituent/condition of existence, 224, 225–6, 238–49, 251–2 258–61, 264; as 'the unconscious', 243–4
bhikkhu – mendicant, monk, 14
Bodhisatta (Skt *Bodhisattva*) – Buddha-to-be, 151, 194–5
brahmaloka – *brahma*-world, 51–2
brahman – cosmic spirit, 'absolute', 9, 50, 59–60, 62, 74, 76, 81, 209, 215
brāhmaṇa – Brahmin, 32–3, 148, 155, 157, 200, 219, 260

caraṇa – conduct, 53
cetanā – intention, 82, 201
cetas – mind, awareness, 80
citta – mind, 214, 215, 235
cuti-citta – death-moment, last thought, 244–5

dakṣiṇā – sacrificial gift/fee, 44
devaloka – World of the Gods, 45–6
dhamma – impersonal element, 77, 80, 87, 91, 112, 115, 121, 124–5, 139, 155–6, 179–81, 229, 263
dhamma – Buddhist doctrine (q.v. *dharma*), 219, 221–2
dharma – the way things are and/or should be, cosmic order, 39, 41, 53
dharmanairātmya – selflessness of things, 123–7, 154n
dhātu – element, 112, 154
dīkṣa – sacrificial initiation, 47–8
diṭṭhi – view, 87–143; view in the Noble Eight-fold Path, 89–90
diṭṭhigatam – viewpoint, prejudice, opinion, 103, 119, 127–8, 132, 134–5
doṣa – troubles, humours, 69, 161
dukkha – unsatisfactory, 'suffering', 9, 191–3

Glossary and index of Pali and Sanskrit terms

gandhabba (Skt *gandharva*) – (descending) spirit, 210–13

idapaccayatā – the fact of things having a specific cause, 106
iriyā-pathā – (sequence of four) postures, 159, 230–2
iṣṭāpūrta – merit gained from sacrifice, 54

jhāna – meditation level, 123, 215–18
jīva – life, soul, 36n, 55, 115
jīvitindriya – life-faculty, 227–30, 258, 264

kaivalya – isolation, 63
kāma – pleasure, 39, 58
karma – action and its rewards, 13, 16, 29, 53–8, 64, 67, 68–70, 82, 88–9, 91, 120–1, 155, 193–4, 200–8, 217, 219–24, 229, 232, 239, 262–4
khandha (Skt *skandha*) – category, aggregate, constituent of personality, 9 and n, 21–2, 82, 93, 97, 112, 114, 118–19, 125–6, 132–3, 134, 157, 167–8, 169–70, 179–80, 216–17, 223, 229, 246, 252
khīṇâsava – one whose corruptions are destroyed, 127
kratu – intention, 58
kṣaṇa (Pali *khaṇa*)/*kṣaṇikavāda* – moment/momentariness, 226, 233–8, 241–3, 248, 252–3; three sub-moments (arising, presence, cessation), 234, 237, 241–2, 258
kṣatriya – king, warrior, 34, 51, 52, 155, 260
(a)kusala – (un)wholesome, (bad) good, 90
kuṭī – cell, hermitage hut, 167, 168

loka – world, sphere, rebirth-plane, 45–9, 53, 54, 63, 76–7, 214–15
lokīya/lokuttara – worldly/superworldly, 92

mahāyajñā – great sacrifice, 57
manas – mind, 77, 80, 214, 233, 235
mātika – lists, schedules, 21–2, 122
mokṣa – liberation, enlightenment, 13, 29, 39, 47, 52–3, 63–4, 81, 149

nāma-rūpa – name-and-form, mind and body, 82, 107, 204, 211–12, 223
nibbāna (Skt *nirvāṇa*) – 'blowing-out', enlightenment, liberation, 10–13, 16, 52–3, 68, 81–4, 92, 113, 121, 122–3, 125, 135–6, 151, 164, 171, 175, 206–8, 216, 220, 249–50, 260–1, 262–5
nītattha/neyyattha – of literal/indirect meaning, 154

pabbajjā – going forth (from home to homelessness), 171–2
pañca-kāma-guṇe – five strands of sense-pleasure, 169–70, 220, 251
paññā – wisdom, insight, 90, 102, 221–2
papañca – imagining, false conceptualisation, 141–2
paramattha-sacca (Skt *paramārtha-satya*) – ultimate truth, 19, 71, 147–8, 153–6, 176, 179–82, 199, 263
paṭicca-samuppāda – Dependent Origination, 103–10, 203–5
paṭisandhi(-viññāṇa) – rebirth-linking(-consciousness), 210, 212, 244
peta – ghost, spirit of the dead, 152–3
pitṛloka – World of the Fathers, 45–6
prakṛti – nature, the material world, 81, 100
prāṇa – breath, 50, 80
prārthanā – religious aspiration, prayer, 150
pubbe-nivāsānussati – memory of former lives, 162–3, 168
pudgala-nairātmya – selflessness of persons, 124
puggala-vemattatā – differences between persons, 93, 161
punarmṛtyu – repeated dying, 46–7
puñña – merit, 219
purisa/puggala – person, 71, 73, 74–5, 77, 154, 160–5, 223
puruṣa – (cosmic and/or individual) person, 51, 55, 73, 79, 81, 102
puthujjana – ordinary man, 92, 93, 163

ṛta – cosmic order, law, 41, 54

śabda-brahman – *brahman* as sound, 105
saddhā – confidence, 'faith', 89, 129
sakkāyadiṭṭhi – Personality Belief, 93–4, 101, 132–3, 153
samādhi – concentration, meditation, 90, 111–12, 221–2
samaṇabrāhmaṇa – ascetics and brahmins, religieux, 33–4
samatha – tranquillity, 111
sambhāra – composite, 55
saṃkhāra (Skt *saṃskāra*) – (mental) formation, construction, 55, 82, 108, 118–20, 122–3, 200–8, 236
sammuti-sacca (Skt *saṃvṛti-satya*) – conventional truth, 19, 71, 147–8, 153–6, 176, 179–82, 199, 263

Glossary and index of Pali and Sanskrit terms

saṃsāra – the round of rebirth, 13, 16, 29, 33, 43, 47, 63–4, 88–9, 91, 120–1, 155, 164, 168, 187–8, 193, 200–8, 213–18, 220, 222, 249–50, 259, 262–5
saṃvattanika-viññāṇa – evolving consciousness, 215
saññāvedayita-nirodha – cessation of perception and feeling/'experience', 142, 228, 229–30, 245–6
sassatavāda – eternalism, 35, 104–5, 181–2, 261
sati – mindfulness, 139–42, 173–4
satipaṭṭhānā – (Four) Foundations of Mindfulness, 114
satto – (a) being, 132, 154–5
sekho – learner, 92
sīla – morality, 90, 111–12, 221–2
soma – hallucinogenic drink used in Vedic ritual, 50, 52
śūdra – lowest of the four varnas, 260
sukṛtāṃ/sukṛtasya loka – World of (Those who have acquired) Sacrificial Merit, 45, 46, 55, 200
śūnyatā – emptiness, 116, 124–7
svabhāva – own-being, essence, 124
svargaloka – Heavenly World, 45

tapas – asceticism, ascetic power, 51, 81, 84, 235
Tathāgata – 'thus-gone', title of a Buddha, 106, 131–8, 155
Theravāda – Way of the Elders, distinguished from and compared to the *Mahāyāna* tradition, 20–6, 123–7

ucchedavāda – annihilationism, 35, 104–5, 181–2
upādāna – grasping, attachment, 83, 107, 204, 210
upādi – substrate (of rebirth), 83
upanayana – initiation, 48
upāsaka/upāsika – male/female lay follower, 14, 69–70

vaiśya – third of the four varnas, 52, 260
vaso – power, control, 97
viññāṇa – consciousness, 103–4, 201–2, 204–5, 213–18, 223–4, 235
viññāṇa-sota – stream of consciousness, 257–8
viññāṇa-ṭṭhiti – station(ing) of consciousness, 213–18
vipassanā – insight, 111–12
visuddhi – purity, purification, 112–13, 129–30
viveka – seclusion, 167, 171–5

yajamāna – patron, client for whom sacrifice is performed, 42, 61–2, 63
yama/niyama – self-control, 60
yathābhūta-dassana – seeing things as they really are, 115
yogā – 'bonds' of view, 127
yogakkhema – rest from work (synonym for *nibbāna*), 221
(a)yoniso-manasikāra – (lack of) careful attention, 118–19, 138–43
yuga – cosmic aeon, age, 41

General index

action, and its rewards, 13, 16, 29, 53–8, 64, 67, 68–70, 82, 88–9, 91, 120–1, 155, 193–4, 200–8, 217, 219–24, 229, 232, 239, 262–4
Aesop's fables, 17, 152
Agnihotra, 57
Ajita Kesakambalī, 36–7
Ājīvikas, 35–8
altruism, indistinguishable from self-interest, 188–95
Ames, M., 209
Angirases, 43
annihilationism, 35, 104–5, 181–2
Arnold, Sir E., 261

Bachelard, G., 147, 166, 209
Bareau, A., 11
Basham, A. L., 34, 37, 38
Bergson, H., 253–8
Bhartṛhari, 105
Bhattacharya, K., 10
brahman, cosmic spirit, 'absolute', 9, 50, 59–60, 62, 74, 76, 81, 209, 215
Brāhmaṇas, 30, 41–64, 79, 81, 149, 200, 214
Brahmin, 32–3, 148, 155, 157, 200, 219, 260
'breath-doctrine', 49–50
Buber, M., 166
Buddhaghosa, 22
Buddha-to-be, 151, 194–5
Buddhism (schools other than *Theravāda*), *Madhyamaka*, 115, 124, 234n; *Mahāsaṃghika*, 224; *Pudgalavāda* (Personalist), 11, 162, 178, 181; *Sarvāstivāda*, 21, 110, 189; *Sautrāntika*, 21; *Vijñānavāda*, 224, 241, 247, 259–60
van Buitenen, J. A. B., 100

Carrithers, M. B., 112
Cārvāka (Lokāyata), 38
Chomsky, N., 3
Christ, 97
consciousness, 103–4, 201–2, 204–5, 213–18, 223–4, 235; constructed/constructive, 205–8; evolving, 215; home, 224, 259–60; stationing of, 213–18; stream of, 257–8
constituents of personality, category, aggregate, 9 and n, 21–2, 82, 93, 97, 112, 114, 118–19, 125–6, 132–3, 134, 157, 167–8, 169–70, 179–80, 216–17, 223, 229, 246, 252
Coomaraswamy, A. K., 9
Coulson, M., 23
Cratylus, 253

death, 46–7, 50, 244–5
Demieville, P., 190
Dharmapāla, A., 14, 24
Douglas, M., 112
Dumont, L., 1, 2, 62, 64, 65, 164, 175, 193, 264
Durkheim, E., 6, 20, 43, 48

Edgerton, F., 58
Eliade, M., 166
Eliot, Sir C., 13
enlightened man, saint, 88, 91, 92, 142, 206–8
eternalism, 35, 104–5, 181–2, 261
existence, condition/constituent of, 224, 225–6, 238–49, 251–2, 258–61, 264

'fire-doctrine', 50
Frauwallner, E., 10, 11, 49, 51, 108, 147, 202
Freud, S., 166, 243–4, 259, 264
von Fürer-Haimendorf, C., 31–2

Geertz, C., 2, 262, 264
Gellner, E. A., 84
Gombrich, R. F., 18–19, 66, 83, 94n, 150, 151
Gonda, J., 45, 214
Gramsci, A., 32
Grimm, G., 10
Gunaratna, V. F., 254

Heesterman, J. C., 51, 60-1
Heidegger, M., 199
Heraclitus, 225, 248, 252–3
Hume, D., 225, 254–5

Humphries, C., 8

'I am', conceit of, 94–5, 96, 100–3, 119, 141–2, 153, 189, 263
imagery, 19–20, 23, 84, 148, 165–76, 185–8, 200, 218–24, 225–6, 230–3, 247–61, 264–6
'I-maker', the utterance 'I', 100–3, 263
immortality, non-dying, 42–4, 46
individuality, 74, 132 and n, 148, 156–60, 167, 190, 223, 239; acquisition of, 138, 158

Jainism, 33, 37–8, 52
James, W., 87, 112, 173, 189, 253–8
Jātaka stories, 17, 67, 70, 151–2
Joyce, J., 253

Kālidāsa, 23
Kāmasūtra, 39
Kant, I., 182, 225
Kathāvatthu, 109, 178–82
Kauṭilya (*Arthaśāstra*), 39
king, warrior, 34, 51, 52, 155, 260

life, 36n, 55, 115; -faculty, 227–30; a full, 44–7; -formations, 227–8
liberation, enlightenment, 13, 29, 39, 47, 52–3, 63–4, 81, 149; *see also nirvāṇa*
lives, memory of former, 162–3, 168
Locke, J., 177

Mahāyāna Buddhism, 8, 20, 23, 24–6, 106, 110, 116, 123–7, 135, 154n, 194
Makkhali Gosāla, 35–6
Malalasekera, G. P., 4
Malamoud, C., 63
Mann, T., 262–3
Marriott, McK., 17
Mauss, M., 2, 3
meditaton, 90, 111–15, 122–3, 139–42, 172–3, 215–18, 221–2
Metteyya Buddha, 16, 151
Mill, J. S., 240
mind, 77, 80, 214, 215, 233, 235
moment, momentariness, 226, 233–8, 241–3, 248, 252–3; three sub-moments (arising, presence, cessation), 234, 237, 241–2, 258
Monier-Williams, Sir M., 13

Ñāṇamoli Thera, 22, 112, 178
Ñāṇajīvako Bhikkhu, 254
Ñāṇānanda Bhikkhu, 141
nirvāṇa, 'blowing-out', enlightenment, liberation, 10–13, 16, 52–3, 68, 81–4, 92, 113, 121, 122–3, 125, 135–6, 151, 164, 171, 175, 206–8, 216, 220, 249–50, 260–1, 262–5
non-violence, 139–42
Norman, K. R., 96
not-self, concept introduced, 4–5, 7–12; doctrine of, 87–143; linguistic form discussed, 95–6; relationship to ordinary language use of 'self', 70–8; later scholastic arguments for, 178–82; self and other(s), 188–95
Nyanaponika Thera, 173, 239
Nyanatiloka Mahāthera, 5, 213, 227, 261

Obeyesekere, G., 69
Oldenburg, H., 11, 29

Pakudha Kaccāyana, 36
Pali Text Society, 7
Pañcatantra, 152
Parfit, D., 177 and n
Personality Belief, 93–4, 101, 132–3, 153
persons, 71, 73, 74–5, 77, 154, 160–5, 223; essence of cosmic and/or individual, 51, 55, 73, 79, 81, 102; differences between, 93, 161
Pocock, D., 15
Poussin, L. de la Vallée, 15, 108, 193, 202, 211, 239
Prajāpati, 42, 81
Prajñāpāramitā, 24, 115, 124
Pūraṇa Kassapa, 36
purity, purification, 112–13, 129–30

Radhakrishnan, Sir S., 9
Rāhula, W., 4, 106, 192, 252–3, 266
Ṛbhus, 43
rebirth, *see under saṃsāra*
Redfield, R., 17
Rhys Davids, C. A. F., 7, 8
Rhys Davids, T. W., 8, 35n, 106, 162
Richardson, D., 253
Robinson, R. H., 192

Śaṃkara, 23
Sāṃkhya-Yoga, 73, 79–80, 81, 99, 100, 102, 174
saṃsāra, the round of rebirth, 13, 16, 29, 33, 43, 47, 63–4, 88–9, 91, 120–1, 155, 164, 168, 187–8, 193, 200–8, 213–18, 220, 222, 249–50, 259, 262–5
Sarvadarśanasaṃgraha, 38–9
Schweitzer, A., 195n
self, 71–4, 76, 79–81

General index

selflessness, of persons and of things, 123–7, 154n
Silburn, L., 42, 199, 201
Smart, N., 133
Spiro, M. E., 6, 16, 150, 153
Stcherbatsky, T., 11, 234
Steiner, F., 183
Steiner, G., 116
'suffering', unsatisfactory, 9, 191–3

Tambiah, S. J., 17, 67–8
time, 41–53, 58–64, 200–8, 214–18, 234–8, 252–8
truth, conventional and ultimate, 19, 71, 147–8, 153–6, 176, 179–82, 199, 263

Upaniṣads, 8, 30, 31, 41, 43, 49–64, 79–81, 149, 154, 168, 184, 208–9, 211, 215, 232–3, 261

Vedānta, 9
Vedas, 30, 41–50, 59, 149, 219
  Ṛg Veda, 41, 43, 81, 232
  Atharva Veda, 41, 44, 55, 59, 81, 232
view, 87–143; in the Noble Eight-fold Path, 89–90
viewpoint, prejudice, opinion, 103, 119, 127–8, 132, 134–5

'water-doctrine', 49
Weber, M., 12, 38n, 89, 195n
Wittgenstein, L., 3
Woolf, V., 253
world, sphere, rebirth-plane, 45–9, 53, 54, 63, 76–7, 214–15
Worsley, P., 65

Yajñavalkya, 58, 80
Yama, 44, 80

Zaehner, R. C., 9, 14–15
Zeno, 256